for
c.r.h.

Each person, withdrawn into himself, behaves as though he is a stranger to the destiny of all the others. His children and his good friends constitute for him the whole of the human species. As for his transactions with his fellow citizens, he may mix among them, but he sees them not; he touches them, but does not feel them; he exists only in himself and for himself alone. And if on these terms there remains in his mind a sense of family, there no longer remains a sense of society.

—TOCQUEVILLE

THE FALL
OF PUBLIC MAN

BOOKS BY RICHARD SENNETT

The Hidden Injuries of Class
(with Jonathan Cobb)

The Uses of Disorder

Families Against the City

19th Century Cities
(editor, with Stephan Thernstrom)

Classic Essays on the Culture of Cities
(editor)

THE FALL
OF PUBLIC MAN

by

RICHARD SENNETT

CAMBRIDGE UNIVERSITY PRESS

CAMBRIDGE · LONDON · MELBOURNE

Published by the Syndics of the Cambridge University Press
The Pitt Building, Trumpington Street, Cambridge CB2 1RP
Bentley House, 200 Euston Road, London NW1 2DB
296 Beaconsfield Parade, Middle Park, Melbourne 3206, Australia

First published in the U.S.A. by Alfred A. Knopf, Inc., 1976
First published in Great Britain by the Cambridge
University Press 1977

Portions of Chapter 13 first appeared in the Afterword to *Forest
Hills Diary* by Mario Matthew Cuomo (New York: Random
House), 1975.

Library of Congress Cataloguing in Publication Data

Sennett, Richard, (Date)   The fall of public man.

Includes bibliographical references and index.
1. Social History. 2. Community life. 3. Social
interaction. 4. Social life and customs. 5. Alienation (Social psychology)   I. Title.
HN13.s45   309   76–25131
ISBN 0 521 21642 7 hard covers
ISBN 0 521 29215 8 paperback

Printed Offset Litho in Great Britain by
Cox & Wyman Ltd
London, Fakenham and Reading

CONTENTS

CONTENTS

Contents

CONTENTS

ACKNOWLEDGMENTS

I wish to thank Clifford Curzon and Murray Perahia for helping me first define the purpose of this book. During the course of writing it, I was helped by discussions with Peter Brooks, Clifford Geertz, Richard Gilman, Caroline Rand Herron, Anne Hollander, Herbert Menzel, Orest Ranum, Carl Schorske, Richard Trexler, and Lionel Trilling. I want to thank Ben Barber, Juan Corradi, Marion Knox, Leo Marx, and David Riesman for their comments on the manuscript. I owe a special debt of thanks to Davis Herron, who gave me the benefit of his close reading of the text.

Research for this book was conducted with the assistance of Marcia Bystryn, Bernard McGrane, Mark Salmon, and Christina Spellman. I should particularly like to thank Marcia Bystryn for her very patient and competent work.

Finally, I should like to thank Robert Gottlieb and Angus Cameron for editorial guidance. Bobbie Bristol guided the book through production, and Jack Lynch helped me refine the language of the text.

I wish to thank librarians and curators for assistance at the libraries of the Institute for Advanced Study, the Lincoln Center for the Performing Arts, the Metropolitan Museum of New York, Harvard University, the Bibliothèque Nationale, Cambridge University, and New York University. Financial support for the research and writing of this book came through the generous assistance of the Institute for Advanced Study, the John Simon Guggenheim Foundation, and the Ford Foundation. The manuscript was typed by the staff of the Center for Policy Research, and I wish to thank them for their collective efficiency and good humor.

A NOTE ABOUT THE AUTHOR

Richard Sennett is Professor of Sociology at New York University and Senior Research Fellow, Center for Policy Research. He is the author of several books on urban family life and on social psychology, including *The Uses of Disorder* and (with Jonathan Cobb) *The Hidden Injuries of Class*. Before entering academia, he studied the cello and still plays in chamber music groups in New York City. *The Fall of Public Man* brings together his interests in the psychology of urban life and the sociology of performing.

PART ONE

THE PUBLIC PROBLEM

CHAPTER 1

THE PUBLIC DOMAIN

Modern times are often compared to the years the Roman Empire went into decline: Just as moral rottenness is supposed to have sapped Rome's power to rule the West, it is said to have sapped the modern West's power to rule the globe. For all the silliness of this notion, it contains an element of truth. There is a rough parallel between the crisis of Roman society after the death of Augustus and present-day life; it concerns the balance between public and private life.

As the Augustan Age faded, Romans began to treat their public lives as a matter of formal obligation. The public ceremonies, the military necessities of imperialism, the ritual contacts with other Romans outside the family circle, all became duties—duties in which the Roman participated more and more in a passive spirit, conforming to the rules of the *res publica*, but investing less and less passion in his acts of conformity. As the Roman's public life became bloodless, he sought in private a new focus for his emotional energies, a new principle of commitment and belief. This private commitment was mystic, concerned with escaping the world at large and the formalities of the *res publica* as part of that world. This commitment was to various Near Eastern sects, of which Christianity gradually became dominant; eventually Christianity ceased to be a spiritual commitment practiced in secret, burst into the world, and became itself a new principle of public order.

Today, public life has also become a matter of formal obligation. Most citizens approach their dealings with the state in a spirit of resigned acquiescence, but this public enervation is in its scope much broader than political affairs. Manners and ritual interchanges with strangers are looked on as at best formal and dry, at worst as phony. The stranger himself is a threatening figure, and few people can take great pleasure in that world of strangers, the cosmopolitan city. A *res publica* stands in general for those bonds of association and mutual commitment which exist between people who are not joined together by ties of family or intimate association; it is the bond of a crowd, of a "people," of a polity, rather than the bonds of family or friends. As in Roman times, participation in the *res publica* today is most often a matter of going along, and the forums for this public life, like the city, are in a state of decay.

The difference between the Roman past and the modern present lies in the alternative, in what privacy means. The Roman in private sought another principle to set against the public, a principle based on religious transcendence of the world. In private we seek out not a principle but a reflection, that of what our psyches are, what is authentic in our feelings. We have tried to make the fact of being in private, alone with ourselves and with family and intimate friends, an end in itself.

Modern ideas about the psychology of this private life are confused. Few people today would claim that their psychic life arises by spontaneous generation, independent of social conditions and environmental influences. Nevertheless, the psyche is treated as though it has an inner life of its own. This psychic life is seen as so precious and so delicate that it will wither if exposed to the harsh realities of the social world, and will flower only to the extent that it is protected and isolated. Each person's self has become his principal burden; to know oneself has become an end, instead of a means through which one knows the world. And precisely because we are so self-absorbed, it is extremely difficult for us to arrive at a private principle, to give any clear account to ourselves or to others of what our personalities are. The reason is that, the more privatized the psyche, the less it is stimulated, and the more difficult it is for us to feel or to express feeling.

The post-Augustan Roman's pursuit of his private, Oriental gods was separated in his mind from the public world. He finally imposed those gods upon the public world, by subjugating military law and social custom to a higher, clearly different principle. Under the modern code of private meaning, the relations between impersonal and intimate experience have no such clarity. We see society itself as "meaningful" only by converting it into a grand psychic system. We may understand that a politician's job is to draft or execute legislation, but that work does not interest us until we perceive the play of personality in political struggle. A political leader running for office is spoken of as "credible" or "legitimate" in terms of what kind of man he is, rather than in terms of the actions or programs he espouses. The obsession with persons at the expense of more impersonal social relations is like a filter which discolors our rational understanding of society; it obscures the continuing importance of class in advanced industrial society; it leads us to believe community is an act of mutual self-disclosure and to undervalue the community relations of strangers, particularly those which occur in cities. Ironically, this psychological vision also inhibits the development of basic personality strengths, like respect for the privacy of others, or the comprehension that, because every self is in some measure a cabinet of horrors, civilized relations between selves can only proceed to the extent that nasty little secrets of desire, greed, or envy are kept locked up.

The advent of modern psychology, and of psychoanalysis in particular, was founded on the faith that in understanding the inner workings of the self *sui generis,* without transcendental ideas of evil or of sin, people might free themselves from these horrors and be liberated to participate more fully and rationally in a life outside the boundaries of their own desires. Masses of people are concerned with their single life-histories and particular emotions as never before; this concern has proved to be a trap rather than a liberation.

Because this psychological imagination of life has broad social consequences, I want to call it by a name that may at first seem inapt: this imagination is an intimate vision of society. "Intimacy" connotes warmth, trust, and open expression of feeling. But precisely because we have come to expect these psychological benefits throughout the range of our experience, and precisely because so much social life which does have a meaning cannot yield these psychological rewards, the world outside, the impersonal world, seems to fail us, seems to be stale and empty.

In a sense, I am turning around the argument David Riesman made in *The Lonely Crowd.* Riesman contrasted an inner-directed society, in which men pursued actions and made commitments based on goals and sentiments they felt within themselves, to an other-directed society, in which these passions and commitments depend on what people sense to be the feelings of others. Riesman believed American society, and in its wake Western Europe, was moving from an inner- to an other-directed condition. The sequence should be reversed. Western societies are moving from something like an other-directed condition to an inner-directed condition—except that in the midst of self-absorption no one can say what is inside. As a result, confusion has arisen between public and intimate life; people are working out in terms of personal feelings public matters which properly can be dealt with only through codes of impersonal meaning.

This confusion might appear to be a peculiarly American problem. The value American society places on individual experience might seem to lead its citizens to measure all social life in terms of personal feeling. However, it is not rugged individualism which is now experienced; rather, it is anxiety about individual feeling which individuals write large in terms of the way the world works. The source of this anxiety lies in broad changes in capitalism and in religious belief. These are not narrowly national in their boundaries.

Anxiety about what one feels might also be seen as the spread, and the vulgarization, of the Romantic "quest for personality." Such a quest has not been conducted in a social vacuum; it is the conditions of ordinary life which have propelled people into this Romantic search for self-realization. Further, it has been beyond the scope of literary studies of this quest to weigh up the costs to society which result, and these costs are great.

The erosion of public life also demands a kind of study apart from the usual modes of social history. To talk about expression in public leads naturally to the question: what kinds of expression is the human being capable of in social relations? When a man pays a stranger a compliment, for example, does he act expressively in the way a stage actor acts? It is difficult to talk about an emptiness of expression in public life without some theory of what expression is. Is there, for example, a difference in the expression appropriate for public relations and that appropriate for intimate relations?

I have tried to create a theory of expression in public by a process of interplay between history and theory. Concrete changes in public behavior, speech, dress, and belief are used in this book as evidence for making a theory about what expression is in society. As the history has suggested clues to a theory, I have tried to take the abstract insights gained as clues in their turn for new questions to ask the historical record.

A dialectical inquiry means the argument is complete only when the book has come to an end. You cannot state "the theory" all at once and then lay it like a map over the historical terrain. To have at least some clarity at the start, however, I should like to discuss in the present chapter the social and political dimensions of the public problem as it has developed in modern society, and in the next chapter present the dimensions of a theory of expression in public. In the subsequent pages of this book, the historical and theoretical questions will be played back and forth.

LOVE OUTSIDE THE PUBLIC DOMAIN

The public problem of contemporary society is two-fold: behavior and issues which are impersonal do not arouse much passion; the behavior and the issues begin to arouse passion when people treat them, falsely, as though they were matters of personality. But because this two-fold public problem exists, it creates a problem within private life. The world of intimate feeling loses any boundaries; it is no longer restrained by a public world in which people make alternative and countervailing investment of themselves. The erosion of a strong public life therefore deforms the intimate relations which seize people's wholehearted interest. No more graphic instance of this deformation has occurred in the last four generations than in the most intimate of personal experiences, physical love.

In the last four generations, physical love has been redefined, from terms of eroticism to terms of sexuality. Victorian eroticism involved social relationships, sexuality involves personal identity. Eroticism meant that sexual expression transpired through actions—of choice, repression, interaction. Sexuality is not an action but a state of being, in which the physical act of love follows almost as a passive consequence, a natural result, of people feeling intimate with each other.

The terms of eroticism among the 19th Century bourgeoisie were almost entirely couched in fear, and therefore expressed through the filter of repression. All sexual action was shaded by a feeling of violation —a violation of the woman's body by the man, a violation of the social code by two lovers, a violation of a deeper moral code by homosexuals. Large segments of modern society have rebelled against the fear and the repression, and this is all to the good. But because of the way ideals of intimacy color the modern imagination, there has also been a reaction against the idea that physical love is an action people engage in, and like any other social action might have rules, limits, and necessary fictions which give the action a specific meaning. Instead, sex is a revelation of the self. A new slavery is therefore substituted for the old.

Sexuality we imagine to define a large territory of who we are and what we feel. Sexuality as an expressive state, rather than an expressive act, is entropic, however. Whatever we experience must in some way touch on our sexuality, but sexuality *is*. We uncover it, we discover it, we come to terms with it, but we do not master it. That would be manipulative, instrumental, unfeeling—and it would also put sexuality on an equal footing with emotions we attempt to mold rather than to submit to. The Victorians, who viewed sex in this latter way, could therefore speak of learning from their erotic life, although the learning was so painfully difficult because of the filters of repression. We do not today learn "from" sex, because that puts sexuality outside of the self; instead, we unendingly and frustratingly go in search of ourselves through the genitals.

Think, for instance, of the different connotations of the 19th Century word "seduction" and the modern term "affair." A seduction was the arousal of such feeling by one person—not always a man—in another that social codes were violated. That violation caused all the other social relations of the person to be temporarily called into question; one's spouse, one's children, one's own parents were involved both symbolically through guilt and practically if discovery of the violation occurred. The modern term "affair" tamps down all these risks because it represses the idea that physical love is a social act; it is now a matter of an emotional affinity which *in esse* stands outside the web of other social relations in a person's life. It would seem illogical now for a person conducting an affair, whether inside or outside the bounds of a marriage, to see it innately connected to parental relations, so that whenever one makes love to another person one's status as someone else's child is altered. This, we would say, is a matter of individual cases, of personality factors; it is not a social matter. Among freer spirits the same argument would be made of an affair in relation to a marriage. The very word "affair"—so blank, so amorphous—indicates a kind of devaluation of sexuality, as an image which can be socially shared through speech. In rebelling against sexual repression, we have rebelled against the idea that sexuality has a social dimension.

Why should efforts at sexual freedom, so well meant in spirit, end as insoluble, magical puzzles of self? In a society where intimate feeling is an all-purpose standard of reality, experience is organized in two forms which lead to this unintended destructiveness. In such a society, the basic human energies of narcissism are so mobilized that they enter systematically and perversely into human relationships. In such a society, the test of whether people are being authentic and "straight" with each other is a peculiar standard of market exchange in intimate relations.

Narcissism in the clinical sense diverges from the popular idea of love of one's own beauty; more strictly, and as a character disorder, it is self-absorption which prevents one from understanding what belongs within the domain of the self and self-gratification and what belongs outside it. Thus narcissism is an obsession with "what this person, that event means to me." This question about the personal relevance of other people and outside acts is posed so repetitively that a clear perception of those persons and events in themselves is obscured. This absorption in self, oddly enough, prevents gratification of self needs; it makes the person at the moment of attaining an end or connecting with another person feel that "this isn't what I wanted." Narcissism thus has the double quality of being a voracious absorption in self needs and the block to their fulfillment.

Narcissistic character disorders are the most common sources of the forms of psychic distress therapists now see. The hysterical symptoms which were the dominant complaints of Freud's erotic and repressive society have largely disappeared. This character disorder has arisen because a new kind of society encourages the growth of its psychic components and erases a sense of meaningful social encounter outside its terms, outside the boundaries of the single self, in public. We must be careful to specify the kind of distress it is, in order not to falsify the milieu in which it has acquired a social form. This character disorder does not lead inevitably to psychosis, nor do people under its sway live in an acute state of crisis all the time. The withdrawal of commitment, the continual search for a definition from within of "who I am," produces pain but no cataclysmic malaise. Narcissism, in other words, does not create the conditions which might promote its own destruction.

In the realm of sexuality, narcissism withdraws physical love from any kind of commitment, personal or social. The sheer fact of commitment on a person's part seems to him or her to limit the opportunities for "enough" experience to know who he or she is and to find the "right" person to complement who he or she is. Every sexual relationship under the sway of narcissism becomes less fulfilling the longer the partners are together.

A primary relation between narcissism and sexuality can be drawn in terms of images people have of their own bodies. An interesting study conducted in Paris over many years has shown that as people come to take their bodies as more and more complete definitions of their own sexuality, the "symbolizing" of the body becomes less and less easy for them. As sexuality becomes an absolute state fixed in the form of the body, the people who are those bodies have increasing difficulty imagining phallic forms in natural organisms such as plants or feeling a relationship between bodily movement and the action of a cylinder or a bellows. The enshrining of the body as an absolute sexual state is narcissistic because it makes sexuality exclusively an attribute of the person, a state of being rather than an activity, and therefore essentially isolated from the sexual experience the person may or may not have. The study concludes that the result of this narcissism is a decrease in "metaphorical" imagination of the body, which is to say an impoverishment of the cognitive activity of creating a symbol out of a physical thing. This is one reason why, as a society shifts from eroticism to sexuality, from belief in emotional actions to belief in emotional states of being, destructive psychological forces are brought to the fore. It is a sign of the destructiveness unleashed when a society denies even to Eros a public dimension.

The most common form in which narcissism makes itself known to the person is by a process of inversion: If only I could feel more, or if only I could really feel, then I could relate to others or have "real" relations with them. But at each moment of encounter, I never seem to feel enough. The obvious content in this inversion is a self-accusation, but buried beneath it is the feeling that the world is failing me.

A second destructive force reinforces this fruitless search for an identity composed of materials from within. This force can best be described by giving an example of it in the training of apprentice diagnostic interviewers.

In their first sessions, beginning interviewers are often anxious to show that they regard their subjects as real people, not just as "data sources." The interviewers want to deal with their subjects as equals making joint discoveries. This laudable desire results in a peculiar initial situation: every time the subject reveals some detail or feeling of his private life, the interviewer will counter by revealing a detail from his own. Treating someone else as a "real person" in this situation becomes like a market exchange of intimacies; they show you a card, you show them one.

Interviewers tend to grow out of this marketing of mutual revelations when they begin to see that, exposing themselves, they are losing the opportunity to find out about the subject's feelings. This opportunity will arise if the interviewer asks questions, or just sits silent, waiting for the other person to go on. After a time, sensitive interviewers begin to be uncomfortable with the idea that to treat someone else as an emotional equal you must have a reciprocal relationship with him, reacting to whatever he shows you by revealing something to him. And at this point, the interviewers are on the way from an ideal of intimacy based on market exchange to a more genuine intimacy. In it, boundaries around the self are not isolating, but can actually encourage communication with others.

Interviewers receive their initial notions of intimacy as market exchange from assumptions which rule the larger society. If people are close to each other to the extent that they know about each other, then interpersonal knowledge becomes a matter of reciprocal revelation. When two people are out of revelations, and the market exchange has come to an end, all too often the relationship comes to an end. It is exhausted because "there is nothing more to say," each person comes to take the other "for granted." Boredom is the logical consequence of intimacy as an exchange relationship. This exhaustion perfectly complements the narcissistic conviction that whatever gratifications one is receiving at the moment are not all that one could receive, or, inverted, that one is not really feeling enough for the relationship to be "real."

Narcissism and the market exchange of self-revelations structure the conditions under which the expression of feeling in intimate circumstances becomes destructive. There is a never-ending search for gratification, and at the same time the self cannot permit gratification to occur. Some measure of the power of this self language can be glimpsed in the code words used today to measure the "authenticity" of relationships or other persons. We speak of whether we can personally "relate" to events or other persons, and whether in the relation itself people are "open" to one another. The first is a cover word for measuring the other in terms of a mirror of self-concern, and the second is a cover for measuring social interaction in terms of the market exchange of confession.

The 19th Century bourgeois family attempted to preserve some distinction between the sense of private reality and the very different terms of the public world outside the home. The line between the two was confused, often violated, it was drawn in the erotic sphere by a hand impelled by fear, but at least an attempt was made to maintain the separateness and complexity of different domains of social reality. There was a quality about the bourgeois life of the last century all too easy to forget—its essential *dignity*. There was an effort—diseased and destined to collapse, to be sure—to make distinctions between realms of experience, and thus to wrest some form out of a society of enormous disorder and harshness. Marx perceived that dignity no less than did Weber; the early novels of Thomas Mann are celebrations of it in the same measure that they are studies in its inevitable disintegration.

If entrapment in questions of self had occurred even as people continued to lead active lives with people they could never know, in politics and large-scale bureaucracies, we might sensibly conclude that the dimensions of the problem lay in the increasing importance of psychology in bourgeois life; this psychological problem could be seen as divorced from sociological questions of participation and group action. But in fact a trade-off has occurred. As concern for questions of selfhood has grown greater, participation with strangers for social ends has diminished—or that participation is perverted by the psychological question. In community groups, for instance, people feel they need to get to know each other as persons in order to act together; they then get caught up in immobilizing processes of revealing themselves to each other as persons, and gradually lose the desire to act together.

This desire to reveal one's personality in social dealings, and to measure social action itself in terms of what it shows of the personalities of others, can be labeled in two ways. It is first a desire to authenticate oneself as a social actor through display of one's personal qualities. What makes an action good (that is, authentic) is the character of those who engage in it, not the action itself. When some one person is judged to be authentic, or when society as a whole is described as creating problems of human authenticity, the language reveals one way in which social action is being devalued in the process of placing more weight on psychological matters. As a matter of common sense we know that good men perform bad acts, but this language of authenticity makes it hard for us to use common sense.

The desire to authenticate oneself, one's motives, one's feelings, is secondly a form of Puritanism. For all the liberating of our sexuality, we are within the orbit of self-justification which defined the Puritan's world. And this is so for a particular reason. Narcissistic feelings often focus themselves on obsessive questions of whether I am good enough, whether I am adequate, and the like. When a society mobilizes these feelings, when it deflates the objective character of action and inflates the importance of subjective states of feeling of the actors, these questions of self-justification in action, via a "symbolic act," will come systematically to the fore. The trade-off now occurring between public and private concern, by mobilizing these obsessive questions of the legitimacy of the self, has reawakened the most corrosive elements of the Protestant ethic in a culture which is no longer either religious or convinced that material wealth is a form of moral capital.

The trade-off between greater psychic absorption and lessened social participation can easily be mistaken as a psychological issue itself. It could be said that people are losing the "will" to act socially, or that they are losing the "desire." These words as pure psychological states mislead because they do not explain how a whole society could lose its will together, or change its desires. They further mislead in suggesting a therapeutic solution, to shake people out of this self-absorption—as if the environment which has eroded their social will and transformed their desires might suddenly welcome changed individuals with open arms.

DEAD PUBLIC SPACE

Intimate vision is induced in proportion as the public domain is abandoned as empty. On the most physical level, the environment prompts people to think of the public domain as meaningless. This is in the organization of space in cities. Architects who design skyscrapers and other large-scale, high-density buildings are among the few professionals who are forced to work with present-day ideas of public life, such as they are, and indeed are among the few professionals who of necessity express and make these codes manifest to others.

One of the first pure International School skyscrapers built after World War II was Gordon Bunshaft's Lever House on Park Avenue in New York. The ground floor of Lever House is an open-air square, a courtyard with a tower rising on the north side, and, one story above the ground, a low structure surrounding the other three sides. But one passes from the street underneath this low horseshoe to penetrate to the courtyard; the street level itself is dead space. No diversity of activity takes place on the ground floor; it is only a means of passage to the interior. The form of this International-type skyscraper is at odds with its function, for a miniature public square revivified is declared in form, but the function destroys the nature of a public square, which is to intermix persons and diverse activities.

This contradiction is part of a greater clash. The International School was dedicated to a new idea of visibility in the construction of large buildings. Walls almost entirely of glass, framed with thin steel supports, allow the inside and the outside of a building to be dissolved to the least point of differentiation; this technology permits the achievement of what S. Giedion calls the ideal of the permeable wall, the ultimate in visibility. But these walls are also hermetic barriers. Lever House was the forerunner of a design concept in which the wall, though permeable, also isolates the activities within the building from the life of the street. In this design concept, the aesthetics of visibility and social isolation merge.

The paradox of isolation in the midst of visibility is not unique to New York, nor are the special problems of crime in New York a sufficient explanation of the deadness of public space in such a design. In the Brunswick Centre built in the Bloomsbury section of London and in the Defense office complex being built on the edge of Paris, the same paradox is at work, and results in the same dead public area.

In the Brunswick Centre two enormous apartment complexes rise away from a central concrete concourse; the apartment buildings are stepped back story after story, so that each looks like a Babylonian terrace city sited on a hill. The terraces of the Brunswick Centre apartments are covered in glass for the most part; thus the apartment dweller has a greenhouse wall letting in a great deal of light and breaking down the barrier between inside and outside. This permeation of the house and the outside is curiously abstract; one has a nice sense of the sky, but the buildings are so angled that they have no relationship to, or view out on, the surrounding buildings of Bloomsbury. Indeed, the rear end of one of the apartment blocks, faced in solid concrete, gives on, or rather ignores, one of the most beautiful squares in all of London. The building is sited as though it could be anywhere, which is to say its siting shows its designers had no sense of being anywhere in particular, much less in an extraordinary urban milieu.

The real lesson of Brunswick Centre is contained in its central concourse. Here there are a few shops and vast areas of empty space. Here is an area to pass through, not to use; to sit on one of the few concrete benches in the concourse for any length of time is to become profoundly uncomfortable, as though one were on exhibit in a vast empty hall. The "public" concourse of the Centre is in fact shielded from the main contiguous Bloomsbury streets by two immense ramps with fences edging them; the concourse itself is raised several feet above street level. Everything has been done, again, to isolate the public area of Brunswick Centre from accidental street incursion, or from simple strolling, just as the siting of the two apartment blocks effectively isolates those who inhabit them, from street, concourse, and square. The visual statement made by the detailing of the greenhouse wall is that the inside and the outside of a dwelling have no differentiation; the social statement made by the concourse, the siting of the complex, and the ramps is that an immense barrier separates "within" the Brunswick Centre from "without."

The erasure of alive public space contains an even more perverse idea—that of making space contingent upon motion. In the Defense Center, as with Lever House and Brunswick Centre, the public space is an area to move through, not be in. At Defense, the grounds around the mass of office towers which compose the complex contain a few stores, but the real purpose is to serve as a pass-through area from car or bus to office building. There is little evidence that the planners of Defense thought this space to have any intrinsic value, that people from the various office blocks might want to remain in it. The ground, in the words of one planner, is "the traffic-flow–support-nexus for the vertical whole." Translated, this means that the public space has become a derivative of movement.

The idea of space as derivative from motion parallels exactly the relations of space to motion produced by the private automobile. One does not use one's car to see the city; the automobile is not a vehicle for touring—or, rather, it is not used as such, except by joyriding adolescent drivers. The car instead gives freedom of movement; one can travel, uninhibited by formal stops, as in the subway, without changing one's mode of motion, from bus, subway, or elevated to pedestrian movement, in making a journey from place A to place B. The city street acquires, then, a peculiar function—to permit motion; if it regulates motion too much, by lights, one-ways, and the like, motorists become nervous or angry.

Today, we experience an ease of motion unknown to any prior urban civilization, and yet motion has become the most anxiety-laden of daily activities. The anxiety comes from the fact that we take unrestricted motion of the individual to be an absolute right. The private motorcar is the logical instrument for exercising that right, and the effect on public space, especially the space of the urban street, is that the space becomes meaningless or even maddening unless it can be subordinated to free movement. The technology of modern motion replaces being in the street with a desire to erase the constraints of geography.

Thus does the design concept of a Defense or a Lever House coalesce with the technology of transportation. In both, as public space becomes a function of motion, it loses any independent experiential meaning of its own.

"Isolation" has so far been used in two senses. First, it means that the inhabitants or workers in an urban high-density structure are inhibited from feeling any relationship to the milieu in which that structure is set. Second, it means that as one can isolate oneself, in a private automobile, for freedom of movement, one ceases to believe one's surroundings have any meaning save as a means toward the end of one's own motion. There is a third, rather more brutal sense of social isolation in public places, an isolation directly produced by one's visibility to others.

The design idea of the permeable wall is applied by many architects within their buildings as well as on the skin. Visual barriers are destroyed by doing away with office walls, so that whole floors will become one vast open space, or there will be a set of private offices on the perimeter with a large open area within. This destruction of walls, office planners are quick to say, increases office efficiency, because when people are all day long visually exposed to one another, they are less likely to gossip and chat, more likely to keep to themselves. When everyone has each other under surveillance, sociability decreases, silence being the only form of protection. The open-floor office plan brings the paradox of visibility and isolation to its height, a paradox which can also be stated in reverse. People are more sociable, the more they have some tangible barriers between them, just as they need specific places in public whose sole purpose is to bring them together. Let us put this another way again: Human beings need to have some distance from intimate observation by others in order to feel sociable. Increase intimate contact and you decrease sociability. Here is the logic of one form of bureaucratic efficiency.

Dead public space is one reason, the most concrete one, that people will seek out on intimate terrain what is denied them on more alien ground. Isolation in the midst of public visibility and overemphasis on psychological transactions complement each other. To the extent, for instance, that a person feels he must protect himself from the surveillance of others in the public realm by silent isolation, he compensates by baring himself to those with whom he wants to make contact. The complementary relation exists because here are two expressions of a single, general transformation of social relations. I have sometimes thought about this complementary situation in terms of the masks of self which manners and the rituals of politeness create. These masks have ceased to matter in impersonal situations or seem to be the property only of snobs; in closer relationships, they appear to get in the way of knowing someone else. And I wonder if this contempt for ritual masks of sociability has not really made us more primitive culturally than the simplest tribe of hunters and gatherers.

A relation between how people view their love-making and what they experience on the street may seem farfetched. And even if one grants there are such connections between modes of personal and public life, one might reasonably object that they have shallow roots historically. It is the generation born after World War II which has turned inward as it has liberated itself from sexual constraints; it is in this same generation that most of the physical destruction of the public domain has occurred. The thesis of this book, however, is that these blatant signs of an unbalanced personal life and empty public life have been a long time in the making. They are the results of a change that began with the fall of the *ancien régime* and the formation of a new capitalist, secular, urban culture.

THE CHANGES IN THE PUBLIC DOMAIN

The history of the words "public" and "private" is a key to understanding this basic shift in the terms of Western culture. The first recorded uses of the word "public" in English identify the "public" with the common good in society; in 1470, for instance, Malory spoke of "the emperor Lucyos . . . dictatour or procurour of the publyke wele of Rome." Some seventy years later, there was added a sense of "public" as that which is manifest and open to general observation. Hall wrote in his *Chronicle* of 1542, "Their inwarde grudge could not refrayne but crye out in places publicke, and also private." "Private" was here used to mean privileged, at a high governmental level. By the end of the 17th Century, the opposition of "public" and "private" was shaded more like the way the terms are now used. "Public" meant open to the scrutiny of anyone, whereas "private" meant a sheltered region of life defined by one's family and friends; thus Steele, in an issue of the *Tatler* in 1709, "These effects . . . upon the publick and private actions of men," and Butler in the *Sermons* (1726), "Every man is to be considered in two capacities, the private and the publick." To go "out in publick" (Swift) is a phrase based on society conceived in terms of this geography. The older senses are not entirely lost today in English, but this 18th Century usage sets up the modern terms of reference.

The meanings accorded *le public* in French show something similar. Renaissance use of the word was largely in terms of the common good and the body politic; gradually *le public* became also a special region of sociability. Erich Auerbach once made a thorough study of this more modern definition of "the public," first appearing in France in the middle of the 17th Century, as it was related to the public that was the audience for plays. The theatrical public was referred to in the time of Louis XIV by the catch-phrase *la cour et la ville,* the court and the city. Auerbach discovered that this theatrical public in fact consisted of an elite group of people—an obvious finding in terms of court life, not so obvious in terms of urban life. *La ville* of 17th Century Paris was a very small group, whose origins were non-aristocratic and mercantile, but whose manners were directed to obscuring this fact, not only out of shame but in order to facilitate interchanges with the court.

The sense of who "the public" were, and where one was when one was out "in public," became enlarged in the early 18th Century in both Paris and London. Bourgeois people became less concerned to cover up their social origins; there were many more of them; the cities they inhabited were becoming a world in which widely diverse groups in society were coming into contact. By the time the word "public" had taken on its modern meaning, therefore, it meant not only a region of social life located apart from the realm of family and close friends, but also that this public realm of acquaintances and strangers included a relatively wide diversity of people.

There is a word logically associated with a diverse urban public, the word "cosmopolitan." A cosmopolite, in the French usage recorded in 1738, is a man who moves comfortably in diversity; he is comfortable in situations which have no links or parallels to what is familiar to him. The same sense of the word appeared in English earlier than in French, but was not much employed until the 18th Century. Given the new terms of being out in public, the cosmopolitan was the perfect public man. An early English usage foreshadowed the commonplace sense of the word in 18th Century bourgeois society. In one of Howell's *Letters* (1645), he wrote, "I came tumbling out into the World, a pure Cadet, a true Cosmopolite, not born to Land, Lease, House, or Office." Without inherited wealth or inherited feudal obligation, the cosmopolitan, whatever his pleasure in worldly diversity, of necessity must make his way in it.

"Public" thus came to mean a life passed outside the life of family and close friends; in the public region diverse, complex social groups were to be brought into ineluctable contact. The focus of this public life was the capital city.

These changes in language were correlated with conditions of behavior and terms of belief in the 18th Century cosmopolis. As the cities grew, and developed networks of sociability independent of direct royal control, places where strangers might regularly meet grew up. This was the era of the building of massive urban parks, of the first attempts at making streets fit for the special purpose of pedestrian strolling as a form of relaxation. It was the era in which coffeehouses, then cafes and coaching inns, became social centers; in which the theater and opera houses became open to a wide public through the open sale of tickets rather than the older practice whereby aristocratic patrons distributed places. Urban amenities were diffused out from a small elite circle to a broader spectrum of society, so that even the laboring classes began to adopt some of the habits of sociability, like promenades in parks, which were formerly the exclusive province of the elite, walking in their private gardens or "giving" an evening at the theater.

In the realm of necessity as in the realm of leisure, patterns of social interaction grew up which were suited to exchange between strangers and did not depend on fixed feudal privileges or monopolistic control established by royal grant. The 18th Century urban market was unlike its late medieval or Renaissance predecessors; it was internally competitive, those selling in it vying for the attention of a shifting and largely unknown group of buyers. As the cash economy expanded and modes of credit, accounting, and investment became more rationalized, business was carried on in offices and shops and on an increasingly impersonal basis. It would, of course, be wrong to see either the economy or the sociability of these expanding cities replacing at a stroke older modes of business and pleasure. Rather they juxtaposed still-surviving modes of personal obligation with new modes of interaction, suited to a life passed amidst strangers under conditions of poorly regulated entrepreneurial expansion.

Nor would it be correct to imagine that forging a social bond suited to an expanding city and expanded bourgeois class was either painless or just. People anxiously sought to create modes of speech, even of dress, which would give order to the new urban situation, and also demarcate this life from the private domain of family and friends. Often in their search for principles of public order they resorted to modes of speech, dress, or interaction logically suited to a vanishing era, and tried to force these modes to signify under new and antipathetic conditions. In the process many inequities of late medieval society, now transplanted to alien terrain, became all the more painful and oppressive. There is no need to romanticize the public life of the *ancien régime* cosmopolis to appreciate it; the attempt to create a social order in the midst of confusing and chaotic social conditions at one and the same time brought the contradictions of the *ancien régime* to a point of crisis and created positive opportunities for group life which have yet to be understood.

As in behavior, so in belief, the citizens of the 18th Century capitals attempted to define both what public life was and what it was not. The line drawn between public and private was essentially one on which the claims of civility—epitomized by cosmopolitan, public behavior—were balanced against the claims of nature—epitomized by the family. They saw these claims in conflict, and the complexity of their vision lay in that they refused to prefer the one over the other, but held the two in a state of equilibrium. Behaving with strangers in an emotionally satisfying way and yet remaining aloof from them was seen by the mid-18th Century as the means by which the human animal was transformed into a social being. The capacities for parenthood and deep friendship were seen in turn to be natural potentialities, rather than human creations; while man *made* himself in public, he *realized* his nature in the private realm, above all in his experiences within the family. The tensions between the claims of civility and the rights of nature, epitomized in the divide between public and private life in the cosmopolitan center, not only suffused the high culture of the era but extended into more mundane realms. These tensions appeared in manuals on child-rearing, tracts on moral obligation, and common-sense beliefs about the rights of man. Together, public and private created what would today be called a "universe" of social relations.

The struggle for public order in the 18th Century city, and the tension between the claims of public and private life, constituted the terms of a coherent culture, though there were, as there are in any period, exceptions, deviations, and alternative modes. But a balance of public and private geography in the Enlightenment did exist, and against it there stands out in relief the fundamental change in the ideas of public and private which followed upon the great revolutions at the end of the century and the rise of a national industrial capitalism in more modern times.

Three forces were at work in this change. They were, first, a double relationship which industrial capitalism in the 19th Century came to have with public life in the great city; second, a reformulation of secularism beginning in the 19th Century which affected how people interpret the strange and the unknown; third, a strength which became a weakness, built into the structure of public life itself in the *ancien régime*. This strength meant that public life did not die an instantaneous death under the weight of political and social upheaval at the end of the 18th Century. The public geography prolonged itself into the 19th Century, seemingly intact, in fact changing from within. This inheritance affected the new forces of secularism and capitalism as much as they were at work on it. The transformation of public life can be thought of as parallel to the collapse which comes to athletes who have been especially strong, so that they survive beyond youth with seemingly undiminished powers, and then all at once make manifest the decay which has been continuously eroding the body from within. Because of this peculiar form of survival, the signs of *ancien régime* publicness are not so far from modern life as might at first be imagined.

The double relation of industrial capitalism to urban public culture lay first in the pressures of privatization which capitalism aroused in 19th Century bourgeois society. It lay second in the "mystification" of material life in public, especially in the matter of clothes, caused by mass production and distribution.

The traumas of 19th Century capitalism led those who had the means to try to shield themselves in whatever way possible from the shocks of an economic order which neither victors nor victims understood. Gradually the will to control and shape the public order eroded, and people put more emphasis on protecting themselves from it. The family became one of these shields. During the 19th Century the family came to appear less and less the center of a particular, nonpublic region, more an idealized refuge, a world all its own, with a higher moral value than the public realm. The bourgeois family was idealized as life wherein order and authority were unchallenged, security of material existence could be a concomitant of real marital love, and the transactions between members of the family would brook no outside scrutiny. As the family became a refuge from the terrors of society, it gradually became also a moral yardstick with which to measure the public realm of the capital city. Using family relations as a standard, people perceived the public domain not as a limited set of social relations, as in the Enlightenment, but instead saw public life as morally inferior. Privacy and stability appeared to be united in the family; against this ideal order the legitimacy of the public order was thrown into question.

Industrial capitalism was equally and directly at work on the material life of the public realm itself. For instance, the mass production of clothes, and the use of mass-production patterns by individual tailors or seamstresses, meant that many diverse segments of the cosmopolitan public began in gross to take on a similar appearance, that public markings were losing distinctive forms. Yet virtually no one believed that society was becoming thereby homogenized; the machine meant that social differences—important differences, necessary to know if one were to survive in a rapidly expanding milieu of strangers—were becoming hidden, and the stranger more intractably a mystery. The machine production of a wide variety of goods, sold for the first time in a mass-merchandising setting, the department store, succeeded with the public not through appeals to utility or cheap price, but rather by capitalizing on this mystification. Even as they became more uniform, physical goods were endowed in advertising with human qualities, made to seem tantalizing mysteries which had to be possessed to be understood. "Commodity fetishism," Marx called it; he was only one among many who were struck by the confluence of mass production, homogeneity of appearance, and yet the investing in material things of attributes or associations of intimate personality.

The interaction of capitalism and public geography thus pulled in two directions; one was withdrawal from the public into the family, the other was a new confusion about the materials of public appearance, a confusion which, however, could be turned to a profit. It might therefore be tempting to conclude that industrial capitalism alone caused the public realm to lose legitimacy and coherence, but the conclusion would be inadmissible even on its own terms. What after all prompted people to believe these physical goods, so uniform, could have psychological associations? Why believe in a thing as though it were human?

The fact that this belief was profitable for a few does not explain why it should be held by a multitude.

This question involves the second force which changed the public life inherited from the *ancien régime,* a change in the terms of belief about worldly life. This belief is secularity. As long as the secular is thought opposed in some way to the sacred, the word becomes one-dimensional and fixed. It is better used as the imagery and symbols which make things and people in the world understandable. I think the following definition best: secularity is the conviction before we die of why things are as they are, a conviction which will cease to matter of itself once we are dead.

Secular terms changed drastically from the 18th to the 19th Century. "Things and people" were understandable in the 18th Century when they could be assigned a place in the order of Nature. This order of Nature was not a physical, tangible thing, nor was the order ever encapsuled by worldly things. A plant or a passion occupied a place in the order of Nature but did not define it in miniature and whole. The order of Nature was therefore an idea of the secular as the transcendental. Not only did this idea permeate the writing of scientists and other intellectuals, it reached into such daily affairs as attitudes toward the discipline of children or the morality of extramarital affairs.

The secularism which arose in the 19th Century was of a wholly antithetical sort. It was based on a code of the immanent, rather than the transcendent. Immediate sensation, immediate fact, immediate feeling, were no longer to be fitted into a pre-existent scheme in order to be understood. The immanent, the instant, the fact, was a reality in and of itself. Facts were more believable than system—or, rather, the logical array of facts became a system; the 18th Century order of Nature in which phenomena had a place but in which Nature transcended phenomena was thus overturned. This new measure of what could serve as materials for belief ruled psychology as much as it ruled the study of physical objects. By 1870 it appeared plausible to study "an emotion" as having a self-contained meaning, if one could find out all the tangible circumstances in which "the emotion" appeared and the tangible signs through which "the emotion" made itself manifest. No circumstance or sign could therefore be ruled out, a priori, as irrelevant. In a world where immanence is the principle of secular knowledge, everything counts because everything might count.

This restructuring of the code of secular knowledge had a radical effect on public life. It meant that appearances in public, no matter how mystifying, still had to be taken seriously, because they might be clues to the person hidden behind the mask. Any appearance a person made was in some way real, because it was tangible; indeed, if that appearance were a mystery, all the more reason for taking it seriously: on what grounds, a priori, would one put it out of mind, on what grounds discriminate? When a society dedicates itself to the principle of things having meanings in themselves, it thus introduces an element of profound self-doubt into its cognitive apparatus, for any exercise of discrimination may be a mistake. Thus arose one of the great and enriching contradictions of the 19th Century; even as people wanted to flee, to shut themselves up in a private, morally superior realm, they feared that arbitrarily classifying their experience into, say, public and private dimensions might be self-inflicted blindness.

To fantasize that physical objects had psychological dimensions became logical in this new secular order. When belief was governed by the principle of immanence, there broke down distinctions between perceiver and perceived, inside and outside, subject and object. If everything counts potentially, how am I to draw a line between what relates to my personal needs and what is impersonal, unrelated to the immediate realm of my experience? It may all matter, nothing may matter, but how am I to know? I must therefore draw no distinction between categories of objects and of sensations, because in distinguishing them I may be creating a false barrier. The celebration of objectivity and hardheaded commitment to fact so prominent a century ago, all in the name of Science, was in reality an unwitting preparation for the present era of radical subjectivity.

If the impact of industrial capitalism was to erode the sense of public life as a morally legitimate sphere, the impact of the new secularity was to erode this sphere by a contrary route, posing to mankind the dictum that nothing which arouses sensation, puzzlement, or simple notice may be excluded a priori from the realm of the private life of a person, or be bereft of some psychological quality important to discover. However, capitalism and secularism together still provide only an incomplete view of what agents of change were at work on the public domain, or rather a distorted picture. For the sum of these two forces would have added up to complete social and cognitive disaster. All the familiar catastrophic clichés—alienation, dissociation, etc.— would have to be trundled out. Indeed, if the story of how a public dimension was shattered stopped at this point, we should expect that there would have occurred among the bourgeoisie massive upheavals, political storms, and rages of a sort equal in passion, if different in substance, to those which socialists hoped would arise among the 19th Century urban proletariat.

The very extension of an established urban culture into the world of these new economic and ideological forces counterbalanced them, and maintained some semblance of order for a time in the midst of very painful and contradictory emotions. Historians promote blindness about this inheritance. When they speak of a revolution being a "watershed," or the coming of industrial capitalism as being a "revolution," they often suggest to the imagination of their readers that beforehand there was one society, that during the revolution society stopped, and that afterward a new society began. This is a view of human history based on the life cycle of the moth. Nowhere, unfortunately, has the chrysalis theory of human history reigned to worse effect than in the study of the city. Phrases like "the urban-industrial revolution" and "the capitalist metropolis" (employed by writers of contrary political views) both suggest that before the 19th Century the city was one thing, after capitalism or modernism did its work, entirely another. The error is more than that of failing to see how one condition of life blurs into another; it is a failure to understand both the reality of cultural survival and the problems this legacy, like any inheritance, creates in a new generation.

The bourgeoisie continued to believe that "out in public" people experienced sensations and human relations which one could not experience in any other social setting or context. The legacy of the *ancien régime* city was united to the privatizing impulses of industrial capitalism in another way. Out in public was where moral violation occurred and was tolerated; in public one could break the laws of respectability. If the private was a refuge from the terrors of society as a whole, a refuge created by idealizing the family, one could escape the burdens of this ideal by a special kind of experience, one passed among strangers, or, more importantly, among people determined to remain strangers to each other.

The public as an immoral domain meant rather different things to women and men. For women, it was where one risked losing virtue, dirtying oneself, being swept into "a disorderly and heady swirl" (Thackeray). The public and the idea of disgrace were closely allied. The public for a bourgeois man had a different moral tone. By going out in public, or "losing yourself in public," as the phrase occurred in ordinary speech a century ago, a man was able to withdraw from those very repressive and authoritarian features of respectability which were supposed to be incarnate in his person, as father and husband, in the home. So that for men, the immorality of public life was allied to an undercurrent of sensing immorality to be a region of freedom, rather than of simple disgrace, as it was for women. For instance, in the restaurants of the 19th Century, a lone, respectable woman dining with a group of men, even if her husband were present, would cause an overt sensation, whereas the dining out of a bourgeois man with a woman of lower station was tacitly but studiously avoided as a topic of conversation among any of those near to him. For this same reason, the extramarital liaisons of Victorian men were sometimes conducted more publicly than one would in retrospect imagine, because they occurred in a social space which continued to be far away from the family; they were "outside," in a kind of moral limbo.

Moreover, by the middle of the last century, experience gained in the company of strangers came to seem a matter of urgent necessity in the formation of one's personality. One's personal strengths might not develop if one did not expose oneself to strangers—one might be too inexperienced, too naïve, to survive. In the child-rearing manuals and primers for juveniles of the 1870's or 1880's, we encounter again and again the contradictory themes of avoidance of worldly perils in the company of strangers and the command to learn so thoroughly the dangers of the world that one becomes strong enough to recognize these hidden temptations. In the *ancien régime,* public experience was connected to the formation of social order; in the last century, public experience came to be connected to the formation of personality. Worldly experience as an obligation for self-development appeared in the great monuments of the last century's culture, as well as in its more everyday codes of belief; the theme speaks in Balzac's *Illusions Perdues,* in Tocqueville's *Souvenirs,* in the works of the social Darwinists. This pervasive, painful, unreasonable theme was the conjunction of a surviving belief in the value of public experience with the new secular creed that all experiences may have an equal value because all have an equal, potential importance in forming the self.

We need finally to ask what hints we have in ordinary experience at the present time of the transformations which occurred in the last century. In what ways do seemingly abstract forces like privatization, commodity fetishism, or secularism bear upon our lives? Within the realm of current beliefs about personality itself, four of these connections with the past can be discerned.

THE PAST IN THE PRESENT

In ordinary language today, people speak of doing something "unconsciously" or making an "unconscious" slip which reveals their true feelings to someone else. No matter that the usage is meaningless in any strict psychoanalytic sense. What it reveals is a belief in the involuntary disclosure of emotion, and that belief took form in the last century as the weighting of public and private life became imbalanced. By the end of the last century, the notion of the involuntary disclosure of character states showed itself most clearly in the flourishing practice of phrenology—the reading of character from the physical shape of the head—and the Bertillon measurements in criminology, by which psychologists attempted to identify future criminals through cranial and other physical traits. In both, what a person is psychologically was thought to show both physically and involuntarily; personality is a state not subject to guided, sure shaping. In more refined notions, like that of Darwin's, transitory emotional states were also thought to be involuntarily disclosed; indeed, much early psychoanalytic investigation was based on a principle derived from Darwin—namely, that primary process could be studied in adults because it escaped adult control and will. At a broader level, in the high Victorian era people believed their clothes and their speech disclosed their personalities; they feared that these signs were equally beyond their power to mold, but would instead be manifest to others in involuntary tricks of speech, body gesture, or even how they adorned themselves.

The result was that the line between private feeling and public display of it could be erased beyond the power of the will to regulate. The boundary between public and private was no longer the work of a resolute human hand; thus, even as the separate reality of the public realm remained believable, its governance no longer seemed a social act. What is today popularly misnamed "unconscious" behavior was foreshadowed by these ideas of involuntary disclosure of character in public.

The second trace of the 19th Century crisis lies in ordinary political speech today. We are likely to describe as a "credible" or "charismatic" or "believable" leader someone who can make appeals to groups whose interests are alien to his own beliefs, constituency, or ideology. In modern politics it would be suicide for a leader to insist: Forget about my private life; all you need to know about me is how good a legislator or executive I am and what action I intend to take in office. Instead, we get excited when a conservative French President has dinner with a working-class family, even though he has raised taxes on industrial wages a few days before, or believe an American President is more "genuine" and reliable than his disgraced predecessor because the new man cooks his own breakfast. This political "credibility" is the superimposition of private upon public imagery, and, again, it arose in the last century as a result of the behavioral and ideological confusions between these two realms.

Psychological imagery, it has already been noted, was superimposed on things for sale in public. The same sort of process began in the behavior of politicians in front of street crowds, first strikingly manifest in the revolutions of 1848. What was perceived when people watched someone behave in public was his intentions, his character, so that the truth of what he said appeared to depend on what kind of person he was. If the person observed on these terms in public was a politician, this superimposition had a profoundly anti-ideological effect, in the pure political sense of that word. How can a view of social ills or the vision of a better society ever signify in and of itself, and motivate sustained action, if its believability depends on how much an audience at a given moment sympathizes with the character of the man who champions the cause? Under these conditions, the system of public expression became one of personal representation; a public figure presents to others what he feels, and it is this representation of his feeling which arouses belief. This superimposition of private upon public had a particularly strong appeal among bourgeois audiences, but to the extent that others lower in the social scale could be made to believe in its terms, there could occur class domination through the imposition of bourgeois canons of "respect" for a genuine personality. In short, the present-day ideas of "authenticity" in public have their root in an anti-ideological weapon, one which began to be used in the last century in the warfare between the classes.

The third connection involves the defense mechanisms people used one hundred years ago against their own belief in involuntary disclosure of character and against the superimposition of public and private imagery. By an odd route, these defenses came to encourage people to elevate artistic performers to the special status as public figures which they occupy today.

If one can't help showing what one feels, and if the truth of any emotion, statement, or argument in public depends on the character of the person speaking, how are people ever to avoid being fathomed? The only sure defense is to try to keep oneself from feeling, to have no feelings to show. Today, the repressiveness of Victorian society is condemned as a mixture of social snobbishness and sexual fear. But behind these motivations, there was something, if not more appealing, at least more understandable. In a milieu where sensation and feeling, once aroused, are thought to be displayed beyond the power of the will to conceal them, withdrawal from feeling is the only means of keeping some measure of invulnerability. For instance, people tried to shield their characters from others by wearing as little as possible jewelry, lace, or trimmings of an unusual kind, so as not to draw attention to themselves; this was one of the reasons why only a few machine dies for clothes were popular at any one time, although technically a variety of patterns might easily have been employed on the same machines.

At the same time that people sought to appear as unremarkable as possible, they began to demand that in the theater clothes be exact indicators of the characters, histories, and social positions of the *dramatis personae.* In the historical plays performed in midcentury, the actors were supposed to represent exactly what a medieval Danish prince or Roman imperator was supposed to look like; in melodrama, costume and stage gesture became so stylized that by looking at a man entering the stage with rapid, mincing steps you could instantly tell he was the villain before he had spoken a word. More generally, in a performing art, unlike life, one was to see a person strongly declared, see personality regnant. The actor and musician rose in social status far beyond the level of servanthood which they occupied in the *ancien régime*. The performer's social rise was based on his declaration of a forceful, exciting, morally suspect personality, wholly contrary to the style of ordinary bourgeois life, in which one tried to avoid being read as a person by suppressing one's feelings.

In this society on its way to becoming intimate—wherein character was expressed beyond the control of the will, the private was superimposed on the public, the defense against being read by others was to stop feeling—one's behavior in public was altered in its fundamental terms. Silence in public became the only way one could experience public life, especially street life, without feeling overwhelmed. In the mid-19th Century there grew up in Paris and London, and thence in other Western capitals, a pattern of behavior unlike what was known in London or Paris a century before, or is known in most of the non-Western world today. There grew up the notion that strangers had no right to speak to each other, that each man possessed as a public right an invisible shield, a right to be left alone. Public behavior was a matter of observation, of passive participation, of a certain kind of voyeurism. The "gastronomy of the eye," Balzac called it; one is open to everything, one rejects nothing a priori from one's purview, provided one needn't become a participant, enmeshed in a scene. This invisible wall of silence as a right meant that knowledge in public was a matter of observation—of scenes, of other men and women, of locales. Knowledge was no longer to be produced by social intercourse.

The paradox of visibility and isolation which haunts so much of modern public life originated in the right to silence in public which took form in the last century. Isolation in the midst of visibility to others was a logical consequence of insisting on one's right to be mute when one ventured into this chaotic yet still magnetic realm.

To speak of the legacy of the 19th Century's crisis of public life is to speak of broad forces such as capitalism and secularism on the one hand and of these four psychological conditions on the other: involuntary disclosure of character, superimposition of public and private imagery, defense through withdrawal, and silence. The obsessions with selfhood are attempts to work out these conundrums of the last century, by denial. Intimacy is an attempt to solve the public problem by denying that the public exists. As with any denial, this has only made the more destructive aspects of the past the more firmly entrenched. The 19th Century is not yet over.

CHAPTER 2

ROLES

The shifting weight between public and private life has attracted the attention of many writers on modern society, and has also puzzled them. The puzzlements have been of two sorts.

The subject is so vast it is hard to shape. Concerned are issues as diverse as the erosion of public space in cities, the conversion of political discourse into psychological terms, the elevation of performing artists to a special status as public personalities, and the labeling of impersonality itself as a moral evil. As part of the same problem, it is hard to know what kind of specific experience, what kind of "data" are germane to the general theme. Common sense suggests, for example, that the replacement of city streets and squares as social centers by suburban living rooms might have something to do with an increased absorption in questions of self. But what is the exact sense of such a connection, and what are its ramifications?

The second difficulty is more elusive. For all the generality of these themes, writers who take them on often seem to be writing about, or at least groping toward, another subject, embedded in the idea of the erosion of a public domain but not immediately apparent in those terms of discourse. That problem is the social terms on which human beings are expressive. What social conditions encourage people to display their feelings to others in such a way that some sympathetic response, some arousal occurs? Under what conditions do human beings tap their creative powers to make ordinary experience expressive? These questions are ways of asking when, if ever, the human being naturally and without fuss calls on the energies which today seem isolated in the very special preserves of Art. Much of the contemporary writing on society's obsession with the self proclaims the fact that this obsession cuts people off from being expressive to one another, that we are artists without an art. But what is the art which intimate obsessions erode?

There is a relation between the question of method and the question of aborted expression. The artfulness which is squandered in self-absorption is that of playacting; playacting requires an audience of strangers to succeed, but is meaningless or even destructive among intimates. Playacting in the form of manners, conventions, and ritual gestures is the very stuff out of which public relations are formed, and from which public relations derive their emotional meaning. The more social conditions erode the public forum, the more are people routinely inhibited from exercising the capacity to playact. The members of an intimate society become artists deprived of an art. These modes of playacting are "roles." Thus, one method of making sense of the shift between public and private in modern culture would be to investigate the historical changes in these public "roles." That is the method of this book.

Because social analysis today is conducted in a Babel of languages, it might be helpful to begin by clarifying some of the ideas currently used to describe the imbalance of psychological and social claims in modern culture. Those who have directly addressed themselves to this problem fall into two rather distinct camps. In one are writers who are concerned with the moral condition of a society given over to psychological vision; in the other are those who seek to explain the historical origins of such a change by employing the terms of the Marxian tradition.

The moralists have been the more concerned with the questions of human expression which are raised by this historical imbalancing; their concerns are, however, not so much with a theory of the creative potentialities of any society, but rather with the specifically modern paradox that when people are concerned with expressing their own feelings, they are not very expressive people. This paradox informs such works as the German sociologist Theodor Adorno's *The Language of Authenticity,* the attacks on subjectivity-as-truth conducted by a number of French psychoanalysts, and most recently, and most powerfully, the last writings of Lionel Trilling.

At the end of his life, Trilling was beginning to write about the belief in a "boundaryless" self in modern culture. In the first of these studies, *Sincerity and Authenticity,* Trilling was concerned to show the terms on which self-revelation is not an act of expression. His inquiry was specifically directed to understanding a shift in language which embodies this truth, a shift from the language of personal sincerity spoken before the 19th Century to a language of individual authenticity spoken after it. By sincerity, Trilling means the exposure in public of what is felt in private; by authenticity, he means the direct exposure to another of a person's own attempts to feel. The modes of authenticity erase distinctions between public and private. That humanity might consist in keeping wounding feeling about another person from him, that disguise and self-repression may be morally expressive—under the aegis of authenticity these ideas cease to signify. Instead self-disclosure becomes a universal measure of believability and truth, but what is disclosed in the revelation to another of oneself? Here Trilling arrives through an analysis of literary texts, above all through a critique of Sartre, at an idea which we have expressed in the psychological concept "narcissism." The more a person concentrates on feeling genuinely, rather than on the objective content of what is felt, the more subjectivity becomes an end in itself, the less expressive he can be. Under conditions of self-absorption the momentary disclosures of self become amorphous. "Look at me feel" is obvious narcissism, but Trilling has perceived that the less obvious formula "I can only show you my attempts to feel" is bound up in the same impulse.

David Riesman's understanding of the issues involved in this historical change is in much the same spirit as Lionel Trilling's, although Riesman's argument in *The Lonely Crowd* was toward an opposing end. (He has since moved toward Trilling's position in his less well-known but equally important work on the sociology of education.) The American generation which grew up with *The Lonely Crowd* was prone to misread the author's intentions. They thought he was criticizing the tendency of American society to replace the Protestant culture of inner direction and private need by a culture in which people demand more openness to the needs and desires of others. In fact, for all its difficulties, Riesman thought this other-directedness was a change for the better in American life, and in European society if it followed the same path. The misreading of Riesman's values was a logical consequence of the culture in which his audience lived; for that generation was dominated by the desire to use psychological life as an escape from and rebuke to an empty social world. The rebuke, and the subsequent revolts of those elements of the generation of the 1960's which put the same premium on "getting your head together" before you act, were neither of them challenges to the dominant culture, but in fact unwitting intensification of the imbalance between an empty public domain and an intimate domain overburdened with tasks it could not fulfill.

The importance of Riesman's work lies not simply in how it was misread. Nor is it that Riesman himself misread a pattern of historical movement, since in fact there has been a movement from something like his society of other direction to a society of inner direction. Riesman's achievement was to create a social-psychological language for this general and manifold problem. Moreover, Riesman was the first to show why those who are concerned about the overburdening of intimate life, as this affects the expressive power of people obsessed with themselves, belong within a particular tradition of social thought. It is the tradition established in the 19th Century by the writings of Alexis de Tocqueville.

Tocqueville initiates this modern critique at a specific point in his writing, in the second volume of *Democracy in America*, published five years after the first. The first volume saw the dangers of democracy, which was equated with equality, to lie in the suppression of deviants and dissidents by the majority who rule. In Tocqueville's second volume, the emphasis is on the conditions of everyday life in a state of equality, rather than on politics, and now the danger of suppression of deviants is replaced by a danger more complex and nuanced. The dangers are now among the mass of the citizens rather than their enemies. For under a rough equality of conditions, Tocqueville believed, the intimacies of life would become increasingly important. The public being composed of others like oneself, one could entrust public affairs to the hands of bureaucrats and state functionaries, who would look out for common (i.e., equal) interests. The engaging issues in life would then become more and more psychological in character—as citizens, trusting the state, would abandon their concern for what was occurring outside the intimate realm. What would be the result?

Tocqueville saw it as a twofold constriction. The degree of emotional risk-taking men would be willing to engage in would grow less and less. Men would be continually ambitious but harbor no great passions, much less vent them, because passion would threaten the stability of intimate life. Second, gratifications of the self would become increasingly difficult, since, Tocqueville argued, *any* emotional relationship can be meaningful only when it is perceived as part of a web of social relations, rather than the "lonely inexpressive end" of individualism.

Few of those who write today within the Tocquevillian tradition accept its genetic base—the belief that these psychic evils are the result of a society of equality of conditions. Neither in Trilling's nor in Riesman's work is there the belief that equality "causes" intimate vision. But if not equality, what then does? This is the difficulty faced by this school in modern times, for all the complexity of its moral insight and its humane concern for the expressive choking which intimacy creates.

The second modern approach to the problems of intimate vision has indeed been concerned with these causes, and much less concerned with the resulting moral and psychological complexities. This approach is embodied in the work done by members of the Institute for Social Research (the "Frankfurt school") after World War II. In its prewar days, the Institute's members, notably Theodor Adorno, attempted full-scale analyses of the concept of authenticity of feeling, both at an everyday level of experience and in terms of more philosophic notions, such as those of Hegel. After the war, younger members like Jurgen Habermas and Helmut Plessner took up this work in terms of a shift in meaning of "public" and "private." Habermas conducted studies of opinion surveys to deduce what people thought about the public dimension of social life; Plessner tied the changing weights between public and private to shifts in the character of the city. This younger generation moved away from some of the psychological depth of Adorno and Max Horkheimer to a more "economic" emphasis—if economics be understood in the broad sense of production of the means of life. In so doing they relied on notions developed by Marx about "privatization" in bourgeois ideology, that is, about the compensatory tendency in modern capitalism for people working in impersonal market situations to invest feelings in the realm of family and child rearing which they could not invest in work itself.

What resulted was a great refinement of the terminology of "privatization," but these writers, especially Plessner, paid a heavy price for it. As they came more within Marxian orthodoxy, the resultant evils they depicted became ever more one-dimensional: man became an alienated, suffering creature in the hands of a horrid system, a system internalized in his very feelings—rather than a creature whose own propensities for self-destructiveness and expressive failure were reinforced by a destructive system. The language of pure victimization appeared. Since a pure victim is a passive receiver of the blows of fate, all the complexities of real victimization, and especially the active participation in one's own degradation which writers of the Tocquevillian school perceived, were lost.

Each of these schools has a strength which the other lacks. The first has a descriptive power and insight into the phenomena of intimate vision; the second has a refined language, although narrowed to the Marxian topic of privatization, of how these phenomena were produced. However, the first school has been attuned to the fact that behind the issue of self-absorption there stands a more fundamental issue. They see that the expressive potential of human beings can be encouraged by a set of social conditions and also that these conditions can reinforce the person's own self-destructive urges. The younger generation of the Frankfurt school gradually became deaf to this hidden problem, the ills of modern society becoming couched in all the familiar catastrophic clichés of alienation, depersonalization, and the like.

To overcome these problems—to be both historical and sensitive to the complexities of historical result—demands a method and a theory at the same time. Social scientists often mislead others, and themselves, by writing as though a method were a neutral means to an end, so that the scientist "applies" a theory to a problem. In studying the erosion of public roles, we are adopting a mode of inquiry, which at the same time is a theory about our subject—namely, that the subject contains more than meets the eye, that it contains the hidden problem of the conditions under which human beings are able to express themselves forcefully to each other.

ROLES

A "role" is generally defined as behavior appropriate for some situations but not for others. Crying as such is behavior which cannot be described as a "role"; crying at a funeral is behavior which can be so described —it is expected, appropriate, specific to that situation. Much of the study of roles has been a catalogue of what kind of behavior is appropriate to what kind of situations, and the theories of roles now current are of how society creates definitions of appropriateness. Usually overlooked in such catalogues, however, is the fact that roles are not just pantomimes or dumb shows in which people mechanically trot out the right emotional signs at the right place and moment. Roles also involve codes of belief—how much and on what terms people take seriously their own behavior, the behavior of others, and the situations in which they are engaged. Beyond all the cataloguing of how people behave, there is the question of what value they place upon "situation-specific" behavior. Codes of belief and behavior together make up a role, and this is exactly what makes it so difficult to study roles historically. For sometimes new patterns of behavior will continue to be interpreted with old codes of belief, and sometimes the same sort of behavior will continue over time, even as people arrive at new definitions of what it means.

Special kinds of beliefs are involved in roles. This may be seen by distinguishing such a belief from two allied words, "ideology" and "value." Belief can be separated from ideology in a simple-minded way. The statement "Workers are screwed by the system" is an ideological sentence. Such an ideological statement is a formula of cognition, logical or illogical, for a given set of social conditions. The ideology becomes belief at the point at which it becomes consciously involved in the behavior of the person who holds it. Ideology is often confused with belief because cognition is confused with belief. "I love you" is as a piece of language a coherent cognitive expression; whether it is believable or not depends on factors other than that it is a complete sentence, it is uttered at an appropriate moment by one person to another, and so forth.

Much of the opinion which people hold about social life never touches on or strongly influences their behavior. Ideology of this passive sort often shows up in modern opinion polls; people tell a pollster what they think about urban default or the inferiority of blacks, the pollster thinks he has arrived at a truth about their feelings because these opinions can be rationally related to the informant's social status, education, and the like, and then the people involved behave in a way at odds with what they have professed to the pollster. A graphic example of this occurred in the United States in the early 1970's: labor-union bureaucrats were at the same time loudly condemning protesters against the Vietnam War as "unpatriotic" and putting the strongest concrete pressure on the government to end the war. The study of belief as opposed to opinion is therefore an inquiry into those feelings and dispositions which are tied to actions, and influence concretely those actions. Codes of belief in roles can formally be defined as the activation of ideology, and this activation comes about through the influence of social conditions, not through the dictates of linguistic coherence.

The phrases "social values" and "value systems" are barbarisms the social sciences have inflicted on ordinary language. I confess I have never understood what "a value" is. It is not a thing. If it is part of the language by which people rationalize their social world, then it should be treated as a part of ideology. If "a value" is a "prized idea," then the term is a complete mess. "Liberty" and "justice" are prized ideas which mean different things to different people at different times; to call them social values per se gives no clue as to the grounds on which they are valued.

So a belief will be taken as an activation of the logical cognition of social life (ideology); this activation occurs outside the linguistic rules for coherence; the term "value" is abandoned as unclear. The beliefs germane to roles, furthermore, center not on the nature of God or the physiological constitution of man; they are tied to specific acts of behavior. They concern what a person believes he experiences when he prays in church as opposed to his praying spontaneously on a walk through the fields. His notion of what surgery will accomplish in ridding his body of a malign fluid and his general views on surgery are different kinds of belief. It is reasonable to object that there may be no logical distinction between a general belief in God and the belief in Him when one is able to pray to Him in a church; true enough, there may be no difference—or there could be one. By focusing on specific situations, it is possible to investigate whatever shadings of belief derive from its relation to action, and these may elude the student of "world-views," "cultural mentalities," and the like.

The study of roles has a long (although by sociologists unrecognized) history in Western thought. One of the oldest Western ideas of human society is to see society itself to be a theater. There is the tradition of *theatrum mundi*. Human life as a puppet show staged by the gods was Plato's vision in the *Laws;* society as a theater was the motto of Petronius' *Satyricon*. In Christian times the theater of the world was often thought to have an audience of one, a God who looked on in anguish from the heavens at the strutting and the masquerades of His children below. By the 18th Century, when people spoke of the world as a theater, they began to imagine a new audience for their posturing—each other, the divine anguish giving way to the sense of an audience willing to enjoy, if somewhat cynically, the playacting and pretenses of everyday life. And in more recent times, this identification of theater and society has been continued in Balzac's *Comédie Humaine,* in Baudelaire, Mann, and, curiously, Freud.

The image of society as a theater has no single meaning, passing through so many hands and so much time. But it has served three constant moral purposes. The first has been to introduce illusion and delusion as fundamental questions of social life, and the second has been to detach human nature from social action. Man as actor arouses belief; outside the conditions and the moment of performing, that belief might otherwise not be forthcoming; therefore, belief and illusion are tied together in this image of society. Similarly, an actor's nature cannot be inferred from any single role he plays, for in a different play or in a different scene, he may appear in a wholly different guise; how then infer human nature from actions in the theater of society?

Third, and most important, the images of *theatrum mundi* are pictures of the art people exercise in ordinary life. This is the art of acting, and people who exercise it are playing "roles." For a writer like Balzac, these roles are the various necessary masks people wear in different situations. Man as a creature of masks perfectly suits Balzac's belief, as it has other writers who have perceived human affairs as some species of *comédie,* that neither human nature nor some single definition of morality can ever firmly be deduced from behavior.

Ironically, as modern sociologists have grown more and more interested in the masks themselves (inelegantly defined as "situation-specific behavior"), the classical moral concerns have disappeared. Perhaps this is a simple failure in knowledge. All too often, role analysts write as though in the "prescientific" era kindred ideas were unknown. Perhaps it is that "scientists" of society are disposed to believe that human behavior and human morals are somehow distinct, and that science addresses itself only to the former. But, I think, there is something more at work in this diminution of insight, this narrowing of the ground, which modern sociologists have effected in the *theatrum mundi* tradition. It is related to the very shift in weights between public and private life, and is graphically revealed in the work of the leading contemporary role analyst, Erving Goffman.

Goffman has studied a wide range of human situations, from farmers in the Shetland Islands, to mental patients, to the problems of physically deformed persons; he has investigated traffic patterns in cities, advertising, gambling casinos, and surgical operating rooms. He is an extremely sensitive and acute observer, noticing little fragments and exchanges which in fact play a large part in structuring the interactions of people. The difficulties in his work come when he seeks to formulate these observations into a theoretical system.

Each of the "scenes" in his purview is a fixed situation. How the scene came into being, how those who play roles in it change the scene by their acts, or, indeed, how each scene may appear or disappear because of larger historical forces at work in the society—to these questions Goffman is indifferent. The static, historyless society of scenes in his books derives from his belief that in human affairs people seek always to establish a situation of equilibrium; they give and take with one another until they create enough stability to know what to expect by mutually balancing their actions; the balanced actions are the "roles" of a given situation. The element of truth in the approach is lost because Goffman has no ear for, indeed no interest in, the forces of disorder, disruption, and change which might intervene in these arrangements. Here is a picture of society in which there are scenes but no plot. And since there is no plot in this sociology, no history, there are no characters in it, as that term has any meaning in the theater, for their actions cause no change in the lives of his people; there are only endless adaptations. In Goffman's world, people behave but they do not have experience.

The attention to static behavior in roles, at the expense of attention to experience learned in such situations, derives from a fundamental moral supposition of this seemingly amoral kind of inquiry. These roles do not admit of much commitment. Save for deviants like the insane and the deformed, little investment of feeling appears among the various players. In fact, if a particular role involves any pain, Goffman portrays those caught as not challenging their social circumstances, but rather "the individual constantly twists, turns, and squirms, even while allowing himself to be carried along with the controlling definition of the situation . . . the individual . . . is a juggler and synthesizer, an accommodator and appeaser. . . ."

Since the "controlling definitions" are fixed, juggling is what makes experience complex. In other words, writers of the Goffman school present less a general theory of society than a prime symptom of the modern malaise which forms the subject of this book—the inability to imagine social relations which would arouse much passion, an imagination of public life in which people behave, and manage their behavior, only through withdrawal, "accommodation," and "appeasement."

PUBLIC ROLES

How has it occurred that the terms of role-playing changed so that they became less and less matters of expression, more and more matters of neutralization and appeasement of others? To raise the question is first to revive the moral concern contained in the classical school of *theatrum mundi,* especially its belief that role-playing is expressive, that when people invest feeling in their roles, they acquire something of the power of an actor. But, then, to what do people commit their passions when they play roles?

In the theater, there is a correlation between belief in the persona of the actor and belief in conventions. Play, playacting, and acting, all require belief in conventions to be expressive. Convention is itself the single most expressive tool of public life. But in an age wherein intimate relations determine what shall be believable, conventions, artifices, and rules appear only to get in the way of revealing oneself to another; they are obstructions to intimate expression. As the imbalance between public and intimate life has grown greater, people have become less expressive. With an emphasis on psychological authenticity, people become inartistic in daily life because they are unable to tap the fundamental creative strength of the actor, the ability to play with and invest feeling in external images of self. Thus we arrive at the hypothesis that theatricality has a special, hostile relation to intimacy; theatricality has an equally special, friendly relation to a strong public life.

How do experiences an audience of strangers have in the theater or music hall compare with the experiences they have on the street? In both domains, expression occurs in a milieu of relative strangers. In a society with a strong public life there should be affinities between the domains of stage and street; there should be something comparable in the expressive experience crowds have had in these two realms. As public life declines, these affinities should erode. The logical setting for studying this relation of stage and street is the great city. It is in this milieu that the life of strangers in crowds is most in evidence and that transactions between strangers acquire a special importance. In short, the subject of the changing weights between public and intimate life ought to be illuminated by a historical comparative study of the changing of roles on stage and in the street in a setting where modern public life, based on an impersonal, bourgeois, secular society, first took hold: the cosmopolis.

To compare the arousal of belief within the performing arts to the arousal of belief on the streets must cause unease, because it means associating art with society, and since the 19th Century that association has been an uneasy one. When, in the late 19th Century, historians used the arts as tools for studying social life, it was usually the social life of a small elite—patrons, leading personalities of the age, and the like—to which they referred. We may think of writers like Matthew Arnold or Jakob Burckhardt, who saw art as a key to understanding the whole of a society, but these men were in their time exceptions to the connoisseur's assumption that great art at a given moment bore a relation only to a very select region within society.

It was the anthropologist who in the present century began naturally to see art in relation to society as a whole. But as this relationship became popular outside anthropology, the view of art became trivialized, in a kind of reverse snobbism. One moved from art of a people, usually handicrafts and taken seriously as genuine aesthetic production by the anthropologist, to "people's art," in which only a restricted class of artwork has a relation to society as a whole, to "media." Media is or are formulations of people's art in which any purposive attempt at expression is replaced by the more neutral, functional notion of communication. "The medium is the message" is a dictum sensible only when expression itself is reduced to a flow of messages. In general, as the relationship to society has grown larger, all too often the art which qualifies for this relation has been diminished; serious art and social life remain as disjunct as in the 19th Century, only the terms are reversed.

Therefore, in associating performing arts and social relations, one must be open, simply, to the idea that serious, real, genuine art can assist in understanding a social condition widespread in society. It is equally important to get away from a language of cause and effect. For instance, there are affinities between Parisian stage costume and Parisian street dress in 1750. Instead of asking which determined the other —a meaningless exercise—it is more valuable to inquire what the similarities between stage and street dress, both markedly different from clothing considered appropriate for the home, tell about images of the body in public. When in the 19th Century stage and street dress began to diverge, a change in belief about the body in public was occurring, and the dimensions of this change can be studied by studying the divergence.

PUBLIC ROLES IN CITIES

If cause and effect, influence, and the like are poor ways to describe the relation between public life and the public (performing) arts, there is nonetheless a logical relationship between the stage and the street. This logical relationship has four parts. First, the theater shares a problem not with society in general, but with a peculiar kind of society—the great city. The problem is one of *audience*—specifically, how to arouse belief in one's appearance among a milieu of strangers. Second, there can arise in a city rules for making believable appearances before strangers that have a *continuity of content* with the rules governing response to the stage at the time. The audience thus can play a common role in both realms. Third, to the extent a common problem of audience is solved through a common code of believability, *a public geography is produced*, according to two criteria of publicness: the world external to immediate surroundings and personal loyalties becomes consciously defined, and movement through diverse social circumstances and groups of strangers with the aid of this common code becomes comfortable. Fourth, to the extent a public geography exists, social *expression* will be conceived of *as presentation* to other people of feelings which signify in and of themselves, *rather than as representation* to other people of feeling present and real to each self. The four structures typified here are thus of audience, of continuity in rules of belief, of public geography, and of expression. There is concrete human experience embedded in this abstract set of logical relations.

There are probably as many different ways of conceiving what a city is as there are cities. A simple definition therefore has its attractions. The simplest is that a city is a human settlement in which strangers are likely to meet. For this definition to hold true, the settlement has to have a large, heterogeneous population; the population has to be packed together rather densely; market exchanges among the population must make this dense, diverse mass interact. In this milieu of strangers whose lives touch there is a problem of audience akin to the problem of audience an actor faces in the theater.

In a milieu of strangers, the people who witness one's actions, declarations, and professions usually have no knowledge of one's history, and no experience of similar actions, declarations, and professions in one's past; thus it becomes difficult for this audience to judge, by an external standard of experience with a particular person, whether he is to be believed or not in a given situation. The knowledge on which belief can be based is confined to the frame of the immediate situation. The arousal of belief therefore depends on how one behaves—talks, gestures, moves, dresses, listens—within the situation itself. Two people meet at a dinner party; one tells the other he has been depressed for weeks; to the degree the listener as audience can judge the truth of such statements only by the way the stranger enacts the feeling of depression, to that degree appearances like this have an "urban" quality. The city is a settlement in which such problems of enactment are most likely to arise as a matter of routine.

What is impossible in the city is impermissible in the theater. Whatever knowledge an audience has of a performer's private life will not suffice to arouse belief in what he or she does on the stage. Knowing an actor has signed the right peace petitions cannot alone make us take him seriously as a Coriolanus; if he has publicized his private love affairs, that will not make him per se a credible Romeo. There are poor performers who coast for a time on their status as "star personalities," but not very far for very long. In urban situations, we usually lack the external knowledge to judge the reality for a stranger's behavior; in the theater we make as if we were strangers to the actor, so that he must arouse belief in a part; an audience's memory of how he played it five years, months, days ago will not carry. Belief in the theater, therefore, like belief in a stranger, is a matter of taking the immediate encounter as the limit of knowable reality. In both, external knowledge on the part of the audience is not involved—in the city by necessity, in the theater by fiat.

Thus, resemblances between theatrical costume and street clothing, or between the style of acting a tragic figure like Coriolanus and the style in which politicians comport themselves before a street crowd, have more than a casual relationship, because there is more than a casual relationship of audience in the two domains.

The idea that men are like actors, society like a stage, was enshrined in the traditional school of *theatrum mundi,* because in fact this common problem of audience has in the past frequently been solved through a common code of believable appearances. That is not to say that the common codes of Plato's time were replicated in the time of Marivaux, but that the fact of a bridge reappears. The problem with this tradition is that it is all too easy to assume that what is common is therefore innate. There is a great variety to be observed from society to society in the nature of those rules which bridge between belief on the stage and belief in strangers on the street. In societies with quite strict etiquettes of hierarchical status, for instance, the behavior of a stranger will be scrutinized until, by clues of gesture or speech, others can place where he belongs on the ladder; usually he will not be directly asked for this information about himself. Such was the case in many medieval Indian cities. In them, the same scrutiny of gesture and speech appeared in popular plays. In societies which lack this strict etiquette of hierarchy, or in which the facts of rank do not alone determine the parameters of a believable appearance, a bridge between stage and street can be built in other ways. In mid-18th Century Paris, for instance, both clothes for the street and costumes for the stage treated the body as a neutral frame, an inanimate mannequin, on which wigs, elaborate hats, and other adornments were to be placed; the body aroused interest, and the character dressing his body belief, to the extent that the body was treated as an object to be decorated. Within the private family circle, a more *négligée* and entirely animate sense of bodily dress prevailed.

When a bridge between stage and street arises, in response to the problem of audience, a public geography is born. For then it is possible to believe in the reality both of unknown people and of imaginary characters as in a single realm.

Balzac once spoke of the differences between provincials and cosmopolitans in these terms: a provincial believes only in what he observes among those whom daily exposure makes familiar, while a cosmopolitan is willing to believe in what he can only imagine about ways of life and people he has yet to experience himself. Of course, it would be unreal to argue that, in the centers of Western society since the Middle Ages, people literally conflated stage actors with real people— although, again, in many societies today more innocent, if that is the right word, than our own, the two would be as one. Rather, in a period like the 18th Century, actor and stranger would be judged on the same terms, and what one could learn from the one in the domain of art, one could learn from or apply to the other in the special domain of impersonal social life. And therefore, in a very real sense, art could be a teacher about life; the imaginative limits of a person's consciousness were expanded, just as in an age in which putting others on, posing, and the like seem morally inauthentic, these limits are contracted.

The creation of a public geography has, in other words, a great deal to do with imagination as a social phenomenon. When a baby can distinguish the me from the not-me, he has taken a first and most important step in enriching his symbol-making powers: no longer must every symbol be a projection of the baby's own needs onto the world. The creation of a sense of public space is the adult social parallel to this psychological distinction in infancy, with parallel results; the symbol-making capacity of a society becomes that much richer, because the imagination of what is real, and therefore believable, is not tied down to a verification of what is routinely felt by the self. Because an urban society which has a public geography has also certain powers of imagination, the devolution of the public and rise of the intimate have a profound effect on the modalities of imagination which prevail in that society.

Finally, in an urban society facing a common audience problem for stranger and actor, solving that problem through common codes of belief, creating thereby a sense of a meaningful public domain in society, human expression is likely to be conceived in terms of gestures and symbols which are real no matter who makes the gesture or uses the symbol. Emotions are therefore presented. As changes in the first three structures occur, a change in the structure of expression occurs. Who speaks then determines increasingly the expressiveness of what is said; attempts at representation to others of emotions experienced by a particular speaker, as part of his personality, as an expression of him, come to prevail. This fourth structure embodies the correlation between a strong public life and what is called in psychology the objectivity of expressive signs; as the public disintegrates, the signs become more subjective.

These four logical structures relating theater to society are like irregular verbs; they can be used once one knows how to conjugate them. They comprised together the public life which existed in relatively strong form in the cities of Paris and London in the middle of the

18th Century. As the problem of audience came to be conceived of differently in the city than in the theater, codes of belief and behavior before strangers drew apart in the two realms. As these public roles drew apart, the two conditions for a meaningful public geography were thrown into a state of confusion, and finally in the modern age into a state of dissolution. As the public domain grew more obscure, the terms of how society understood human expressivity moved from presentation to representation.

In this book the elements of public life are first studied in Paris and London in the 1750's. Two cities have been chosen because it is valuable to see what in this public life of a capital cuts across differences of national cultures. The 1750's have been chosen because both cities are relatively prosperous by that decade, and because by then the bourgeois class, whose experiences will be our main concern, began to flourish. This class was more self-confident than in the days when *la ville* hid its social origins. The subjects studied are visual and verbal appearances in public, differences drawn between public and private, ambiguities of that distinction just beginning to appear in a new political movement, contemporary theories of man-as-actor and of the relation of the theater to the city, and finally the material conditions of the *ancien régime* capital.

To chart the disappearance of this world, two decades in the 19th Century are studied, the 1840's and the 1890's. In the 1840's and early 1850's there became manifest the effects of industrial capitalism on visual and verbal appearances in public; in the 1890's there were clearly perceptible revolts in both speech and dress against the terms of public life of the 1840's. For both the 1840's and the 1890's, the subjects studied are, as in the 1750's, images of the body, patterns of speech, man-as-actor, theories of expression in public, and the material conditions of the city. Politics will focus our attention mostly on Paris, because the crises of revolution and reaction in that capital brought to the fore fissures in the public world which were present, but less clear, in less extreme situations elsewhere.

The study of three such widely spaced decades is what historians call "postholing." "Posthole" methods try to depict the sweep of historical forces and at the same time some of the richness of detail which comes from delving into a specific moment. This historical method not only invites theory about why change occurs when seen over such a sweep of time; the method demands theory, I think, because it minimizes explanations of concrete data based on immediate contingencies or sheer chance. Since contingency and accident are as real as capitalism or secularism, what a "posthole" method gains in intellectual vigor, it loses in a certain kind of veracity.

Having established an historical movement, the book in its last part explores what the imbalance of public and intimate means in Western society today. Only a fool could claim himself master of so much material, and that raises the question of what you can and cannot expect as "proof" in this study.

PROOF OR PLAUSIBILITY?

The word "proof" has in empirical social studies come to have an unfortunate meaning: no other explanation but the one advanced after a given process of investigation is feasible. Regression analyses, measures of chi or gamma, are now used in quantitative studies to choose among alternative interpretations, by making a hierarchy of exclusions. Qualitative studies often and mistakenly try to prove arguments in the same way. The researcher must try to exhaust the full range of detail known about a subject. Otherwise there may be data the researcher does not know which "contradict" his argument. On an exclusionary scale of truth, contradiction through the discovery of new evidence must mean invalidation of the original argument, for how can two opposing interpretations of the same subject be equally true?

This empiricism, based on exclusion by the exhaustion of evidence, is in my view opposed to any real notion of intellectual honesty. We arrive at intellectual honesty by admitting, precisely, the reality of contradiction, and eschewing all hope of arriving at an immutable statement. The canon of exhaustion of evidence is in practice a peculiar one; it seems tied to an increasing miniaturization of focus, so that the more we "know" about a subject, the more details we know. Anesthetization of the intellect is the inevitable product of this form of proof, because it requires that no judgments be made until all the facts are in—sometime.

In qualitative research, "proof," if that anxiety-laden word must be used at all, is a matter of the demonstration of logical relationship; the qualitative researcher has laid on him the burden of plausibility. I have come to think that burden is greater and more rigorous than the obligations felt by a researcher excluding one explanation in favor of another, regardless of their respective logical power of coherence. Empirical plausibility is a matter of showing the logical connections among phenomena which can be described concretely. This definition would make a philosopher unhappy, and perhaps put the "scientist" of society out of work, but it should, I hope, serve the expectations of a sophisticated, intelligent general reader. If that reader finds, in the present book, a reasonable analysis of how a malady of modern society has come about, the book has succeeded; if after finishing the book, he thinks of an alternative logic for explaining this distress, so much the better.

Finally, I ought to say a word about the present book in relation to my prior work. I have been writing on the problem of social withdrawal for the last ten years, often without knowing it. *Families Against the City* was a study of how the nuclear family in 19th Century Chicago became a refuge against the larger society, as the city became the center of an industrial region. *The Uses of Disorder* was a study of how personality structures intersect with an economy of affluence, so that people try to purify their experience of the pain, ambiguity, and constraints of necessity which form part of any truly public relationship. *The Hidden Injuries of Class* was a study of how social class is coming to be interpreted as a matter of personality today, and the depoliticizing of class which results. The present book has become for me a general framework which encompasses these particular studies; it is their historical and theoretical setting. I hope the reader will forgive me if in an occasional paragraph, therefore, I correct the errors of interpretation or argument in those particular works, as a result of seeing them now as parts of a whole.

PART TWO

THE PUBLIC WORLD
OF THE
ANCIEN RÉGIME

CHAPTER 3

THE AUDIENCE:
A GATHERING OF STRANGERS

To understand the fall of public life requires that we understand the times in which it was vigorous and the terms on which it was maintained. The four chapters which follow depict the formation, presence, trials, and consequences of public life in Paris and London during the middle of the 18th Century. It may be helpful to say something about two phrases which are used in that description: the first, *"ancien régime"*; the second, "bourgeoisie."

The term *ancien régime* is often used as a synonym for feudalism; it thus could refer to a time period from before 800 to after 1800. I prefer to follow the usage established by Tocqueville: the *ancien régime* refers to the 18th Century, specifically to the period when commercial and administrative bureaucracy grew up in nations side by side with the persistence of feudal privileges. England thus had an *ancien régime* as well as France, though neither bureaucracy nor feudal privilege was the same in the two countries. Sometimes when we think of "the old order," we are prone to imagine a decaying society, blind to the rot within it; the real *ancien régime* had none of this sleepy indifference to its contradictions. Two principles which could never be reconciled were, for a long time, held in an uneasy tension together.

About the use of the term "bourgeoisie" I confess myself somewhat uneasy. There are too many conspiracy stories of the virtuous proletariat done in by the forces of evil led by the bourgeoisie, whether in Augustan Rome, medieval Benares, or modern-day New Guinea. This mechanical class analysis is so stupid that it quite logically induces in the reader a desire never to hear the words "class" and "bourgeoisie" mentioned. Unfortunately, the bourgeoisie existed, class is a fact, and we must somehow speak of them as real, without resort to demonology. No study of the 18th Century city could possibly avoid an analysis of the urban bourgeoisie, because they were its rulers, administrators, financial support, and a good part of its population. Furthermore, the term "bourgeoisie" is a more comprehensive description than "middle class"; "middle class" indicates someone in the middle of a ladder of positions in society, but not how he got there. "Bourgeoisie" indicates that someone occupied that rank because he was engaged in nonfeudal mercantile or administrative work; the stewards of an estate may occupy a middle position in society but are not part of a bourgeoisie. The bourgeoisie of the 18th Century cities hadn't the same economic functions, sense of themselves, or morals as the bourgeoisie of the 19th Century, of course, but that kind of distinction involves changes in a class; throwing the very word out because it is so easily abused has the disadvantage of making it appear as though this class had no history.

Let me finally say what the order of the chapters is. Chapter 3 is about the problem of audience, Chapter 4 about codes of belief, Chapter 5 about the distinction between public and private, Chapter 6 about expression. It should be kept in mind that these subjects are not four different experiences so much as four dimensions of one kind of experience, public experience. And, above all, it should be kept in mind that public life did not *begin* in the 18th century; rather, a modern version of it took form, a public life centered around a bourgeoisie on the rise and an aristocracy on the wane.

A city is a milieu in which strangers are likely to meet. However, "the stranger" can be a figure of two very different sorts. Italians may regard Chinese who move into their neighborhood as strangers, but they know how to think about these intruders; by skin color, the eyes, language, food habits, an Italian can recognize and place a Chinese as unlike himself. In this case, the stranger is synonymous with the outsider, and appears in a landscape where people have enough sense of their own identities to form rules of who belongs and who does not. There is another sense of stranger in which these rules do not apply: the stranger as an unknown, rather than an alien. A stranger can be experienced on these terms by someone who does have rules for his own identity, such as an Italian meeting someone he cannot "place"; the stranger as an unknown can dominate, however, the perceptions of people who are unclear about their own identities, losing traditional images of themselves, or belonging to a new social group that as yet has no clear label.

The city as a collection of strangers of the first sort is best typed by the ethnic city, like modern New York outside Manhattan, or Cape Town, race or language providing instant distinctions. A city of the second sort, in which strangers are unknown quantities, arises when a new, as yet amorphous social class is forming in this city and the city is reorganizing around that social group. Such was the case with Paris and London in the 18th Century. The new class was that of the mercantile bourgeoisie.

"The rise of the bourgeoisie" is a hackneyed phrase, so much so that one historian has been moved to comment that the only historical constant is that the middle classes are always everywhere rising. The sheer familiarity of the image obscures an important fact about class change; a rising or developing class usually doesn't have a clear idea of itself. Sometimes a sense of its rights comes to it before a sense of its identity; sometimes the facts of economic power march ahead of appropriate manners, tastes, and morals. The appearance of a new class can thus create a milieu of strangers in which many people are increasingly like each other but don't know it. There is a sense that the old distinctions, the old lines between one group and another, no longer apply, but little sense of new rules for instant distinctions. The expansion of the bourgeois mercantile and commercial classes in the 18th Century capital was accompanied by both the appearance of many unclassifiable people, materially alike but not cognizant of their similarities, and the loosening of traditional social rankings. Absent was a new language for "us" and "them," insider and outsider, "above" and "below" on the social ladder.

The audience problem of a milieu of strangers has been identified with the problem of audience in the theater: how to arouse belief among those who do not know you. This problem is much more pressing in a milieu of strangers as unknowns than in a milieu of strangers as outsiders. For an outsider to arouse belief, he must penetrate a barrier, marking himself credible on the terms familiar to and used by those inside. But strangers in a more amorphous milieu have a more complex problem, one of arousing belief by how they behave in a situation where no one is really sure what appropriate standards of behavior for a given sort of person are. In this second case, one solution is for people to create, borrow, or imitate behavior which all agree to treat arbitrarily as "proper" and "believable" in their encounters. The behavior is at a distance from everyone's personal circumstances, and so does not force people to attempt to define to each other who they are. When this occurs, a public geography is on the way to being born.

Let us look, then, at the forces in the mid-18th Century capitals which created a milieu of strangers as unknowns. We shall explore the size and migration of population, its density in the city, and its economic character, in the decades of and preceding the 1750's.

WHO CAME TO THE CITY

In 1750 London was the largest city in the Western world; Paris the next largest. All other European cities were far behind in size. It would be nice to make the simple statement that in the century 1650 to 1750 Paris and London were growing in population. The statement is true, only it must be hedged with all kinds of conditions.[1]

Here is how London grew. In 1595, it contained about 150,000 souls; in 1632, 315,000; in 1700, about 700,000; at the middle of the 18th Century, 750,000. The growth of London in the Industrial period of the last two centuries makes these changes seem pale; in the 19th Century London grew from 860,000 to 5 million. But the people of the 18th Century didn't know what was to come. They could only see what had happened, and the city, especially after the great fire in the middle of the 17th Century, appeared to them to be becoming extraordinarily populous.[2]

To arrive at the population of Paris during this period is more difficult, because politics got in the way of census-takers in the century from 1650 to 1750. The best estimates run as follows: Cardinal Richelieu's census of 1637, about 410,000; 1684, about 425,000; 1750, 500,-000. These seem small changes over the course of the century, especially when compared to London. However, they have to be set in the context of the nation; as Pierre Goubert points out, population in France as a whole was at least stagnant, probably in real decline, through much of the early and middle 18th Century. Growth in the population of Paris was slowly occurring while population in France as a whole lapsed.[3]

"Growth" appeared different in London than in Paris, then, but what does urban growth itself mean? If births are greater than deaths in a city, then over time the increases can come from within; if births are fewer than deaths, a swelling of the city's size can occur only if outsiders are entering in greater numbers than the city is itself losing through its death-birth ratio. In studies of death and birth in the 18th Century, a sharp debate exists between Talbot Griffith and H. J. Habakkuk about how much improvements in medicine and public health brought down the death rate and increased the birth rate. But no matter how this scholarly question is settled, it is certain that the increase in the size of both Paris and London during the century before 1750 depended greatly on migration from the outside, from smaller towns and the country. The demographer Buffon puts this succinctly. As of 1730, he tells us, "London needs to supplement (from the provinces) the number of its births by more than half in order to maintain itself, whereas Paris is self-sufficient to about one-seventy-fifth."*[4]

In both Paris and London, external migration is the source of their different forms of population strength. Thanks to the work of E. A.

---

*Not a reversible formula; there are not seventy-five times more deaths than births. Buffon is talking about what is needed to maintain or increase the population, given all relevant factors.

Wrigley, we have a clear idea of the numbers and patterns of migration to London for the century from 1650 to 1750. He estimates that for London to swell its ranks, it needed 8,000 in-migrants each year during this period. The people moving were young—Wrigley estimates their average age at twenty—and usually unmarried. That is, unlike the great peasant migrations to American cities a century and a half later, it was unusual for whole families to move to London. Using material gathered by C. T. Smith in 1951, the places people came from can be mapped out; most moves are from points fifty miles or more from London, and fifty miles was at that time a matter of at least two days' travel.[5]

Migrations to Paris were similar. It is known that after the death of Louis XIV more use was made of Paris by the nobility, but these people were never, even in the Sun King's time, entirely cut off from the city as a refuge from the stilted court life of Versailles. Their return would hardly provide the population necessary to replenish a Paris continually drained by the death of its own infants and children. From some research of Louis Henry, it seems reasonable to say that Paris, like London, drew its population sustenance from migrants who lived at least two days' journey from the city, who were young and single, who, as in England, were not pushed by famine or war into the city, as would occur later, but rather who had left the countryside of their own accord to better their lot. The picture of London is thus of an enormous city, for its time, growing at least by half through the in-migration of young and unattached people. The picture of Paris, too, is of a lesser, but relatively enormous city, growing slowly while the population outside it stagnates, and drawing almost all of its population replenishment and growth from the in-migration of the same type of person.[6]

Thus, in the population formation of both cities, a special sort of stranger played a critical role. He or she was alone, cut off from past associations, come to the city from a significant distance. Indeed, in describing the population of their cities, Londoners and Parisians in a decade like the 1720's resort to images of these outsiders as "motley," "amorphous," "questionable," "unformed." Defoe describes London as "overgrown," the appearance of so many people from the provinces making it so, and so requiring governmental offices and regulations. He can find no words to describe these newcomers, save that they are a "motley mass." With the exception of the "Irish horde," there seems to be no social order among them. And since they have no form, he expects them to wash away from the city in the same way they have come: "Then, I say, will be a time to expect the vast concourse of people to London will separate again and disperse as naturally as they have now crowded hither."[7]

Marivaux's *La Vie de Marianne* and *Le Paysan Parvenu* turn, similarly, around the idea of Paris as a city built on a streaming together of these strangers. In both novels, Marivaux describes Paris as a place where people of unknown origins can "pass" because the whole city has grown through the migration of "unknown quantities." The "true nature of those with whom they discourse" was becoming increasingly difficult for older Parisians to assay.

Contrast these images to the image of the stranger as outsider given by New Yorkers or Bostonians in 1900. In the American cities, strangers were interpreted through ethnic stereotypes, rejected as unfit or dangerous to know because of the negative connotations involved. There was no stereotyping in Defoe or Marivaux; the city of strangers they knew was not divisible into ethnic, economic, or racial types (save the London Irish). The fact that most of the immigrants were lone rather than in family clusters made them even more "unknown quantities."

London was often described as a "great Wen." The early 18th Century meaning of this word is not pretty, a wen being an open sore out of which all sorts of pussy liquids flow, but it accurately captures some of the feeling behind the more elegant phrases like "unknown quantities" used to describe the new populace. How are these people going to make sense of each other? They are cut loose, they have not even the marks of a past life as adults, nor the categorizable strangeness of immigrants from another land. On what terms are they to judge their communications with each other, to what knowledge, to what parallels in past experience does one appeal in dealing with a motley mass?

When the term "growth of population" is used to describe both these cities, it is not just a neutral matter of numbers. It specifies a certain social fact. As the city became larger, its population became problematic.

WHERE THEY LIVED

One might expect that this population would soon sort itself out into different territories in the city, each territory marked by certain economic and social characteristics. Then the classifying of strangers would become easier. This ecological process, however, was subject to checks and confusions from the 1670's on, in both Paris and London—confusion, ironically, due to planned attempts to deal with the increasing urban population.

Cities with increasing populations logically ought to handle them in one of two ways: the area of the city can be enlarged, or a greater number of people can be concentrated in the same place. Almost no city known has so simple a growth pattern that it either spreads out in space or grows denser on its old terrain. And it is not just a question of having land area and density increase at the same time, because population increase is not an "additive" phenomenon, so that little steps of reorganization accommodate each rise in the level of population. Increases in population usually instigate a reorganization of the whole ecology of a city; cities have to be thought of in terms of crystals which re-form their structure each time more substance of which the crystal is composed is introduced.

If we were to walk through Paris in the 1640's or London before the great fire of 1666, we would be struck by the sheer concentration of people in a geographic space minuscule by modern standards. Houses were packed together in streets no more than ten or twelve feet wide, with sudden gaps of vast open space. Indeed, as we approached new buildings near the walls of Paris or at the no-man's-land between the City of London and Westminster, we would perceive not a gradual diminution in the concentration of houses, but a sudden abrupt break between teeming streets and isolated houses arranged almost as country estates.

After the great fire in 1666 in London and in the 1680's in Paris, the massing of population in both cities began to take on a new form. Burnt or fallow land was not simply filled in. It was reorganized on a new principle, that of the square, a square radically unlike the squares of medieval towns both in appearance and in function. The principles of square design in London broke with the medieval past in quite a different way than the squares of Paris did. But these two contrary revolts against the past led to the same social end.

The square building which began in Paris in the 1680's was conditioned by two prior events. The first was the work of Bernini in Rome, the second the work of Louis XIV and his architects at Versailles. Bernini's Piazza Obliqua in front of St. Peter's in Rome was a challenge to the whole thrust of planned square building in the Renaissance. Bernini wanted to use the square to suggest the vastness of space through formal design, rather than its enclosure and taming, as the Renaissance had sought. The idea of immense space made by man in the very midst of a dense urban settlement is what the architects of Paris picked up in the 1680's, the Place des Victoires (1685–86) being the first expression.[8]

What such an effort meant for the city of Paris was that the human mass of population and the humanly contrived illusion of limitless space now were to be joined together. The illusion of great space in the midst of great mass is the governing principle of the Place Vendôme (built 1701) and the Place des Invalides (finished 1706), culminating in Jacques-Ange Gabriel's Place de la Concorde in 1763.

The architects of some of these grand urban spaces were trained for work at Versailles; Hardouin-Mansard became involved in the building of the Place Vendôme after overseeing the construction of the Palace of Versailles, for example. But just as Versailles was conceived of originally as an antidote to the Paris of the 1660's, a place of order whose very rooms, suites, and gardens would instill a hierarchical attitude among the inhabitants, the Paris of the early 18th Century was to be a corrective to Versailles. The great urban *places* were not to concentrate all activities of the surrounding streets; the street was not to be a gateway to the life of the square. Rather than a focus as all the architecture at Versailles is a focus, the square was to be a monument to itself, with restricted activities taking place in its midst, activities mostly of passage or transport. Above all, these squares were not designed with a lingering, congregating crowd in mind. Hardouin-Mansard struggled therefore to eliminate stalls, bands of acrobats, and other forms of street trade from the squares, sought as well to keep the cafes on them contained behind their doors and the posthouses out of the squares altogether.[9]

The result was to weaken the life of the square as it was known in both medieval and Renaissance Paris. Where once the squares had a multiplicity of functions, what Arnold Zucker calls the "overlay" of all the activities of the city occurring in one place, the crowd life of the city was now fragmented and dispersed.[10]

Indeed, the very demolition and construction activities needed to clear these vast spaces forced clusters of population in Paris away from the centers of 1660 into more spread-out areas. The cluster of noble families and their extensive servant and service population around Invalides moved in the early 18th Century back to the Marais; cleared land in front of St.-Sulpice moved another knot of nobles and attendants into the empty spaces of St.-Germain-des-Prés. As the population of Paris gradually grew, the areas around the grand places became more dense, but these centers no longer served as points where the crowd could knit together in diverse activities in the same place.[11]

The medieval and Renaissance squares were free zones in Paris, as opposed to the controlled zone of the house. The monumental squares of the early 18th Century, in restructuring the massing of population in the city, restructured the function of the crowd as well, for it changed the freedom with which people might congregate. The assemblage of a crowd became a specialized activity; it occurred in three places—the cafe, the pedestrian park, and the theater.

In London, the square as a free zone for crowds also came to an end during the period 1666–1740, but through an entirely opposite route. After the great fire of 1666, many plans were put forward for the rebuilding of the City of London, the greatest being that of Christopher Wren. These plans were rejected by Charles II almost immediately. The plans, had they been realized, would have given London the ornamental focal points of the kind Bernini was creating in Rome or which Hardouin-Mansard would later create in Paris. Indeed, the repudiation of Wren's plan was a rejection of a kind of town square London had recently seen in its midst, the Covent Garden work planned by Inigo Jones.[12]

But the idea of accommodating population in the city through the building of squares was not abandoned. In the Covent Garden district the Duke of Bedford and in Bloomsbury the Earl of Southampton began building blocks of houses on the side, the squares "irrationally scattered over a site, separated and yet not quite cut off from each other." The essential feature of these squares was that they were not to be filled with street vendors, acrobats, flower sellers, and the like, as was Covent Garden; they were to be filled with shrubs and trees.[13]

It is often said that in massing housing around an enclosed floral territory, the English were attempting to preserve the sense of country-side in building the city. That is only half true. These houses in Blooms-bury were urban in character and built in groups; they resembled houses being built in the center of the unburned portion of the City of London. If a modern person can imagine a skyscraper with parking lots, traffic lights, and all the attendant services suddenly placed in the midst of a cornfield in expectation on the builder's part that soon other sky-scrapers would be built up around it, he will have some sense of the mentality of Bedford and Southampton in developing their estates.[14]

The creators of the scatter squares were very intent upon keeping commerce out of the square area. Bedford applied to the government for the legal right to evict peddlers and hawkers from the squares. Although in the 1690's this prohibition was hard to enforce, by the 1720's it was effective. The square itself had become a museum of nature in the midst of housing of the most sophisticated sort. And indeed, the expectations of the developers were realized. People built houses near the squares, and gradually the area became as dense as the old City.

In London as well as in Paris, then, the restructuring of population through the planning of squares held back the square itself as a central place of multiple use, of meeting and observing. What did this restriction of the square as a free zone feel like to people at the time? Defoe gives a vivid picture for the 1720's:

> It is the disaster of London, as to the beauty of its figure, that it is thus stretched out in buildings, just as the pleasure of every builder . . . and as the convenience of the people directs . . . and this has spread the face of it in a most straggling, confused manner, out of all shape, uncompact and unequal.[15]

The city's growth meant it lost a center, a focus. The growth did not seem to Defoe a matter of time's necessities slowly ripening. It felt sudden, abrupt:

> It is, in the first place to be observed, as a particular and remarkable crisis, singular to those who write in this age . . . that the great and more eminent increase of buildings in and about the city of London, and the vast extent of ground taken, and now become streets and nobles' squares of houses, by which the mass or body of the whole is become so infinitely great, has generally been made in our time, not only within our memory, but even within a few years. . . .[16]

The social question raised by the population of London and Paris was the question of living with or being a stranger. The social question raised by the new terms of density in the city was where these strangers were to be visible routinely, so that images of types of stranger could be formed. The old meeting ground, the multi-use square, was being eroded by space as a monument to itself in Paris, by a museum of nature in London. Thus was demography creating a milieu in which the stranger was an unknown.

Strangers as an audience for each other might even so have avoided much of the burden of enactment, the necessity of arousing belief only within the framework of an immediate scene, if the hierarchical structure of social groups had remained untouched by the city. For the images of place, duty, and politeness in this hierarchy would have afforded people standards of reference to bring to specific encounters; hierarchy might still serve as a sure yardstick of belief. But the economy of the capital city associated with these demographic changes eroded the yardstick of hierarchy as a clear measure of the relations between strangers. Because hierarchy became an uncertain measure when dealing with a stranger, the problem of audience arose.

CHANGES IN THE URBAN BOURGEOISIE

In the first half of the 18th Century, the English and French economies experienced a sharp growth in international trade. England's foreign trade doubled from 1700 to 1780; the market shifted from Europe as the main buyer to England's own overseas colonies. The French stepped into the void, carrying on much of the trade with other European countries that England once had done.[17]

This increase in trade had a great effect on the capital cities of both countries. London and Paris were major ports, as well as the centers of mercantile finance for overseas shipping and the commercial distribution points for goods flowing in and out of the country and between various provinces within the country. The vigorous growth of trade had both physical and social results. In London, growing trade on the

Thames had the effect of stretching out the city to the west, just as the new squares did. In Paris, the growth of trade on the Seine also stretched the city to the west, and more and more docks and warehouses were packed onto the quais in the center of the city, along the Tuileries and surrounding the Île de la Cité.[18]

Socially, the growth of trade created jobs in the financial, commercial, and bureaucratic sectors of city society. To speak of the "growth of the bourgeoisie" in either city is to refer to a class engaged in activities of distribution rather than production. The young people coming to the city found work in these mercantile and commercial pursuits; in fact, there was something of a labor shortage, for there were more posts that demanded literate workers than there were people who could read. Like the balance of density in a city, the balance of jobs in it behaves like a crystal: The new trade activity in the 18th Century capitals was not added onto what had been there before; the whole economic structure of the city recrystallized around it. Shop space on the quais became too dear for small-time artisans, for instance; they began moving out of the center, and thence out of the capital itself, as the commercials moved in.

The issue which concerns us in the growth of this middleman bourgeoisie is the question of a clear class identity, for the lack of it reinforced the sense of the stranger as unknown.

One writer has remarked of Paris that its bourgeoisie knew they were something new, but not what they were. Self-confidence can be detected in the mercantile ranks of the middle 18th Century, unlike the self-effacing impulses of their forerunners in the days of *la cour et la ville* in the 17th Century. There was a lack of focus, though, in what these burghers perceived themselves to be: they were the new men, but what was that? In Diderot's plays about the bourgeois life of his day, such as *Le Père de Famille*, the characters treat their survival without roots in land, even their prosperity, as something of a mystery.

One explanation for this absence of proclamations of "who we are" is that the mercantile classes had perhaps yet to move from confidence to smugness. Another is that secure self-definitions were difficult given the economic formation of this class. It was a class into which people stepped, a new and expanding class; it was a matter of mobility rather than inheritance. It was a class far more blurred in outline than the older Renaissance or post-Renaissance mercantile classes, in that as trade in the city expanded, the nature of the urban market changed. In the early 18th Century this market moved from competition for monopoly of trade in a given area or commodity to competition of trade within that area or commodity. It was this change in the market which made middle-class identity unstable throughout the echelons of commerce.

In both London and Paris, for example, open-air markets which sold enormous quantities of goods took hold at this time. They sold goods from the ships; they operated in special districts of the city. Unlike the medieval *foires,* the Foires de St.-Germain and the Foires des Halles were permanent operations, with licenses given by government patent to each seller. With the building of Covent Garden in the 1640's the same regularization of urban open-air markets arose in London. However, the licenses of urban trade were unlike the older export or import licenses. A particular company would no longer hold an exclusive right to deal in a particular commodity, as the East India Company did for a time in tea, but a number of companies by fair and often by illegal means had the same goods to sell. Thus, the nature of competition was transformed from a contest for monopoly in a particular area to contests of trade within each area. As both cities became hubs of international buying and selling, their internal markets became overlapping.[19]

In *The Economy of Cities,* Jane Jacobs has argued that the result of this kind of urban growth was the continual search for territories not yet touched by competition, for new kinds of goods and services to sell, in order to get away from the pressure of competing with others. The argument in its general form makes most historians irate; changed slightly, it makes sense of a certain phenomenon in these two cities. When territories of work were destroyed, it became much more difficult for fathers to transmit to their sons their own work. The reason was simple: the fathers had only half the work to give. They could bequeath capital or a skill, but not a community of assured customers, an assured source of supply, and so on. Even more, under conditions in which fathers were forced to compete strenuously for work, the sons attempted to break away, to create a new market for their skills by work in trades or jobs which appeared to them less crowded (an appearance all too easily unreal in fact). The expansion of trade in London and Paris at the turn of the 18th Century fragmented the continuity of work within the family. The result was that it became difficult to place "who" a stranger was simply by his family background.[20]

The dislocations of rank caused by the overlapping market were spreading down from mercantile to manual labor as the crystal of the 18th Century urban economy re-formed. This was most apparent in the guilds. In both Paris and London, guilds encompassed large numbers of laborers in the late 17th Century; by the middle of the 18th Century the number of guild laborers had declined. The usual explanation—by Sombart, for example—is that guilds did not fit in with the mobile labor pool required by an industrial society. But to adopt such an explanation is to view the history of the 18th Century city as a preparation for what had not yet come. Within the lives of urban workers, as Kaplow has pointed out, there were immediate reasons to encourage them to abandon guild work for more floating occupations. While the move from journeyman to master was theoretically possible within a lifetime, practically it was remote. In the 18th Century Paris guilds, "whether as eternal journeymen or *chambrelans*, the poverty of these workers was likely to be extreme and their mobility nil, a condition they may have resented even more intensely than did their brothers outside the guilds." Even if it is true that guilds in the 18th Century declined functionally for Sombart's reasons, it is also true that the guilds were emptied more intentionally because, for the young involved, the right to work in a trade given by a father's membership in it did not guarantee the son that he would have any work to do, much less any "prospects."[21]

Among the lower working classes, the competition to sell services became overlapping in the same way that the competition to sell goods overlapped among the middle classes. The pool of servants was far greater than the number of places for servants in Paris and London at the end of the 17th Century, and this excess of labor became worse during the 18th Century. For servants, supply so exceeded demand that it was difficult to induce patrons to take on one's children—it was cheaper to maintain a household by taking on fresh adult servants as required rather than keeping entire the families of the old. As international trade via the city expanded, the service economy within the city became fragmented, and intra-craft, intra-service competition grew stronger; the very concept of territories of work separating people was destroyed.[22]

The demography and economics of these two vigorous cities served, in sum, to define the stranger as an unknown, at least in a short time, an unknown who could not easily be placed through factual inquiries. When people broke a family tie to come to the city, family names, associations, and traditions did not help. When population was distributed by new urban forms massing large numbers of people around squares not meant as places of easy congregation and sociability, knowing those strangers through routine observation became more difficult. When the complexity of overlapping markets destroyed stable territories of economic activity, occupational "place" did not help. Status breaks between the generations became more frequent; the inheritability of position succumbed to the creation of position, lower as well as higher.

Thus the domain of appearances was not ruled easily by standards such as where you came from, where you belong, or what you are doing when I see you on the street. Again, contrast this to the demography of New York at the opening of the 20th Century: The migrants to New York, placed instantly by the language they spoke, often migrated as whole families, or brought their families in train; they clustered together in ethnic subareas of the city, even to the point of living on blocks within their ethnic area according to the locale or even their village in the old country. Once in New York, each of these ethnic subgroups used the area in a manner analogous to the medieval and Renaissance use of squares in Paris. The street was shopping area, meeting group, scene of casual observation, with the church built at a central point along the street. The strangers of mid-18th Century Paris and London lacked such automatic modes of organization.

Let us be clear about this lack of sure rules, for the portrait left here might indicate that the cosmopolitans of the *ancien régime* inhabited a Kafkaesque, abstract universe in which mankind was faceless and blank. This was hardly the case; the 18th Century capital was a place in which people made great efforts to color and define their relations with strangers; the point is, they had to make an effort. The material conditions of life in the city weakened any trust people could place in the "natural," routine labeling of others by origin, family background, or occupation. The effort to color one's relations with others, the attempt to give these social exchanges a form, was an effort to create a meaningful sense of audience. An idea of the amount of work needed to create this meaningful audience out of a milieu of strangers may be gained by comparing a piece of social etiquette in the new urban society with the same etiquette in the older society of the court. This social nicety concerns the questions, greetings, introductions, and gossip as the first stage of sociability for two strangers who have not met before.

INTERCHANGES AT COURT AND IN THE CITY

Observers of the manners of Parisians and Londoners in the 1750's were struck less by the differences between the two cities than by the difference of both from provincial terms of courtesy. They also noticed how similar the cities had become, compared with the disparate court life of England and France.

The court life beginning under Charles II in England was set on an exactly opposite course from the court life developing in France under Louis XIV. The English, after the austerities of Puritan rule, saw a court life take form in their society dedicated to informal pleasure, bonhomie, and a great measure of administrative and political disorder; this lasted from 1660 to 1688. The French under Louis, after the disorders of the Fronde, saw take form a court life purposely formal and orderly, highly disciplined, increasingly prim; this continued until 1715. In England, the surge of urban growth from the 1690's onward was accompanied by an increasing stabilization of both politics and court life; that is, the growth of London and the growth of a stable, limited monarchy went hand in hand. In France, the strength of the king and the strength of Paris were antagonistic. Louis created Versailles, and abandoned the Tuileries as a permanent residence, that he might better control his nobility, that the court might become a rigid hierarchy with no places or scenes of escape. Upon the death of Louis XIV in 1715, the shift to Paris under Louis XV was at the expense of the Versailles institutions. Thus, politically the court histories of England and France are comparable only as opposites. Socially, there were certain parallels.[23]

In the courts of the mid-17th Century, not only in France but in Germany, Italy, and England, greetings between people of different ranks involved elaborate flattery based on interpersonal knowledge. It was the superior who was to be flattered, of course; in dealings between people not of quality with those of quality, titles indicating rank were *de rigueur* on both sides: *Monsieur le Marquis* spoke to *Monsieur l'avo-cat.* Compliments paid under these circumstances were a matter of extolling the other's known qualities to his face. In Saint-Simon's memoirs, we find people "honoring" each other in such terms as "I am delighted to meet the man who . . ." after which follows a list of exploits in war, family connections, or—when dealing with people of slightly lower rank—character strengths which give the man a reputation. Telling a person the most flattering thing about him or her at a first meeting was a way of establishing a social bond.[24]

The structure of a court-dominated society makes greetings and compliments of this sort easy. With the exception of Versailles, these courts were small, so that the repute of a person and his background could easily be spread among the small community. Estimates of the number of people at Versailles at its peak vary enormously, but it is clear from Saint-Simon and from such modern writers as W. H. Lewis that within ranks likely to meet at court, the subgroups were again small enough so that the facts about a person could be spread by word of mouth before one was introduced. In addition, the importance of precedence promoted intense inquiry about the status of strangers one was to meet.[25]

Patterns of gossiping flowed naturally from such a situation. Gossip was unrestrained exchange of information about other people; their sins, affairs, or pretenses were dissected in the greatest detail because in the court most of these intimacies were common knowledge. Furthermore, gossip had a clear relationship to social rank. An inferior in Saint-Simon's pages never indicates to a superior that he knows of, or has actually heard, gossip about the superior, while the superior in speaking to a lesser person may without insult indicate that he has heard gossip about that person and indeed discuss its truth or falseness even during a first meeting.

In London and Paris seventy years later, the pattern had changed.

For purposes of clarity, let us analyze the same social class as would before have oriented itself to a court. In 1750, Lord Chesterfield cautions his son never to allude to the family of a person to whom one is being introduced, because one never knows for sure what emotional relationship exists between a person and his family, nor can one, in the "confusions" of London, even be sure one has the family patterns straight. In a populous environment filling and refilling with strangers, greetings which flatter the person and his known qualities became a difficult business. Generally there were now to be found stock phrases of greeting, whose acceptability was a matter of how nonparticular and flowery they were as figures of speech all their own; the fact that they could be, and were, applied indiscriminately to any person in no way detracted from their civility. Indeed, the essence of a compliment was to honor another person without having to be direct and personal.[26]

When, for instance, Marivaux's Marianne, in *La Vie de Marianne*, goes to her first great dinner party in Paris, she is struck by how inviting and open the company there is, how little they talk of people whom she might not have heard of, what care they take to draw her out to speak without prying into her own life. In the urban society of the 18th Century courtesy became the reverse of the styles of court society in the mid-17th. The initial social bond was established by forms of courtesy based on a recognition that people were "unknown quantities."[27]

Gossip took on a peculiar character under urban conditions. If you gossip too early in your acquaintance with a man, Voltaire wrote, you insult him. Rather than an instant terrain of topics to share, gossip became the mark of friendship at a certain stage. There was great risk otherwise of talking about people whom your listener would be well disposed toward; or even, as in one of the popular stories of the 1730's, relating a licentious tale about a woman unwittingly to the very woman herself. The great city thus ruled out talk about personality as a way of first making contact with others.[28]

The consciousness of a distance between oneself and one's traffic with the world became an overriding theme for many writers in the 1740's, of whom Lord Chesterfield was perhaps the most famous example. In Chesterfield's letters to his son the emphasis was all on learning to survive in the world by hiding one's feelings from others. In 1747, Chesterfield counseled:

> People of your age have, commonly, an unguarded frankness about them which makes them the easy prey and bubbles of the artful and the experienced. . . . Beware, therefore, now that you are coming into the world, of these proffered friendships. Receive them with great civility, but with great incredulity too; and pay them with compliments but not with confidence.[29]

A few days later, Chesterfield amplified his advice—indeed, this year marks the beginning of a lifelong peroration, in which Chesterfield tells his son that he can survive the "snares" of great cities like Paris and London only by wearing a mask. Chesterfield's words were stark:

> Of all things, banish the egotism out of your conversation, and never think of entertaining people with your own personal concerns or private affairs; though they are interesting to you, they are tedious and impertinent to everybody else; besides that, one cannot keep one's own private affairs too secret.[30]

Again and again Chesterfield cites his own mistakes as a youth, when, sheltered from the realities of London, he grew up to think that directness and frankness were moral qualities; the price of these virtues was "great harm done to myself and to others" when he began to live an adult life in London. Brought up in an aristocratic milieu similar to Madame de Sévigné's, Chesterfield regarded her *"spiritualité"* by the 1740's to be a positive danger, as the social life he lived shifted from court and estate to a life passed among strangers in the cosmopolitan city.

The mid-18th Century was one of the great ages of sociability, but its citizens were unlikely candidates for such an honor. The material conditions of life made people question marks to each other, and this uncertainty was no emotionally neutral affair. The fear of others as unknown prompted remarks like Chesterfield's counsel that "one cannot keep one's own private affairs too secret," the very fear of these material changes thus reinforcing their effect, which was a cloak thrown over strangers so that they could not be "placed" by virtue of their material circumstances. How then did these unlikely candidates create a society of such intense sociability? What were the tools they used to build relations with each other?

CHAPTER 4

PUBLIC ROLES

One way in which 18th Century urban society made social encounters meaningful was through codes of belief that worked in both the theater and everyday life. In retrospect, we may wish to be more cautious about this bridge than people at the time were. In both Paris and London in the mid-18th Century, people spoke of the city as having changed the basic terms of the age-old imagery of *theatrum mundi.* Fielding in 1749 spoke of London as having become a society in which stage and street were "literally" intermixed; the world as a theater, he said, was no longer "only a metaphor" as it had been in the Restoration. Rousseau in 1757 wrote a treatise to show that the conditions of life in Paris forced men to behave like actors in order to be sociable with each other in the city. As we shall see two chapters hence, these declarations of a new *theatrum mundi* were not quite what they seem; in retrospect, it would be better said that a bridge was built between what was believable on the stage and what was believable on the street. This gave the life of the street a form. Just as the actor touched people's feelings without revealing to them his own character offstage, the same codes of belief he used served his audience to a similar end; they aroused each other's feelings without having to attempt to define themselves to each other, a definition the material conditions of life would have made difficult, frustrating, and probably fruitless. This bridge, in turn, gave men the means to be sociable, on impersonal grounds.

It was in this way that the first of the four structures of public life —the audience problem—came to have a logical relationship to the second structure—the codes of belief bridging theater and society. The first was a matter of material disorder; the second an emotional order built upon it; the order was a response to the disorder, but also transcendence of it.

The structural bridge between belief in the theater and on the street was formed by two principles, one concerning the body, the other the voice. The body was treated as mannequin; speech was treated as a sign rather than a symbol. By the first principle people visualized clothes as matters of contrivance, decoration, and convention, with the body serving as a mannequin rather than as an expressive, living creature. By the second, they heard speech which signified in and of itself, rather than by reference to outside situations or to the person of the speaker. By both principles, they were able to detach behavior with others from personal attributes of physical or social condition and so had taken the second step in creating a geography of "out in public."

THE BODY IS A MANNEQUIN

A modern city dweller suddenly transported back to Paris or London in the 1750's would find crowds whose appearance was at once simpler and more puzzling than the crowds of our time. A man in the street now can distinguish the poor from the middle class by sight and, with a little less precision, the rich from the middle class. Appearances on the streets of London and Paris two centuries ago were manipulated so as to be more precise indicators of social standing. Servants were easily distinguishable from laborers. The kind of labor performed could be read from the peculiar clothes adopted by each trade, as could the status of a laborer in his craft by glancing at certain ribbons and buttons he wore. In the middle ranks of society, barristers, accountants, and merchants each wore distinctive decorations, wigs, or ribbons. The upper ranks of society appeared on the street in costumes which not merely set them apart from the lower orders but dominated the street.

The costumes of the elite and of the wealthier bourgeoisie would puzzle a modern eye. There were patches of red pigment smeared on nose or forehead or around the chin. Wigs were enormous and elaborate. So were the headdresses of women, containing in addition highly detailed model ships woven into the hair, or baskets of fruit, or even historical scenes represented by miniature figures. The skins of both men and women were painted either apoplexy-red or dull white. Masks would be worn, but only for the fun of frequently taking them off. The body seemed to have become an amusing toy to play with.

During his first moments on the street, the modern interloper would be tempted to conclude that there was no problem of order in this society, everybody being so clearly labeled. And if this modern observer had some historical knowledge, he would give a simple explanation for this order: people were just observing the law. For there existed on the statute books in both France and England sumptuary laws which assigned to each station in the social hierarchy a set of "appropriate" clothes, and forbade people of any one station from wearing the clothes of people in another rank. Sumptuary laws were especially complicated in France. For instance, women of the 1750's whose husbands were laborers were not permitted to dress like the wives of masters of a craft, and the wives of "traders" were forbidden certain of the adornments allowed women of quality.[31]

Laws on the statute books, however, do not indicate laws observed or enforced. By the opening of the 18th Century, very few arrests were made for violation of the sumptuary laws. Theoretically, you could go to jail for imitating another person's bodily appearance; practically, you need have had no fear by 1700 of doing so. People in very large cities had little means of telling whether the dress of a stranger on the street was an accurate reflection of his or her standing in the society, for all the reasons elaborated in the last chapter; most of the migrants to the cosmopolitan centers came from relatively far away, following new occupations once in town. Was what the observer saw on the street then an illusion?

According to the logic of an egalitarian-minded society, when people do not have to display their social differences, they will not do so. If both law and strangerhood allow you to "get away" with being any person you choose to be, then you will try not to define who you are. But this egalitarian logic breaks down when applied to the *ancien régime* city. Despite the fact that sumptuary laws were seldom enforced throughout western Europe, despite the fact that in the great cities it would be difficult to know much about the origins of those one saw in the street, there was a desire to observe the codes of dressing to station. In doing so, people hoped to bring order to the mixture of strangers in the street.

The clothing of most urban middle- and upper-class Frenchmen and Englishmen showed a remarkable stability in cut and general form from the late 17th Century to the middle of the 18th Century, certainly more stability than in the previous eighty years. With the exception of the female's pannier (a flattened-out skirt) and the gradual change in the ideal male build—from corpulent to thin and narrow-waisted—there was a clinging in the 18th Century to the basic shapes of the late 17th. However, the use of these forms was changing.[32]

Clothing which in the late 17th Century was worn on all occasions was by the middle of the 18th Century conceived of as appropriate only on stage and in the street. In the 18th Century home, loose-fitting and simple garments were the growing preference of all classes. There appears here the first of the terms of the divide between the public and the private realm: the private realm being more natural, the body appeared as expressive in itself. Squire remarks that, during the Régence,

Paris saw the complete adoption of a negligé appearance. The costume of the boudoir had descended to the drawing-room.

The "private" quality of dress was emphasized by the general
use of forms distinctly "undress" in origin.[33]

On the street, by contrast, clothes were worn which recognizably
marked one's place—and the clothes had to be known, familiar bodily
images if the markings were to be successful. The conservation of the
late 17th Century gross forms of bodily appearance cannot thus be
viewed as a simple continuity with the past. The attempt was to use
proven images of where one belonged in the society in order to define
a social order on the street.

Given the changes in urban life, this attempt was bound to encounter difficulties. For one thing, many of the new mercantile occupations
had no 17th Century precedent, so that those who worked in the accounts-receivable section of a shipping firm had no appropriate clothing
to wear. For another, with the collapse of the guilds in the great cities,
much of the repertoire of familiar clothing based on guild markings was
useless, because few people were entitled to it. One way people solved
these difficulties was by taking as street wear costumes which clearly
labeled a particular trade or profession but had little relation to the
trade or profession of the wearer. These people were not necessarily
dressing above themselves. In fact, the records indicate that lower-
middle-class people seem to have been only sporadic counter jumpers
in the matter of clothes. Nor, if these old clothes were donned by
someone of a different but equivalent trade or profession, was there
much thought given to altering the garments to suit or to symbolize
their own particular station. That would have been idiosyncratic; the
clothes would not have meant much to a person on the street who did
not know their wearer, much less the reason why he might have altered
a familiar form. Whether people were in fact what they wore was less
important than their desire to wear something recognizable in order to
be someone on the street.[34]

We would say of a shipping clerk in a poultry firm who dressed like
a butcher or falconer when he went out for a walk that he was wearing
a costume; that notion of costume would help us comprehend his behavior as having something to do with the dress of an actor in the
theater, and we could easily understand that such a mode of dressing
could be called observing a convention.

What makes 18th Century street wear fascinating is that even in
less extreme cases, where the disparity between traditional clothes and
new material conditions had not forced someone into an act of imper-
sonation, where instead he wore clothes which reasonably accurately
reflected who he was, the same sense of costume and convention was
present. At home, one's clothes suited one's body and its needs; on the
street, one stepped into clothes whose purpose was to make it possible

for other people to act as if they knew who you were. One became a figure in a contrived landscape; the purpose of the clothes was not to be sure of whom you were dealing with, but to be able to behave as if you were sure. Do not inquire too deeply into the truth of other people's appearances, Chesterfield counseled his son; life is more sociable if one takes people as they are and not as they probably are. In this sense, then, clothes had a meaning independent of the wearer and the wearer's body. Unlike as in the home, the body was a form to be draped.

In articulating this rule, we should specify "men" in place of "people." For women were rather more carefully scrutinized for a relationship between their rank and their clothing: within a general rank, like men, they might adopt one street face or another, but they could incur hostility for jumping the line between ranks. The problem was most acute in the shades of ranking, none too clear themselves, between middle-middle levels and upper-middle levels, and the reason for this lay in the means by which fashion was disseminated at the time among the female population.

France was the model for feminine London's taste in both the middle and upper ranks of society. In this decade, middle-rank English-women usually wore what upper-rank Frenchwomen had been wearing ten or fifteen years before. French clothes were disseminated by means of dolls; the dolls were dressed in exact replicas of current fashion, and then salesmen, their cases packed with fifteen or twenty perfect mannequins in miniature, would travel to London or Vienna. In Paris itself something of a similar time lag existed between classes, though, of course, the dolls were unnecessary.[35]

The cast-off system would have created a tremendous blurring of class lines if the dolls were brought back to human size exactly, or, rather, the differences between middle and upper classes would have been that the former were exact echoes of what the fashionable ladies wore when they were much younger. In fact, when the dolls were brought back to life-size proportions, the dresses were systematically simplified. In Paris, where the dolls were not needed, the same simplifying pattern also occurred. The result was that middle-class women were faint echoes of their aristocratic contemporaries when they were younger, but also simplified versions of them.[36]

Codes of dress as a means of regulating the street worked by clearly if arbitrarily identifying who people were. The cast-off pattern could threaten this clarity. The following is the reaction of one middle-class husband, an oil merchant, to his wife's dressing above herself, reported in the *Lady's Magazine* of a slightly later period, 1784:

When down dances my rib in white, but so bepukered and plaited, I could not tell what to make of her; so turning about,

I cried, "Hey, Sally, my dear, what new frolic is this: It is like none of the gowns you used to wear." "No, my dear," crieth she, "it is no gown, it is the *chemise de la reine.*" "My dear," replied I, hurt at this gibberish . . . "let us have the name of your new dress in downright English." "Why then" said she, "if you must have it, it is the queen's shift." Mercy on me, thought I, *what will the world come to, when an oilman's wife comes down to serve in the shop, not only in her own shift, but in that of a queen.*

If the oil merchant's wife or anyone else could wear a *chemise de la reine,* if imitation was exact, how would people know whom they were dealing with? Again, the issue was, not being sure of a rank, but being able to act with assurance.[37]

Thus when one saw that a woman was dressing above her station, it was considered only good manners to hold her up to ridicule, even to point out to other strangers that she was an impostor. This shaming, however, was behavior which, like the clothes themselves, had a specific geography: if you found out someone dressing above station in a social gathering in your home, it would be the height of bad taste to subject her to the treatment you felt entitled to inflict on the street.

The clothing of the aristocracy and the higher bourgeois classes can now assume its place in relation to that of the lower orders. The principle of dressing the body as a mannequin, as a vehicle for marking by well-established conventions, drew the upper and lower realms of society closer together than a casual visitor might first surmise from the actual costumes, or more precisely, the upper classes drew this principle to its logical conclusion; they literally disembodied bodily imagery. If that casual visitor were to stop for a moment, indeed, and consider in what the playfulness and fantasy of the upper-class clothing lay, he would be struck by the fact that the wig, the hat, the vest-coat, while attracting attention to the wearer, did so by the qualities of these adornments as objects in themselves, and not as aids to setting off the peculiarities of his face or figure. Let us move from tip to toe to see how the upper orders arrived at this objectification of the body.

Headdresses consisted of wigs and hats for men, and tied and waved hair, often with artificial figurines inserted, for the women. In commenting on the evolution of wigs by the middle of the 18th Century, Huizinga writes:

> . . . the wig is swept up into a regular panache of high combed hair in front with rows of tight little curls over the ears and tied at the back with laces. Every pretence of imitating nature is abandoned; the wig has become the complete ornament.

The wigs were powdered, and the powder held in place with pomade. There were many styles, although the one Huizinga describes was the most popular; the wigs themselves required great care to maintain.[38]

Women's approach to dressing their hair is best illustrated by *La Belle Poule*. A ship of that name defeated an English frigate and inspired a hairdo in which hair represented the sea and nestled in the hair was an exact replica of *La Belle Poule*. Headdresses like the *pouf au sentiment* were so tall that women often had to kneel to go through doorways. Lester writes that

> the *pouf au sentiment* was the favorite court style, and consisted of various ornaments fastened in the hair—branches of trees representing a garden, birds, butterflies, cardboard cupids flying about, and even vegetables.

The shape of the head was thus totally obscured, as was much of the forehead. The head was support for the real focus of interest, the wig or hairdo.[39]

Nowhere was the attempt to blot out the individual character of a person more evident than in the treatment of the face. Both men and women used face paint, either red or white, to conceal the natural color of the skin and any blemishes it might have. Masks came back into fashion, worn by both men and women.[40]

Marking the face with little patches of paint was the final step in obliterating the face. The practice was begun in the 17th Century, but only by the 1750's had it become widespread. In London patches were placed on the right or left side of the face, depending on whether one were Whig or Tory. During the reign of Louis XV, patches were placed to indicate the character of the Parisian: at the corner of the eye stood for passion; center of the cheek, gay; nose, saucy. A murderess was supposed to wear patches on her breasts. The face itself had become a background only, the paper on which these ideograms of abstract character were mounted.[41]

The surfaces of the body followed the same principles. In the 1740's women began displaying more of their breasts, but only as a background on which to place jewels or, in only a few cases, let us hope, patches. The male at the same time used lace at the edges of sleeves, and other sewn-on adornments, more and more delicate. With the slimming of the body, the body frame became simpler, so that it permitted more plasticity and variety in adornment.[42]

Women's skirts largely hid their legs and feet. Men's breeches did not hide the feet. On the contrary, during this period, leggings divided the limb in half visually, and attention was focused on the shoe rather than, as in the early 1700's and again at the end of the century, on the leg as a whole. The bottom extremity of the body was, as were the face and upper torso, an object on which were placed decorations.[43]

The body as an object to be decorated bridged stage and street. The bridge between the two had an obvious and a not so obvious form. The obvious bridge was in the replication of clothes in the two realms; the not so obvious bridge was the way in which stage designers still conceived of allegorical or fantastic characters through the principle of the body as mannequin. In addition, it is important to note one area in which the clothing already described, which was street clothing, was forbidden to be replicated upon the stage.

Above the level of degrading poverty, the street clothing of all ranks was usable almost intact as stage costume. But its use in the mid-18th Century theater produced certain anomalies, at least to a modern observer. In plays with relatively contemporary settings, like Molière's comedies, mid-18th Century audiences saw characters dressed for the street even when the scene was a boudoir. Intimate dress for intimate scenes was out. In plays with historical settings, the clothing of the street was the clothing of the stage, no matter whether the play performed was set in ancient Greece, medieval Denmark, or China. Othello was played by David Garrick dressed in a fashionable, elaborate wig; by Spranger Barry in a gentleman's cocked hat. Hamlet, as played by John Kemble, appeared in gentleman's attire and a powdered wig. The idea of historical presentation, of what a Dane or a Moor looked like in a certain place at a certain time, was largely absent from theatrical imagination. A critic wrote in 1755 that "historical exactitude is impossible and fatal to dramatic art."[44]

The bridge between stage costume and street clothing cannot thus be thought of as part of a general desire for art to mirror life. The bridge in images of the body distorted a mirror, of setting or of time. In addition, similarity between stage and street in the clothing itself was limited by one fact of social position.

The theater audiences of this decade demanded a sharp discontinuity between the two realms when stage characters were those of the lower orders of society; these wretches people turned a blind eye toward in the city; they wanted to be equally blind in the theater. Occasionally, some respectable manual occupations were also prettied up— especially servants. The servants dressed by the designer Martin in Paris "were all silks and satins with ribbons everywhere: the type has been preserved for us in the porcelain figures of the period." In 1753 Madame Favart appeared once on the stage in the sandals, rough cloth, and bare legs of a real working woman of the provinces; the audience was disgusted.[45]

Within these class limits, and within the generally conservative lines of dress, stage costume was often the proving ground of new wig

styles, new face patches, new jewelry. Just as in the Renaissance designers would often try out new architectural forms first as stage backdrops,
couturiers in the middle of the 18th Century would often experiment
with new styles on the stage before they attempted to make them into
everyday street clothing.

If one moves from specific costumes to the principles of costuming
employed by the great costume designers of the time, Martin and
Boquet in Paris, there appears a less obvious way the theater bridged
the rule of appearance which governed the street.

Martin gave theater costumes a lightness and delicacy unknown in
the days of Louis XIV; his costumes for Roman characters began to show
an exaggeration which is whimsical. This element of fantasy was picked
up by Boquet, his successor in the mid-18th Century. Allegorical figures
ceased to be creatures; they became an assemblage of decorative elements draped on the body but wholly unrelated to its movements or
form. The actress Mlle Lacy would appear in the role of Amour dans
l'Eglé with exposed breasts, but the breasts were not exposed by intent.
The costumer simply had no drapery he wanted to put under the lace
garlands which were to be draped across the chest. The bare upper
torso was like a background for the real focus of interest—the lace frills.
The actor Paul would appear as Zéphire with drapery tied at an awk-
ward point on his chest—no matter, it is not the chest the costumer is
dressing, he is rather presenting a beautiful and delicate arrangement
of cloth.[46]

It is the rule of appearance in the everyday world—the body as
mannequin—that this theater costuming elaborated. Allegorical figures
were "fantastications of contemporary dress," street dress which itself
expressed freedom and social dominance in terms of fantasy.

Costume's "fundamental lines changed with the fluctuations of
fashion," Laver writes. That is true as well in terms of actual clothes; the
bridge between the street and the stage also existed when a woman
would think of showing herself on the street as Amour dans l'Eglé. The
rules of bodily appearance in London and Paris in the 1750's show an
almost pure type of a structural continuity between the street and the
stage.[47]

To peek ahead for a moment, when street clothes and stage costume come to be seen as having something to do with the body, as did
the house clothing of the mid-18th Century, they will also come to
appear to have something to do with the character of the person wearing them. At that point, this rule for marking oneself in a public milieu
will go weirdly out of control: reading "more" into the appearance of
strangers, men and women will have less of a sense of order in their
perceptions of strangers. The uses of artifice in the mid-18th Century
thus should be treated with respect, even if today no one would wish
to revive the society in which they appeared.

SPEECH IS A SIGN

Men and women weeping over a hero's death on stage; loud catcalls at an actor who forgets his lines; riots in the theater when a play takes an unpopular political line—we should expect these things in a Romantic setting, or among the citizens of the Revolution, but that is not when the behavior is most often to be found. It exists rather in that audience of wigs and fripperies of the mid-18th Century. It is the woman wearing the *pouf au sentiment* who exclaims against the rhymed politics of Beaumarchais; it is the pomaded man who weeps so unself-consciously at the misfortunes of Lekain.

How can people whose lives are governed by impersonal and abstract convention be so spontaneous, so free to express themselves? All the complexity of the *ancien régime* city lies in that seeming paradox. Their spontaneity rebukes the notion that you must lay yourself bare in order to be expressive. To conceive of the natural man as an expressive creature, and the social man as a being whose thoughts and feelings are weak, fractured, or ambivalent because they are not truly his own, became Romantic common sense after the Great Revolution, and then passed into both intellectual and popular culture. This point of view is Pastoralism. Its latest expression was found in the 1960's among those small numbers of people who actually left (and large numbers who wanted to leave) the city and in the natural setting of the country tried to get "back in touch" with themselves. Even the most cursory glance at the behavior of cosmopolitan theater audiences of the 1750's raises some disturbing questions about this recurrent pastoral ideal. Here were people who for the first time were drawing a firm line between the private and natural, on the one hand, and the public and conventional, on the other. In that latter realm, they could be almost embarrassingly emotional. Can it be that the freedom to feel is greater when one's personality and one's identity in society are quite clearly separated? Can spontaneity and what we have learned to call "artificiality" have some hidden and necessary relationship? They do; that relationship is embodied in the principle of speech as a matter of signs rather than symbols.

In the 1750's, this rule of expressive speech was continuous between stage and street, but in the theater it was distilled, more neatly codified, and is therefore more easily comprehended in retrospect. To understand audience speech of the mid-18th Century, it is necessary to know first in rough outline how a theater was run as a business.

In the 1750's, both London and Paris had official established theaters, the "patent" or "licensed" houses and theaters with a more popular base struggling to achieve an equality of status. In Paris the two commercial fairs (the Foire de St.-Laurent and the Foire de St.-Germain) of the city had from the end of the 17th Century housed acrobats, circus acts, and a species of *commedia dell'arte*. From this source came the Théâtre Italien. In both cities there was opera; in both cities, managers of the sanctioned theaters mixed entr'actes of ballet or farce in the midst of even the most serious tragedy.

The Comédie Française in its old quarters (pre-1781) appears to have housed 1,500 spectators, and in its new, perhaps 2,000. Hogan puts the numbers in mid-18th Century London at around 1,500. Harbage's estimates for the Elizabethan theaters range between 1,750 and 2,500, so that the 18th Century house was somewhat smaller. By comparison, the Metropolitan Opera House holds 3,600; Covent Garden somewhat less.[48]

How many people went to the theater? Better data exist for Paris than for London. In the middle of the 18th Century, the Comédie Française was making an enormous gain in audience attendance; from under 100,000 spectators a year in 1737, the numbers rose steadily to about 160,000 in 1751 and about 175,000 in 1765. But these figures contain an interesting story. The French were not going in greater numbers to see new plays. From 1730 to 1760, very few new plays were introduced into the repertoire—and this was true of the English stage too. In 1750, more people were going to see more regularly dramas with which they were perfectly familiar.[49]

We need one more initial set of facts about the audience: who was in it? In both London and Paris, the presence of many workers can be ruled out in either the Comédie Française or Garrick's theaters—the tickets cost too much. London legitimate-theater audiences tended to be more a mixture of the middle and upper ranks than did Parisian audiences, which tended to be dominated by the elite. But there were places in the French theater for members of the middle ranks, for students, and for intellectuals. These places were in the parterre, and the people who occupied the parterre in the old Comédie Française building stood. An interesting fact about audience behavior appeared when the Comédie Française moved into its new building in 1781. Now the parterre had seats, and they were reserved; the middle ranks could now be more comfortable. And yet writers on the stage at the time commented to a man that with the comfort of the parterre had come a certain deadness into the theater. There were no more shouts from the back of the hall, no more people eating food while they stood watching the play. Silence in the audience seemed to diminish the enjoyment of going to a play. And that reaction is a clue to the sense of audience spontaneity and participation.[50]

Although the dramatic literature of London and Paris in the mid-18th Century was quite different (the French then thought Shakespeare barbaric, for instance) the behavior of audiences in the two cities was similar. For instance, when we look at the stage in the 1750's, we see not only actors but numerous spectators—young and members of the upper ranks—who have seats on the stage. And these "gay bloods" parade across the stage as the mood takes them; they wave to their friends in the boxes. They feel no embarrassment at being themselves in full view of the audience, mixed up with the actors—in fact, they rather enjoy it. During the middle of the 18th Century, the openness and spontaneity of audience response are based on their sense that the actor and the spectator are in the same world, that it is real life, something very close to the audience, that is happening there. No matter that Mithridates falls down dead at the foot of one's next-door neighbor sitting up on the stage. The death provoked a display of emotion in the audience that would embarrass a modern spectator:

> . . . they entered intimately into the anguish of the various characters being represented before them. They burst freely into tears. . . . Following a death scene both men and women wept; the women screamed, and sometimes fainted. So immersed did they become that a foreign visitor was astonished not to hear them laugh "when in a tragedy they hear certain words that might strike them as amusing—as do German audiences."[51]

The intermixing of actor and audience, the extreme emotion displayed by the audience when they were touched, may explain why the silence of the parterre, when the Comédie Française moved into its new quarters twenty years later, was disturbing, taken as a sign that the theater design was a "signal failure." But the mixing of the actor and the spectator in the 1750's, like the displays of feeling, was not a Dionysian release, or ritual in which the actor and the audience became one person in the observance of a common rite. At the same time these audiences were involved, they were in control. They were objective and highly critical of the actors and actresses inducing them to weep The audience was willing to interfere with the actor directly; it did so through a system of "points" and a system of "settling."

The state-licensed theaters of both London and Paris were presenting, as we have seen, repertoires of old and familiar plays. There were certain favorite moments in each play well known to the audience, much anticipated. When an actor or actress arrived at such a "point," he or she would suddenly come down to stage front and center, and deliver his or her lines full face to the crowd. The audience would respond to this direct appeal either with hoots or hisses, or, if the actor appeared to have done well, with those "tears, screams, and faints," calling for a repeat. This could go on seven or eight times. It was an instant "encore" outside the dramatic story. The "points" were at once moments of convention, interrupting whatever was the proper stage business, and moments of direct communion between actor and audience.[52]

"Settling" had to do with relations between prompter and actor. If an actor forgot lines, he of course looked down to the prompter. Once the audience became aware of his lapse of memory, they tried to unnerve him further by hissing or booing so loudly that he could not follow the cues of the prompter. They "settled" the actor, often for good.[53]

This spontaneity was not the privilege of privileged audiences only. For a time in the 1740's, the Théâtre Italien was forbidden to present anything but pantomime on the stage. Its popular audience responded by singing out in unison the words that the actors and actresses mimed for them. The English popular houses were so noisy and responsive that many theaters had to be periodically gutted and redecorated, so much damage had the audiences done in showing approval or disdain for what passed on the stage.[54]

This passion and spontaneous audience feeling in part arose because of the social status of actors. They were in this period considered a species of servant, servants of depraved nature. Musicians, indeed all performers, were slotted in this rank. In the 18th Century city, as was true in Louis XIV's Versailles, people spoke with great freedom in front of and to their servants; women showed themselves deshabille in front of menservants because the servants really didn't count. So in the theater: These people who perform are here to serve us; why should we not display ourselves "point" and "settle" then; what is to stop us from being direct? On this ground, spontaneity in the theater was a matter of social rank. The actor exists to give pleasure. He amuses or arouses our pity, but, like a butler or maid, he is under our control.[55]

But an explanation of this controlled spontaneity based alone on the inferior status of the actor is insufficient. Alone, it obscures changes in the profession of acting which were related to changes in the social character of the actor's audience. Alone, it obscures the relation in turn between how this audience behaved and its sense of speech as believable in terms of signs rather than symbols. Because speech as a sign system is foreign to modern ideas of spoken language, let us preface it with a brief account of the tandem changes of actor and audience for whom it made sense.

In the middle of the 17th Century, most professional actors belonged to touring companies. Regular theaters open to the public were beginning to spring up—in Paris there were three—but the profession of acting remained vagabond, moving from court to court, the actor frequently changing his associates, the urban theaters in Paris and London providing only partial employment. The overwhelming need of the actor was to find new patrons.[56]

The economics of performing were such that "the actor"—was tragedian, comedian, singer, dancer—was whatever would be needed at a court where he could find work. More important, the absence of a self-sufficient theater meant that distinctions of place were minimal. The troupes which appeared in Paris appeared in the countryside or at Versailles.[57]

In London, the Restoration brought into being a theater less dependent upon royal or aristocratic patronage, more able to sustain itself, for a relatively brief season each year, by public subscription, but still from a handful of patrons. This was particularly true of opera. Public performances of music by instrumentalists also began earlier in London than in Paris or Rome; the performances originated as part of tavern life, and the performers were accorded a status parallel to that of a barmaid.[58]

Either as a court or an urban activity in the mid-17th Century, performing was thus subject to a great deal of instability, of vagabondage, the ordinary performer being of low status, the highly skilled stage director being the servant either of one patron and his taste or, in London, of a small public who made of the skilled player-director a harassed jack-of-all-trades.

The audiences for theatrical performances were organized in ways far different from what would appear in the mid-18th Century. At all kinds of performances—dramatic, operatic, or vocal—the principal patron of the day was the focal point of audience behavior. Those around him emulated him in his approval or disapproval; the performer sought not to please the audience as a whole, but only a small segment of it. The very design of theater buildings reflected this ranking. The theater was designed so that the best sight lines were always those from a royal or seigneurial box; the sight lines in London theaters of the 17th Century were similarly geared to a few patrons, the others in the audience having a better view of those few than they did of the stage.

At the beginning of the 18th Century, the theater and its audience began to assume a new form. Certain theaters of Paris and London became organizations which received public grants and defined privileges. The theater became, in Duvignaud's words, "little by little an institution and the actor, if not a bureaucrat, at least a regular worker who produced a definite quantity of emotions on regular dates." The necessity for vagabondage thus came to an end. Like other state functionaries, the actor in Paris or London looked for a permanent post in one of these patent theaters, a post which remained his whether public subscription paid for expenses or not.[59]

In the allowed but not licensed theaters, like the Comédie Italienne or the Comédie de la Foire, troupes were also forming on a more stabilized basis with a regular group of patrons, with some under-the-table government money. In London, both patent and allowed theaters became stabilized, though they received little state support.[60]

The reasons for this stabilization of the acting profession are not far to seek. The public began in the *ancien régime* city to treat the theater as it had been in ancient Athens: as a meeting ground for the populace as a whole, not as an occasion occurring under the eyes of, and directed toward pleasing, one or a small number of patrons. The design of theaters built from the 1720's on showed this; more attention was paid to having unobstructed sight lines for a large portion of the audience rather than a few, and the royal boxes became less and less an immediate focus of the audience's attention. Refreshments began to be served during the performance itself by hawkers wandering the aisles, rather than in the private apartments of the patrons. The foyer became a place in which to meet between acts, rather than an entrance. Tickets were sold in the theater building, rather than distributed as a gift of the patron—although the former practice still remained on a smaller scale. These changes were in no sense a democratization of public performance. Patrons were still sought, though they became larger and larger in number for each production; the house itself was still segregated in its seating by rank. What happened was that the theater itself had become more accessible, more of a focus of social life in the city than an entertainment "given" the people by a king or noble at court. The "routinizing" of professional performing was not a sign of its death, of a loss of spontaneity; these new conditions of professional stability made the theater a more reliable medium for an audience that was beginning to treat it as more than entertainment.

As the whole audience began in part to support the work of the performing servants, the audience became more vocal in reacting to the performances. In the 17th Century, to be sure, court-audience passions were intense, but they could be curbed at a nod from the prince or dignitary providing the entertainment; just as the patron controlled the players, he controlled the behavior of the others in the audience who were his guests. With the gradual fragmentation of this exclusive patronage in the 18th Century, the audience was under no such obligatory control.

With this enlarged audience there grew up a new kind of transaction between actor and audience. The work of the actor became more studied, less a heavy-handed recitation of the lines; he sought to reach the whole of the house, not just to make an impression on a few. As the audience became more familiar with the plays, they demanded this finesse; they began, knowing how it would all come out, to concentrate on the details of the actor's work. In the words of one critic, they paid less attention to the play "as a story revealed" and more to the work of "enactment" as an aesthetic experience in itself. The visitor to an opera house in northern Italy today may still see glimpses of this performing situation: it is the moment, not the movement, which counts.

In the mid-18th Century capital, performance as a matter of moments rather than movement involved spoken words as signs rather than symbols. Modern usage defines a "symbol" as a sign which stands for some thing or things else. We speak of symbols having "referents," for example, of having "antecedents." The symbol easily loses a reality of its own in this usage: "When you say that, or use that word, what you really mean is . . ." and so on. One of the social origins of the idea of decoding signs can be traced to a century ago, in the interpretation of appearances which came to be made in the 19th Century city: appearance is a cover over the real individual hidden within.[61]

In the middle of the 18th Century, this conversion of sign to symbol, this assumption of a world standing behind a given expression, would be foreign. To speak was to make a strong, effective, above all self-contained, emotional statement. The fact that this speech was so consciously worked at, or that body imagery was consciously toyed with, in no way detracted from what convention produced. The woman in the *pouf au sentiment* did not feel "artificial," the *pouf* was an expression in and of itself. The actor who fell dead at one's neighbor's feet on the stage was dead, and one reacted to the fact, no matter that we would now decode the situation as "incongruous." Think of the ultimate verbal sign, the point in front of the footlights: this absolute moment, this complete arrest of movement, led men to feel enraged at the actor or made them weep at the point because the gesture was absolutely believable in its own terms. It had no referent to the scene in which it occurred.

This cognitive system of signs was in fact a conservative force. The 18th Century audience, so instant and direct in their judgments, put a terrible check on the actor or playwright who might try to do what had not been done before. Recall the disapproval by the Paris audience of Madame Favart's realistic appearance as a seedy and threadbare servant; it may now make some sense: she was going to make them sympathize with her wretchedness; they wouldn't be able to help themselves because they didn't conceive of her or any actress as "just acting." A play did not "symbolize" reality; it created reality through its conventions. And therefore she had to be driven off the stage, because what would happen to the order of things if one cried for one's servants? Beaumarchais fought battle after battle with his audience for the same reason. It was not because the audience wanted to be in pretend, in never-never land, that they were shocked at the servant Figaro as a protagonist; it was precisely because in the theater they could not help believing in him that Figaro disturbed them.[62]

The task of all theater is the creation of an internal, self-sufficing standard of believability. In societies where expressions are treated as signs rather than symbols, this task is most easily achieved. In such societies, "illusion" has no connotation of unreality, and the creation of theatrical illusion is simply the realization of a certain power of expression in, rather than a forgetting, an obscuring, or a retreat from "real life." A striking instance of this sense of illusion in a society of signs is the interpretation Parisians made of the disappearance of the stage seats for audiences at the end of the 1750's.

There are two versions of how in 1759 they were swept off the stage so that the rest of the audience could have an uninterrupted view. One version says that a wealthy man gave the Comédie Française an endowment to replace the stage-seat income. Another version lays the change to Voltaire, and is more interesting, if true. In plays like *Sémiramis* (1748), he employed great numbers of actors in crowd scenes and spectacles, so many that in the revival of the play in 1759, the stage seats had to be removed. Garrick then followed suit in 1762. The result was to increase the sense of "illusion" on the stage. Here is how Collé, a playwright of the day, put it:

> One hears better and the illusion is greater. No longer does one see Caesar brushing the dust from the wig of some fool seated in the front row of the stage seats and Mithridates expiring in the midst of one's acquaintances.

When Collé spoke of the "illusion" being the greater where those feet were not visible, he meant the perfecting of a sign. He meant that one can believe in the death more fervently when the feet are gone. To say that "it's just a play" and nothing remained to remind one it's not real misses his meaning.[63]

Because the spoken word was real at a given moment, the point believable without reference to what had come before or what was to come, the instantaneous spontaneity of the audience was also released. People did not at every moment have to engage in a process of decoding to know what was really being said to them behind the gesture. This was the logic of the points: spontaneity was a product of artificiality.

Let us now see what bridge this system of speech made between stage and street. The urban institution in which this system of spoken signs ruled was the coffeehouse of the early 18th Century. By the middle of the century, new institutions had arisen where strangers gathered: the cafe or pub serving liquor, the first restaurants, the pedestrian park. In some of these new institutions the speech pattern of the coffeehouse continued intact; in others it fragmented. By the mid-18th Century a new kind of gathering spot, the men's club, was also taking form, one whose notions of sociable speech were opposed to those of coffeehouse, cafe, and pedestrian park alike. In terms of institutions, then, it is clearest to think, on the one hand, of the pure bridge in speech between the mid-18th Century theater and a gathering place of a slightly earlier era; on the other, to think that by the 1750's this bridge continued, but that other institutions with speech of a more fragmented sort also existed. Most importantly, the exterior foyers and appendages to the theater building itself were becoming important social centers, and here speech occurred among the audience on much the same terms as between audience and performer during the play.

The coffeehouse was a meeting-place common to both London and Paris in the late 17th and the early 18th Century, though, due to England's greater control of the coffee market, the coffeehouses were more numerous in London. The coffeehouse is a romanticized and overidealized institution: merry, civilized talk, bonhomie, and close friendship all over a cup of coffee, the alcoholic silence of the gin shop as yet unknown. Moreover, the coffeehouses performed a function which makes it easy to romanticize them in retrospect: they were the prime information centers in both cities at this time. Here papers were read, and at the beginning of the 18th Century the owners of London coffeehouses began to edit and print newspapers themselves, applying in 1729 for a monopoly in the trade. Such business activities as insurance, which relied on information about the likelihood of success in a particular venture, grew up in coffeehouses; Lloyd's of London began as a coffeehouse, for instance.[64]

As information centers, the coffeehouses naturally were places in which speech flourished. When a man entered the door, he went first to the bar, paid a penny, was told, if he had not been to the place before, what the rules of the house were (e.g., no spitting on such and such a wall, no fighting near the window, etc.), and then sat down to enjoy himself. That in turn was a matter of talking to other people, and the talk was governed by a cardinal rule: in order for information to be as full as possible, distinctions of rank were temporarily suspended; anyone sitting in the coffeehouse had a right to talk to anyone else, to enter into any conversation, whether he knew the other people or not, whether he was bidden to speak or not. It was bad form even to touch on the social origins of other persons when talking to them in the coffeehouse, because the free flow of talk might then be impeded.[65]

The turn of the 18th Century was an era in which outside the coffeehouse, social rank was of paramount importance. In order to gain knowledge and information through talk, the men of the time therefore created what was for them a fiction, the fiction that social distinctions did not exist. Inside the coffeehouse, if the gentleman had decided to sit down, he was subject to the free, unbidden talk of his social inferior. This situation produced its own speech pattern.

The generality of much of the discourse in Addison and Steele's reports on coffeehouse talk is not only a product of their minds, but an accurate report of the kind of speech that permitted people to participate on a common ground. As men sit at the long table, telling stories of great elaborateness, describing wars or the demeanor of leading citizens with rodomontade and flourish, they have only to use their eyes and tune their ears to "place" the stories or descriptions as coming from one with the point of view of a petty-minded petty clerk, an obsequious courtier, or a degenerate younger son of a wealthy merchant. But these acts of placing the character of the speaker must never intrude upon the words these men use to each other; the long periodic sentences flow on, the familiar descriptive phrases which everyone has heard a hundred times before are invoked once again, and a frown goes round the table if someone makes an allusion that may be applied to the "person of any one of his hearers." Coffeehouse speech is the extreme case of an expression with a sign system of meaning divorced from—indeed, in defiance of—symbols of meaning like rank, origins, taste, all visibly at hand.

People thus experienced sociability in these coffeehouses without revealing much about their own feelings, personal history, or station. Tone of voice, elocution, and clothes might be noticeable, but the whole point was not to notice. The art of conversation was a convention in the same sense as the dressing to rank of the 1750's, even though its mechanism was the opposite, was the suspension of rank. Both permitted strangers to interact without having to probe into personal circumstances.

By the 1750's the coffeehouses were on the decline in London and Paris. The coffeehouse declined in part for purely economic reasons. In the early 18th Century, the British East India Company became involved in tea imports, on a vastly more profitable scale than the older coffee import arrangements; trade with China and India expanded around tea, and tea became fashionable. The coffeehouse merchants had no royal license for tea and so were eclipsed.[66]

The life of the coffeehouses was continued in the coaching inns of the mid-18th Century capitals, where travelers to the city were often surprised to hear habitués speak "freely and without reserve upon general topics of conversation." It continued in the new establishments in both Paris and London where one could drink spirits. The cafe and the pub are often portrayed as 18th Century institutions of an exclusively manual-laboring clientele, but this was not the case. In the pubs and cafes around the theaters, the clientele was much more mixed:

indeed, as many of these drinking places were physically attached to the theater buildings, they served as pre- and post-performance gathering points for the audience. People who went to the theater in mid-18th Century Paris or London spent an enormous amount of time in or near them; the conversation in these places was both lengthy and general, the speakers sedulous in their phrasing. Indeed, memoirs from the period indicate that versions of pointing and settling were practiced in these cafes, a man standing up suddenly when he had a "point" to make (colloquial usage dates from this practice), and that calls for repetition of phrases were taken as quite proper. A speaker was "settled" by sheer noisemaking on the part of the others when he became tiresome.

But not all cafes worked on the lines of the theatrical ones, nor did speech as sign preserve itself in daily life intact and whole into the mid-18th Century. Some sense of the multiplicity of speech forms was revealed by the best-known Parisian cafe, the Café Procope, an establishment licensed to serve food, wine, and coffee.

This cafe, founded at the end of the 17th Century, was one of approximately three hundred such establishments in Paris in the middle of the 18th Century. Conversations were open to anyone in the Procope, and yet it had at certain tables groups of young men, most of whom possessed stage seats at the Comédie Française, who would flock to the Procope after plays to talk, drink, and gamble, and who, when knocked off the stage in 1759, arranged a protest demonstration at the cafe. Other cafes in Paris differed from it in containing a less literary and racy clientele, but the cluster of friends who withdrew from the general cafe conversation to pursue their special interests could be found in most other cafes as well.[67]

Speech as a system of signs was threatened on two sides by the mid-18th Century. One was the club, the other was the pedestrian promenade. Clubs became popular among a small circle in the 1730's and 1740's. Although the 18th Century club touched on the lives of very few people, it is worth examining in some detail, both because the terms of its speech foreshadow a phenomenon to become more widespread in the next century and because the terms of its sociability did not at first, in the mid-18th Century, provide complete gratification for those whom snobbism impelled to create this social form.

To understand the club, it is necessary to understand the language of the wealthier bourgeoisie and elite. They did not attempt to create specific differences between intimate language and public speech, as they did with the actual clothes they wore; the studied linguistic formulas developed during the early part of the century were still the language of home entertainments, compliments between friends, even of declarations of love. The first institution created specifically for private speech was the men's club.

Coffeehouses occasionally had provided food, but when they did so they encroached on the domain of the taverns. Clubs met at these taverns and *auberges* rather than in coffeehouses, and their meetings were at first centered on sharing a meal. There were more clubs in London than in Paris; in the middle of the 18th Century few clubs in either city had buildings of their own.[68]

The sociability of the club differed from the coffeehouse life in a way graphically revealed by an incident in Boswell's *Life of Samuel Johnson*. Sir Joshua Reynolds mentioned to the members of the Turk's Head Club that Garrick the actor had said of the club, "I like it much. I think I shall be of you." Johnson replied, "He'll be of us! How does he know we will permit him?" Garrick approached the club, that is to say, as though it were a coffeehouse in the old manner. That openness Johnson denies.[69]

The clubs of the mid-18th Century were based on the idea that speech gave most pleasure when one had selected the audience, excluding those whose personal lives were distasteful or alien. In that sense the clubs were private. Privacy meant speech was agreeable only when one controlled whom one was speaking to.[70]

Club talk meant that speech as a sign, put at a distance from the personal circumstances of the speaker, was challenged. The first thing you wanted to know was not what was said, but who was speaking. The immediate result was that the flow of information became fragmented; when you were with friends in your club, the chances of your finding out what was happening in the great world outside were more restricted than in coffeehouse days.

This limitation explains why clubs, for all their exclusiveness, had a hard time in the mid-18th Century. In this age of intense sociability, the limitations of the club soon produced boredom. Oliver Goldsmith put it well in a remark he made to other members of the Turk's Head Club in 1773, arguing that the club's numbers should be enlarged to twenty: "It would be an agreeable variety [to enlarge the club], for there can be nothing new amongst us; we have travelled over each other's minds."[71]

A more general challenge to the speech patterns of coffeehouse and theater cafe came, oddly, from the very pleasure people took in observing and being observed in a milieu of strangers. By the middle of the 18th Century walking in the street as a social activity acquired an importance which in Paris and London it had never had before. The promenade was at the time described as the advent of an Italian taste; in one way it was so. The Baroque city planners in Italy, especially Sixtus V in Rome, had attached great importance to the pleasures of travel through the city, experiencing movement from one monument, one church, one square to another. This sense of the monumental city, translated into the life of London or Paris a century later, became less a matter of seeing sights than seeing other people. Making contact with other people on the street was no simple activity, however. The streets of Paris and London were still largely a tangle of small, very dirty roads, unlike the municipal improvements made in Rome during the 17th Century. Sidewalks were rare, and usually built of loosely fastened wooden planks, so that they survived only a few years of wear. Even in daylight, violent crimes erupted in the most fashionable parts of both cities, the municipal police being at a rudimentary stage.

A new institution in the city was necessary. It was the public park, designed to make carriage rides and pedestrian travel easy. The building of new parks and the renovation of older undeveloped areas into parks and promenades began in great earnest in the 1730's.

In the middle decades of the century, walking and riding in the park—especially St. James's Park—became a daily experience for large numbers of Londoners:

> Foreign visitors saw in the London parks . . . something of the "peculiar genius" of the English people: their passion for the "promenade," the mixture of classes which was so strangely tolerated.

Taking walks in the park became in turn the means of maintaining, en masse, that sociability between classes which the coffeehouses had formerly provided. But the terms of speech had, in the process, changed.[72]

There is an interesting letter of Leopold Mozart's in which he described one such walk in St. James's Park with his family:

> The King and Queen came driving by, and although we were all differently dressed, they knew and saluted us; the King in particular threw open the carriage window, put out his head laughing, and greeted us with head and hands—particularly our Master Wolfgang.

The characteristic of this open encounter was that contact lasted only a moment: the King gestures to the little violinist and his genius son, they do not sit down for several hours over hot mugs of coffee to chat. (Of course, kings never would have, but even dukes in 1700 would.) The walks in St. James's Park were spontaneous encounters, like the spontaneity of talk in the coffeehouse; only now the spontaneous was a matter of the fleeting.[73]

Parisians used the Tuileries as the English used St. James's Park, with two modifications. With the gardens located so close to the Seine —then a working river bustling with ships—the bucolic charm of St.

James's was not reproduced, as wagons of goods frequently cut through; the Tuileries were also more crime-infested. Common to both was the first germination of the idea of silence in public. You will not sit for hours chatting; you are only taking a walk and can pass anything or anybody by.[74]

In both London and Paris, strangers meeting in the parks or on the streets might without embarrassment speak to each other. In the 1740's it was in good taste for all classes of men to make the pantomime motion of tipping their hats to an unknown woman in order to indicate the wish to speak to her. If she wished, she might reply, but on no account were these street exchanges to be understood as giving the man the right to call upon the woman and her family, nor were similar interchanges between male strangers. What occurred on the street was in a different dimension than what occurred at home. By contrast, in Madame de Sévigné's time, the sheer fact of an introduction gave one person at least the right to attempt to call upon another person. Even if rebuffed in another setting, the attempt was not a breach of good taste. The 18th Century codes of speech belong to the middle and upper orders, to be sure, but there is some evidence to suggest that they were imitated among the ranks of household servants.

The spontaneity of speech in the 18th Century theater may now assume its proper and peculiar meaning. In the theater, the audience could be wholly expressive on terms it could not wholly or uniformly experience outside. Outside the theater, in the 1750's, one might make a display of emotion of the same intensity to friends at the Turk's Head Club, to strangers at the Café de la Comédie, but surely not in the course of walking in St. James's Park.

A literary critic of a certain school might now raise an objection: "You talk about speech as a conventional sign in these theaters," he might protest. "You talk about the spontaneity of the highly stylized audience, but don't you realize that the rules of any art, the 'artifices,' make it possible for the audience to feel what they cannot easily feel in the everyday world? You are describing theater, not the peculiar theater of the 1750's in two cities." And this argument might be expanded into the dictum that whenever people interact with each other in terms of convention, they deal in signs rather than symbols.

The objection, intelligent as it is, shows the problem of treating the relation between language and belief outside the terms of history. In all situations where people believe in a sign, they do not become vociferous in demonstrating the fact that they are convinced: there is a world of difference between 18th Century behavior at the Comédie Française and the behavior of modern theater audiences sitting mute when faced with Art. Similarly with rules of speech on the street, with clothes, and costume. The experiencing of a sign—vociferously, silently, etc.—

defines what a sign is. The audience forcing a point is living a different *kind* of sign language than an audience applauding at the end of a play, or at most applauding at the end of a speech.

THE IMPERSONAL REALM IS PASSIONATE

"Public" behavior is a matter, first, of action at a distance from the self, from its immediate history, circumstances, and needs; second, this action involves the experiencing of diversity. This definition has no necessary bounds of time and place, for a hunting and gathering tribe or a medieval Indian city could in principle fulfill its conditions. But historically the modern meaning of "public" jelled around the same time these two codes of belief, the body as a mannequin, speech as a sign, also took form. The confluence was no accident, for each of these codes of belief met the tests of a public phenomenon.

The body as mannequin for clothes was a self-consciously public mode of dress. Clothes which revealed, suited, or gave comfort to the body and its needs were thought proper only for the home. The body as mannequin met the test of diversity in a double sense; this principle of dressing moved from street to stage almost intact, and on the street itself the marking and play with clothes as with a doll was a means of organizing and bringing order to the diversity of the street.

Speech as sign also met the tests of a public phenomenon. It was activity at a distance from the self; on the street a general language about generalities; in the theater one was aroused not according to personal whim or flush of feeling but only at the proper and conventional moments. Speech on these terms met the test of diversity in the same double sense as clothes did; the principle bridged stage and street and also bridged diversity among strangers on the street.

If these two principles of arousing belief served the same ends, they did so by contrary means. The visual principle involved arbitrarily marking the body in terms of rank and in terms of fantasy; the verbal principle involved arbitrarily denying the marks of rank. However, both these principles share a rejection of symbol, a rejection of the idea that behind the convention there lay an inner, hidden reality to which the convention referred and which was the "real" meaning. Both visual and verbal principles therefore sharpen a definition of "public" expression: it is anti-symbolic.

Now, if the public realm were but a certain mode of feeling, any analysis of the public should stop here, for these visual and verbal principles are the means to feeling in public. However, the public also is a geography; it exists in relation to another domain, the private. Publicness is part of a larger balance in society. Furthermore, as part of a larger whole it has meanings, in terms of political behavior, the concept of rights, the organization of the family, and the limits on the state, which are not so far established by an account of the tools by which people feel in public. To the question of the larger geography, the line between public and private around which this society of the 18th Century was organized, we next turn.

CHAPTER 5

PUBLIC AND PRIVATE

The material motivations of public life, and its emotional means of expression, suggest to the modern observer certain qualities for its opposite, private side. Here in the realm of family and friends, close to the self, it seems reasonable that people would be more interested in expressing their peculiarities, their distinct personalities, their individuality. But this quite reasonable expectation is a distortion; it is to view the 18th Century in terms of privacy which took form in the last century. Before the 19th Century, the realm close to the self was not thought to be a realm for the expression of unique or distinctive personality; the private and the individual were not yet wedded. The peculiarities of individual feeling had as yet no social form because, instead, the realm close to the self was ordered by natural, universal human "sympathies." Society was a molecule; it was composed, in part, of expression at a contrived and conscious distance from personal circumstances, family and friends, and, in part, of self-expression which was also "impersonal" as that word is understood today. We need to understand this alien notion of a natural realm of the self because we continue today to believe in notions of human rights which arose because of it.

The modern notion of human rights comes from an opposition between nature and culture. No matter what the customs and mores of a society, every person has certain basic rights, no matter how lowly or disadvantaged he may be placed in those cultural arrangements. What are these rights? We have two clichéd formulations of them, both originating in the 18th Century: life, liberty, and the pursuit of happiness; liberty, equality, and fraternity. Among these rights it is easier to discuss life, liberty, or equality than the pursuit of happiness or fraternity; they seem almost tacked on as benefits of the first set, rather than equally fundamental rights. And the reason we do not perceive them as of an equal weight is that we have lost the assumption, which germinated in the 18th Century, on which they are based. This was that the psyche had a natural dignity; this integrity of psychic needs also sprang from an opposition of nature and culture. If a man's feelings are damaged, if he is made to feel abject or ashamed, this is a violation of his natural rights as surely as seizing his property or holding him in jail arbitrarily is. When a person has received such an injury he is therefore entitled to attempt to heal the wound by changing the social conditions which caused it. The pursuit of happiness was one formulation of this psychic integrity, fraternity was another. It is the natural man who possesses these psychic rights; not the individual. All men could demand fraternity or happiness precisely because the natural was impersonal and non-individual.

The notion that human beings have a right to be happy is a peculiarly modern, Western idea. In societies of great poverty, rigid hierarchy, or strong religious passions, psychic gratification can have little meaning as an end in itself. This peculiar claim of nature against culture began to take form in the 18th Century, particularly in England, France, northern Italy, and northeastern America. Like any complex historical development, it was not born full-grown. Our forebears struggled to find images and experiences which could somehow express this opposition, so as to give the pursuit of happiness a concrete social form. One way they found to express it was through the distinction between public and private. The geography of the capital city served its citizens as one way to think about nature and culture, by identifying the natural with the private, culture with the public. By interpreting certain psychic processes as inexpressible in public terms, as transcendent, quasi-religious phenomena which could never be violated or destroyed by the arrangements of convention, they crystallized for themselves one way, and not the only way, surely, but a tangible way, in which natural rights could transcend the entitlements of any particular society.

The more this opposition of nature and culture through the contrast of private and public became tangible, the more the family was viewed as a natural phenomenon. The family was "a seat of nature" rather than an institution like the street or the theater. The idea here was that, if the natural and the private are united, then every man's experience of family relations will be his experience of Nature. The order of Nature might be definable only by the most highly tuned minds, but this transcendental phenomenon was more generally discussable, because in discussing emotional transactions in the family, one was discussing questions of Nature.

This is why the psychic transactions in the family were viewed in terms we would today call impersonal or abstract. Psychology in the 18th Century was replacing the Renaissance notion of bodily "humors," in which character was manifested in one of four, or in some versions seven, states depending on how much bodily fluid particular organs produced; the newer notion was of natural "sympathies," determined by the functional unity of the human species rather than the functional or dysfunctional processes of the body. Psychology was a science based on natural taxonomy—that is, the classification of the behavior of different species—rather than on physiology. These sympathies all men shared; they became manifest in the seat of nature, the family; their label is a just guide to their meaning: what people shared was a natural compassion, a natural sensitivity to the needs of others, no matter what the differences in their social circumstances. That people have natural rights was a logical consequence of such a definition of human nature.

To explore this private, natural world, we need to make two caveats. The first is that while people in the Enlightenment sensitive to this issue saw Nature as a deity, a transcendental phenomenon of which one tangible expression was love in the family, they did not therefore deify Nature as a state of perfection. In Frank Manuel's happy phrase, the Enlightenment had a "respectful but by no means subservient" relation to its gods; Nature, unlike medieval superstition, gave man, after all, cause for hope, rather than despair in his own powers. This attitude, when expressed in terms of the opposition of private/nature and public/culture, meant that the relations between the two realms were more a matter of checks and balances than absolute hostility. The private realm was to check the public in terms of how far conventional, arbitrary codes of expression could control the whole of a person's sense of reality; beyond these borders he had a life, a form of expressing himself, and a set of rights which no convention could obliterate by fiat. But the public realm was a corrective to the private realm as well; natural man was an animal; the public therefore corrected a deficiency of nature which a life conducted according to the codes of family love alone would produce: this deficiency was incivility. If culture's vice was injustice, nature's vice was its rudeness.

This is why, in speaking of these two realms, they must be thought of as a molecule: they were concurrent human modes of expression, located in different social settings, which were correctives to each other.

The second caveat is a matter of language. Just as the public realm was an evolving phenomenon, taking form over time, so was the private. The family quite gradually became thought of as a special institution. The discovery of the family, and so of a social setting alternative to the street, depended in its turn on another, interior, slow discovery: that of a special, natural stage in the human life cycle, childhood, which could flourish only within the terms of family life. We talk about public and private as fixed states, because picturing them is easier so. They were in fact complex evolutionary chains.

THERE ARE LIMITS ON PUBLIC EXPRESSION

We have already seen how a limit was put, in substance, on visual and, in access, on verbal public expression. Clothing for the home was adapted to the needs, comfort, and movement of the body; clothing for public use was contrived without reference to those needs. Speech at home and in public was similar in substance, but the private realm was the place in which one could control whom one spoke to; thus the members of private clubs spoke of their societies "as akin to the company of the family."

The growing perception of the family as a natural group harboring a special class of beings—children—put more comprehensive limits on public expression. The discovery that two centuries ago people discovered childhood is the work of Philippe Ariès, in his *Centuries of Childhood:* this book opened up a whole new field—the study of the family as a historical form, rather than as a fixed biological form in history. Ariès found, and his findings have since been expanded and refined by David Hunt and by John Demos, that by the middle of the 18th Century adults were beginning to think about themselves as fundamentally different kinds of creatures from those who were their children. The child was no longer thought a little adult. Childhood was conceived as a special and vulnerable stage; adulthood was defined in reverse terms. The evidence Ariès uses is mostly from the family records of urban people in the middle and upper reaches of society. There is a reason for this; this same articulation of life stages served these people in defining the limits of public life. What was occurring in the cosmopolitan centers was that the mature people who inhabited them began to think of the public life, with its complexities, its poses, and, above all, the routine encounters with strangers, as a life which only adults were strong enough to withstand, and to enjoy.

The limiting of public life to adults had an interesting genesis; it came in part from the gradual distinctions made between childhood and adult forms of play.

Until late in the 17th Century there were few lines between the games amusing to children and games amusing to adults; that is, there were few childhood pleasures which adults considered beneath their own interest. Dolls dressed in elaborate costumes interested people of all ages. Toy soldiers similarly amused people of all ages. The reason for this sharing of games, dolls, and toys was precisely that sharp demarcations between stages of life did not then exist. Since, in Philippe Ariès's phrase, the young person was an "incipient adult" from a very early age, his amusements had nothing self-contained about them. At the end of the 17th and the beginning of the 18th Century, with lines between childhood and adulthood being drawn more sharply than they had before, certain kinds of play were reserved to children, certain kinds forbidden to them.

By the middle of the 18th Century, children were prohibited from engaging in games of chance, which the authorities believed suitable only for people with a knowledge of the evil rampant in the world. In 1752 tennis and billiard masters throughout France were forbidden to give classes while children's schools were in session, because a great deal of gambling went on during these games. Children were too naïve, it was thought, to cope with this.[75]

Throughout the 18th Century, as in the two previous centuries, communal sings and music-making numbered children and adults as participants. But during the early years of the 18th Century, adults began to find the practice of reading out loud in groups unsuitable and childish; instead even folk tales, in printed form, became adult material, when enjoyed in silent reading. Conversely, as silent reading, they were considered unsuitable texts for the young. Speech for the adult was a matter of using his own words, in public.[76]

It was partially because of these changing notions of play that cosmopolitan behavior was considered to be fit only for adults. The child was not to mark precisely his station, nor, if of quality, play with images of his body. Indeed, the dressing to station and elaborate aristocratic dress of children of late 17th Century paintings, or still in 18th Century Spanish paintings, were by the 1750's in London and Paris regarded as absurd. Children should rather be dressed in costumes which were peculiar only to children, which set children as an entire class off from the class of adults.

Similarly, in the theater, if children were permitted to accompany their parents at all, they were expected to be silent and invisible. Comparative studies of children in the late 17th Century theater audiences are nonexistent, but we do know that children were in attendance at the plays of Congreve and Wycherley and were considered simply spectators—an equality with adults all the more striking given the plays they were witnessing.

Cafes, clubs, and pubs were also considered adult places, though children were certainly not excluded from them, especially from the pubs or *auberges* which served as coaching houses. Occasional remarks in Addison and Steele suggest that when children entered into coffeehouse talk they were treated with good humor and patronizingly. The club, per se, was not an institution designed to take in children. The taverns of mid-18th Century Paris were considered dangerous places for children because they might get their hands on a bottle of brandy or port—a danger viewed then not in moral terms but in terms of physical health.

This, then, is how the gradual concern with the special state of childhood marked off certain limits to public expression. The limits can be said to be that the public realm was the place in society reserved for adult play, or they can be said to be the boundary outside of which the adult cannot play. By 1750 a father would be embarrassed to dress up his son's dolls, although he in fact played in exactly the same way when he dressed himself for the street.

If the child did not belong in public, what were the terms on which he belonged in a family? What could the family do for him which public life was unfit to do? It was in answering these questions that people began to treat the family as the "seat of nature," and to find new principles of expression.

NATURAL EXPRESSION IS OUTSIDE THE PUBLIC REALM

To understand the tandem growth of childhood and the belief in natural expression within the family, we have to start with the odds against it at the time. When one reads statements like Turgot's that "one is ashamed of one's children" or Vandermonde's (in an *Essay on the Means of Perfecting the Human Species*) that "one blushes to think of loving one's children," the strength of family feeling two centuries ago appears, if anything, faint. Gibbon wrote of the accident of his own survival at the hands of indifferent parents (he was actually rescued by an aunt); Talleyrand never slept in the same house with his parents. The higher one moved up the social ladder, the more frequently would one hear that direct maternal care and expression of love for an infant was a sign of vulgarity. In both Paris and London, children from the middle-middle and upper-middle classes were often handed directly from nurse to "college," an institution charged with the care of those from seven to eleven or twelve—"care" being usually interpreted as continual physical chastisement. The leading pediatricians of the mid-18th Century, James Nelson and George Armstrong, berated their readers for "unnatural neglect and disregard" of their offspring. There can be no doubt, in sum, that Swift's contemporaries read *A Modest Proposal* with more than a little shock of recognition.[77]

Yet the most important thing about the debates over inhumanity to children is that they occurred at all. Similar neglect of infants and children had gone on in western Europe for century after century; in the mid-18th Century it became sufficiently distressing to many people to be argued about. Distress about being saddled with children, no less than reformist distress at the behavior of those who felt saddled, arose from the very growth of the idea of a special stage of life called childhood. People now noticed that a special, *dependent* class of human beings was produced by the workings of the body. It was the perception

94

of the dependency which was new—as was the fear, empathy, or confusion about it.

"The state of nature" is, in political philosophy, an idea with roots going back to the Middle Ages. The growing perception of this vulnerability of the child produced in the early 18th Century a more concrete, experiential idea of what a state of nature consisted of. It was not a hypothesis. It was a fact in every human life.

The perception of juvenile dependency produced a sense of rights of protection—realized in both France and England in the 1750's and 1760's by laws regulating the practice of wet-nursing and curbing the worst evils of the colleges. The justification for protecting the child was that, if in nature one was vulnerable, then one had a right to nurturance and comfort beyond the accidents of one's birth, condition, or the inclinations of one's parents. The family relation thus was magnified. As the stages of natural maturation were perceived to be more important, every human being in the family became more important. This is what the "right to life" meant two centuries ago; more than the right to sheer existence, it was the right to be valued, to be loved. The fact that a child was naturally frail and so unequal to others in society was no justification for his neglect; his very natural frailties gave him rights against a society, beginning with his parents, in which those frailties could be taken advantage of, in which they made the child "of no account."

The order of nature was thus in the Enlightenment a morally charged scheme; nature was allied with the discovery of, the need for, and the right to, nurture. Among those who, in the debate on the right to nurture, espoused the cause of the child, the consequent definition of nurture was twofold: one was leniency of discipline to bring out the kindly disposition of the child; thus Mary Wollstonecraft:

> It is only in the years of childhood that the happiness of a
> human being depends on others [thus the idea of dependence]
> and to embitter those years by needless restraint is cruel. To
> conciliate the affections, affection should be shown.

The other was participation of both the parents of the child in its upbringing; thus the pediatrician Nelson argued that women should nurse their own babies and fathers should not delegate their authority to colleges. In fact, for all the ambivalence about parenthood, both practices were becoming widespread among the middle ranks of society by 1750, and beginning to challenge a significant number of upper-middle-class parents—although, to be sure, truly aristocratic upbringing continued to be based on the alternative two principles of non-nurturance, harsh discipline and parental absence.[78]

The special task the family could perform, nurturance of those who are helpless, came to seem a natural function of "the" family. Nurturance detached the family from social arrangements. Nelson could thus write a book on the functions of the family without reference to primogeniture, marriage contracts, dower rights, and the like. As this natural function crystallized, there coalesced ideas about natural expression within the family. This expression, called natural "sympathy," was diametrically opposed to the terms of expression which made appearances in public believable.

The theory of sympathy has yet to receive real scholarly treatment because psychologists are so prone to consider "early," or "prescientific," theories of the psyche to be of antiquarian rather than intrinsic interest. It can be said of the varied descriptions of natural character which Diderot collected for the *Encyclopédie,* or which informed Beccaria's *Of Crimes and Punishments,* that, at the least, they share two characteristics. The natural sympathies involve "appetites" which do not outstrip the real needs of the person feeling these appetites; in turn, insofar as men possess "measured" appetites, they desire the same things, fecundity, nurturance, companionship, and the like. The measured appetites are, in the words of Youngman, appetites "germane to the species and not to the accidents of the individual."[79]

Along the first of these lines, it became logical to believe that when a person acted naturally, he acted simply. The order of nature was complex—so complex that any given phenomenon or social condition couldn't wholly express it. Nonetheless, the effect of nature upon the individual was to give him a taste for simple, uncomplicated experience. Think for a moment of the growing taste for loose, unadorned garments in the home as expressions of natural feeling; this is so logical in retrospect that it is easily forgotten that in many cultures the importance of the family is accented precisely by people's desire to dress up when in the house. The belief in simplicity made the very idea of convention irrelevant, for public dress or talk makes meaning reside in the gesture, the sign itself, while a sympathetic expression conceives meaning in terms of the relationship of behavior to the restricted class of needs—the natural appetites—of the person behaving.

Second, it became reasonable for people to believe that the natural sympathies did not differentiate one person from another, since all were measuring their activity in accord with the same appetites. Practically, this meant that when a person acted naturally, he was thought not to stand out, to proclaim himself as special or unique. There was an apt 18th Century phrase to encompass both the simplicity and unexceptionality of natural desires: modesty.

The nurturative function of the family had a place in this scheme of natural expression. When family relations were spoken of as "rude" —either praised or condemned as such—the meaning was that the emotional demands made in the family circle, and especially in the nurturance of children, were far simpler than demands adults made on each other in situations outside the family. It is difficult in an age obsessed by the difficulties of parenthood to comprehend that nurturing could ever be seen as less complex than other social entanglements. But the psychic requirements of parenthood seeming then so modest, the family became the proper place for the natural simplicity of adults to express itself.

Here was a dimension of the psyche, and of expression, which possessed an integrity and dignity, no matter what the circumstances of any individual. And from the integrity of this natural psyche there came in turn a set of natural rights. Beccaria in his book on prisons argued that the prisoner had natural rights to humane treatment because, no matter how heinous his crime as society defined it, once in prison he was as dependent as a child and therefore ought to earn a measure of compassion; he had a natural right to elemental nurturance when reduced to total weakness. Benign captors weren't doing him a favor. His jailers, further, ought to realize he was not so far distant a creature from them, because they shared a common palette of moderate desires; whatever his individual crime in society, there was an element of decency in his impersonal character as a human animal. Thus did the recognition of a common nature and the theory of natural dependency become the psychic foundation of certain political rights.

Natural rights, insofar as they sprang from concepts of nurture and the simplicity of natural desire, consisted at the broadest level of limitations on the unequal distribution of pain. In another work, I have tried to show how, in the 18th Century, the idea of human dignity was divorced from the concept of equality; natural dignity put limits only on the opposite extreme, on inequality, and on inequality of a special sort. The conventions of status in the society of early modern Europe separated human beings into such disparate compartments that they had no sense of belonging to the same species; Madame de Sévigné, a compassionate woman toward those of her own station, attended hangings as recreation and found the death agonies of common wretches "amusing." The concepts of a natural obligation to nurture the weak and of a thread of psychic desire among all mankind put a limit of nature on the pain one class of people ought to tolerate or inflict upon another.[80]

But if hierarchy as such had natural limits, then the rituals of hierarchy were conventions, something made up and agreed to. These behaviors, like the idea of hierarchy itself, lose their power as being immutable and absolute in the order of things. From that perception, the next logical step is to see the principles of natural expression as limitations on the very notion of convention. And when that step is taken, then the principle is established that the private natural world could act as a curb on the special world of cosmopolitan public life.

We have already seen signs of this limitation in the prohibition of public life to children, because they could not bear it. Among adults, the same limit on psychic distress prevailed in both visual and verbal behavior. A person caught dressing above his or her station should never be put to shame among family or in one's own home. In this seat of nature, there was a limit on the pain one could cause another person. It was an affront to snub someone in the home, although no affront on the street. These are trivial examples of a much larger issue: the world of public conventions must not weaken the pursuit of happiness, insofar as this pursuit depended on a sense of psychic integrity and respect of oneself or another as "a man."

Conversely, the public world put a limitation on the principle of happiness as a full definition of reality. Although the realm of conventions could not alter or change nature, because *in esse* nature transcended any social situation, public culture served a purpose in taming the effects of nature. Voltaire's famous riposte to Rousseau, that he had long ago lost the taste for walking on all fours which the natural animal called man might have, was echoed in a highly popular treatise published by an English physician a year later, in which he likened natural human society to a pen of happy, loving ducks: nurturance and simplicity prevail, but the "social graces consist of joyful quacks; the satisfied belch is the highest form of discourse."

PUBLIC AND PRIVATE ARE LIKE
A MOLECULE OF SOCIETY

The modes of public and private expression were not so much contraries as alternatives. In public the problem of social order was met by the creation of signs; in private the problem of nurturance was faced, if not solved, by the adherence to transcendental principles. The impulses governing the public were those of will and artifice; the impulses governing the private were those of restraint and the effacement of artifice. The public was a human creation; the private was the human condition.

This balance was structured by what we now call impersonality; neither in public nor in private were "the accidents of individual character" a social principle. And from that comes a second structure: the only limitations on public conventions were those which could be imagined in terms of natural sympathies. When we say today that natural rights are human rights, the cliché seems to us to indicate something as broad and sweeping as it is amorphous. But when natural rights first began to make sense in terms of everyday experience, they were much less sweeping. The principle of natural order was one of moderation: the conventions of society were subject to check only when they produced extremes of distress or pain.

What would happen, then, if an idea of rights in society took hold, outside the context of this principle of natural moderation? When people in the 18th Century began to toy with the notion of liberty, they began to experiment with an idea outside this context. Liberty as a principle, a structure of social relations, could be encompassed neither by the idea of convention nor by the idea of natural sympathy. To be sure, earlier social-contract theorists like John Locke preached an idea of natural liberty, but it could not be practiced easily. When such an idea was introduced into ordinary social life, the molecule of public and private could be broken. The molecule held because individual character was not used to form a social principle. The demand for liberty changed this. How this molecule could be broken, so that the desire for liberty became joined to a belief in individual character as a social principle, I want to describe by recounting the experience of a man in the mid-18th Century who was thought to be—and the words are significant—one of the first "individual champions of liberty." His story is symptomatic of the rupture later to convulse the society of the *ancien régime.* He neither alone nor successfully broke the molecule of nature and culture apart for long, for in fact as an "individual champion of liberty" his career was short-lived, but his experience was a foreshadowing of how that breakup would one day succeed, and how, in the process, liberty itself would perish, but personality would remain a principle of social organization, on new terms of domination.

THE MOLECULE SPLIT

John Wilkes (1727–1797), son of a wealthy distiller in Clerkenwell, became by his early twenties the very model of a London rake. Cross-eyed, afflicted with a bulging forehead and a receding upper lip, this strikingly ugly man was a personage of such great charm and wit that, in giving himself up to a life of dissipation, his difficulties were entirely of choice rather than of pursuit. He drank excessively and belonged to the most notorious club of his day, the Hell-Fire Club, a parody of a medieval order whose members conducted "rites" amalgamating the Black Mass, the Roman banquet orgy, and a burlesque of the Anglican evening service. At twenty, Wilkes married a rich woman twelve years his senior, with little to recommend her but her money, to please his father; the marriage put no noticeable check on his dissipations. And yet Wilkes had by 1763 become the most notorious political figure of his day—by "accident," he said. He became the champion of the principle that the people have the right to choose those who will represent them in government. Philandering without a break through the 1760's, even while in prison, amusing himself with a thousand expensive and aristocratic entertainments, he yet became identified in the minds of London workers and the London lower-middle classes not merely as a defender of liberty but as this high moral principle incarnate. Wilkes was a contradictory phenomenon. He was a representative figure of the divide between public politics and the "accidents of individual" character, as well as one of the first to cross that line, and so transform the very meaning of a public realm.[81]

When we read the political pamphlets and speeches of the 1750's, in both England and France, we as modern readers can only be amazed by the intensity of the rhetoric. The opposition to one's views—to take an English pamphlet of 1758—are "whoremasters to the Devil, bastards without an ounce of charity for their fathers," etc., while in a French pamphlet on floating a foreign loan, the enemies of the writer are described as "scaly monkeys, slaves of the dung hill on which they gibber," etc. And yet this viciously personal language of politics served, curiously, the same self-distanced ends as did the faceless talk of the coffeehouse. Wilkes afforded in part a good example.[82]

Wilkes entered politics by becoming a political pamphleteer. In 1762 he and a group of friends decided to found a newssheet, the *North Briton*, as a voice of opposition to government policies championed in the *Briton*, edited by Smollett, and the *Auditor*, edited by Arthur Murphy. As was the custom of the time, all articles were published anonymously; it was considered unseemly for one person visibly to attack another in print. The attacks Wilkes launched were acidly personal enough, especially his attacks on Samuel Johnson and the artist Hogarth. But in print they came from an unknown hand: that convention meant one could never be sure who exactly accused one of being a whoremaster to the devil. The rhetorical attacks in the *North Briton* had a second characteristic, as was true for the *Briton* and the *Auditor*. A person was attacked personally in terms of his public association with a policy or political faction, or his ability in conducting policy. His character mattered insofar as it could be identified as making the Minister or the Member of Parliament either slack in the performance of his duties, or obtuse, or easily gulled.[83]

These parameters on political discourse led to certain behavioral constraints. An interesting example of how they worked occurred in 1762 when Lord Talbot, the Lord High Steward, felt himself too viciously attacked in the *North Briton*. He challenged Wilkes to a duel, suspecting Wilkes himself to be the author of the slander. Before the moment when shots were exchanged, Talbot worked himself up into a dreadful rage, attempting to get Wilkes to own that he was in fact author of the piece; Wilkes agreed to fight, without, however, admitting the authorship. The duel took place; both men, terrible shots, missed each other from eight yards' distance. At this point Wilkes confessed his authorship; the two exchanged compliments, and retired to a nearby inn to drink a bottle of claret with every appearance of bonhomie.[84]

Public insult, the public satisfaction of honor, rituals divorced from simple interpersonal friendship or companionability—without an understanding of this organization of gesture, much similar political behavior in the mid-18th Century, in both Paris and London, is inexplicable. In the realm of political rhetoric among the ruling classes, there was a code of gesture as firm as the gestures created by clothing. It was impersonal passion, even when vilifying other persons, made possible by conventions such as anonymous authorship.

Issue No. 45 of the *North Briton* appeared, however, to transgress one of the conventions. It appeared to be an attack on the very person of King George III. In retrospect, issue No. 45 seems tame enough, certainly less rabid than others, such as No. 17, but it so incensed agents of the Crown that Lord Halifax, the equivalent of Home Secretary, sent out a warrant for the arrest of the writers, printers, and publishers of the *North Briton*. There ensued a long and complicated struggle. Wilkes was forced to relinquish his seat in Parliament, then to flee to the Continent—where he passed his period of exile alternately in the company of his daughter and in the arms of the most famous courtesan of Italy, Madame Corradini. At the end of the 1760's he returned to England, went on trial for the *North Briton* No. 45, passed a year and a half in jail, was elected four times to Parliament, four times refused a seat in that body by its members, and upon leaving jail found himself the leader of a mass movement of Londoners who had come to associate his trials with the cause of liberty in England.[85]

It is impossible to speak of these events in comprehensive terms. They bore directly, however, on the meanings attached in the mid-18th Century to the concept of a public rhetorical gesture as an expression at a distance from the self.

Wilkes, like others of his generation, drew a sharp line between his family duties, especially his duties as a father to his only legal child, his daughter Polly, and his "pilgrimages in pursuit of pleasure." Although Wilkes and his wife were legally separated after four years, the father kept a constant watch over the education of his daughter, and attempted to shield her from contact with any of his fellow "pilgrims," except his close friend Charles Churchill. Unlike a London libertine of the late 17th Century, Lord Rochester, Wilkes made every attempt to shield his legal child as well from contact with her natural half-brothers and -sisters. In the attempt to keep one's family separate from one's life in the world, Wilkes was very much a man of his time.

Equally, his sexual forays were public in a well-accepted and quite literal way. There was no attempt on Wilkes's part, just as there was no attempt among other gentlemen, to conduct sexual affairs in secret, save with a married woman whose husband was of equal rank and so could call one to account. Otherwise, if the affair was with a married woman, the responsibility for keeping the affair from the husband lay with the woman. With prostitutes or "debauchees," absolutely no rules of discretion were observed.

The language of extramarital sexual affairs showed many of the characteristics of other forms of public discourse. Compliments were judged pleasing to the extent that they were well made or witty in themselves; the depth of the speaker's passion in uttering them was beside the point; indeed, something of an ironic tone in the utterance of these phrases made the speaker all the more seductive. The idea that a lover must find a unique language of talking about his feelings for a particular woman, a language of love specific to two particular people, was also unknown. The phrases carried from one affair to the next to the next; the issue was how these phrases were said, how they were combined, the manner of enacting them.[86]

Wilkes pushed these rules to their farthest extremes and so acquired in his twenties a reputation for libertinage. Here is Ben Franklin's description of him: "an outlaw and exile of bad personal character, not worth a farthing." Here is Burke's: "a lively, agreeable man, but of no prudence and no principle." Here is Horace Walpole's: "Despotism will for ever reproach Freedom with the profligacy of such a Saint."[87]

This reputation was at times turned against him in his political life, and so, many historians have treated him as a man whose personal character was the standard his contemporaries used to judge his political acts. This interpretation is not quite correct. It is true, for instance, that Wilkes's authorship of an *Essay on Woman*, a highly pornographic parody of Pope's *Essay on Man*, was taken up by his enemies as one reason Wilkes should not be seated in Parliament, even though he was overwhelmingly elected by the freeholders of his London borough. Yet, in the last of the four elections of Wilkes Parliament set aside, the election in which the *Essay on Woman* was most often mentioned, the man Parliament decided "ought to have been elected," a certain Colonel Luttrell, was, if anything, a more notorious rake than Wilkes. Many of Wilkes's enemies by this time (mid-1769) were former or, indeed, present *compagnons* on his binges, and well known as such. The uses of Wilkes's character by enemies have to be looked at with a very jaundiced eye, then. They were often laughed at even by those who uttered them. The real join between Wilkes the person and Wilkes the politician, fatal to the public conventions of politics in his time, occurred among those who were his supporters.[88]

A careful study of Wilkes's supporters, conducted by George Rude, concludes that their backgrounds ran the gamut from prosperous merchants to semiskilled laborers, weighted toward the latter. For them, the issues raised by Wilkes and No. 45, deepened by his continual rejections in Parliament, were of the meaning of representation—he stood for the less privileged members of the society who were exercising the liberty of choosing their representatives in government. But in 1763 the meaning of that liberty was not clear. His supporters not so much seized upon an idea of liberty, pristine and distinct, an idea waiting to be employed, as attempted to develop the idea, to find out what liberty meant through the process of returning Wilkes to power. Because they were developing a political principle, rather than applying a principle to their lives, the man, his sheer existence, the sheer fact of his determination to be seated in the House, acquired an overwhelming importance to them. The cry "Wilkes and Liberty!" was a precise indicator; the man and the principle were one because without this man's presence there was no other way to imagine what liberty meant.[89]

This union meant that every action of the person Wilkes had of necessity a symbolic or public character. His sexual philandering had either to be denied, blotted out from the picture of him as a man—as the more prosperous of his supporters were wont—or converted to a sign of rebellion against the established order, a romanticism of a sexual sort more congenial as an interpretation of his behavior among his working-class supporters. A drayman in 1768 described him admiringly as "free from cock to wig." Promiscuity, like all the other actions of the man, had to be interpreted, for the very life of the person John Wilkes had become a symbol of what liberty itself meant.

The attempt to interpret the meaning of a political principle through the operations of character was at a far deeper level, and of far greater import, than the accusations leveled against Wilkes by partisans of the government. These partisans could easily accuse him, on the one hand, and on the other, replace him with a better Member of Parliament like Luttrell, of far more notorious, indeed more violent and well-known sexual tastes. The connection of character and politics made by Wilkes's followers converted parliamentary hypocrisy into something else: a personal insult to each partisan, rather than to a collective movement.

Certainly, from Wilkes's letters and comments in conversation, there comes little sense that the man himself thought in terms of erasing the line between his personality and his politics. He was as ironic about his own fame as he was about his supporters, when discussing them with friends. Indeed he attempted to keep a distance between private and public life, and the personal adulation of his supporters both gratified him and made him profoundly uncomfortable.

After a period of immense popularity, the differences between the identity his followers ascribed to him and the man's sense of himself led both to grief. A particularly ill-starred and well-publicized passion was said by many to be a betrayal of Wilkesism, because so much adverse publicity ensued. If he was an emblem of Liberty to his supporters, they were allowing him less and less liberty to conduct his own life. At the time of the Gordon Riots (a massive popular persecution of Catholics in London), Wilkes was one of the few in the city to attempt to control the riotous crowds. The masses felt that, in becoming an instrument of order, he had betrayed them again and more basically; they explained the betrayal in terms of a change in his personality, rather than in terms of his institutional constraints and obligations as representative of the Lord Mayor, or, indeed, his own belief in liberty as an act of toleration.[90]

During the period of absolute popularity in the early 1770's, what was the effect of Wilkes, perceived as a public person, on the language of political rhetoric? Foremost in the vast newspaper war which Wilkes's activities aroused was the anonymous writer who called himself "Junius." His credo was simple:

> Measures and not men, is the common cant of affected moderation; a base, counterfeit language, fabricated by knaves, and made current among fools . . . gentle censure is not fitted to the present degenerate state of society.

In defending Wilkes, Junius was most effective, and most noticed, when he would attack the personal characteristics of Wilkes's enemies, notably the Duke of Grafton. But these personal attacks were different in tone from the writing of a decade before, different even from the personal attacks in the *North Briton*. While earlier forms of political rhetoric dealt with private character in terms of public issues and public needs, Junius eschewed all talk of "measures." Character in and of itself became the political issue. Just as Wilkes as a person "embodied" liberty, his enemies embodied tyranny. An assassination of their character sufficed to delegitimate the measures with which their names were associated. The very basis of a public gesture was therefore erased: public speeches of both friend and enemy did not signify of themselves; they were only guides to the character of the speaker. To be sure, Junius' figures of speech were still in the old pattern—that is, he used perfectly familiar language, and language of the elaborate, almost stilted sort considered appropriate for public discourse. But this language was now put to an exclusive use: the vocabulary of invective directed only to character assassination; that assassination of itself a political act, a defense of liberty.[91]

It is interesting to contrast Junius to Samuel Johnson, an enemy of Wilkes who entered the war of rhetoric at the end of the 1760's. In his most famous pamphlet on Wilkes, *The False Alarm*, Johnson made every effort to speak of Wilkes the man in relation to "measures," indeed in relation to abstract principles of constitutional right and privilege. Compare Junius with a passage from *The False Alarm* like the following:

> One of the chief advantages derived by the present generation from the improvement and diffusion of philosophy, is deliverance from unnecessary terrors, and exemption from false alarms. The unusual appearances, whether regular or accidental, which once spread consternation over ages of ignorance, are not the recreations of inquisitive security.[92]

As one commentator on this war of rhetoric, James Boulton, has remarked, the differences in style were in part a difference in class: Johnson speaking purposively to an upper-class milieu. But the differences were more than a matter of class; they concern the very nexus between personality and ideology at that moment. Johnson, and with him Edmund Burke, defenders of the established regime, enemies of Wilkes, gesture in their political writings in exactly the same way that others gestured with their clothes or in the theater. The language of politics was at a remove from intimate life; even in Johnson's most vituperative moments, even in his most personal and nasty attacks on Wilkes, the issue is always Wilkes's fitness to participate in government, never Wilkes's character in and of itself. Johnson, like Burke and the others of the established order, had indeed a clear set of ideas, a clear language of government, a realm of objective discourse into which they could fit Wilkes. It was the realm of the established, the past, the known. Wilkes and his followers were rebelling against that established clarity. They were innovators in search of liberty, but the meaning of this new idea had not, could not have, as clear and objectified a character as that with which time and familiar usage had endowed the idea of privilege. The Wilkesites were constrained to see the meaning of the principle as embedded in the very acts of a man.

This was how the molecule split. Liberty was not part of the framework of natural sympathy; it was opposed to the idea of convention as public order. What was it? Few people of Wilkes's time could give an answer to that question; all they could attempt was to make the idiosyncratic personal life of the champion of liberty "symbolic" of liberty itself. If the cry for liberty was the means by which the structure of the molecule split, the real challenge to public life was not liberty but individual personality as a "symbolic" force. From this idea of individual personality as a social principle came ultimately the modern impulse to find political measures worthwhile only to the extent that their champions are "credible," "believable," "decent" persons.

In his politics Wilkes showed how the end would come; but his life also shows the strength of public culture during the century. In his sense of himself and above all in his failure to hold his supporters for long, he demonstrated the power of this midcentury molecule of private and public to withstand the demands for liberty on personal terms.

CHAPTER 6

MAN AS ACTOR

There is a final question to ask about the public realm of the 18th Century. What kind of man inhabited it? The people of the time gave a clear answer to this question: he was an actor, a performer. But what is a public actor? How, say, is he different from a father? It is a question of identity, and identity is a useful but abused word. In the sense Erik Erikson gave it, an identity is the meeting point between who a person wants to be and what the world allows him to be. Neither circumstance nor desire alone, it is one's place in a landscape formed by the intersections of circumstance and desire. The image, two centuries ago, of public man as an actor was a very definite identity; precisely because it was so forthrightly declared, it serves in retrospect a valuable purpose. It is a point of reference; against it, as the material and ideological conditions of public life grow confused, fragmented, and finally blank after the fall of the *ancien régime,* man's sense of himself in public can be charted.

Public man as an actor: the image, however evocative, is incomplete, because standing behind it, giving it substance, is a more basic idea. This is the concept of expression as the presentation of emotion, and from this comes the actor's identity: the public actor is the man who presents emotions.

Expression as the presentation of emotion is really a general principle which includes such practices as the speech signs discussed two chapters ago. Suppose one person tells another about his father's dying days in the hospital. Today the sheer recounting of all the details would be enough to arouse the other person's pity. Strong impressions minutely described are for us identical with expression. But imagine a situation or society in which the sheer reporting of these details of suffering would not signify to another person. The man recounting these moments could not merely relive them, but had to mold them, selecting some details to emphasize, suppressing others, even falsifying his report, in order to fit it into a form or fit a pattern which his listener understood to be what dying was about. Under these conditions the speaker wants to present to his hearer the death so organized in its details that it fits the picture as an event which arouses pity. Similarly, "pity" is not different depending on what death one hears about; pity exists as an independent emotion, rather than varying with and, therefore, depending upon each experience of it.

This theory of expression is incompatible with the idea of *individual* personality as expressive. If the sheer recital of what I've seen, felt, experienced, without any filtering or shaping or falsifying of my experience to fit it to a standard, if this were expressive, then "pity" in my life can hardly be expressive in the same way to you as your own sense of pity, derived from different experience. In the representation of emotion, when I tell you about my particular feelings as they appear to me, there is no expressive work to be done, "just living." No shaping of gesture or tidying of the scene makes it more expressive; just the reverse, because, once shaped to fit into a general pattern the experience would seem less "authentic." Equally, the principle of representation of emotion is asocial, for in not having the same report of pity to make, people do not have a common sense of pity to share as a social bond.

By contrast, under a system of expression as the presentation of emotion, the man in public has an identity as an actor—an enactor, if you like—and this identity involves him and others in a social bond. Expression as a presentation of emotion is the actor's job—if for the moment we take that word in a very broad sense; his identity is based on making expression as presentation work. When a culture shifts from believing in presentation of emotion to representation of it, so that individual experiences reported accurately come to seem expressive, then the public man loses a function, and so an identity. As he loses a meaningful identity, expression itself becomes less and less social.

I apologize for compressing this theory so, but it will be helpful at the outset to know how much underlies the idea of public man as actor. Indeed, a sense of these logical connections is necessary to understand the very peculiar terms in which man as actor was spoken of by people who inhabited the public world of the *ancien régime* capitals. There were three major voices.

The first was the most common voice to be heard among the cosmopolites of the time: if we inhabit a *theatrum mundi*, and have become like actors, then a new, happier morality is upon us. The second was the more probing one of writers like Diderot, who explored acting in relation to public life and in relation to nature. The third was the singular voice of Rousseau. Rousseau's was the greatest theory of the time about the bridge between cosmopolitan life and theater, and a strong condemnation of it. Analyst and critic, he was also prophet, predicting that the public order would succumb to a life based on authentic intimate feeling and political repression combined. Of this new condition—so much like our present-day condition—he approved. Yet he was also a bad prophet, for he believed that the new order would come through the fall of the city and the resurgence of the small town. His ideas are a touchstone to exploring how this public world has come to be lost in modern urban culture, a culture replacing the expressive life and identity of the public man with a new life, more personal, more authentic, and, all things considered, emptier.

THE COMMON-SENSE VIEW OF MAN AS ACTOR

By the opening of Book Seven of *Tom Jones,* the young man's adventures have become centered in London. It is at this point that Fielding presents a little essay called "A Comparison Between the World and the Stage." He begins as follows:

> The world hath been often compared to the theatre . . . this thought hath been carried so far, and become so general, that some words proper to the theatre, and which were, at first, metaphorically applied to the world, are now indiscriminately and literally spoken of both: thus stage and scene are by common use grown as familiar to us, when we speak of life in general, as when we confine ourselves to dramatic performances. . . .

Fielding is apologetic in tone a little later on; of course his readers know that the stage and the street are realms that "literally" translate into each other; he is talking in clichés and he excuses himself. He just wants to remind his dear readers that the mixture of dramatics and ordinary life is real, is no fancy "metaphor" as it was in the Restoration.[93]

"The world as a stage" was indeed an old cliché dressed up in new ways by the mid-18th Century. We have observed that one of the classic functions of the *theatrum mundi* imagery was to detach human nature from social action, by separating actor from act. In the common-sense view of man as actor, personally you were no longer indictable as a bad man for committing a bad act; you just needed to change your behavior. Man as actor bears a lighter moral yoke than either Puritan or devout Catholic: he is not born into sin, he enters into it if he happens to play an evil part.

Fielding himself put it well. In his essay he argued that "a single bad act no more constitutes a villain in life than a single bad part on the stage," and that indeed, as the realms of city and theater have become intermixed, the analogy becomes a literal truth. The character of acts and the character of actors are separate, so that a man of the world "can censure an imperfection, or even a vice, without rage against the guilty party." Further, there is no clear way to tell who men are in the great city, so the emphasis must be entirely upon what they do. Does a man harm others? Then, in the fashion of Garrick, the problem before him is to change his roles. And why should he not reform, since no appearance, no role, is fixed in the great city by necessity or by knowledge others have of one's past?[94]

If, in general, man as actor relieved himself of the burdens of innate sin by divorcing his nature from his acts, 18th Century common sense concluded that he thus could enjoy himself more. Tied in public neither to the realm of nature nor to the Christian duties of the soul, his playfulness and pleasure in the company of others could be released. This is why writings of the time so often allied images of man as actor to cosmopolitan life; their version of *theatrum mundi* did not refer to the relations between man and the gods or to dark pessimism about the meaning of human life, as did the Renaissance Platonists on the one hand and the Elizabethan dramatists on the other. There is a marvelous *Persian Letter* of Montesquieu's, in which his hero, wandering into the Comédie Française one night, cannot distinguish who's on stage and who's supposed to be watching; everyone is parading, posing, having a good time. Amusement, cynical toleration, pleasure in the company of one's fellows, these were the tones of feeling contained in the everyday notion of man as an actor.

But there were those who understood that the prevalent clichés of man as actor depended, in their very sense of sociability, on a deeper and unspoken idea of expression. Greatest of these was Diderot, whose *Paradox of Acting* connected acting to a more general psychological theory.

DIDEROT'S PARADOX OF ACTING

Diderot summed up what he called the paradox of acting quite simply:

> Do not people talk in society of a man being a great actor?
> They do not mean by that that he feels, but that he excels in
> simulating, though he feels nothing . . .

Diderot was the first great theorist of acting as a secular activity. Most 16th and 17th Century French theories of acting correlated how an actor performed with the contents of what he or she performed. The truth of the lines spoken had some relationship to how well the actor could speak. Thus it was possible to subsume the idea of acting under the rubric of rhetoric, and to talk of rhetoric in relation to morals and religion. In this formula the priest became the greatest possible rhetorician because the lines he spoke were absolute truth. No good Christian would dream, of course, of directly comparing priest and actor, but the reason lay precisely in the fact that the priest's rhetoric was innately superior to anything possible on the stage, because he was speaking divine truth.[95]

Diderot broke this connection between acting, rhetoric, and the substance of the text. In his *Paradox* he created a theory of drama divorced from ritual; he was the first to conceive of performing as an art form in and of itself, without reference to what was to be performed. The "signs" of the performance were not for Diderot the "signs" of the text. I put this less clearly than Diderot. He writes:

> If the actor were full, really full, of feeling, how could he play
> the same part twice running with the same spirit and success?
> Full of fire at the first performance, he would be worn out and
> cold as marble at the third.[96]

An actor who believes in his own tears, who governs his performance according to his sentiments, who has no distance from the emotions he projects, cannot act consistently. An actor must not respond to the substance of the text to act it, nor is his art governed by the substance of the text. We know, for instance, that a great actor in a bad play can still give a great performance. The reason lies in the very nature of performed expression: without some work on the emotions to be conveyed, without the exercise of judgment or calculation in showing them, an expression cannot be performed more than once.[97]

The theory Diderot propounds concerns more than the tricks of stagecraft; it addresses itself to the superiority of artifice over nature in expressing an emotion. Diderot puts a question:

> Have you ever thought on the difference between the tears
> raised by a tragedy of real life and those raised by a touching
> narrative?

He answers by saying that tears of real life are immediate and direct, while the tears brought on by art must be produced consciously, by degrees. But while the natural world may therefore seem superior to the world of the actor, it is in fact much more vulnerable and liable to accident. Think of a woman weeping, Diderot says, who has some minor disfigurement which takes your attention away from her woe, or whose accent you find difficult to understand, and so you are diverted, or who shows you her grief at a moment when you are unprepared to receive it. In all these ways the world where people react directly and spontaneously to each other is a world where expression is often perverted; the more natural the expression between two people, the less reliably expressive they will be.[98]

At best, in the world where sympathy and natural feeling govern, if there is an exact representation of an emotion it can happen only once.[99]

Diderot then asks how an expression can be presented more than once, and in answering it he defines the idea of a conventional sign. A feeling can be conveyed more than once when a person, having ceased to "suffer it," and now at a distance studying it, comes to define its essential form. This essence is a subtraction of the accidental: if by chance a rigid posture appears to detract from the scene of a woman expressing sorrow over an absent husband, then the rigid posture is replaced by a stoop. If declaiming loudly occasionally draws attention to the volume of the voice rather than the words spoken, the voice is taught to stay lower. By such studies, the essential character of an emotion is established. In the process of arriving at these signs, an actor has ceased to feel the emotion as the audience to whom he conveys these emotions will feel them. He does not stop feeling: Diderot is often falsely interpreted that way; rather the actor's feelings about the gesture have become different from the feelings the gesture will arouse in the audience.[100]

Gestures of this sort are the only way expressions can be stable, the only way they endure. The purpose of a gesture is to defeat the deformation of time:

> You are talking to me of a passing moment in Nature. I am talking to you of a work of Art, planned and composed—a work which is built up by degrees, and which lasts.

Repeatability is the very essence of a sign.[101]

Diderot's model of a great actor was the Englishman David Garrick. He met Garrick in the winter of 1764–65; in a passage from the *Paradox,* Diderot describes the impression Garrick made on him:

> Garrick will put his head between two folding doors, and in the course of five or six seconds his expression will change successively from wild delight to temperate pleasure, from this to tranquility, from tranquility to surprise, from surprise to blank astonishment, from that to sorrow, from sorrow to the air of one overwhelmed, from that to fright, from fright to horror, from horror to despair, and thence he will go up again to the point from which he started. *Can his soul have experienced all these feelings, and played this kind of scale in concert with his face?*[102]

A cliché of Diderot criticism has it that Diderot set Art against Nature, that the power of an actor like David Garrick was seen to be great to the degree that it was unnatural, almost monstrous. This simple opposition won't do. Diderot believed that all the study of the actor was directed at finding the essential forms which govern the natural world; the actor distills these forms out. By withdrawing his own feelings from the material, he has acquired the power to be conscious of what form is inherent in the realm of natural feeling. Because the performer builds on nature, he can communicate with people who remain in that chaotic state. By finding forms of expression which are repeatable, he brings a momentary sense of order into their own perceptions. The communication is not a sharing of this sign. One person must become master of—and distant from—the feeling to which another will submit. Embedded in the notion of a sustained, repeatable expression, therefore, is the idea of inequality.

This potentially friendly relationship between art and nature in Diderot's theory is important in analyzing performing offstage. Diderot meant to encompass more than the activities of a very few geniuses like Garrick. He meant to use them as models for other expressive social transactions. Social acts which are innately expressive are those which can be repeated. Repeatable social acts are those in which the actor has put a distance between his own personality and the speech or bodily dress he shows to others. Appearances at a distance from self are subject to calculation, and the person making the appearance can change his speech or bodily dress depending on the circumstances in which he is placed. Diderot's is the rationale of such signs as the elaborate, impersonal compliment, repeatable almost indiscriminately to others, an explanation of why such a sign should have continued to give pleasure. The compliment has a life of its own, a form independent of the particular speaker and his particular hearer. It signifies of itself. So does the *pouf au sentiment;* so does the face patch. The impersonality of successful speech between the classes has the same rationale: to the degree that it is purposely elaborate, a world unto itself, a form signifying apart from the circumstances of speaker and audience, it is expressive. In sum, from successful acting Diderot moves to a theory of emotion as presentation. The feelings an actor arouses have form and therefore meaning in themselves, just as a mathematical formula has meaning of its own no matter who writes it. For this expression to occur, men must behave unnaturally, and search for what convention, what formula can be repeated, time after time.

Diderot's ideas in retrospect appear as an intellectual underpinning for the public life of his era. But in no direct sense can Diderot be read as a spokesman for his fellow Parisians; his text, finally finished in 1778, did not appear in print until 1830. In the 1750's there were writers on the theater who explicitly rejected views like Diderot's and instead followed an emphasis on natural sympathies. Indeed, the *Paradox* was itself a response to a well-known treatise of 1747, *Le Comédien*, by Remond de Sainte-Albine, quickly translated into English by John Hill, then translated back into French by Sticotti in 1769—the version Diderot read. *Le Comédien* argued sentiment, and thus the soul of the actor, to be the source of the actor's power; if he were a cold soul, he would be an indifferent actor. But the views Diderot espoused were popular in the 1750's, if less cogently argued. Diderot was anticipated by Riccoboni's *L'Art du Théâtre;* by Grimm's writing on the theater; later, in the *Encyclopédie,* they were codified in an article on Declamation by Marmontel.[103]

It was in the 1750's that the argument theater historians call the war between Sentiment and Calculation first took form. A charming and most unbelievable instance of it is recorded a few years later, in which the two great actresses of Diderot's time, Madame Clairon and Madame Dumesnil, meet at the Théâtre Boule-Rouge. Madame Clairon was in Diderot's eyes the female Garrick; Madame Dumesnil was to him an actress of middling talent because she depended on her own feelings. The two actresses began debating the question of sensibility versus calculation in creating a role. Madame Dumesnil declared, "I was full of my part, I felt it, I yielded myself up to it." To which Madame Clairon replied abruptly, "I have never understood how one could do without calculation." The actor Dugazon jumped in: "[It is not] our object to know whether dramatic art exists . . . but whether in this art fiction or reality is to dominate." Madame Clairon: "Fiction"; Madame Dumesnil: "Reality."[104]

For all the pleasing triviality in which this argument could end up, the most important aspect of it was an assumption both sides shared. From the writing of Remond de Sainte-Albine and Riccoboni in the 1750's to Diderot, and then on into the 19th Century in the reflections of such actors as Coquelin, Diderot's basic premise was accepted by all. This was the independence of the activity of performing—its independence from the text. The war between sentiment and calculation concerns what the actor feels, not the correctness of those feelings in terms of the correctness of the words he or she had to speak. How can you be moved by my eloquence, Bishop Bossuet asked his congregation in a famous sermon of the 17th Century, and not thereby be moved to confess your sins to God? Eighty years later, it was possible to discuss Bossuet's qualities as a great speaker, perhaps hotly arguing how much he was in control, how much he was subject to the fire he heaped upon his parishioners, without troubling oneself too much with the proposition that, if he was a great speaker, one ought to be more devout. Both sides in Diderot's time secularized the phenomenon of performing, cut it loose from external indexes of truth. Diderot's arguments extended the secular idea to its logical conclusion as a theory of expression: if performing was an activity which has meaning independent of the particular text, then it also must have a meaning independent of the particular performer, his private sentiments, his passing moods.

The completion of this idea of secular performing lay in Rousseau's linking of it to the city.

ROUSSEAU'S INDICTMENT OF THE CITY AS THEATER

Oddly, the greatest writer on, the most constant student of, urban public life was a man who hated it. Jean-Jacques Rousseau believed cosmopolitanism was no high stage of civility, but a monstrous growth. More than any other of his contemporaries, Rousseau investigated the great city thoroughly, as though dissecting a cancer. Paris was his main concern, but the theatrical qualities of life in Paris he believed to be spreading to all the capitals of Europe. Rousseau must be read as more than a reporter of his times, more than a moral commentator. In castigating the mixture of stage and street life, he arrived at the first complete and probing theory of the modern city as an expressive milieu.

Rousseau was the first writer to depict the city as a secular society. He was the first to show that this secularism arose out of a particular kind of city—the cosmopolitan capital; that is, he was the first to envision discontinuities in "urban" experience, and thus to arrive at a theory of cosmopolitanism. He was the first to link the public codes of belief in the cosmopolis to basic psychological experiences like trust and play; the first to relate the psychology of cities to a psychology of creativity. And all this, so insightful, so probing, was directed toward a terrible end; from his anatomy of the great city, Rousseau concluded that mankind could achieve psychologically authentic relationships— the opposite of cosmopolitanism—only by imposing on itself political tyranny. And of this tyranny he approved.

The circumstances under which Rousseau came to write down his theory give some clues to what he wrote. Sometime between 1755 and 1757 the French philosopher d'Alembert wrote an article for the *Encyclopédie* on the city of Geneva. D'Alembert noted that there were no theaters in the city. Given the Calvinist traditions of Geneva, this did not much surprise d'Alembert; he knew the Genevans feared "the taste for adornment, dissipation, and libertinism which the actors' troops disseminate among the young." But as an outsider he saw no reason why this strict and ascetic city could not tolerate a theater; in fact, he thought a theater could do the citizens some good. "A finesse of tact, a delicacy of sentiment," he wrote, "is very difficult to acquire without the help of theatrical performances."[105]

D'Alembert's sentiments were much like Fielding's: the theater has lessons of behavior for ordinary life. These sentiments roused Rousseau, a citizen of Geneva, who had passed some years in Paris; in 1758 he published the *Letter to M. d'Alembert.* This letter is a reply to much more than d'Alembert intended to say. To justify political censorship of the drama, Rousseau had to show that d'Alembert's values were those of a cosmopolitan; he then had to show that the spread of cosmopolitan values to a small town would destroy its religion and that as a result people, in learning how to behave with the "delicacy of sentiment" of actors, would cease having a deep and honest inner life.[106]

All of Rousseau's opposites—cosmopolitan, small town; acting, authenticity; liberty, just tyranny—come from a theory of corruption, the corruption of *moeurs. Moeurs* can be rendered in modern English as a cross of manners, morals, and beliefs. Eighteenth Century writers use the word in a sense that terms like "value orientation," "role definition," and the rest of the sociological lexicon cannot encompass; *moeurs* concern the complete manner, the style a person possesses.[107]

Moeurs are corrupted, Rousseau maintains, when people form a style that transcends work, family, and civic duty. To step outside the context of functional survival, to think of pleasures that do not contribute to begetting and maintaining life—this is corruption. One way to read Rousseau is that he identified corruption with what we think of as abundance.[108]

How easy is it to corrupt a man or woman? At the opening of the *Letter,* Rousseau claims it is hard: "A father, a son, a husband, and a citizen have such cherished duties to fulfill that they are left nothing to give to boredom." But then Rousseau amends himself immediately, for clearly the enemy—frivolous pleasure, foreign amusement, idle gossip in cafés—is everywhere. The habit of work can be undone by "discontent with oneself, the burden of idleness, the neglect of simple and natural tastes." In other words, man is in rather constant danger of corruption.[109]

The historian Johan Huizinga defines play as a release from the economic, by which he means activity which transcends the world of daily necessity, of survival duties and tasks. Play in this sense is Rousseau's enemy. Play corrupts.[110]

Play takes place in at least a temporary condition of leisure. The Protestant relationship between leisure and vice is that when men have no necessary duties pressing on them, they give way to their natural passions, which are evil. The sloth, the glutton, the seducer, and the libertine are natural man, revealed by his or her play. Such was Calvin's idea, and Geneva was organized by him to give man no rest, and therefore no chance for sin.

Calvin's idea of the small city as a perfect theocracy was straightforward. Here was an economically viable environment, a physical place offering protection in time of war, still small enough to permit constant surveillance of the populace. From a religious point of view, the advantage of the small city is that it is the most secure political tool to repress man's natural baseness. Rousseau struggled to view mankind as naturally good and yet view the political control as legitimate; therefore his view of the relationship of *moeurs* to the small city is more complicated than Calvin's.

What would happen, he asked, if people were freed of the rigidities of small-city life? What would happen if men and women possessed genuine leisure? Freedom from the duties of survival would mean that men and women had more chance for social interactions—for visits in cafés, walks on promenades, and the like. Sociability is the fruit of leisure. The more people interact, however, the more they become dependent on one another. Thus the forms of sociability we have called public Rousseau thought of as social relations of mutual dependence. In the *Letter,* the mutual dependence of people, cut loose from bonds of necessity, is portrayed as terrifying.

People come to depend on others for a sense of self. One manipulates one's appearance in the eyes of others so as to win their approval, and thus feel good about oneself. Lionel Trilling has summarized Rousseau's argument in the *Letter* in this way:

> . . . the spectator contracts by infection the characteristic disease of the actor, the attenuation of selfhood that results from impersonation . . . by engaging in impersonation at all the actor diminishes his own existence as a person.[111]

In a state of leisure, men and women develop the *moeurs* of actors. The seriousness of losing independence is masked because people are at play: they experience pleasure in losing themselves. In Rousseau's words,

> . . . the principal object is to please; and, provided that the people enjoy themselves, this object is sufficiently attained.[112]

It is no accident that Rousseau entered the lists when a theater was proposed for his city. The theater, rather than licentious books or pictures, is a dangerous art form because it promotes the vices of men and women who do not have to struggle to survive. It is the agent of loss of self.

Now enters the capital, cosmopolitan city: its public culture is the realm where this loss of self occurs.

All cities are places with large numbers of people living closely packed together, a central market or markets, and the division of labor carried to a high degree. These conditions ought to influence the *moeurs* of people in all cities. For the small city, Rousseau believes, the influence is direct.[113] The small city is a place which brings to fruition all the virtues of good, decent people struggling to survive. By contrast, in London or Paris, economics, family background, and other material conditions have an indirect influence on styles of life; they directly influence the *volonté*, the will, of city men. *Moeurs* then result from what this will desires.[114]

Why make this distinction? For two reasons. First, by inserting this middle term, Rousseau gets to talk about the large city in special moral terms. He gets beyond modern liberal formulas of bad urban behavior as the result of bad social conditions—with the noble soul of the offender waiting in the wings for liberation. Large cities matter to Rousseau because they corrupt the very center of a human being, corrupt his or her will.

Second, the very complexity of social and economic relations in the great city means you cannot tell what kind of man you are dealing with in any given situation by knowing what work he does, how many children he supports—in short, by how he survives. The very complexity of social relations in the city makes reading character from material conditions difficult. Equally, the economic nature of a cosmopolitan center is to accumulate what would now be called "surplus capital." It is the place where rich men enjoy their fortunes through leisure activities and poor men imitate them; the very concentration of capital means a few people have genuine leisure and many people out of envy become "idle"—that is, sacrifice their material interests for the sake of having a leisure "style."

The great city Rousseau thus perceived as an environment wherein you cannot tell what kind of man a stranger is in a given situation by finding out how he survives. The situations, indeed, in which you are likely to meet him are those in which you are not meeting for some functional purpose, but meeting in the context of nonfunctional socializing, of social interaction for its own sake. And on this insight he imposes his analysis of the nature of leisured play. For in a state of leisure, people interact more and more for the sheer pleasure of contact; the more they interact outside the strictures of necessity, the more they become actors. But actors of a very special sort:

> In a big city, full of scheming, idle people without religion or principle, whose imagination, depraved by sloth, inactivity, the love of pleasure, and great needs, engenders only monsters and inspires only crimes; in a big city, where *moeurs* and honor are nothing because each easily hiding his conduct from the public eye, shows himself only by his reputation . . .[115]

Reputation—being known, being recognized, being singled out. In a big city this pursuit of fame becomes an end in itself; the means are all the impostures, conventions, and manners which people are so free to toy at in the cosmopolis. And yet these means lead inexorably to the end, for when one has no fixed "place" in a society, dictated by the state which in turn is but the instrument of a Higher Power, then one makes up a place for oneself by manipulating one's appearance. Because playacting is corrupt, all one wants to get from playing with one's appearance is applause. For Rousseau, the cosmopolis, in turn, destroys the believability of religion, because one can make up one's own place, one's own identity, rather than submit to the identity the Higher Power has assigned one. The pursuit of reputation replaces the pursuit of virtue.

There are many Rousseaus, because many of the works Rousseau wrote contradict each other or possess divergent points of view. The Rousseau of *Émile* is not exactly the Rousseau of the *Letter* as concerns these ideas of play, reputation, and religion. The Rousseau of the *Confessions* is a man who has partially broken free of the strictures of the *Letter*. The *Letter* is an extreme position, argued to its logical conclusion.[116]

Nonetheless, throughout Rousseau's work this accusation of cosmopolitan public life recurs. From *Julie:*

> Just as clocks are ordinarily wound up to go only twenty-four hours at a time, so these people have to go into society every night to learn what they're going to think the next day.[117]

And here is another extraordinary passage from the same novel in which, Ernst Cassirer comments, "nothing is 'invented'; every word is drawn from Rousseau's own experience" of Paris:

> People meet me full of friendship; they show me a thousand civilities; they render me services of all sorts. But that is precisely what I am complaining of. How can you become immediately the friend of a man whom you have never seen before? The true human interest, the plain and noble effusion of an honest soul—these speak a language far different from the insincere demonstrations of politeness (and the false appearances) which the customs of the great world demand.[118]

The great city is a theater. Its scenario is principally the search for reputations. All city men become artists of a particular kind: actors. In acting out a public life, they lose contact with natural virtue. The artist and the great city are in harmony, and the result is a moral disaster.[119]

But some questions should be asked at this point. Paris is a theater,

a society of men and women posing to one another. But poses sometimes heal deformities of nature or the wounds of circumstance. Rousseau tells us the pursuit of reputation is rife in cities. So what, if men
are spurred to produce great things in hopes of being praised? In *Émile*
there is a scornful passage in which Rousseau speaks of role playing in
the great city as a means for people to forget their often humble origins,
but, on the scale of sins, this would hardly seem to rank with rape or
murder.

Rousseau's critique of the city seems headed, from a brilliant beginning, to a vulgar end—the celebration of the simple, truthful yokel.
Rousseau saves his argument from banality by suddenly and dramati-
cally within the text changing its terms.

Rousseau began with the paradigm of virtue/work, vice/leisure.
Obviously the big city bustles; it has an electric energy which the sleepy
everyday round of home, work, church, home can scarcely have had in
Geneva. In the middle of the *Letter,* a new scale of action is introduced:
frenetic coming and going, actions without meaning characterize the
great city, because without the pressures of survival, man spins crazily.
In the small city, action proceeds at a slower pace; this permits leisure
to reflect on the true nature of one's actions and self.[120]

Rousseau makes this sudden shift because now he can show the
effect of a city on the general pattern of human expression. Truly
creative expression is done by the man in search of a true self; he
expresses this discovery in words, music, and pictures. The works of art
are like reports of a psychological inquest. Art of the great city, which
starts with an interdependent set of social relations, produces fictions
and stylizations of self. These conventions exist on their own; they have
no relation to personal character. Rousseau detests the presentation of
emotions on these terms; he wants a more inward-turning probe of
character. Here is part of Rousseau's contrast between presentation and
representation:

> ... true genius ... knows not the path of honors and fortune
> nor dreams of seeking it; it compares itself to no one; all its
> resources are within itself.[121]

Rousseau has performed a sleight of hand: expression will be determined by how honest—*honnête*—a man is, and honesty is defined by
how unique he or she is. Honesty for the Calvinist is making an inven-
tory of how-I-have-sinned-today; for Rousseau it is losing a consciousness of how one appears to the world at large.[122]

Thus arises a marvelous paradox. What's wrong with the actor is
that he or she, sensitive to insult and to praise, moves in a world in
which there exist definitions of good and bad, virtue and vice. Similarly,

the trouble with the great city is that there is *too much* community. The values of the community, whatever they are, count for too much, because people try to win reputation from others by acting out these values. The small town has better values, survival virtues, but by the end of the *Letter* Rousseau has developed a second virtue of the small town. It permits more isolation, it permits people to ignore the community's standards and search out their own hearts to "see whatever there is, just to see." Here is Rousseau's summation of the small town:

> . . . more original spirits, more inventive industry, more really
> new things are found there because the people are less imita-
> tive; having few models each draws more from himself and
> puts more of his own in everything he does.[123]

Censorship of an art, the theater, is therefore justified, for the same reason that thought reform is justified. Indeed, if the theater flourishes, the legislation of morality cannot. In a city like Geneva, the theater could seduce people into having models for behavior. In Geneva, in the midst of political tyranny, men should become creatively unique. In a large city, censorship is useless; what plays are produced is less important than the fact that plays are produced at all. The actor on the stage becomes the model of what every Parisian aspires to achieve in private life.[124]

ROUSSEAU'S PROPHECIES

These are the outlines of a great, and frightening, argument about public life. Its very contradictions are a part of that greatness, contradictions which have dogged all those who followed in Rousseau's wake. Political tyranny and the search for individual authenticity go hand in hand. That is the essence of Rousseau's prophecy, and it has been fulfilled. By contrast, when men pose to win fame, accommodate others, or even to be kind, each appears to end up having no soul of his own. That also has become modern belief.

But Rousseau was also a very bad prophet of modern times. Perhaps the most revealing error is seen by comparing his theory with the behavior of Wilkes and the Wilkesites. The Wilkesites, the first mass movement of the 18th Century city, of all shades of rank from wealthy merchant to penniless hackboy, overturned the dramatics of the *ancien régime* metropolis in a manner Rousseau did not dream of. For him, destruction of convention would occur only as the environment in which men lived became more controlled. For them, the destruction would develop only as their freedom from control expanded. Rousseau could imagine the end of public life only in a small town—that is, he could imagine an alternative to the metropolis, but not its historical growth. Coherence, political control, a perfect fit of tyranny with the needs of the natural man: this was his vision. It was a retreat into a past, a mythical past at that, a withdrawal from the great city. But the forces within that city which were overturning the principles of appearance of the *ancien régime* were directed to contrary ends, to the achievement of a lack of constraint, a liberty within the great city. This boundary-less liberty men hoped to understand through the symbolization of personal experience.

PART THREE

THE TURMOIL
OF PUBLIC LIFE
IN THE 19TH CENTURY

To an old woman of Paris, born in the *ancien régime,* surviving into the 1880's, the contrasts between the city of her youth and the city of her old age might appear to her as the feverish growth of public life in the 19th Century. Spectacle was rampant on the city's streets: she might think of Nadar's ascents in a balloon which brought hundreds of thousands to the Champ de Mars; of the appearance of a giraffe in the Jardin des Plantes which drew such large crowds that several people were crushed to death; of a dog named Munito, who supposedly talked, attracting a vast throng at the Jardin Turc, waiting in vain day after day for Munito to hold forth. If a serious soul, she would have noted some of the same spectacle quality during the revolutionary days; she would have read novels of Balzac in which the urban crowd as a human circus formed the principal theme. The fevered search for excitement by the denizens of 19th Century Paris she could have set in memory against the elaborately careful interchanges between strangers she had witnessed as a child, in the days before the first revolution.[1]

To tell her that the city was ceasing to be a public culture would have drawn a snort of derision. Yet the very surfaces of life in the great city were more puzzling than her memories might first suggest. Those who lived in the city of spectacle knew that these moments of enthusiasm in public were ephemeral; Maxime du Camp put it neatly: ". . . it is as if people's heads are turned by a wind of madness. Parisian enthusiasms are sudden, and they are sometimes tremendous, but they don't last long." The terms of the spectacle were also becoming onesided. The masses watching Nadar's balloon witness an act outside everyday experience—that, precisely, makes it spectacular. In the face of this feat, how are they to judge him? How are they to participate? As the *flâneur* parades down the street, people watch him; they do not feel free any longer to go up and speak to him. The passive spectator, the onlooker silent and amazed: the city may be in fever, yet even in this surface excitement the signs of a change appear.[2]

This era, at once so prim in its habits and so unbuttoned in its momentary enthusiasms and dreams, is difficult today to imagine in all its complexity and all its grandeur. We see the primness as a slavery from which we have barely recovered a century later, the fantasy as false and perverse, a world of imagined passions and inflated perceptions which were only "compensation" for the rigors of propriety. It is difficult to perceive Balzac's entrepreneurs, the *flâneurs* who walk the streets of Paris in Baudelaire's poems, as both great and fatally diseased. It is difficult to understand how, despite our rebellion against them, their struggle with the eroding line between privacy and publicness was the seed of the present-day struggle with intimacy.

It is equally difficult to connect this fevered and fearful public world of a century ago to what came before. The city of passive spectacle was new; it was also a consequence of the public civility established in the *ancien régime.* That prior culture had to exist for the bourgeoisie to inflate it into spectacle, and so ultimately rob the public realm of its meaning as a form of sociability.

Four questions should be posed about 19th Century public life. The first is, what effect had material conditions—the population and economy of the 19th Century capital city—on the public realm? The second is, how did individual personality become a social category? Recall that even in the *ancien régime* the question of individual personality could profoundly if temporarily shake the public realm, as in the Wilkesite movement. In the 19th Century the individual and his peculiar strengths, desires, and tastes became permanently enshrined as a social idea, from rugged individualism, survival of the fittest, and similar fierce justifications of the new economics to more subtle and more troubling beliefs in which society was supposed to work through, exist for, or strengthen personality. How this belief in individual personality realized itself in behavior within the public realm, how personality in public was understood—this is the import of the second question.

The third question is, what happened to the identity of man in public, if people now took personality to be a social category? Specifically, what happened to the image of man as actor? Here we will be dealing not only with the fate of an 18th Century cliché, but with the most profound change of the 19th Century, that of silent observation as a principle of public order.

The fourth and final question is, in what way did personality in public plant the seed of the modern rule of intimacy? If the first three questions are about what the last century inherited and deformed, the fourth is about how it in turn prepared the ground for the modern erasure of the *res publica.*

Each of the four chapters which follow takes up one of these questions. Chapter 7, focusing on the relation of material conditions to public life, deals with the population, ecology, and economy of the 19th Century capitals, particularly a new form of public economy in the city.

Chapter 8, concerned with the advent of individual personality as a social category, begins by showing how one writer, Balzac, interpreted personality as a social category; the effect of personality on the public realm is then explored in terms of clothes on the street and on the stage in the 1840's; the chapter concludes by contrasting a revolt against *ancien régime* bodily imagery in 1795 with a revolt a century later against Victorian images of the body in public. Chapter 9, probing images of public identity, shows how this personalizing of the public realm created a new domain of speech and silence, and how within that domain only a special kind of person could continue to be an actor in public. Chapter 10, addressing the ways in which the personalizing of public space paved the way for the modern deadening of the *res publica,* is concerned with politics; its two themes are leadership defined as public personality, and community struggle as an attempt to form a collective personality. While the chapter on material conditions depicts general trends over the course of the century, the last three chapters follow the "posthole" method, treating these public phenomena in the 1840's and 1890's.

The beginning of this book sketched three forces of change at work in the 19th Century which altered public life: a double change wrought by industrial capitalism, a change in the terms of public belief wrought by a new secularity, a change in public behavior wrought by the very survival of one facet of *ancien régime* public ideology. These forces together form one explanation, hopefully a coherent one, of the effects of material change on public life, of personality in public, of why a new image of public man was born, and of how the 19th Century traumas of public life prepared for the 20th Century denial of the public itself. The reader might reasonably ask, why then proceed in the Talmudic fashion of asking questions; why not simply devote a chapter to each agent of change, and show its effects on manners and mores?

A language of causes works in one of two ways. It works mechanically; if X is done or exists, Y results. It also works historically, but then is more complicated. From a set of concrete phenomena which change over a period of time, the analyst tries to piece together and build up a theory of change. A good example of the difference comes in the presentation of a particular person's life history in a therapy. A "therapeutic honeymoon" comes very early on in the therapy; the patient gives a nice, clear picture of all the X's in his life which produced his neurotic symptoms, his Y's. Clear: but the very lack of ambiguity, the very static quality, makes the explanation meaningless, "I know what my problems are" being a way to remain stuck in them. As the therapy proceeds, the piecing together of changes in specific phenomena gradually leads to a theory of why they happened. The patient may in fact arrive at something like his original explanations during the therapeutic honeymoon, but now they have a different, experiential meaning.

Composing the history of a culture has an analogous problem to composing the picture of a life. The problem is mechanical clarity, not clarity per se. The essence of the three forces at work in the 19th Century was that, when each intruded into different areas of public life, it did so in somewhat different ways. The inheritance of the idea of meaningful public visual appearances was, for example, similar to but not exactly the same as the inheritance of belief in public speech as a special experience. Equally, changes in a particular phenomenon of public life never sprang from one single and pure source. The language of cause and effect is like the language of class, real but easily abused. Without it, society is a vast ocean of phenomena; everything exists but nothing has a reason for being. The problem therefore is to be neither mechanical nor mindless. I have tried to ask questions about historical change which, by posing the effects of change in concrete terms, will gradually bring forward the complexity of these three sources and thus build toward a theory of change.

What is true of the sources is true also of four barometers of distress which can be used in evaluating the changes. These four signals that the entrance of individual personality into public life caused difficulty are: the fear of involuntary disclosure of feeling, the superimposition of inappropriate private imagery on public situations, the desire to repress one's feelings in order to be shielded in public, the attempt to use the passivity inherent in silence as a principle of public order. Fear of involuntary disclosure of feeling would obviously mean something different to a woman being stared at silently by men on the street than it would to a politician about to lie to an audience. The complexities of distress, like those of source, are like themes in fugues.

A final prefatory note on the usage of the word "urban" and on the city of Paris itself.

In urban studies the words "urban" and "urbanize" are difficult to use and easy to confuse. Ordinary usage takes "urban" to refer to a place on the map and its life; "urbanize" to refer to the spread of this life to places other than the physical city. Charles Tilly has well shown the inadequacies of this ordinary usage as one moves into 19th Century society; what made "the city" was an administrative, financial, and legal system international in scope. Urbanization in the 19th Century was also more than the diffusion of urban habits; it stood for a more general diffusion of "modern," anti-traditional forces. And yet it was not all of a piece: the city was still a distinctive culture, especially the capital city. Its public life was diffusible, but here was a special point from which diffusion began.[3]

An urban situation has been taken as one in which strangers are likely to meet routinely. We have been concerned with the social psychology of encounters between strangers; in the 19th Century this social psychology came to apply to a brutal demographic issue. In the 19th Century in western Europe as well as southern and southeastern Europe, a sharp rural dislocation occurred. Partially a matter of famine, partially one of new forms of rural property ownership and the capitalization of farming, this upheaval sent masses of peasants and villagers out of their traditional homes, displacing them either to cities in Europe, to unknown provincial localities, or to the United States, Argentina, and Brazil. These displaced persons were thus also coming to experience encounters with strangers—routinely, as part of the more general trauma of their uprooting.

In this way, the demography of the 19th Century countryside meant that city life was going to have a meaning beyond the city's borders. It was not that whatever happened to public behavior in the capital city was instantly disseminated to the provinces; rather that, for people who were themselves becoming nomadic and landless, the life of the city, appearing as a condition of permanent uprooting, no longer seemed wholly alien, wholly foreign. The countryside too faced the problem of a life passed amidst strangers; in that sense it was connected to the problem of audience in the city, though filtering this problem through the memory of past tradition, or the forming of little nuclei of villagers or native speakers when the peasant himself was thrust into the city. This 19th Century connection between city and country paved the way for a much stronger erasure of geographical boundaries in the present century, so that the denial of public life today in the great city can become entwined, through a new technology of communication, with that same denial in the larger society.

Our present focus is upon the capital city itself in the 19th Century, and gradually upon Paris alone. In the first two of the four following chapters, the emphasis is on what Paris and London shared, materially and in terms of belief in individual personality in public. In the last two chapters, as we move closer to politics, Paris is more the sole subject. Walter Benjamin wrote of Paris as both "the capital of the 19th Century" and "intractably unique." It was the relation of politics to culture that made Paris Benjamin's capital of the 19th Century. Here ideological conflicts were brought to an extreme; revolutionary upheavals feared elsewhere played an actual part in the experience or the memory of each Parisian generation. Paris was the place in which all the fears and fantasies of the 19th Century bourgeoisie were concentrated. In focusing the tensions sweeping through all of western Europe, Paris made their structure and consequences manifest, and thus the city was, like modern New York, a place of both fascination and horror to others. It was as though in Paris Europeans saw a disease creeping into all their lives, and yet could not avert their gaze from the sick patient.

CHAPTER 7

THE IMPACT
OF INDUSTRIAL CAPITALISM
ON PUBLIC LIFE

"The urban revolution" and "the industrial city" are two quick, misleading ways to portray the changes of a century ago. The first misleads
by suggesting the growth of cities in the 19th Century to be so enormous
that they had little relation to the cities which existed before. The
second misleads by suggesting this growth typically occurred in places
where manufacturing in giant factories was the life the city's populace
knew. In fact, the greatest growth of population occurred in cities with
few large-scale industries; it occurred in the capitals. The sheer enlargement of population was, to be sure, unprecedented. Older patterns of
handling this population and sustaining it economically were magnified
until they became unrecognizable; in this way changes in number gradually produced changes in form. The new population was ordered at
first by established patterns of the city's ecology; these changed, but by
a gradual process. The people who poured in also had recognizable
roots in the past. They were still mostly young and single, slowly as a
group becoming older and composed of family units, as the century
progressed and the dislocations of agriculture grew more widespread
outside the city.

In part, the economics of the 19th Century capitals also magnified
what existed in the *ancien régime* city. Trade, finance, and bureaucracy
remained the main activities of the capitals. Factories are land-hungry
operations; in general, if they exist in cities at all, they are at the fringes
where land is cheaper. The sweatshop is a more common center-city
operation; it is both less mechanized and smaller. In the 19th Century
capitals, such indigenous industries as these were connected to trade,
to the rapid, small-scale, often highly specialized conversion of raw
goods from the colonies or other European nations into retail items.

The internal economy of these capitals did give birth to a new
economic pursuit. With population so greatly increased in the city,

retail trade became profitable as never before. The mass of buyers opened up a new form of public commerce centered in the department store, at the expense of the classic open-air markets and small shops. In this new form of retail commerce, all the complexities and problems of 19th Century public life emerged; this trade was a paradigm of the changes to come in the public realm. To understand this new public trade, let us first see the manner in which material life magnified what had come before.

WAS THE 19TH CENTURY URBAN DWELLER A NEW PERSONAGE?

The growth in population in the 19th Century capitals was so great that the numbers themselves make interesting reading. Here is how the demographer A. F. Weber portrayed the growth of Paris:

1801	547,756
1821	713,966
1841	935,261
1861	1,174,346
1881	2,269,023
1896	2,536,834

And here is one way of understanding what such figures meant: Take a population group in 1801 and make it a base of 100; then show subsequent growth of population during the century as a ratio to this base. The ratios for France's population as a whole, for the twelve largest cities other than Paris, and for Paris itself, during the 19th Century, were as follows:

Year	France	12 Cities	Paris
1801	100	100	100
1821	110	120	130
1841	120	154	171
1861	133	268	306
1881	140	354	414
1896	143	405	463*

*This ratio does not quite balance with a ratio computed from the raw population data on Paris above because of certain annexations of territory to Paris from 1852 to 1865 which were not treated uniformly by statisticians.

The picture of growth is clear: the twelve largest cities grew much more rapidly than France as a whole; Paris itself in turn grew more rapidly than these cities.[4]

The growth of London was as vigorous as that of Paris during the century, but to picture it is more difficult, because "London" had no neat demographic, administrative, or social borders. There was the administrative county of London; an outer ring beyond this which transformed London into "greater London"; and even beyond the ring more sprawl. This smeared mass of humanity stood, however, in exactly the same relationship to other cities in England, and to England's population as a whole, as did Paris to Lille or to France. Between 1871 and 1901, Asa Briggs writes, "the population of Greater London rose faster than that of any of the provincial conurbations and far faster than that of the national population as a whole."[5]

If we stay within the administrative county of London, London's growth in the 19th Century can be computed as follows:

1801	864,845
1821	1,225,694
1841	1,873,676
1861	2,803,989
1881	3,834,354
1891	4,232,118

It was, as in the 18th Century, a much larger city than Paris, though both were, in turn, much larger than other European capitals. The rates of growth in London and Paris, in relation to their national cultures, were similar. Here are the London, other-large-city (over 100,000), and national (England and Wales) ratios:

Year	Nation	Other Large Cities	London
1801	100	—	100
1821	134	100	141
1841	178	158	216
1861	226	153	324
1881	292	136	443
1891	326	166	489

The difference in French and British patterns lay in the growth of their provincial cities, those in France growing more, and more steadily, than those in England. The step-by-step ratios of growth in Paris and London during the century were remarkably parallel.[6]

To appreciate the human meaning of these numbers, one has to recall the fact that up to that time, the only city to begin to approach the size of either Paris or London was imperial Rome, sixteen hundred years before. Or again, that no other urban settlement known has ever before grown so fast in so short a time.

Why these capitals grew so big is a complicated matter. It is fairly certain that in both Paris and London the birth-to-death ratio during the century became more favorable to the living. Improvements in medicine and public health removed the constant threat of plague—the great scourge of urban populations—so that more of the children born into city families lived to start families of their own. If the city increased from within somewhat, the major source of its expansion continued to be in-migration. During the first half of the century, this flow was still of the young and unattached who came some distance from the city; the crisis of the countryside did not begin in earnest until the 1850's. When it did, the peasant family didn't crowd the voluntary migrant out of the picture; the new family migrants joined the ranks of the still continuing older flow of individuals.

A caution has to be made about these immense numbers. The outflow from the city was also enormous; many of those who were counted in one year in an urban census disappeared by the next, as they washed like a tide back into provincial towns and countryside—especially true of the uprooted peasants. A study by Peter Knights and Stephan Thernstrom suggests that the real picture of 19th Century urban growth should be of a sharp, steady growth in the number of permanent urban residents in the midst of or buried under a much larger, much more unsteady growth of people flowing into the great cities who would soon leave, their places taken and their numbers swelled by then another wave of unstable migrants.

THE LOCALIZING OF THE CITY

Simply not enough is known about the differences between stable and unstable migrants to the city to know if they had different experiences of residence—the basic condition of density. My own research on Chicago suggests that middle-class people long resident in that city were as likely to move around as workers of shorter residence in it; one study of 19th Century Paris shows the same result, another does not.[7]

As in the 18th Century, 19th Century Paris and London handled their general problems of increasing density in quite different ways; again, as in the *ancien régime,* these different patterns produced a similar social result.

To imagine the experience of population growth within Paris in the first half of the 19th Century, one would have to think of a box filled with pieces of glass; more and more glass is stuffed into the box, the pieces of glass themselves begin to break under the pressure, yet the sides of the box hold. By 1850, nothing more can be added; the box is not broken apart, but entirely remade along larger, though equally rigid, lines. The pressure process begins again. Paris was not a city of sprawl, as was London; it was a city in which urban form was always strained to the limit by population growth.

The box which contained Paris throughout its history was its wall. The wall served different purposes in the city at different points in time. In the 18th Century, the wall ceased to serve the city as a defense against invasion; indeed, by the 1770's the wall's purpose was to control the populace within. Through the sixty gates of the wall would pass the goods and manufactures of the city, all of which could be subject to a tax called the octroi. This was the "Wall of the *Fermiers Généraux*" (the wall of the tax collectors). It was the legal limit of the city until 1840. Baron Haussmann began to build a new legal, administrative, residential wall for the city in the late 1850's, a wall that was unlike the previous walls only in that it was no longer a physical structure.

In the first half of the 19th Century, the increasing population of Paris had to find space within the Wall of the *Fermiers Généraux*. The available housing was quickly filled up. Houses then began to be subdivided into multiple dwellings; when this new breakup of space became insufficient, upper stories were added to the old buildings. If the emptying of public squares in the previous century is recalled, one can imagine those vast open *places* remaining unfilled in the early 19th Century and now surrounded by districts where the population was choking on itself. Americans can form some picture of this extreme by imagining Central Park bordered by an urban area with a population density higher than that of the Lower East Side immigrant communities of the 1930's.[8]

Much debate exists among historians about the degree to which the social classes were intermixed and unsegregated in these teeming streets. The classic image of the early 19th Century Parisian house is of a wealthy family on the first floor, a respectable family on the next floor, and so on, until one reached the servants in the garret. The image of course is misleading, but dismissing it is also misleading. For in the remaking of the city by Haussmann in the 1850's and 1860's the intermixing of classes within districts was reduced by design. Whatever heterogeneity occurred spontaneously in the division of private houses into apartments in the first half of the century was now opposed by an effort to make neighborhoods homogeneous economic units; investors in new construction or in renovation found this homogeneity rational in that they knew exactly what kind of area they were putting their capital into. An ecology of *quartiers* as an ecology of classes: this was the new wall Haussmann erected between the citizens of the city as well as around the city itself.

The fundamental problem of density in Paris remained as before; fixed size allotted to numbers which rapidly congested the space. Behind the *grands boulevards,* away from the new *places,* residential and commercial choking remained. But the reorienting of the *quartiers* so that they acquired a more homogeneous class character changed the very terms of localism and cosmopolitanism.

David Pinckney has observed that "Parisians of a century ago ordinarily lived, worked, and found their pleasures within the confines of a few blocks." Haussmann's physical reordering of the city was but one expression and concretization of a larger process, a process of what the Chicago urbanist Louis Wirth called the "segmenting" of the city, what his colleague Robert Park called the forming of social "molecules" in the city during the course of the 19th Century. These segments complemented the growing division of labor in the industrial economy. The population of Paris, becoming more and more dense, became at once homogenized on a small turf and differentiated from turf to turf.[9]

In *ancien régime* Paris there were, of course, rich and poor districts —but the meaning of a "rich" district was that many rich people lived there. The term did not mean that prices for food or drink or housing would be consistently higher than in a district with less rich people. Today's urbanite is so accustomed to think that the economy of an area "fits" the level of affluence of its inhabitants that it is difficult to picture the pre-19th Century neighborhood as it actually was, with an intermixing of diverse classes in neighboring buildings if not in the same house, and an intermixing of different qualities of stalls, shops, and even little fairs to serve these various clienteles.

The molecular process occurring in the population distribution of Paris in the last century magnified a process we have already seen begun in the *ancien régime* city in the case of the public square. As the city continued to fill up with people, these people increasingly lost functional contact with each other outside. There were more strangers and they were more isolated. The problem of the square was magnified to the problem of *quartier* and neighborhood.

The isolation of social classes from each other in the city occurred also in London during the last century, but by the extension of the city rather than by the internal compression of classes which occurred in Paris. As new territory was added to the city, the builders constructed vast tracts of housing to meet the needs of economically homogeneous groups. As in Paris, the investment seemed surer and more secure if the property was uniformly inhabited by the members of one class; in the case of bourgeois housing, uniformity in building a new district meant that the neighborhood property values were likely not to go down; in the case of building workers' housing, a homogeneous grade of construction within the shades of choice available to a working-class population of buyers meant that costs could be kept down by bulk purchases of raw materials and fittings.

As London smeared itself across a larger and larger territory, the same localism arose by sheer physical separation and distance as was accomplished in Paris by differences between relatively close areas in the price of apartments, food, and amusement. Demographers have some evidence that the "center" of London (above St. James's Park and, oddly, Mayfair) remained an economically and socially integrated environment, but the center was losing its meaning; London was becoming the string of connected residential villages it is today. The sheer size of London meant that the minority of London workers who commuted some distance to a factory spent much of their free time in transit; this in turn reinforced the importance accorded the locality—as a place which was respite from the world of work.

We have noted that capital cities of the industrial era were not industrial. Industry itself meant something different in France than in England, though; but again this difference ended in a similar result for each capital. Clapham, the great historian of the French and German economies in the 19th Century, doubts that by 1848 France as a whole had much of a factory system, on the English scale, at all; more goods and services were being produced in that year than in 1815, but in enlarged workshops. In the second half of the 19th Century, as true factories did develop, they did so at a distance from Paris. The reason was simple: land in or even near Paris was too expensive to be used for the purpose. Land was not a scarce commodity in greater London, but, for reasons which are not clear, although factories did develop in the ring of "greater London" there developed no factory economy of the intensity of Manchester or Birmingham.[10]

The writers of the Chicago school of urban studies believed that a movement from neighborhood to neighborhood, from scene to scene, was the essence of "urban" experience. An urbanite to them was someone who knew not only one *quartier,* one locality, but many at the same time. That experience, however, did not belong to all urbanites of the last century equally; it had a class character. As the structure of *quartier* and neighborhood homogenized along economic lines, the people most likely to move from scene to scene were those with interests or connections complicated enough to take them to different parts of the city; such people were the more affluent. Routines of daily life passed outside the *quartier* were becoming bourgeois urban experience; the sense of being cosmopolitan and membership in the bourgeois classes thus came to have an affinity. Conversely, localism and lower class fused. The only routine trips working-class Parisians were likely to make to non-working-class sectors of the city, or indeed to other working-class neighborhoods, were for the purposes of shopping, as at one of the new department stores. Cosmopolitanism—as the experience of diversity in the city—was therefore passed to the working classes as an experience of consumption.

The contrast between working-class local and middle-class cosmopolitan should not be overdrawn. There were few respectable people who wanted to leave their own safe corners of the city; especially among middle-class women the desire to be shielded from the masses of strangers was strong. But the complexity of the business, pleasure, and sociability of the affluent was at least likely to draw them out of the confines of a small piece of turf; the woman visited her milliner, her dressmaker, went to the Woman's Institute, went home to tea, then out to dine; the man went to office, to club, perhaps to a theater, to a meeting.

It is important to see that this "right to the city," as Henri Lefebvre calls it, was becoming a bourgeois prerogative, because today there is so much celebration of the *vie du quartier*. Those who today romanticize the *vie du quartier* or the virtues of localism perceive the "color" of working-class life, at the cafe, or in the streets, but fail to perceive that this "color" is the product of an economic simplification of urban territory in the last century. The working-class person of the *ancien régime* city, who wore quite different but equally onerous chains, found that they did not confine his movement—for pleasure, excitement, or work—about the city. The celebration of localism and of the small-scale neighborhood on the part of well-meaning planners today is an unwitting reinforcement of a new form of domination, a deprivation of the city, imposed on workers in the last century.

Being "out in public" was for our great-grandfathers a more meaningful question, therefore, if they were bourgeois than if they were not. It is something of an irony about the troubles they were having: would the distress occasioned in public perhaps have been less if the range of people routinely in public had been greater?

CHANCE AND BOURGEOIS LIFE

In a society breaking feudal ties, it is the bourgeoisie who are the critical class. In 18th Century Paris and London, commercial and bureaucratic work did not involve fulfilling an obligation set down from time immemorial. As the 19th Century progressed, these same cosmopolitan bourgeois occupations acquired a new context.

As a working rule, we can identify the bourgeois classes of London and Paris beginning with proprietors of businesses with at least one other employee, with office workers, clerks, bookkeepers, and the like, and with the professional and managerial strata above them. They were a surprisingly large group of people; with their families they comprised between 35 and 43 percent of London's population in 1870, between 40 and 45 percent of Paris in the same year. There were proportionately more middle-class families in the capitals than in the rest of either country; in England as a whole in 1867, about 23 percent of the population was middle-class.[11]

Just as industrial capitalism meant something different in England than it did in France, the consciousness of oneself as a "respectable" Londoner had connotations and undertones different from the consciousness of oneself as a "bourgeois" Parisian. Yet, from capital to capital, such differences were not as extreme as differences from nation to nation. As in the *ancien régime* capital, cosmopolitanism cut across national lines, but in the 19th Century to speak of such affinities is to speak of the worldliness of only a part of the city. The cosmopolitan bourgeoisie took on in the last century some of the characteristics of an international class; it was not the proletariat of the industrial countries which did so. "Sophistication": in the 18th Century, in both France and England, the word was derogatory; but in the 19th Century it became a compliment among those bourgeois. It denoted those whom one could recognize as "well brought up" or having "good manners" despite the barriers of language, national custom, and age.

By one account, the increase in Paris between 1770 and 1870 in the percentage of bourgeois workers was not great, perhaps a third more. But the real change in context was in what they traded and administered—a system of machine-made, mass-produced goods. It is important to understand how those who experienced this new system understood it. They did not understand it very well, partly because they brought many attitudes of the old city to bear on the new. But the way in which they tended to misunderstand the industrial order is important, for it reveals a fundamental view of industrial life which conditioned all attitudes toward the public realm: this was that bourgeois respectability was founded on chance.

The businessmen and bureaucrats of the last century had little sense of participating in an orderly system. Moreover, since they directed the new system, we tend to assume they understood at least their own work, and nothing could be farther from the truth. The new principles of making money and directing large organizations were a mystery even to those who were very successful. The workers in the large-scale enterprises of Paris and London in the 1860's and 1870's used to picture their activities in terms of the gamble, the game of chance—and the appropriate scene was the stock exchange.

To understand the new economic stimuli which affluent people felt challenged by, we need to know the meaning of speculation at the time. It was possible in fact to make or to lose a great deal of money very quickly. Families with capital tended to put it into one or, at most, a very few enterprises. A bad investment, therefore, and decent, respectable families faced ruin; a good investment, and suddenly one inhabits a whole new world. What were the rules for making a good and bad investment? Investors of a century ago possessed far less information than their counterparts today on which a decision could be made. For instance, few firms published annual statements of profit and loss. Most "information" was in the form of gossip. The stock exchanges, the City, the *bourse* and its subsidiaries in Paris had no real principles of governance such as even *pro forma* assurances that companies being traded in actually existed; the commodity exchanges were, if anything, worse. Major national investments were equally a matter of chance, and followed no real rationality in the ordinary sense. Railroads were built into absolute wilderness in France because it was "suspected" that someday iron would be found there; the great scandals like the Panama affair had their echo in yearly fiascos equally, if less spectacularly, fraudulent. The existence of so much fraud depended on an investment class which had almost no standards in its own mind of how industry developed, and therefore of what was a rational investment decision.

It was not even until the end of the 1860's that people began to connect the succession of good and bad times and to think, therefore, of something called a business cycle. But what caused this cycle? Today we can give a good account of it via the contemporaneous writings of Marx, but few brokers were reading him a century ago. Businessmen were most apt to explain business cycles in mystical terms. A banker from Manchester, John Mills, believed the business cycle depended on "the science of mind"; in 1876 William Purdy advanced the theory that business cycles occurred because young investors grew middle-aged and therefore hadn't the physical strength to keep capital circulating vigorously. In France the understanding of the cycle was no better. And what made this failure of self-analysis so critical at the time was that the economic shifts of the last century were so much more abrupt and sudden than they are today, so that within a space of a few months industrial France could plunge from expansion to depression and after a period of stagnation, in which nothing seemed to work to make things better, suddenly and inexplicably begin an upswing.[12]

The inexplicable instabilities which governed the investment sectors governed in turn the bureaucracies. Operations like the Crédit Foncier, mammoth in scale, would appear, become involved in major and what seemed long-term projects, and suddenly collapse; their work would then be taken over by another organization, with new personnel. Some historians of France are tempted to contrast its bureaucratic history favorably to that of England, arguing that the greater state control of the economy in France gave bureaucrats more security. The argument may hold in terms of provincial life; in terms of London and Paris it does not, because, paradoxically, while the central organs of the French state were all located in Paris, the economy of the city itself was subject to much less low-level state control than that of the provinces or the countryside. The rebuilding of Paris by Haussmann, which caused enormous financial and commercial losses, would have been impossible in a provincial city because the dead hand of bureaucracy would have inhibited the frenetic (and disorderly) accumulation of capital, workers, and material.

Respectability founded on chance: that is the economic fact of the 19th Century which was associated with a demography of expansion and isolation. The dignity of the bourgeoisie appears again: to set against this economy a stable home, to force the family as a group into a life of rigid propriety, was an act of will, and took a certain strength. The rigidities seem stifling today; perhaps it is the very fact that the capitalist economy has grown relatively more orderly and has a firmer hold on us which permits us to scorn 19th Century propriety.

If people's consciousness of their times was directly a product of the material conditions under which they lived, then the bourgeois citizens of the 19th Century capitals ought to have believed they lived in a time of permanent cataclysm. In retrospect, it is possible to see how the material conditions of the city were rooted in and were magnifications of material patterns which existed prior to the reign of the industrial order. As experienced at the time, however, the increases of population, the changes in ecology, the fluctuations of the new industrial order, were so great that they were traumatic. The city therefore should have been every man's image of a life to avoid, with masses of people aimless, rootless, and threatening, the sustenance of a decent life a matter of chance rather than will.

These material conditions did not induce that perception. A consciousness of material disorder in the great city reigned among its citizens and in the provinces, yet in fact many people longed to move to the capital, fearsome as life was there. Over the course of the century as a whole, the majority of migrants to the city came voluntarily, as young single people, not as displaced groups. The inhabitants of different kinds of cities, provincial cities in the two countries, were more likely to see themselves plunged into the abyss. In part this was because these provincial cities were the body of the new industrial capitalism. In Lille, in Lyons, in Manchester or Birmingham, were the factories; they created the economy and demography of Manchester, a new city.

In other, older towns the tissue of provincial social life was fragile, and easily rent by the factory and the effect of capitalism on agriculture. The pages of *Middlemarch* show "the coming of a great change" to a town; in *Little Dorrit* similar new material facts are married to London, and are to be understood within the city's ongoing life. *Middlemarch* is about what happens to a provincial town; *Little Dorrit* is about what happens in London.

The reason why material changes did not induce the perception of utter chaos, why middle-class people could feel that survival was possible in the city, why cosmopolitan life was important and meaningful for all its terrors, was precisely that the citizens did not have to invent a culture in the city with images of what urban life was about, how to cope with the unknown, how to behave in front of strangers. There was an inherited culture. This culture was the public realm. Just as it grew in the *ancien régime* in response to material changes of population and demography, it survived for our great-grandfathers as a tool for attempting to preserve order in the midst of much greater material shifts in the city. The gifts our great-grandfathers received they in time, like any heir, wasted. Eventually, the bourgeoisie deformed, to the point where nothing remained, the modes developed in the 18th Century of conducting a meaningful life at a distance from the uncertainties of personal circumstance. But the impulse to conduct such a life remained strong, even as the means for doing so were crumbling. This is the great paradox by the end of the last century: as material conditions finally became more known and regular, the public world became less and less stable.

How then was public life conducted in the midst of, as a response to, as a defense against, these new material conditions?

PUBLIC COMMODITIES

There is no better introduction to this public life than the curious story of how retail trade was transformed in the 19th Century capital cities. The rise of the department store, mundane a subject as it may seem, is in fact in capsule form the very paradigm of how the public realm as an active interchange gave way in people's lives to an experience of publicness more intense and less sociable.

In 1852, Aristide Boucicault opened a small retail store in Paris called Bon Marché. The store was based on three novel ideas. The markup on each item would be small, but the volume of goods sold large. The prices of goods would be fixed, and plainly marked. Anyone could enter his shop and browse around, without feeling an obligation to buy.[13]

The principle of a fixed price for retail goods was not entirely original with him. Parissot's Belle Jardinière was selling linen on this basis as early as 1824. But Boucicault was the first to apply the idea to a full range of retail goods. One measure of the originality of fixed prices is that, until the last decades of the *ancien régime,* it was forbidden by law for retailers to give out handbills showing a fixed price for their wares. Another, more human measure is the effect of fixed prices on the experience of shopping.[14]

In a market where retail prices float, sellers and buyers go through all kinds of theatrics to up or lower the price. In Middle Eastern bazaars, displays of outraged feeling, impassioned declarations of pain and suffering occasioned by the loss or purchase of this so beautiful rug, are part and parcel of the sale. In the Paris meat markets of the 18th Century, hours could be spent on maneuvers to up the price of a side of beef by a few centimes.[15]

Haggling and its attendant rituals are the most ordinary instances of everyday theater in a city, and of the public man as an actor. The end of the line of production and distribution in a society without fixed prices is posturing, jockeying for position, the ability to notice chinks in an opponent's armor. The stylized interplay weaves the buyer and the seller together socially; not to participate actively is to risk losing money.

Boucicault's fixed-price system lowered the risk of not playing a role. His notion of free entrance made passivity into a norm.

In the retail establishments of *ancien régime* Paris and the early 19th Century, to enter a store was understood to mean one would buy something, no matter what. The browser looking casually around belonged in the open market, not inside a shop. This "implicit contract" to buy makes perfect sense in terms of the dramatic efforts required by the open-price system. If a seller is going to invest his time in glowing speeches about his goods, in declarations that he is on the verge of bankruptcy and cannot go a penny lower, he has got to know that you will make it worth his while. This dramaturgy takes time, and therefore tends to discourage rapid sales volume. Boucicault, envisioning low markup, high volume, had therefore to do away with such theatrical behavior.[16]

Why did Boucicault and his imitators, Burt in London, Potter Palmer in Chicago, begin to sell on high volume, low markup? The simplest answer concerns the production system. Machine-made goods could be made more quickly and in much greater volume than goods produced by hand. The department store on this account is a response to the factory. A complementary explanation is given by C. Wright Mills in terms of industrial bureaucracy. In *White Collar,* he gives this rationale for the fixed-price system: in a store dealing in volume sales, there must be a large number of employees, and therefore, "if the entrepreneur himself does not sell, he has to have one price; he cannot trust clerks to the bargain successfully."[17]

As complement to the factory, as a product of impersonal bureaucracy, the department store still could not have succeeded without a mass of buyers. It was here that the population influx to the capital entered the picture. But the economics of real estate development was more and more localizing this mass of potential buyers. The sheer physical complexity of the old city streets was also an obstacle to assembling this mass of consumers. It is estimated that because of the twisted, narrow streets of Paris at the opening of the 19th Century, a journey by foot which today could take fifteen minutes, at that time required an hour and a half. To leave one's *quartier* was a time-consuming affair, and yet for the department stores to achieve their volume they had to draw customers from all over the city. The creation of the *grands boulevards* in the 1860's in Paris helped make this possible. The creation of a transport system in Paris and in London made it even more feasible. In Paris, horse-drawn buses were introduced in 1838, but the 1850's was their great period of growth; in 1855 they carried 36 million passengers; in 1866 they carried 107 million. The same union of quick transport and retail commerce marked the development of Chicago after the Great Fire of 1871. This public transport was not designed for pleasure, nor did its routes intermix the social classes. It was for moving workers to work and to the stores.[18]

Mass-produced goods, handled by a large bureaucracy, with a mass of buyers, all deal with what might induce the seller to abandon the old patterns of retail commerce in order to make more profit. They do not explain why the buyer was willing to change parts. Profit for the seller does not explain, above all, why the buyer in Paris was willing to become a passive figure when it came time to hand over his money.

Let us rule out first the simple and obvious explanation of why the buyer might be willing to abandon active participation in retail commerce. Prices in general did not become cheaper in department stores than in the old-time shops. The price levels of a few items went down, but that saving was more than canceled out because people of even modest means were buying items they had never thought of owning before. The level of consumption throughout the middle classes and upper working classes expanded. One instance: with the coming of the department store, the idea of owning several sets of clothes, all quite similar and machine-made, for street wear took hold. Another: in these stores people began buying pots and pans which served specialized purposes, the all-purpose stewpot and skillet now seeming inadequate.

There was a relationship between the new, passive role of the buyer and what appears as a new stimulus to consumption. D'Avenel gives a succinct description of the quality of goods sold in the new department stores:

> Instead of selling with an exaggerated mark-up first-class merchandise, or low-grade merchandise with a reduced mark-up, they [the department stores] sold merchandise of good or sufficient quality with a mark-up which was formerly used only for low-grade merchandise.

Medium-grade objects with markup once appropriate only to objects of poor quality and consumers spending more to own more—this is what the "standardization" of physical goods was about. The retailers of the time, Boucicault and Palmer most explicitly, knew they had a problem in stimulating people to buy such nondescript goods. They tried to solve this problem by creating a kind of spectacle out of the store, a spectacle which would endow the goods, by association, with an interest the merchandise might intrinsically lack.[19]

The first means the retailers used was that of unexpected juxtaposition. A visitor to Bloomingdale's furniture floor in New York would have the best sense of what these 19th Century stores attempted. Rather than one hundred pots of the same size by the same manufacturer on the floor, there would be one example only, put next to a pot of a different shape. Zola wrote that "the strength of the department stores is increased tenfold by the accumulation of merchandise of different sorts, which all support each other and push each other forward." D'Avenel made the same point: "It seems . . . that the most dissimilar objects lend each other mutual support when they are placed next to one another." Why should this be? The use character of the object was temporarily suspended. It became "stimulating," one wanted to buy it, because it became temporarily an unexpected thing; it became strange.[20]

The stimulation produced by jumbling dissimilar objects together the retail owners reinforced by the continual search for exotic *"nouveautés"* to put on sale in the midst of the most prosaic wares. Strange goods, the export of the colonized states, are useful, says Bertrand Gille, not only as articles of trade in themselves. They accustom the buyer to the notion that he will find in the store what he did not expect and thus be willing to leave the store with merchandise he did not enter in search of. Volume, that is to say, was achieved in the retail trade through an act of disorientation: the stimulation to buy resulted from the temporary well of strangeness, of mystification that the objects acquired.[21]

There was a logical conclusion to this process of stimulation. High volume meant objects appeared and disappeared rapidly in the store. This fact the retailers seized on, to create an illusion of scarcity of supply among what were in fact mass-produced goods. A buyer was stimulated when he or she was presented with objects whose existence seemed fleeting, and whose nature was veiled by associations out of the context of normal use.

In the latter decades of the 19th Century, department-store owners began to work on the spectacle character of their enterprises in quite deliberate ways. Plate-glass windows were inserted on the ground floors of the stores and the arrangement of goods in them was made on the basis of what was most unusual in the store, not what was most common. The window decorations themselves became more and more fantastic and elaborate.[22]

By stimulating the buyer to invest objects with personal meaning, above and beyond their utility, there arose a code of belief which made mass retail commerce profitable. The new code of belief in trade was a sign of a larger change in the sense of the public realm: the investment of personal feeling and passive observation were being joined; to be out in public was at once a personal and a passive experience.

Karl Marx had an apt phrase for the psychology of consumption itself: he called it "commodity fetishism." In *Capital* he wrote that every manufactured object under modern capitalism becomes a "social hieroglyphic"; by that he meant that inequities in the relations of owner and worker producing this object could be disguised. Attention could be diverted from the social conditions under which the objects were made to the objects themselves, if the goods could acquire a mystery, a meaning, a set of associations which had nothing to do with their use.[23]

Boucicault and other department-store owners were creating that meaning. By mystifying the use of items in their stores, giving a dress "status" by showing a picture of the Duchesse de X wearing it, or making a pot "attractive" by placing it in a replica of a Moorish harem in the store window, these retailers diverted buyers, first, from thinking about how or even how well the objects were made, and second, about their own roles as buyers. The goods were all.

But why did commodity fetishism work? That question begins to raise the matter of the relationship between capitalism and public culture. The capitalist order had the power to throw the materials of appearance into a permanently problematical, permanently "mystifying" state, to use Marx's term. Imagine that Boucicault had a new kind of pot for sale: he knew that the way to move it off his shelves in high-volume sales was not to suggest exactly what it could be used for, and how the housewife ought to do so; he knew instead that he had to suggest its possibilities for use were infinite and unspecifiable, display it in his window rigged up as a Moorish harem, and convey the idea it was disappearing so quickly off the shelves that soon this pot would acquire the status of a collector's item. In the manufacture of clothes, we will observe the mystification of appearance proceeding by much simpler means: the cheapest machine-made clothes were those which used only a few materials and were cut from a few basic dies, so that large numbers of people came to look very much the same. Who were they? You now have difficulty telling from how they looked.

But what the new economics will not explain about 19th Century urban culture is why and how the people of the great cities came to take their mystifying, unresolvable appearances so seriously; why in the store they believed that wearing a ten-franc dress worn by the Duchesse de X made one a little more "aristocratic," or believed that a new cast-iron pot had a personal meaning to the buyer in terms of his fantasies of Moorish pleasure. If one great theme of the time is the growth of homogeneous, machine-made objects, the other is the increasing importance the denizens of Carlyle's London and of Balzac's Paris accorded to these exterior appearances as signs of personal character, of private feeling, and of individuality.

Marx was himself continually attacked during his lifetime for arguing that goods were consumed according to their value as status objects, or expressions of the personality of the buyer. Today these ideas have become so familiar that it is difficult to place ourselves in the frame of mind of Marx's utilitarian critics, who saw every man and woman as rationally in pursuit of rational economic interest, buying only what was needed or of use. This was the great duality of 19th Century thought: the insistence in the abstract on utility and hard fact, the perception in practice of a psychomorphic world. In the same way that Marx self-consciously perceived goods becoming an "appearance of things which expresses the buyer's personality," other fleeting appearances were being interpreted by others less sure of their perceptions as signs of inner and permanent character.

John Stuart Mill conceived of a science of "ethology," a science of reading character from minute behavior; this was popularized into deducing character from external appearances like the shape of the skull or the slope of one's handwriting. Carlyle wrote a book, *Sartor Resartus*, which was a theory of clothes as "emblems of soul"; Darwin published a great work on psychology, *The Expression of Emotion in Man and Animals*, which discussed the meaning of grief in terms of the minutiae of crying, or the feeling of anger in terms of the appearance of anger which facial muscles produce upon the face. Criminological methods like the Bertillon measurements of "criminal-type" skulls were but one popular reflection of this new science of ethology. Fielding's world, in which masks do not express the nature of the actors, was over; masks were becoming faces.

Here, in the world of retail commerce, appeared a sign of the first force of change in the public realm of the last century, and also a problem which this force cannot explain. One of the two major effects of capitalism on public life was to mystify public phenomena, but the mystification could succeed only if people were willing to believe that objects were invested with attributes of human character; profits for the seller do not indicate why people were so willing to believe. To understand the belief, we shall need to understand a new idea of character itself in the making.

Here, too, is the first appearance of one of the psychic symptoms of this new public life: the superimposition of imagery in realms which had in the *ancien régime* been kept apart. A dress in 1750 was not a matter of what you feel; it was an elaborate, arbitrary marking of where you stood in society, and the higher you stood in society, the more freedom you had to play with that object, your appearance, according to elaborate, impersonal rules. By 1891, owning the right dress, no matter that it was mass-produced and not very pretty, could make you feel chaste or sexy, for your clothes "express" you. In 1860, you are stimulated to buy a black cast-iron pot measuring ten inches in diameter because it is shown in a store window holding "the mysterious, seductive cuisine of the East." Industrial advertising works by an act of disorientation, which depends on this superimposing of imagery, which in turn depends both on a distinctive mode of production and on a distinctive belief about the universal presence of human character.

Industrial capitalism had a second effect upon the public realm, in addition to that of mystification. It changed the nature of privacy; that is, it affected the realm which counterpoised the public. Signs of this second effect can also be detected within the commerce of the city, in the changes which occurred in the small shops and markets which the department stores challenged.

Up to the late 17th Century, the central market of the city was a source for Parisians of all agricultural and handmade goods. Around the time of Louis XIV's death, Les Halles began to become a more specialized market, a market for food. Well in advance of the industrial century, Les Halles was losing its character as a *foire;* as commerce became more specialized, there waned the pageants and festivals of the late Middle Ages which celebrated market activity. The Industrial Age completed this specialization of Les Halles, did not cause it.[24]

What changed in the 19th Century was the social terms on which food was bought or sold. During the period of strong market conditions in the 1740's, the laws treated the seller at Les Halles as a potential delinquent, and strong constraints were put on the variety of actions he could undertake: certain forms of advertisement were prohibited, the buyer was guaranteed certain rights of redress, what a seller could sell was fixed by law.[25]

These restrictions on the seller in Les Halles were lifted in the 19th

Century. To speak of the free market as the gospel of the last century, as Karl Polanyi does, is to speak of a market in which the seller's person became beyond the law. The sale itself was not "freed" in the same way. For it is in the 19th Century that the fixed price invaded the retail transactions of Les Halles in the wake of the mass merchandising of the department store.[26]

Open-price trading did not disappear in Les Halles in the 19th Century; it continued in wholesale transactions. But these sales were for the first time treated as business which must be kept secret. If the "public" who bought retail knew what open prices were, they might object to fixed prices, thus throwing the high-volume retail market into chaos. What defines a wholesale situation socially, then, is the fact that it is "private" in a new sense: in private, people are free to engage in the postures and interaction that a century before marked public commerce.[27]

Here, too, economic practice in 19th Century Paris gives a clue to larger changes. In "public," one observed, one expressed oneself, in terms of what one wanted to buy, to think, to approve of, not as a result of continuous interaction, but after a period of passive, silent, focused attention. By contrast, "private" meant a world where one could express oneself directly as one was touched by another person; private meant a world where interaction reigned, but it must be secret. At the end of the 19th Century Engels spoke of the private family as the expression of a capitalist ethos; he should have been more specific. The family parallels not the public world of capitalism, but the wholesale world; in both, secrecy is the price of continuous human contact.

But here, too, there are puzzles not immediately explicable. That code of secrecy of the 19th Century is completely baffling. The family, especially the middle-class family, was to be absolutely sheltered from the tremors of the outside world. It seems illogical that appearances in the public world of the city would be taken seriously in terms of personal character if the family was so strongly felt to be a place whose very shelter from the world permitted people to be expressive. It should, logically, be only within the confines of the family, or only in the private wholesale deal, that appearances would have a psychological character. But this logic was not practiced. Privacy as the realism of interactive expression—yet a culture where a stranger could tell your character from how you looked and dressed; the city as a fevered *"comédie"*—yet in the spectacle few men play an active role.

The belief that secrecy is necessary when people are fully interacting gives the key to a second of the barometers of psychic distress in the society: the desire to withdraw from feeling in order not to show one's feelings involuntarily to others. Only by making your feelings a secret are they safe, only at hidden moments and places are you free to interact. But precisely this fearful withdrawal from expression puts more pressure on others to get closer to you to know what you feel, what you want, what you know. Flight and the seed of compulsive intimacy are absolutely joined: the sheer expression of an emotion, any emotion, becomes ever more important as so much work becomes necessary to penetrate another's defenses to the point where he is willing to interact.

These signs of contradiction in public and private puzzled those who experienced them no less than they puzzle and frighten us in retrospect. The world of retail commerce indicates the terms of the most basic of these puzzles, the effects and the limits of capitalism on public life, in terms of mystification and in terms of privatization. To get further into these issues we shall now explore the question of how personality became a social category, and so intruded into the public realm. I think it is important to say that in the very confusion and seriousness of this world going askew there was something heroic. If Balzac's Paris is less civilized than Marivaux's, less attractive, it is more compelling. The seeds of modern life are there, but there is struggle; nothing as yet could be taken for granted.

CHAPTER 8

PERSONALITY
IN PUBLIC

In asking what effect new material conditions had on public life, in particular the effects of industrial capitalism upon it, we find ourselves having to ask a second question, how personality entered the public realm. The system of profits couldn't succeed without this intrusion of personality, and the system of profits won't explain why it arose.

Personality appeared in public because a new secular world-view appeared in society as a whole. This world-view replaced an Order of Nature by an ordering of natural phenomena; belief in the first arose when a fact or event could be placed in a general schema; belief in the second began earlier, when the fact or event was understood, and so seemed real, in and of itself. The first was a doctrine of secular transcendence, the second a doctrine of secular immanence. Personality was one form of this belief in immanent meaning in the world.

It is easy to imagine "capitalism" as a historical force, because tangible actions and changes, in production, prices, or power, come to mind. It is not easy to imagine "secularity" in the same way, because it is hard to conceive of it as anything but an abstract product of other forces in society. The inability to imagine secularity as an independent social force comes, I think, precisely from the present-day inability to conceive of the act of belief as real in itself. And this in turn derives from our peculiar inability to comprehend the sociological realities of religion—religion, as Louis Dumont has observed, being *the* primary social structure for most of human society during most of its existence. Because today the gods have fled from our minds, we therefore easily imagine that the process of belief itself has ceased to be a fundamental social category and is instead a social product. The followers of Lévi-Strauss, for instance, seize upon his notions of general structures of thought and are blind to the vision from which these notions sprang, that impulses of faith produce the linguistic and economic and family structures which knit seemingly diverse societies together.

Some people have argued that the god of nature in the 18th Century was still a god, and that therefore to speak of secular society is to speak of a society beginning in the 19th Century. It is better to see the 18th and 19th Centuries as two stages in a process of secularization. "Nature and Nature's god" was a deity without a face; one could honor it but not pray to it. Although Nature was transcendent, belief in it did not bring to the faithful life after death; that is, belief did not make them transcendent beings. This is why a good definition of secularity is "the reason things are as they are in the world, reasons which will cease to matter in themselves, once we are dead." (See Chapter 1.)

That a change in secularity occurred between the 18th and the 19th Century is clear. More than just scientific positivism, it encompassed Darwin's theory of evolution, attitudes toward art, and everyday convictions, as well as profound changes in the field of psychology itself. Why the change occurred is a book of its own, but I want to state one way of conceiving it.

Belief remains a fundamental social condition, nor is the will to belief erased, even as mankind loses a belief in gods. We are not a peculiar age in our scientific and rationalistic proclivities; we are peculiar only in that our science is used as the enemy of idolatry. This enmity began in and has steadily progressed since the Enlightenment. In the 19th Century the will to believe passed from a non-idol religion to a more reflexive condition: beliefs become more and more centered on the immediate life of man himself, and his experiences as a definition of all that he can believe in. Immediacy, sensation, the concrete—only here can belief finally flourish, once idolatry is forbidden. This reflexive principle then goes a step beyond the first, 18th Century break. As the gods are demystified, man mystifies his own condition; his own life is fraught with meaning, yet it remains to be played out. Meaning is immanent in it, yet the person is unlike a stone or a fossil which is fixed and so can be studied as a form.

It is here that personality enters the scheme of immanent belief. Personality became in the last century the way to think about the meaning implicit in human life, when in every life the concrete form, the self as a complete object, had yet to crystallize. Just as it used to be thought that "the family" was a fixed biological form in history, it is still easy to imagine personality as a constant in human affairs, for there have always been differences in feeling, perception, and behavior among people. The issue is what people are likely to make of those differences. As the gods fled, immediacy of sensation and perception grew more important; phenomena came to seem real in and of themselves as immediate experience. People in turn were disposed to make more and more of differences in the immediate impressions they made upon each other, to see these differences, indeed, as the very basis of social existence. These immediate impressions different people produced were taken to be their "personalities."

Personality came in the 19th Century to diverge from the Enlightenment belief in natural character in three important ways. First, personality is seen to vary from person to person, whereas natural character was the common thread running through mankind. Personality varies because the appearances of emotion and the inner nature of the person feeling are the same. One is what one appears; therefore, people with different appearances are different persons. When one's own appearances change, there is a change in the self. As the Enlightenment belief in a common humanity is eclipsed, the variation in personal appearances becomes tied to the instability of personality itself.

Second, personality, unlike natural character, is controlled by self-consciousness. The control an individual practiced in relation to his natural character was the moderation of his desires; if he acted in a certain way, modestly, he was bringing himself into line with his natural character. Personality cannot be controlled by action; circumstances may force different appearances and so destabilize the self. The only form of control can be the constant attempt to formulate what it is one feels. This sense of controlling the self is mostly retrospective; one understands what one has done after the experience is over. Consciousness always follows emotional expression in this scheme. Personalities, therefore, are not only composed of variations in rage, compassion, or trust between people; personality is also the capacity to "recover" one's emotions. Longing, regret, and nostalgia acquire an importance in 19th Century psychology of a peculiar sort. The 19th Century bourgeois is always remembering what it was like when in youth he was really alive. His personal self-consciousness is not so much an attempt to contrast his feelings with those of others as to take known and finished feelings, whatever they once were, as a definition of who he is.

Modern personality, finally, diverges from the idea of natural character in that freedom of feeling at a given moment seems like a violation of "normal" conventional feeling. The mid-18th Century did not set social convention against spontaneity; the woman in the pouf "pointing" Mme Favart was engaged in one form of spontaneity, and at home in her natural gown she was engaged in another. Spontaneity of personality, however, is set against social convention, and makes free spirits seem like deviants. Spontaneity and involuntary disclosure of character overlap in their meaning, but can be separated in one way; spontaneity is *safe* involuntary feeling which seems to do neither others nor oneself harm. Psychologists in the 19th Century came to believe, as did their patients, that ordinary people who were involuntarily expressive were often insane people; this is another form of the fear of spontaneous feeling as abnormal. This same principle has also come to be turned around. Self-consciousness about being different inhibits spontaneity of expression.

Personality created by appearances, controlled if at all by self-consciousness about one's past, spontaneous only by abnormality: these new terms of personality began to be used in the last century to understand society itself as a collection of personalities. It was within that general context that personality entered the public realm of the capital.

What is the principle giving rise to these terms of personality? The clue to all three is contained in the first. Personality varies among people, and is unstable within each person, because appearances have no distance from impulse; they are direct expressions of the "inner" self. That is, personality is immanent in appearances, in contrast to natural character, which, like Nature itself, transcends every appearance in the world.

> All visible things are emblems; what thou seest is not there on its own account; strictly taken, is not there at all: Matter exists only spiritually, and to represent some Idea, and *body* it forth. Hence *Clothes*, as despicable as we think them, are so unspeakably significant.

These words from Thomas Carlyle's *Sartor Resartus* would make no sense in the age of the wig and *pouf au sentiment*. For Carlyle clothes had become "unspeakably significant," because appearances made in the world are not veils but guides to the authentic self of the wearer.[28]

One really knew about a person by understanding him at the most concrete level—which consisted of details of clothes, speech, and behavior. In the clothes and speech of Balzac's Paris, appearances were therefore no longer at a distance from self, but rather clues to private feeling; conversely, "the self" no longer transcended its appearances in the world. This was the basic condition of personality.

It was the conjunction of this secular faith in personality, a faith in immediate appearances as a guide to inner feeling, with the economics of industrial capitalism which thrust personality as a social category into the public realm. These two forces have since carried on a dialogue. In the last chapter we saw from the side of profit some of the results of personality in public: passivity, human exchange as a secret, mystification of appearance itself. The new secular faith brought a logic of its own to that public realm which produced sympathetic results. To know, one must impose no coloration of one's own, of one's own commitments; this meant silence in public in order to understand it, objectivity in scientific investigation, a gastronomy of the eye. Voyeurism was the logical complement of 19th Century secularity.

To understand the voice of secularity, and its place in this dialogue,

I think it best to begin as concretely as possible, with one man interpreting the world on these terms. Let us begin, therefore, with Balzac. Alive to all the new material conditions of the modern city, he sought to interpret them through these new codes of personality.

BALZAC'S VISION OF PERSONALITY AS A SOCIAL PRINCIPLE

"Wherever in Balzac's novels Paris is not directly presented, she is even more vividly implied," Henry James once wrote. Surfeit, isolation, and chance—these were the new stimuli of the capital cities, and these were Balzac's subjects. They radiate from a central, almost obsessive concern of Balzac, his absorption in Paris as a place where fortunes are made and broken, as a milieu open to talent and then talent mysteriously ignored. The entrepreneurial is the basic mode of human relations. The man of calm judgment, if he enters Balzac's world at all, as does David in *Illusions Perdues*, can be no more than the passive victim of entrepreneurial society. Images like the following from *Splendeurs et Misères des Courtisanes* thus typify Balzac's sense of Paris as the locale for a new material order:

> You see, Paris is like a forest in the New World, where a score of savages roam—the Illinois, the Hurons, who live on the proceeds offered them by the different social classes. You are a hunter of millions; to capture your million you use snares, limed twigs, decoys. Some hunt heiresses, others a legacy; some fish for consciences, others sell their clients bound hand and foot. The man who comes back with his gamebag well stocked is hailed, feted, received into good society.

To survive in this milieu, a person must abandon any attachment, any stable commitment:

> A man who prides himself on following a straight line through life is an idiot who believes in infallibility. There are no such things as principles: there are only events; there are no laws but those of expediency.[29]

The image Balzac used to express the effect of material conditions upon the quality of life in this milieu was that of the wheel of fortune. He put the image to a use which Renaissance writers, who also resorted to it to picture their societies, would not have accepted. Fortune is in Balzac no longer the sport of the gods with man, nor Machiavelli's "Woman of Chance" at war with religion. Balzac based *Père Goriot* on

King Lear, but in transposing the plot to a modern city, Balzac dethroned the idea of the wheel of fortune from its Renaissance nobility and majesty and thrust it into the dirt of scandal, vulgar compromises, and false expectations. As chance is dragged down from the realm of the gods into the minutiae of everyday affairs, as it is secularized, "fortune" itself becomes a matter of total change, from absolute success to absolute failure, with no gradations at which the wheel stops in between. Thus in *Père Goriot:*

> Yesterday at the top of the wheel at a Duchess' . . . today at the very bottom begging a moneylender: this is what it is to be a woman of Paris.

Ignoble and absolute: this is what chance has become.[30]

Balzac's desire to portray the new conditions of urban life has led some critics to reproach him, in his singlemindedness, for being a bad reporter. Thus Charles Lalo:

> The *Comédie Humaine* slighted the main thing, which was production, and overestimated the accessory—which was speculation.

Of course such criticisms are innately silly, in that no one man can be held to account as an encyclopedia, but they raise an important point: why did Balzac care so much about instability, chance, and extreme changes in mid-19th Century Paris? One obvious answer is that Balzac was simply chronicling the new stimuli of the city proper, but behind this answer stands another.[31]

To Balzac, the modern city with its culture of voracious mobility was really a revelation of the human psyche fully emancipated from stable obligations, duties, feudal contacts, traditional ties. In the city, petty corruptions, little mindless cruelties, seemingly insignificant slights became inflated to moral absolutes: there was no longer any transcendent principle of King or God to oppose these cruelties. The city exposed thus all the possibilities of human psychology; that is, every scene had a meaning, because no principle outside of human desire made it happen. A segment of writing in *La Comédie Humaine,* titled successively *Scenes of Private Life, Scenes of Provincial Life, Scenes of Parisian Life,* Balzac explained in an introduction, portrayed stages in the life cycle, with mankind fully matured only in the city. What does the city ripen when ties of dependence and obligation are finally broken? Balzac's answer is perhaps the most famous picture of Paris in all his work:

[In Paris] genuine feelings are the exception; they are broken by the play of interests, crushed between the wheels of this mechanical world. Virtue is slandered here; innocence is sold here. Passions have given way to ruinous tastes and vices; everything is sublimated, is analysed, bought and sold. It is a bazaar where everything has its price, and the calculations are made in broad daylight without shame. Humanity has only two forms, the deceiver and the deceived. . . . The death of grandparents is awaited; the honest man is the fool; generous ideas are means to an end; religion appears only as a necessity of government; integrity becomes a pose; everything is exploited and retailed; ridicule is a means of advertising oneself and opening doors: the young men are one hundred years old, and insult old age.[32]

Thus, in Balzac, we might seem to arrive at an instance of the larger problem raised in the last chapter, an indictment of the city based on its material circumstances. Yet Balzac is more than conscious of these conditions; he interprets them with a new yardstick. He calls Paris "the most delicious of monsters" in the opening of *Scenes of Parisian Life;* and indeed, each of its horrors he savors. We find in Balzac a passion for examining the city in every revolting particular, a pleasure in showing the reader just how terrible it is, a love for this "delicious" monster not at odds with the genuine disgust Balzac feels toward Parisian life, but rather superimposed over his disgust. The double vision, not the indictment, is what makes Balzac a great reporter of the mentality of the city. The basis of this double vision is Balzac's belief that personality has become the fundamental social category of the city, and this belief he in turn derives from analysis of the details of appearances. It was at this level that Balzac spoke to and speaks for his contemporaries.

Balzac's attention to detail used to be thought a matter of his "style," as opposed to his "subjects"; it now is thought to be the very substance of his art. At present, Balzac's absorption in detail is interpreted either as "romantic realism" or as "melodrama." These two interpretations do not conflict, but they contain some important differences. The idea of Balzac's romantic realism, as it is interpreted by Donald Fanger, is that the novelist concentrates on the details of personal daily life because each of these, if picked over, and apart, and turned around from every angle, will reveal not just the person's character or even personality in a myriad of different guises, but will give up a secret, which is that of a picture of the whole society. All of society is miniaturized in every small concrete manifestation of life, but the novelist and the reader of novels must force themselves to strain every faculty, to invest more feeling in details than they could logically ever warrant, in order to prise out this secret. Little acts, little things of life do not have any clear signification without that inflation. This approach to the minutiae of variations of human personality and action has been best summarized by George Lukacs in the following words: "What [Balzac] did was to depict the typical characters of his time, while enlarging them to dimensions so gigantic . . . that they can never pertain to single human beings, only to social forces." The concern for detail is that of a "realist"; the strength of feeling about it is that of a "romantic"; when the two combine, the result is to make of each personality in each scene a statement about the social order of the city as a whole.[33]

Here then is Balzac's formulation of personality as a social category: if it is immanent, everywhere in social life, it is also a mystery, a secret which will not of itself speak. His is the reverse side of Marx's coin: personality is everywhere present in social relations but is mystifying. How then to make it speak? The observer can do so, first, only by a force of interest which inflates and magnifies details into symbols. But passionate interest alone does not explain the process by which the details of life are magnified in psychic symbols.

This symbol-making procedure Peter Brooks has called melodrama —not only because Balzac was throughout his life attracted to the stage, and wrote several plays or play-scripts (the earliest being *Le Nègre: Mélodrame en Trois Actes*), but because the procedure by which Balzac inflated his details into symbols was the same procedure by which stage melodramatists shaped their characters. This was to present in the description of the detail of behavior or feeling only what can easily and immediately be connected to another detail; the detail in itself, the sign which has no referent, is death to this kind of description. The reader must apprehend a fact only as it belongs to a type, and a person's behavior only as it belongs to a type of behavior. In this way we can quickly, in a stage melodrama, recognize the villain, the damsel in distress, the young rescuer.[34]

But on the stage the connection is such that individual characters have a meaning only as they fit general character types. In the novels of Balzac, the flow is reversed. The web of details is constructed such that general social forces have a meaning only as they can be reflected in individual cases. In Balzac, the procedure permits us to see, as Lukacs put it, "social forces" embodied in the trivial doings of everyday life; once embedded, however, they are hard to detach. Balzac's art is to make us believe in capitalism only by arousing belief in particular capitalists, to analyze "the artist in Paris" only by showing us every detail about specific artists at work at specific times and places in the city. In this way, social categories arouse belief only as we see them as immanent in a particular person's life. That he so aroused belief is Balzac's mark as a great artist: the expectation that social life is believable only on these terms marks Balzac as representative of a new, a more general mentality.

There is a famous scene from the opening of *Père Goriot,* a description of the dining room of Madame Vauquer's *pension* and of Madame Vauquer herself, and a famous interpretation of this scene, by Erich Auerbach in *Mimesis,* which perfectly illustrates Balzac's way of making society into a set of psychological symbols, each of which is based on little, insignificant details. The description begins with the room at seven in the morning and the cat who arrives in it before its mistress. Then Madame Vauquer enters. Each feature on her face is noted by a metaphor; then the whole face is described all over again in different metaphors. Then we have an exact picture of each layer of her clothes, then six sentences, each of which restates something about her character which has been stated previously, but slightly altered. Auerbach calls this exhausting intensity of attention to detail "demonic"; this passion to see, never to stop feeling, what it means for this tawdry woman to walk into the dining room in the morning, to sum up the whole of her life in her first momentary appearance—this demonism is the romantic realism of which Fanger speaks. It is the investment of all the observer's passion in the smallest facts.[35]

But how exactly does Balzac make us see each fact? Auerbach points out that Balzac makes each physical detail imply another and larger phenomenon, as in the phrase *"sa personne explique la pension, comme la pension implique sa personne,"* and then by association, as Balzac after this sentence immediately compares the *pension* to a prison. Or the minute facts are made to speak by juxtaposition: "Her loose, floppy bodice [is] in harmony with the room, whose walls ooze misfortune"; or the minutiae are thrust into a general description, so that they are suddenly forced to have a meaning which of themselves they do not carry:

> Madame Vauquer resembles all women *who have had troubles.* She has the glassy eye, the innocent expression of a bawd who is about to make a scene in order to get a higher price, but who is at the same time ready for anything in order to soften her lot.

We do not expect the image of a middle-aged, complaining woman to be suddenly associated with the image of a complaining whore; thrust between these two, mediating them, is that tiny detail of a woman with "a glassy eye." By being so placed, this little phrase becomes associated with each of these characters; this detail of physical appearance is the only concrete "proof," as it were, that these two character types are related. By placing the physical detail so, Balzac forces it to have a metaphoric as well as a linguistic meaning as a transition between unlikes. It becomes inflated, to signify something greater than itself. By such procedures, Balzac, the devoted observer of facts, lifts them out of the realm of the factual. This scene, like all of Balzac's description, in Auerbach's words, "is directed to the mimetic imagination of the reader, to his memory-pictures of similar persons and similar *milieux* which he may have seen." By being so very detailed about this boardinghouse, Balzac makes us think we are reading about "a boardinghouse in Paris." Yet this boardinghouse is not portrayed as a representative type, something typical rather than something individual. All the tissues connecting it to "similar persons and similar *milieux*"—the *pension* related to the dusty silence of the Paris prison; the doyenne of the house, smothered in her lace and her misfortunes, related to the brashest whore working the Madeleine—make the scene more important in and of itself. Inflating the detail by making it seem so innately connected to everything else in the social world, the detail becomes pregnant, a fact crucial to decode and demystify. The way of seeing then naturally disposes the observer to see all the city as bursting with meaning in every particular, a *comédie* waiting to be fathomed if one seizes hold violently of each of its scenes as a world all its own.[36]

Inflation and miniaturization at the same time; from this personalizing of society come two results, one an instability in what is perceived, the other a passivity in the perceiver.

In Balzac's own work, clothes are a favorite subject for showing the presence of individual personality in all appearances. Not only do clothes reveal the character of those they drape; changes in clothing prompt Balzac's characters to believe they have become new persons. In *Peau de Chagrin*, Rastignac seems *"metamorphosé"* by his new clothes at one point; in *Illusions Perdues*, Lucien, newly arrived in Paris, feels if he can only wear the right clothes somehow he will behave less gauchely and feel less anxiety; new clothes will "give him strength." In *Père Goriot*, changes in clothing are the means by which we see a moral decay take place. In all, it is by an analysis of the details of clothing, following the principles of perception used in analyzing the boardinghouse of Madame Vauquer, that these shifts in character are conveyed.[37]

The shifts clothes make in character led Balzac to a particular theme: appearances are masks in which the man behind the mask has the illusion of a separate and stable character but is in fact prisoner of his momentary appearances. This is a subtle formulation of a more general theme of his society: the fear of involuntarily disclosing character. You see no barrier between inner character and outer, momentary details of appearances; those appearances change; therefore changes in you are disclosed to anyone who scrutinizes you. There are no disguises;

each mask is a face. Immanence of personality, instability of personality, involuntary disclosure of personality: this trinity of his times Balzac reveals to be a prison. In popular commentary of the day on Balzac's writing, this question of disguises seems in fact to have troubled his public most. To say masks are faces touched a raw nerve.

If there is attachment to the act of seeing, and to the city as a whole, there is in Balzac no attachment to any particular scene. Balzac speaks of the "gastronomy of the eye," his love of the city for its scenes to observe. Balzac moves from molecule to molecule in the city, but is not defined, as narrator or commentator, by anyone. He does not speak from the point of view of belonging to a part of the city. His art in this reveals a second consequence—a peculiar passivity—which results from perceiving society in psychological symbols.

We saw earlier that the increasing fragmentation of the capital along class and ethnic lines drew, to some extent, a difference between bourgeois and worker in terms of cosmopolitanism. It was the bourgeois who was more likely to be able to move from scene to scene; the worker whose lesser economic circumstances were more likely to confine him to a locale. Balzac's lack of attachment to any scene, the absence in his writing of speaking, as it were, from the vantage point of one molecule about the rest, is the realization of a bourgeois cosmopolitanism. Contrast him to Daumier; Daumier was rooted to a particular culture, that of the urban proletariat of a particular neighborhood. Most of his figures "are based on people I see from my window." His vision of the classes was fixed in the same way: he was more likely to see the worker as victim than as sinner. Social relations are known, have only to be shown. For Balzac, everyone is a sinner. To understand human vices in all their variety, one had to roam all over the city, never taking the behavior of one molecule of society as a standard for the rest. One can never understand a specific life except "on its own terms." This rootlessness, this absolute relativism, this lack of commitment is what makes Balzac's a bourgeois view of the city. The bourgeois writer suspends his commitments to particular beliefs, and commits himself instead to the act of seeing. Passion and a peculiar passivity: this "gastronomy of the eye" defines a class culture, whose compass moves, as we shall see, from perception in the arts to perception of the social groups in the city.

Juxtapose Balzac now with the new forms of retail commerce in the city, and there emerges an outline of the public world of the mid-19th Century. In his writing the perception of personality in society is revealed to have a definite structure. Social relations are embedded in details of personal appearance; instability of the personality perceived is related to the floating passivity of the perceiver. The retail commerce shows how the perception of personality everywhere in society could be turned to a profit. The origins of Balzac's world lie in a secular doctrine of immanent meaning; the origins of the department store lie in mass-production and mass-distribution capitalism.

Without getting enmeshed in the question whether a writer of genius is representative—how easy it is now to believe that only medio-cre art is representative of an era—it is proper to ask about the grounds on which Balzac's contemporaries shared, if only as an expectation of what is believable, his view of the world, and the grounds on which their desire to perceive and believe as he did led the bourgeois audi-ence to different ends than those of the artist.

PERSONALITY IN PUBLIC: NEW IMAGES OF THE BODY

The decades of the middle of the 19th Century bore most historians of clothing and costume, as indeed they should. Squire's judgment is short and damning: "The dullest decade in the history of feminine dress began in 1840. An insipid mediocrity characterized an entirely middle-class epoch." Seldom had the female body appeared in more ungainly form, seldom had male dress been so drab. But these decades are all-important. In them, personality entered the public realm in a struc-tured way. It did so by meshing with the forces of industrial production, in the medium of clothes. People took each other's appearances in the street immensely seriously; they believed they could fathom the charac-ter of those they saw, but what they saw were people dressed in clothes increasingly more homogeneous and monochromatic. Finding out about a person from how he or she looked became, therefore, a matter of looking for clues in the details of his costume. This decoding of the body on the street in turn affected the bridge between stage and street. The codes of belief about street appearances began to be fundamentally different from the belief in appearances on the stage. In these ways, the cosmopolitan bourgeoisie were trying to see in terms comparable to Balzac's, but their vision led to a divorce between art and society.[38]

Terms like "homogeneous," "uniform," or "drab" must be used with caution. Compared with the garb of modern-day Peking, with its single military costume for all ages and both sexes, the clothing of the 1840's would hardly appear uniform or drab. Compared with the 1950's in the United States, it would be a celebration of style. But compared with what came before it, either in the *ancien régime* or in the Roman-tic era, it was homogeneous, it was drab. As numerous writers com-ment, it was the beginning of a *style* of dressing in which neutrality—that is, not standing out from others—was the immediate statement.

The epoch's clothes pose two problems. The first is how and why clothing became more neutral. The second is the insistence on read-ing personality from neutral appearances. The first problem involved a new relationship between clothing and the machine.

The sewing machine made its appearance in 1825, was worked on by various American and European firms, and was finally patented by Singer in 1851. In the 1840's, watches became a mass-production item. In 1820, hats became the same when an American developed a machine for producing felt. By the middle of the 19th Century, almost all shoes sold in cities were made by machine.[39]

The impact of these production changes on the clothes of Paris and London cannot be understood apart from a new means of disseminating fashion in the city. One hundred years before, there were two ways in which a Parisian fashion was broadcast: within the city, the most effective was direct contact on the streets or in public gardens; and dolls were used, dressed in exact replica of what Countess so-and-so was wearing at the moment. By 1857, this had all changed. Through "fashion plates" the pages of the newspaper disseminated fashion instantly, fashion depicted in its exact original form. The 1840's were the first great age of the mass-circulation newspaper; the sheer size of the newspapers' circulation meant that most buyers, indeed, no longer needed to make contact with a living salesman in order to know what to buy. Fashion dolls were still being made in the 19th Century, but had lost their purpose; they were treated as archaic objects, interesting to collect, but were no longer used by salesmen of clothes. What happened within the department store was thus echoed within the world of clothes; active interchange between buyer and seller was transformed into a more passive and one-sided relationship.[40]

By 1857, these changes in mass production and dissemination of clothes had penetrated the world of high fashion. In that year L. Worth opened up his fashion salon in Paris. He was the first high-fashion designer to use machine-made, mass-reproducible clothes. Today the technical quality of the Worth clothes, rather than their beauty, holds the eye. One hundred and twenty years ago, they made an impact because his "good taste" and "beautiful design" were realized in patterns which could easily be copied by the new clothing machines, just as Worth used these machines on a limited scale to prepare costumes for his royal and aristocratic patrons. As a result, there died out the simplifying process that operated in the 18th Century, as clothes passed from elite originators to middle-class imitators. After Worth, such simplification was rendered mechanically obsolete. Differences between upper- and middle-class appearance moved to a new and more subtle terrain.[41]

In the 1830's and 1840's the feminine silhouette came to be defined by the wasp waist and the leg-of-mutton sleeve. The extremely thin waist was achieved only by straitjacketing the body in a corset. The appeal of this imprisonment was, to bourgeois ladies, that it smacked of the dignity of bygone court years when royalty wore tight corsets and full dresses. By 1840, almost all of the female body below the collarbone was covered with clothing of some kind, for by this time the skirt had gradually descended to cover up the feet once again.[42]

In the 1830's the male costume began to subside from the flowing and exaggerated lines of Romantic dress. By 1840 the cravat lost its flamboyance and lay close to the neck. Masculine lines became simpler in these two decades, and the color of clothing more drab. Above all, broadcloth of a black color became the basic material for the streetwear of middle- and upper-class men and the "Sunday clothes" of the working class when they went to church.[43]

Now all these garments were cut by machine from patterns; if a gentleman or a lady could afford a tailor or seamstress, the patterns for hand-sewn clothes followed those of the machine-made patterns, unless the client was very rich or very eccentric. And eccentricity in dress was itself frowned upon increasingly in these decades.

We come here to a "puzzle of taste," in François Boucher's words, which was in fact a sign of a deep-seated and complex belief. In public, people did not want to stand out in any way; they did not want to be conspicuous. Why?

Historians of fashion have ascribed this fear of standing out to rather trivial causes. They speak, for instance, of the influence of Beau Brummell. While Romantics like the Comte d'Orsay dressed flamboyantly, Brummell presented himself as clean, neat, and immaculately controlled. Just as bourgeois ladies deformed their bodies in pursuit of a vanished royal *bon ton,* gentlemen thirty to forty years after Brummell's fall from fashion in 1812 could imagine that in being prim and drab they were showing good taste.[44]

But that is not enough as an explanation. Consider, for instance, a painting in the Royal Museum of Fine Arts in Copenhagen of a street crowd in that city, done by the painter A. M. Hounoeus in the middle of the century. The children's garb is purely Danish, the adults are dressed "Parisian fashion." It is a bad painting but an extraordinary document. Here is a crowd of people, all rather somberly dressed, a large crowd. Who are they? How could we divine their work, their specific status, their backgrounds? By sight it is impossible. They are shielded.

Differences between cosmopolitan and provincial life were involved in this taste for anonymity. It became in the 1840's a sign of middle-class cosmopolitan breeding, or the desire for urbanity among provincials. During the decade on the Continent, people outside the great cities, conversely and in another mood, began to place emphasis on conserving their "native" dress, as opposed to dressing "Paris style." The growing ideas of a folk and a folk spirit, which gave nations their rationale and rights, produced in part this consciously delineated line between Paris and "native" fashion. The idea of the folk began in Herder's generation, and survived as Herder's romantic contemporaries passed from the scene—the folk being always rural or village, the cosmopolitan city being anti-folk.

This new nativism produced extraordinary contrasts in the realm of fashion. If one looks at male fashion plates in Lyons and Birmingham newspapers, one finds in both countries that provincial ideas of good taste were far more colorful, more various, and, to put it finely, more interesting than cosmopolitan ideas. To dress up in a sophisticated way, a cosmopolitan way, meant to learn how to tone down one's appearance, to become unremarkable.

One can make then an easy connection. Given all the material upheaval in the city, people wanted to protect themselves by blending into the crowd. The mass-produced clothes gave them the means to blend. If the story were left here, one could sensibly conclude that now machine society controlled the expressive tools of the culture of the city. And if this were true, then all our familiar friends—dissociation, alienation, and the like—come into the picture: people must have felt dissociated from their bodies because their bodies were expressions of the machine, there was alienation because man no longer expressed his individuality through his appearance, and so on. These descriptions have become so familiar that they are almost comforting; they tell so easily what went wrong.

Yet dissociation is exactly what people so dressed did not do. As the images became more monochromatic, people began to take them more seriously, as signs of the personality of the wearer. The expectation that even blank or trivial appearances had great importance as clues to personality, an expectation which Balzac seized on in his work, his audience also maintained in their own lives. Cosmopolitans, more drab in appearance, tended to use clothes more than their provincial opposites as psychological symbols. The contradiction of their lives in public was that they wanted to shield themselves from individual attention, and the machines provided them the means to do so, yet they scrutinized the appearances of others so shielded for revealing clues about states of personal feeling. How does a black broadcloth suit come to seem a "social hieroglyphic," to use Marx's phrase? The answer lies in seeing the new ideas of immanent personality mesh with the mass production of appearances in public.

The two phenomena which bourgeois people personalized in public appearances were class and sex. Through reading details of appearance strangers tried to determine whether someone had metamorphosed economic position into the more personal one of being a "gentleman." Sexual status became personalized in public as strangers tried to determine whether someone, for all her seeming propriety, gave out little clues in her appearance which marked her as a "loose" woman. Both the "gentleman" and the "loose" woman lurking behind the respectable lady were visually meaningful only as public phenomena. The gentleman and the loose woman out of the public light, at home, had wholly different connotations. A gentleman at home was an attentive person, especially to the needs of his wife. His appearance was not the issue. The perception of a woman's looseness within the family was a perception of her behavior, not of giveaway clues in how she looked or dressed.

How do you recognize a gentleman when you meet a stranger? In *La Diorama*, a popular story set in Paris in the 1840's, a young man suddenly comes into an inheritance. He immediately resolves to buy some good clothes. When he has finished outfitting himself, he encounters a friend on the streets who is a republican, scornful of privileged wealth. And this friend does not by looking at him recognize that he has suddenly acquired wealth, because the clothes do not obviously proclaim the facts. But here there is a second step. He is hurt because, as a young man initiated, he can tell whether the clothes are those of a gentleman or not. Since the friend doesn't know the rules, he can notice nothing. This works in reverse too. When the young man goes to a factory he cannot read the rank of the various workers, although his friend can instantly. That is to say, this clothing does speak socially; it has a code which can be broken.

In 1750, the use of color, emblems, hats, trousers, breeches were instant signs of social place that everyone on the street could know; they may not have been an accurate index, but they were clear if arbitrary signs. These young people of the 1840's inhabit a world where the laws are accessible only to initiates. The clues the initiate reads are created through a process of miniaturization.

Details of workmanship now show how "gentle" a man or woman is. The fastening of buttons on a coat, the quality of fabric counts, when the fabric itself is subdued in color or hue. Boot leather becomes another sign. The tying of cravats becomes an intricate business; how they are tied reveals whether a man has "stuffing" or not, what is tied is nondescript material. As watches become simpler in appearance, the materials used in their making are the mark of the owner's social standing. It was, in all these details, a matter of subtly marking yourself; anyone who proclaims himself a gent obviously isn't.[45]

A Russian visitor to the Jockey Club asked his hosts to define a gentleman: was this an inherited title, a caste, or a question of cash? The answer he received was that a gentleman disclosed his quality only to those who had the knowledge to perceive it without being told. The Russian, a rather abrupt soul, demanded to know what form these disclosures would take, and one member replied to him, as though breaking a confidence, that one could always recognize gentlemanly dress because the buttons on the sleeves of a gentleman's coat actually buttoned and unbuttoned, while one recognized gentlemanly behavior in his keeping the buttons scrupulously fastened, so that his sleeves never called attention to this fact.

Miniaturization extended down into the ranks of the petite bourgeoisie and upper working classes. The use of lace frills becomes in the 1840's a mark of social standing, a mark gentlemen could not pick up. The sheer cleanliness of small articles of clothing like the neckband may be enough for a shopkeeper, inspecting someone to whom he is introduced, to decide whether he is one of us or not.

The characters of loose and respectable women were read through the same combination of inflation and miniaturization. In his study of Victorian sexuality, *The Other Victorians,* Steven Marcus has shown how the medical and social picture of the mid-19th Century prostitute laid great stress on her resemblance to the ordinary respectable woman. Here is Acton, a physician, on the physical similarities:

> If we compare the prostitute at thirty-five with her sister, who perhaps is the married mother of a family, or has been a toiling slave for years in the over-heated laboratories of fashion, we shall seldom find that the constitutional ravages thought to be necessary consequences of prostitution exceed those attributable to the cares of a family.

Nor in street behavior do loose women show themselves specially. They give off small clues only, a glance held too long, a gesture of languor, which a man who knows how to read will understand.[46]

This similarity worked from the other side as well. How was a respectable woman to set herself off from a loose one, let alone a fallen woman, if the resemblance was so close? How could she, presumably innocent and pure, pick up the knowledge to guide her? There arose out of this dilemma a need to pay great attention to details of appearance and to hold oneself in, for fear of being read wrong or maliciously; indeed, who knew, perhaps if one gave off miniature signals of being loose, one really was.

Miniaturization operated, in the perception of "looseness," in terms of the body itself. Since the major limbs of the body were covered, and since the shape of the female body dressed bore no relationship to the body undressed, little things like the slight discoloration of the teeth or the shape of the fingernails became signs of sexuality. Furthermore, inanimate objects which surrounded the person could in their details be suggestive in such a way that the human being using or seeing them felt personally compromised. Some readers may remember the piano-leg covers in their grandfather's homes, or the dining-room table-leg covers; it was considered improper for the legs of anything to show. The idiocy of such prudery can so cloud the mind that its source is forgotten. All appearances have personal meanings: if you believe that little gestures with the eyes may involuntarily betray feelings of sexual license, it becomes equally rational to feel that the exposed legs of a piano are provocative. The root of this indiscriminate fear is as much cultural as sexual, or, better, it was the change in culture which permitted the Victorian bourgeoisie to become more prudish than their 18th Century forebears. And that cultural change, leading to the covering of piano legs, has its roots in the very notion that all appearances speak, that human meanings are immanent in all phenomena.

One's only defense against such a culture was in fact to cover up, and from this came the stony feminine fear of being seen in public. To be shielded from light, from the streets, from exposure of the limbs, was the rule for bodily appearance. Here is how one writer describes it:

> Few Victorians were seen closely in strong light once they had passed their youth. At night they were aureoled by oil lamps and gaslights; during the day they lay in semi-darkness. They undressed in the dark; the rich woman would breakfast in bed and come down to the main part of the house when her husband had left for his office, his club, or his estate.

The 1840's were an age in which the hooded bonnet reappeared as an article of genteel dress; later the thick veil appeared as a feature of middle-class garb, one which shielded the face almost completely.[47]

As people's personalities came to be seen in their appearances, facts of class and sex thus became matters of real anxiety. The world of immanent truths is so much more intense and yet so much more problematical than the public world of the *ancien régime* in which appearances were put at a distance from self. In the coffeehouse, in the theater, in one's clothing, the facts of social standing were so suspended or so stated, even if false, that they needn't of necessity raise questions in a social situation. A man might or might not be what his clothes proclaimed, but the proclamation was clear. Through convention, the anxiety about whom you were talking to was less than in the Victorian situation, where a process of decoding had become necessary. Investigative logic is necessary as a means of making contact with the individual who might or might not flourish behind the façade of appearance. If, however, one did not know the rules that governed particular appearances, did not know how to "read" a cravat tied, or the existence of a kerchief worn over the chignon, you could never be sure of your deductions about whom you were meeting on the street. The compulsive attention to detail, the anxiety for facts which has since come to obsess us in so many ways, was born out of this anxiety about what appearances symbolize.

Closely tied to a code of personality immanent in public appearances was a desire to control these appearances through increasing one's consciousness of oneself. Behavior and consciousness stand, however, in a peculiar relationship; behavior comes before consciousness. It is involuntarily revealed, difficult to control in advance, precisely because there are no clear rules for reading the miniature details; they are clear only to initiates, and neither in acting as a gentleman nor in appearing as a woman of absolute respectability is there ever a stable code to use. In sexuality as in fashion, once "anyone" could pass on a certain set of terms, those terms became meaningless. A new set of clues, a new code to penetrate arises; the mystification of personality is as continued as the mystification of new goods in stores. Consciousness becomes therefore retrospective activity, control of what has been lived —in the words of G. M. S. Young, the work of "unraveling" rather than "preparing." If character is involuntarily disclosed in the present, it can be controlled only through seeing it in the past tense.

A history of nostalgia has yet to be written, yet surely this past-tense relationship of consciousness to behavior explains a crucial difference between 18th and 19th Century autobiography. In 18th Century memoirs like Lord Hervey's, the past is nostalgically recalled as a time of innocence and modest feeling. In the 19th Century memoir, two new elements are added. In the past one was "really alive," and if one could make sense of the past, the confusion of one's present life might be lessened. This is truth via retrospection. Psychoanalytic therapy comes out of this Victorian sense of nostalgia, as does the modern cult of youthfulness.

In a more happy light, it thus arose that during the 19th Century in both Paris and London the detective and the mystery novel became a popular genre. Detectives are what every man and woman must be when they want to make sense of the street. Take, for example (although the example comes from later in the century), passages from Conan Doyle's Sherlock Holmes stories—like the following—which so delighted us as children. In "A Case of Identity," a young woman walks into Holmes's Baker Street flat; he takes one glance at her.

> "Do you not find," he said, "that with your short sight it is a little trying to do so much typewriting?"

The girl and, as always, Watson are amazed that Holmes could deduce this. After she has left, Watson remarks:

"You appeared to read a good deal upon her which was quite invisible to me."

To which Holmes makes the famous reply:

"Not invisible but unnoticed, Watson. You did not know where to look, and so you missed all that was important. I can never bring you to realize the importance of sleeves, the suggestiveness of thumbnails, or the great issues that may hang from a boot-lace."[48]

That sentence could easily have served Balzac as a motto; his methods of characterization, too, were based on decoding isolated details of appearance, magnifying the detail into an emblem of the whole man. Indeed, that magnification he practiced upon himself, as with his famous canes, writing to Madame Hanska one day, for instance:

You cannot exaggerate the success my latest cane has had in Paris. It threatens to create a European fashion. People are talking about it in Naples and Rome. All the dandies are jealous.

Remarks like this were, unfortunately, innocent of any irony.[49]

The difference, however, between Conan Doyle's prose and the ethology of Balzac or Flaubert or Thackeray is that the science of reading character from appearances in these "serious writers" was everywhere tinged with the portrayal of anxiety in the acts of reading; it was not delightful, as Conan Doyle made it seem; among these latter writers, it was made to seem a dangerous necessity, one which could easily go wrong, and so lead their characters into blunders, insults, or the loss of favor.

People who lived so that they would avoid detection on the street, sought, as Thackeray so beautifully put it, to "deny to probing eyes a knowledge that should come to none indiscriminately in the city." Theirs was a world of shaded lamps, hooded bonnets, rides in closed carriages. Indeed, beyond all the mystification produced by the machine, the very belief that appearance is an index of character would prompt people to make themselves nondescript in order to be as mysterious, as little vulnerable, as possible.

The theory of this new sense of personality in public appearances can be read in works of great and continuing power which have survived the last hundred years, as in more popular works and popular practices, like phrenology, which today seem senseless.

In the middle of the 19th Century, at a sophisticated level, the word "ethology" was used by J. S. Mill and other writers to mean "the science of human character as deduced from human appearances" rather than, as the word is used by biologists today, the study of animal genetics as deduced from animal behavior. The significance of clothes in this framework was the subject of Carlyle's *Sartor Resartus*, the first "philosophy" of clothes. *Sartor Resartus* is a complicated, bitter satire: Carlyle invents a Professor Teufelsdröckh, to whom he acts as editor, a professor who spouts all sorts of crude idealistic philosophy. Once the reader is ready to laugh at him, Carlyle begins to introduce, step by step, little pieces of common public belief, like the virtue of order and stability, the importance of piety, and so on, so that the reader is drawn into laughing at himself. Gradually, also, Teufelsdröckh begins to say serious things which are not arrant nonsense, but radical ideas—like his belief in an agnosticism untinged with public ritual. As the reader begins to see himself in Teufelsdröckh, he also sees a new Teufelsdröckh, a man becoming a philosophical radical.

This is a complicated game of persuasion, in which clothes and imagery of the body play the central role. The idea of a philosophy of clothes, as Teufelsdröckh originally puts it forward, is made to be sheer nonsense, a vast, flatulent abstraction. By Chapter 8 of the first book, the idea has become much more compelling. The professor says that by ignoring clothes, by laughing at them, by not taking appearance seriously, men

> shut their eyes to plainest facts; and by the mere inertia of Oblivion and Stupidity, live at ease in the midst of Wonders and Terrors.

If clothes are emblems of inner states, what then will men see?

> For my own part, these considerations of our Clothes and how, reaching inwards even to our heart of hearts, it tailorises and demoralises us, fill me with a certain horror at myself and mankind.

Clothes reveal our corruption then, but Carlyle goes a step further. They themselves have the power to corrupt. Appearances are very serious, not only because of what they make "transparent," but also because the wrong appearance, in destructive social conditions, can make you into a bad man or woman.[50]

By the end of *Sartor Resartus*, Carlyle has established a coherent social critique: if men and women would only look at each other, really look at each other's appearance, they would be forced to think of transforming social conditions. They would be appalled at what they saw. Carlyle's tract, like any great piece of irony, has ceased to be ironic by its end: not only are men and women willfully blind, but sight itself has the power to create a moral indictment; all society's ills are *visible*.

Philip Rosenberg has called *Sartor Resartus* "a sort of *jeu d'esprit* but it is the *jeu d'esprit* of a man in very bad spirits." The book appeared at a time in Carlyle's life when he despaired of himself and the burden of the self that each person carried—a dark moment of a hatred of the web of desire in men now become so transparent, so immanent in their appearances. That clothes will reveal a self unbearable to contemplate —this abyss Carlyle can write about only with the aid of irony.[51]

Yet the same method of reading man's character through his physical appearances recurred in a far different book, one whose tone was sober, scientific inquiry, one whose purpose was to demystify that dark self of Carlyle's—Charles Darwin's *The Expression of Emotion in Man and Animals*. Darwin wanted to show that animals have an emotional life, that the means of expressing emotion in animals and men are similar, that the reasons for the similarity can only be explained by evolution. By showing the physiological origins of human emotion in animals, Darwin hoped to move his analysis of evolution into the realm of the evolution of "values and commitments."[52]

The new codes of appearance surface in Darwin's work in the scientific method he employs. This scientific procedure brought the practice of ethology—that is, of reading character from physical appearances—to its most sophisticated point. Darwin focused on the human body itself. He asked: What are the organs, the muscles, and reflex motions of the body which create on its surface an appearance to which an emotional term is attached? Why when men are sad do they cry, why do the brows knit together when someone is deep in thought, why does feeling happy pull the muscles around the face up, but feeling glum pull them down? They are all questions Diderot's actor would ask himself; Darwin took such expression out of the area of high art, however, and showed the natural form which that actor would attempt consistently to reproduce.

Darwin's method is strikingly illustrated in his analysis of grief in Chapter 7. He begins by posing a problem: how can we recognize someone experiencing grief, but whose suffering "is somewhat mitigated, yet prolonged"? He does not answer the question at first by classifying the kinds of stimuli—a death in the family, the loss of a job —which might induce this controlled grief, nor does he try to describe the social behavior of a person who is coping with death or enforced idleness; no, the phenomenon is to be recognized as follows:

> ... the circulation becomes languid; the face pale; the muscles flaccid; the eyelids droop; the head hangs on the contracted chest; the lips, cheeks, and lower jaw all sink downwards from

their own weight. Hence all the features are lengthened; and the face of a person who hears bad news is said to fall.

Darwin is doing nothing so simple as equating grief with drooping eyelids; rather, if "grief" is felt, the organism expresses its feeling by that drooping eyelid. What then is a "feeling," and why does it express itself in these physical terms?[53]

To answer this question, Darwin seems to become even more physical. He describes a set of "grief muscles" in the face, muscles which, when the eyebrows are drawn oblique to each other, depress at the same time the corners of the mouth.[54]

About these muscles Darwin makes two claims: first, that they develop in all young creatures as the creature attempts to shield itself against physical pain caused to the eyes; second, that these muscles work involuntarily, except in the rare case when they are employed by great actors. Darwin's first claim makes sense in terms of the theory of evolution. A "higher" form of life will carry in its structure anatomical features which served lower forms of life in different settings; if the organism continues to use those features, it will often apply them to ends which make no sense in terms of their first appearance in the lower organism. Thus the horse developed, through natural selection, "grief muscles" as a way of shading its eyes from too much sun; those muscles survived in higher evolutionary forms because the same physiological response makes sense in terms of new environmental conditions. Darwin thus understood grief as too much light flooding into one's existence. This to him was no Sophoclean metaphor; the method of explaining surface appearances provides an exact, scientifically arrived at point of origin for the feeling of being overwhelmed, of having too much pain pour in on oneself. That one can portray being overwhelmed on one's face is due to the fact that previously an animal had too much light pour in on his eyes but possessed an anatomical defense.[55]

From the first principle of this method comes the second: if we locate the anatomical rationale for a feeling, we see why, when the feeling is genuinely experienced, it makes an involuntary appearance. This involuntary appearance of feeling was very important to Darwin, as it is in retrospect in comprehending the intense fear people of the 19th Century had of being exposed to one another, of appearing outside the shelter of home. In concluding his argument, Darwin states the idea of involuntary expression at its strongest:

> . . . only a few expressive movements . . . are learnt by each individual. . . . The far greater number of the movements of expression, and all the more important ones, are, as we have seen, innate or inherited; and such cannot be said to depend on the will of the individual.

As concerns the grief muscles, Darwin insists that even among those who can manipulate them voluntarily, the power is usually an inherited one; he cites as his example a family of actors, in which this power of control passed from generation to generation.[56]

To the extent that the expressive powers of man are inherited from lower evolutionary forms, to that extent he cannot prevent his feelings from showing. These muscles of grief, in the appropriate circumstances, will operate beyond his control, as will the tear ducts, the muscles of the fingers, and so on. Darwin has at once succeeded in demystifying the source of sentiment and having created an image of man as so very vulnerable to being fathomed by others: if a man or woman is genuinely moved, that emotion will show, beyond any power of the person to control it. Appearances have become in this great work of anatomical psychology an absolute revelation of character states. Darwin robbed the human being of a sense of having the power to put impression at a distance from expression.

Darwin's work typifies his age, not in his interpretation of emotion through the principles of evolution, but in terms of his method, the method of using appearances as indices of history, character, or moral predisposition. In the medical schools, this method appeared in such "sciences" as that of the Bertillon measurements, in which disposition to criminal behavior was predicted by cranial shape. The phrenology which the young Sigmund Freud studied was merely the logical application of these Bertillon measurements to the interior of the skull: passion of a sexual nature being thought by 1890 to be concentrated in the right frontal lobe, anger at the middle of the base of the medulla, and so on. Indeed, at an early point in his thinking, Freud thought that the id, ego, and superego were located in different parts of the brain. The idea of the involuntary appearance of character upon the body surface was, above all, expressed in the sexual imagery of the mid-19th Century. Male masturbation, as a sign of degenerate weakness, involuntarily produced hair on the palm of the masturbatory hand; female masturbation, by contrast, was thought to cause the hairs of the pubis to fall out.

Is it any wonder that women should be afraid of showing themselves in public, overdressed as they were, if the principle of involuntary expression were true? One shielded oneself from the gaze of others, because one believed that they could read the innermost secrets of one's feelings at a glance.

Today, a person trying not to feel seems headed toward disaster. A century ago, perhaps a whole class of people did experience a psychic disaster because of their attempts to ignore or suppress their impulses. But the reason they attempted to do this was logical. This was their way of coping with the confusion of public and private life. If once an emotion is clearly felt it is involuntarily shown even to strangers, then the only way to shield oneself is to try to stop feeling, in particular to suppress one's sexual feeling. The physical deformation of the body through clothing makes sense in the same terms: when the body is twisted out of any natural shape, it will cease to speak; if one has effaced all traces of nature, one has reduced one's vulnerability in the eyes of others. Perhaps Victorian prudery was an "irrational passion in the name of denying passion" (Lytton Strachey), perhaps it was the "complement of the repression of others to repress oneself" (Bakunin); it was also a simple attempt to protect oneself from others—a protection thought necessary, given the new psychological sense of public life.

This is a far cry from Fielding, who believed that appearances, at a distance from the self, ought therefore to accustom us to praising or blaming the appearance, the act, and not the actor. Carlyle's readers were no more willing to be radicalized by him than to be forced to accept the theory of evolution by Darwin, but the method of these great writers had its popular reflection in medicine, in criminology, and in religious counsel about sex, as in clothing.

THE STAGE TELLS A TRUTH THE STREET NO LONGER TELLS

The intrusion of personality into the public realm radically altered the bridge in codes of belief between stage and street. In the late 1830's public taste began to demand that the appearances actors made on stage be subject to none of the trials of ethology in the street. The public began to demand that, in art at least, one really could tell, and without difficulty, who someone was by looking at him or her. This desire for believable and true appearances on the stage first surfaced as a demand for accuracy in historical costuming.

In the 1830's there occurs on the stage a passionate if often inept attempt to have characters in plays wear costumes which were absolutely correct and accurate re-creations from the period in which the plays were set. The attempt as such was not new. Ever since the days of Madame Favart—who, we have already seen, appeared on the boards as a peasant accurately dressed, and in 1761 as a Turkish princess dressed in a costume actually imported from Turkey—the impulse existed on both the London and the Paris stage. But in the 1830's, and for the next several decades, historicism acquired a force it had not previously had. The public demanded accuracy in order to create the "necessary illusion" of the theater—a phrase of Moyr Smith's we shall have to ponder at some length.[57]

Here is how Charles Kean, the son of the great 18th Century actor, mounted Shakespeare in the middle of the 19th Century. In *Macbeth* (1853), *Richard III* (1854), *Henry VIII* (1854), and *The Winter's Tale*

(1856) he attempted an exact reconstruction in both costume and scenery of the epochs in which each play was set. Months of research were spent on each task of reconstruction, and an Oxford don was enlisted in the effort, one who agreed to accept Kean's handsome fees only if his name were kept secret in the "mummer's work." In the playbill for *Richard III,* Kean informed the audience, in James Laver's words, "that he had chosen the play because it offered an opportunity of depicting a different historical epoch from those already produced. He names his historical authorities . . . and vouches for the absolute authenticity of all his details."[58]

It would be a mistake to view this historicism as an isolated incident of costume history. The same insistence on a believable appearance extended even into allegorical or mythological costuming. Le Compte's collection of mid-18th Century costumes showed mythological characters like Zephyr or Eros who were dressed in terms of material draped over an inert body. By contrast, in the drama collection of the Lincoln Center Library of the Performing Arts in New York, there is an extraordinary collection of costumes from the Théâtre de la Porte St.-Martin and its productions in the middle of the 19th Century. Gravures 131 and 132 show how characters in a mythological play, *The Kingdom of the Fishes,* were dressed a century after Zephyr and Eros.[59]

Each actor portraying a fish wore a mask which rather exactly reproduced the head of a fish, and the particular variety of fish at that, rather than "fish" in general. One woman appeared in the head of a sea bass, several men appeared in the head of lungfish, and so on. Furthermore, the body costumes were covered with scales, so that you really knew this was a fish in front of you, not just a fantastic figure who happened to be portraying a fish. The king of the fish, in the center of these gravures, wore a crown. The crown had a tail on top and its shape corresponds to the tail of the real fish whose head the king's own head mask was based on.[60]

In this same collection are pictures of the costumes worn in *Les Mystères de Paris,* a popular melodrama of the 1830's and 1840's based on Mercier. The characters in *Les Mystères de Paris* were presented as enigmas of lower-class Paris not easily understood by the bourgeois outsider; the costumes were painstaking attempts to produce figures from the working and lower-middle classes. We are far from the beautiful servants and "picturesque rustics" of the mid-18th Century theater. Edith Dabney's collection of historical costumes, also at the Lincoln Center archives, shows middle-class women's dress reproduced for the stage without any attempt to change or theatricalize the garments— quite the reverse. What you see on the stage is what that person really is. Stage gestures acquired the same logic: the body was to be moved exactly the way bodies moved in "real life"; even in melodrama, melodramatic motion on the part of an actor was in bad taste in the 1850's.[61]

Critics like Carlos Fischer consider the passion for veracity in costume to have been inimical to freedom and imagination in staging a play. We shall for the moment have to put aesthetic judgment aside. On one side of the footlights were men and women dressed so that you couldn't "know" a person by casually looking at him or her. Yet these people believed intimate "knowledge" was contained in clothes. What these people tried to find in the theater was a world where you could indeed be absolutely sure that the people you saw were genuine. The actors really represented what they played. There was no possible deception, no act of deduction which might go wrong. In the theater, unlike the street, life was unshielded; it appeared as it was.

Now this was a remarkable occurrence. Theater historians like Richard Southern speak of the mid-19th Century as the "age of illusion." But in the world of illusion there was certainty. The cosmopolitan city was a world in which physical appearance had no certainty. That is to say, under conditions of illusion, consciously worked at, there was more accessible truth about men and women than there was in the streets. When Moyr Smith spoke of the search for the "illusion necessary" that all these historical forays entailed, what he meant was that for a play to be believable it had to establish a truth of time and place—a truth the players and the audience could not establish in their own lives.

Aristotle tells us that the theater involves a "willing suspension of disbelief." The stage costume of the mid-19th Century capitals transcended this dictum. In the city, society must depend on art to end mystification, to tell a truth which men and women can otherwise arrive at only by an often faulty process of deduction from miniaturized clues. That is to say, the relation between the audience and this art form began to be one of dependence. The theater was doing for them that which in the modern capital they could not do easily for themselves. The divisions between mystery, illusion, and deception on the one hand and truth on the other were in the mid-19th Century drawn into a peculiar form: authentic life, which requires no effort of decoding, 'appeared only under the aegis of stage art.

Thus the new terms of personality altered the relation of stage and street within the public realm. These terms, equally, altered the relationship between public and private. They did so, not only by making private feeling involuntarily manifest in public, but by affecting the basic institution of privacy, the family.

PERSONALITY AND THE PRIVATE FAMILY

At the opening of this book, I mentioned that its preparation has revealed to me problems in my previous work. One of these needs to be raised here. It concerns a change in the institution of the mid-19th Century seen as the antithesis of public life and its discontents, the stable bourgeois family.

The sociologist P. I. Sorokin was the first to perceive that changes in the city in the 19th Century were linked to basic changes in the family. He believed that urban growth caused the family's form to change, from "extended" family to "nuclear" family. An extended family has more than two generations, or more than one conjugal couple within the same generation, in a household. Sorokin believed that the complexities of cosmopolitan culture made it hard to keep the extended family together, and that the simpler nuclear family survived, in Sorokin's phrase, as the "fallout" of broken extended families. Sorokin's student Talcott Parsons picked up on his basic idea and extended it in an odd way. The nuclear family became in Parson's writing a more "efficient" family form than the extended family; rather than the survivor of the wreckage of the extended family, the nuclear family was a positive response to a new society, symbolized by the great city, structured by impersonal bureaucracy, social mobility, and great division of labor. The nuclear family was supposed to be more efficient in this milieu because it tied down the individuals in the family less. Instead, for example, of thinking what a change of job would do to a grandfather with whom one has worked for years and years, now, with one's family being oneself, one's spouse, and children, one has only to think about the job itself and its personal advantages and disadvantages. Thus Parsons brought together individualism, the nuclear family, and the new industrial society.[62]

Fifteen years ago, this was the reigning theory of the modern family—it was modified, challenged, but in sociological circles it was the focus of attention. The trouble was, historians knew it was factually wrong. Bourgeois people in the 19th Century nuclear families never thought of them as instruments of greater efficiency, nor did an unseen hand impel people to behave more efficiently in these families than in extended ones. Indeed, without the support of relatives, people often spun without direction and quickly collapsed in the sudden economic disasters so frequent at the time.

Sorokin's idea of a fallout from disaster seemed closer to the historical record, but didn't suggest much about how life was structured in the family. Furthermore, enough was known to be able to say that the nuclear family, as a form, was nothing new or unique to the 19th Century, nor, as a form, was it peculiar to the big city. What seemed to be changing in the 19th Century was the function of the urban nuclear family.

Writers with an interest in both history and sociology like myself were thus confronted with a problem of connecting family process to family form. As the historical study of the family began in earnest fifteen years ago, we quickly, rather too quickly, arrived at a formula to guide our researches on the 19th Century family: the nuclear family was the tool people used to resist the economic and demographic changes of society, rather than the means of participating in them. The family function was seen as a shelter, a refuge, was not a means of "adaptation and integration" as Parsons said. In a study I conducted of middle-class families in Chicago, *Families Against the City*, I found some evidence to show that the nuclear family might in fact have been counterproductive, for people in it were less stable occupationally, and tended to be less upwardly mobile, than people in the city who lived in extended families. Other researchers, concerned with the position of women, came to view the functions of the 19th Century nuclear family in the same light, as a place for removing women and their children from society, at once suppressing and sheltering them. Marxian notions of privatization were given new life by the theoretical work of such people as Juliette Mitchell and Margaret Bensman, and an exhaustive study of 19th Century writings on child care, conjugal problems, and family imagery has shown the ideology of withdrawal to have grown stronger and stronger during the century. Finally, all this work had as its background the work of Ariès on the family of the *ancien régime,* a work which tended to overemphasize the nuclear family as a new form, but which convincingly showed how by the 19th Century it was ready to assume a new function.[63]

The trouble with this view is not that it is wrong, but that it is analytically incomplete. It lends itself to a static picture of family process, of which the following formulation, from a study of bourgeois family life in Vienna in the later 19th Century, is an instructive example:

> ... *stability* had a high place in the list of virtues. The concrete embodiment of these ideas was a man's home ... the father was the guarantor of order and security, and, as such, possessed absolute authority. And the significance of the home did not end in its being the reflection of a man's success. It was also a *refuge* from the world outside, a place where the tedious details of the workaday world were not permitted entry. For one who was not of the era it is difficult to imagine just what it was like to be born and grow into maturity in such an *iso-*

lated environment, with all the *cares of life* so punctiliously circumvented.[64]

I have italicized the four terms in this statement which add up to a static picture of bourgeois family processes: stability is valued because society is unstable; the family becomes an agent of stability by serving as a means of withdrawal from society; it is therefore isolated; it succeeds in this isolation by encouraging its members consciously, willfully, to avoid intruding the cares of life into family relations. Such an account is unreal in two ways: First, it assumes that the economics of bourgeois life were manageable enough that people could exclude them from family relations simply by a common, tacit agreement not to discuss them. In an age when respectability was founded on chance, economics were not out of mind, even if money was an improper subject at the dinner table. Second, and more crucially, the "isolated, withdrawn" family might make sense in the 18th Century, given its ideas of natural character expressed in the family alone; this family could only be a dream in the 19th Century, given its ideas of personality immanent in all social relations. Of course, bourgeois families wanted to withdraw from the tremors of society; of course, they believed those tremors could be fled. However:

Human relations in the public world were formed according to the same rules which determined human relations in the family. These rules made little, changeable details of personality into symbols; these symbols were supposed to tell everything about the character of a person, but the "data" for these symbols were always going out of focus or disappearing. The family was supposed to be a place in which people could express their personalities; but if they inflated details of family interaction into psychic symbols, they would, against desire, against their will, be experiencing the instability of social relations all over again. In public, it was not the brute facts of economic upheaval which alone produced a sense of upheaval. It was also the new terms of perceiving these facts, of treating society itself as a vast human "hieroglyphic." If family members treated their relations with each other as hieroglyphics, to be understood by wresting a meaning from the details of unstable appearances, then the enemy had come within the place of hiding. Personality would produce again the very disorientation which people were seeking to flee.

Thus, in a book like T. G. Hatchard's *Hints for the Improvement of Early Education and Nursery Discipline* (the sixteenth edition appearing in 1853), the rules for creating order within the family are rules for stabilizing the appearances family members make to each other. Hatchard wrote down all the childhood rules current at the time—"little children should be seen and not heard," "a place for everything and everything in its place," "fortitude is built by early rising." All are cautions against spontaneous behavior. Hatchard explained that only by creating in the child a sense that he must make an "orderly presentation" of himself would his emotions develop, all his emotions from love to obedience to sensitivity for others. But the mother and father are bound by this same rule. For the child to love them, they too must regularize their behavior in front of him. By knowing what to expect, the child develops trust.[65]

Absent in Hatchard is any of the sense of natural sympathy between parents and children found in the 18th Century pediatricians. Emotions are developed, instead; they arise out of the formation of personality; to have a stable personality, family processes must become fixed into "orderly presentations" of people to each other. The parents must be "vigilant" about their own behavior at the same time they are vigilant about the child's behavior. Precisely because personality is created by appearances, relaxation is a danger, for there is no order of nature to fall back on in a relaxed mood. Here is the great difference between the older theory of natural sympathy and the new theory of personality development. Created love demands fixed appearances.

These were the terms on which the modern idea of a personality developed, rather than a natural character expressed, intruded, into the private realm. It was for this reason that order in the family was something more than a reaction to material disorder in the world. The struggle for order in the family process was generated by the same rules of cognition which made people see the workings of the society in personal terms. This struggle for order in family processes, however, has a peculiar affinity with the nuclear family form.

The nuclear family simplifies the problem of order by reducing the number of actors and thereby reducing the number of roles any person in the family must play. Each adult need have only two, spouse and parent: with no grandparents in the house, the child will never see them as someone else's children. The child himself will have only one image of adult love and adult expectation before him; he will not have to sort out what is different about the way you are supposed to behave in front of parents from the way you behave in front of grandparents or uncles. In other words, the nuclear form permits orderly human appearances to resolve into a matter of simplified human relationships. The less complex, the more stable; the less one has to cope with, the more one's personality can develop.

Such beliefs appeared most strikingly in the 19th Century documents which were precursors of the famous "Moynihan Report" on the black family of the 1960's. In the 1860's, social workers in both London and Paris were also worrying about the demoralization of the poor, and linking that demoralization to the family conditions in which the poor lived. In the 1860's, as in the 1960's, a "broken home" was usually taken to be the specific culprit, again with a female as the usual head of household. And in the 1860's, as in the 1960's, what was perceived to be a broken home was in fact a segment of an extended family. The widow or deserted wife was in fact not isolated, but part of a network in which children were passed around from mother to uncle to aunt, in which husbands might disappear to work in another town and then return. The family group became so multi-dimensional as the only possible means of coping with the changes in family fortunes of the poor. Rather than perceiving the extended family as a kind of defensive network, rather than imagining what in fact the catastrophic changes in working-class fortunes would mean to a family if it were indeed a nucleated unit, the middle-class social workers spoke of the uncertain love and there-fore broken spirit of children in the home. Perhaps the broken spirit was there in fact; the point was that in their interpretations these social workers obscured the disruptive power of economics by images of the simple nuclear family as the only medium through which the child could become stable emotionally.[66]

A pattern of historical forces has been at work in modern society which arouses the belief that personality development occurs only through the stabilization of personal interactions; nuclear family life has seemed well suited as a medium for people to attempt to put the belief into practice. If every detail of appearance and behavior "symbolizes" a whole personality state, however, personality itself can come unglued, as the details of behavior change. Order in outward appearance becomes requisite for a personality which coheres over time. Elemental feeling is taken to be "good" feeling. Complicated feeling becomes threatening; it can't be stabilized—to know who you really are, you must sort out the parts, get down to the essentials; in the stripped-down environment of the nuclear family the child will develop his personality traits by removing variety and complexity from his own appearances, and learning to love and trust only fixed and simple images of parents. He can "count on them" to be believable by being consistent. Hatch-ard's advice, echoed by experts in juvenile delinquency like Frederic Demety and Johann Wichern, by a new generation of pediatricians at London Hospital, by Lord Ashley in his arguments to Commons on abandoned children, was to strive to create social relations which re-move the child from the threats of ambiguous or conflicting experience. This was the only means of forming, or re-forming, him into a strong person.[67]

To the extent that people saw complexity as the enemy of durable character, they formed an attitude hostile to the idea, no less the con-duct, of a public life. If complexity is a threat to personality, complexity is no longer desirable in social experience. There is an historical irony in this; the public world of the *ancien régime,* for all its impersonal complexity, was more stable. The very practice of artifice, the very observance of convention, created a clarity, even a formal rigidity, in public.

How well stabilization in the nuclear family worked may be judged from the catalogue of "complaints" in 19th Century family medicine. Complaints were non-catastrophic physical distress with their origins in anxiety, prolonged nervous tension, or paranoiac fear. The "green sickness" was a common name for chronic constipation in women; Carl Ludwig, a physician on the faculty of the University of Marburg, thought its origins lay in the fear women had of accidentally farting after eating, leading to a constant tensing of the buttocks. The "white sickness" came to women who were afraid of being out of doors, even in their gardens, for fear of being spied on or observed by strangers; they therefore exercised so little that the face acquired a pallor. In Breuer's work on hysteria (pre-Freud), such symptoms as compulsive laughing are presented as reactions to depressions at home which prevented the person from being consistently pleasing; the reaction was "so common a complaint among respectable women" as to be almost normal behavior. To be sure, the medical analyses of these complaints were physiological, but the diagnostic reports all radiate from a common scene: a fear of involuntarily, erratically expressing oneself, from one's bodily needs to one's feelings in the family circle. The catalogue of "complaints" found in 19th Century medical textbooks is a testament to the trials of trying to create order in behavior and expression in the home. This may be put another way: when a society proposes to its members that regularity and purity of feeling are the price for having a self, hysteria becomes the logical, perhaps the only means of rebellion. When one reads passages like the following, from Trollope's *The Way We Live Now,* one cannot refrain from a sense of horror:

> [Paul Montague] had been true to her from the first hour of their acquaintance. What truth higher has any woman to desire? No doubt she gave him a virgin heart. No other man had ever touched her lips, or been allowed to press her hand, or to look into her eyes with unrebuked admiration . . . in taking him, all that she wanted was that he should be true to her now and henceforward.

Virginity, purity, permanence of feeling, absence of any experience or knowledge of other men—of these were the hysterical complaints of later life to come.[68]

If hysteria was the sign of the trials of personality in the family, it is no accident that Freud and others should try to counteract it through therapy consisting of self-consciousness about behavior. Most talking therapies before Freud were oriented simply to making the symptoms themselves go away, and allowing the patient to return to a "regular" life, by a representation of the hysterias in great detail to the doctor, thereby, supposedly (and infrequently), purging them in the patient. The idea was that once you talked about your feelings, they were over and done with; they went into your past. Self-consciousness about symptoms was thought a regulatory device; a plunge into the psychic depths was not the purpose of pre-Freudian medicine. "Mastery" was the purpose. Tension resulting in the family through the fear of involuntary expression of feeling, dictated control of surface behavior through self-consciousness. The difference between Freud and his predecessors lay in Freud's willingness to have his patients encounter their deeper, disorderly impulses through talking about the hysterical symptoms.

We are now in a position to state how the modern concept of personality affected the balances between private and public life. A certain line between family and public life was drawn in *ancien régime* society; in the last century the desire to underline it grew greater, but the means of drawing the line grew more confused. The family of the Enlightenment derived its order from a sense of nature; the family of the last century derived its order from human will. Modesty of desire was the impress of nature on character; purity of desire was the impress of will upon personality. The principle of personality created instability in a domain—the family—people were resolved to fix into a tableau.

REVOLTS AGAINST THE PAST

By the end of the last century, people were resolved to tone down some of the anxieties and drabness of this psychological culture. In clothes, the process of de-Victorianizing is supposed to have begun in the 1890's, gathered force in the years just before the Great War when Paul Poiret freed women from their corsets, became full-scale revolt in the 1920's, the forces of liberation losing the battle for roughly the next thirty years, but emerging triumphant in the last decade, an age of see-through blouses, hip-hugger pants, and the like. Such a historical picture is inspiring but misleading. For while there has been a steady revolt against the restrictive clothes of the Victorians, as part of a revolt against their sexual repression, there has been no revolt against the source of these restrictions, the entrance of individual personality into the public domain. Clothes still are taken as a sign of character, and reading the personality of a stranger from the clothes he or she wears still depends on an aesthetic of details. The break between the street world and the stage world of costume has continued to widen, again not in terms of the specific body images we see on the stage, but in terms of the way we decide what those body images mean.

More generally, a revolt against repression which is not a revolt against personality in public is not a revolt. A "cultural revolution" occurs, a "counterculture" arises, and yet all the vices of the old order reappear, unbidden and unexpected, in the new. The persistence has been so common in modern bourgeois revolts against bourgeois life that the observer is tempted to conclude that cultural revolt as such is meaningless. Such an observation is not quite right. Rebellions in *moeurs,* in manners broadly conceived, fail because they are insufficiently radical in terms of culture. It is still the creation of a believable mode of personality which is the object of cultural revolt, and, as such, the revolt is still chained to the bourgeois culture it seeks to overturn.

A good example of this self-defeat when personality forms the goal comes from contrasting two rebellions in fashion, separated in time by the 19th Century. The first was a revolt against the language of the body in the *ancien régime;* this revolt occurred in Paris in 1795, and its purpose was to liberate natural character—to permit *"la nature spontanée"* to express itself in public. The second revolt was in the mid-1890's; it was a revolt against Victorian repression and prudery, but its purpose was to permit people to express their own personalities in public. From making this comparison, we may gain some sense of the difficulty of joining personality and spontaneity, of making liberation of the self a creed, in modern times.

What does the term "revolutionary clothing" mean? In Paris during the Great Revolution, it meant two contradictory ideas of dress, one dominating the years 1791–94, the other dominating the years of Thermidor beginning in 1795.

The first of these ideas is familiar in our own time. Dress in modern China is based on the same principle as dress in Robespierre's Paris, although the actual clothes are different. Clothes are to become uniforms, symbolizing the fact that society is striving toward equality. The drab blouse, the culotte of simple cut, the absence of jewels, decorations, or other adornments, all signified in Paris the absence of social barriers. Robespierre's Paris was a direct attack on the labeling of social station which occurred in the Paris of the *ancien régime;* the labels were simply removed. The body was desexualized—that is, no "frills" were to be worn to make it attractive or remarkable. By making the body neutral, the citizens were "free" to deal with each other without external differences intruding.

Shortly after Robespierre's fall, this idea of revolutionary dress gave way to something much more complicated. Rather than an erasure of the body and its features, people began to dress so as to expose their bodies to one another on the street. Liberty was no longer expressed concretely in uniforms: now there appeared an idea of liberty in dress which would give the body free movement. The natural, spontaneous motion of each other's bodies was what people wanted to see in the street. The *negligée* appearance of the mid-18th Century home was to go public.

A woman's body under the *ancien régime* was a mannequin to be draped. In the first year of Thermidor, it was undraped to the point of near-nudity and became flesh. The *merveilleuse*, the woman of fashion, dressed this way, wore a light muslin drapery which revealed the shape of her breasts fully, covered neither her arms nor her legs below the knees. Audacious women like Madame Hamelin took promenades in the public gardens completely naked, covered only by a thin shawl of gauze. Madame Tallien, the leader of fashion in Thermidor Paris, appeared at the opera wearing only a tiger skin. Louise Stuart wrote from Paris that these "transparent dresses . . . leave you certain there is no chemise beneath."[69]

Mesdames Hamelin and Tallien were the extreme, to be sure. For women further down the social scale, women who had been dressing themselves in uniforms only the year before, these *merveilleuses* set a fashion which was instantly imitated. In less extreme forms, a chemise was added under the muslin. Muslin showed not only the shape of the breasts but, more important, the movement of the other limbs when the body changed position.[70]

To show this motion, it was common for both men and women to wet down their muslin garments, to make them cling as tightly to the body as possible. Dripping wet, they would then sally forth into the streets, in winter as well as in summer. The result was a tremendous outbreak of tuberculosis among the Parisian population. Doctors appealed for dryness in the name of sanity and Nature—presumably the last appeal. Few people listened.[71]

The fripperies of the 1750's wig, the hairdos of vegetables and miniature ships, Parisians of that time found amusing. There was no hint of self-mockery, however, no intended irony in even the most outrageous dress. The idea of play born in Paris in the Thermidor is one in which self-mockery became dominant. It is graphically revealed by the masculine counterpart of the *merveilleuse,* the *incroyable.*

The *incroyable* was a man dressed in the form of a cone with its tip on the ground. Very tight pants, often made of the same muslin as feminine negligees, led up to short coats, and ended in high and exaggerated collars, brightly colored cravats, the hair above worn disheveled or cut close in the style of Roman slaves.[72]

This ensemble was meant to be a parody of fashion. The *incroyables* parodied the *macaronis,* stylish dressers of the 1750's, by using lorgnettes and walking with mincing steps. The *incroyables* expected to be laughed at on the street; they were amused by the envy they attracted; their bodies they and the onlookers both treated as a joke. Bitter parody also occasionally marked the dress of women; the *style du pendu*, or *à la victime*, was a haircut in the fashion of those whose heads were being prepared for the guillotine. A popular entertainment was the *bal des pendus*, where men and women came dressed for the guillotine or painted red rings around their necks.[73]

There are moments in the history of all cities when inhibitionary rules are suspended. Sometimes the inhibitions are lifted for a day or so, as in the Mardi Gras of certain countries, or feast days. Sometimes the city can be for a few years a place where inhibitions established by a dominantly rural society are lifted as people migrate into an urban center that has as yet no restrictive codes of its own. These moments when inhibitions are temporarily removed, or the rules exist but can effectively be ignored, Jean Duvignaud calls moments of urban negative liberty.[74]

Social life in Paris during the Thermidor could be classed as one such moment, and shows what the problem of such liberty is. If one is freed from inhibition, what is one free to be and do? The Thermidorians had no sense that they were taking a vacation, that the rules were being lifted only for a moment so that people could breathe. No less than Robespierre, the man of 1795 believed he was witnessing the birth of a new society. The Thermidorians believed they would bring nature into the public realm. The sense of nature was of the physical, bringing it into public meant people can be spontaneous in their social relations. "Do you think we felt without check when we had no faces, no breasts, no thighs?" a shopgirl remarked to Talleyrand.

From this importation of physical nature into the public sphere came a burst of enthusiasm for physical activity in public. In 1796, it is estimated, over six hundred dance halls opened in Paris; people came to them at all hours of the day and night, unheated and fetid as they usually were. To be in the streets constantly, freely, was a desire the Parisians seldom checked. The sheer importance of the street grew; many all-night cafes were started during that year in the city, with their windows opened to the street; in the winter the windows were undraped. The previous arrangement was for heavy curtains to shield the denizens of the cafe from the gaze of people in the street.[75]

On the streets of Paris in the 1750's the badges of rank were not taken to be indices of character. Now the body became a badge. To be seen, as one was, on the street, to be visible and unshielded: from the sheer muslin draping the body to the removal of drapes on cafe windows, a similar impulse governed. The streets of Thermidorian Paris were to be places without masks.

Some of the elements of Thermidorian dress, the muslin chemise, the flowing frock coat and trousers, continued to be worn throughout the first two decades of the 19th Century. During these decades, however, gradually more and more cloth, adornment, and layers of clothing are placed on the body. The Parisian on the street in 1795, seeking to emulate the simplicity and directness of ancient Greece, began calling clothes by Latin names. This practice, too, gradually disappeared, as did the use of clothing for irony.[76]

The lasting importance of Thermidor dress is not how long the specific clothing remained an influence. It is that here truly was a revolution in culture, a revolution in its essence. Revolutionary experience was available to anyone who wanted it, because the grounds on which the revolution was based were impersonal grounds. Showing one's body in public does not, as an idea, depend on a prior sense of whether or not one is a revolutionary; by performing this specific action, one participates. When a revolution is conceived of in impersonal terms like this, it becomes a realistic matter, because practical activity can make it happen.

When a revolution is conceived of in personal terms, it becomes more impracticable. One has to be "a revolutionary" in order to participate in the revolution. Since most revolutions are confused affairs, and the revolutionary groups have confusing identities, this fundamental intrusion of personality is quite likely to make the revolution not so much a matter of concrete activity as one of symbolic gestures and of change experienced only in fantasy. The same difficulty can attend less extreme desires to change what has existed. This is what happened a century after Thermidor. Once personality had come to govern the terms of culture, personal revolt became in the 1890's a matter of deviance from social norms. Most people who revolted against Victorian prudery in clothes were confused by their own acts, and believed the "real" rebels to be people fundamentally unlike themselves.

In the years which preceded the 1890's, the constriction of the female body reached a new low. The bustle became common in the 1870's and 1880's; it required a cage and numerous stays for its support. The corset also became elaborate and constricting, so that the woman's body was literally in prison. Poke bonnets which deformed the head, and ugly shoes, completed the picture. Male appearance, although not constricted, became equally unappetizing. Shapeless trousers with large checks, sloppy greatcoats, and the low polo collar gave men a rather hangdog look.[77]

In both London and Paris in the 1890's, there was an attempt to rescue the body from these physical deformations. In 1891 the bustle went suddenly out of fashion and was replaced by skirts which were tight-fitting at the hips. Color by the middle of the 1890's began to reign again in women's clothes and in men's. The revolt against drabness for men consisted of a new exuberance in details of dress, in canes, in the color of spats and cravats. When Londoners and Parisians wore these clothes into the provincial towns and countryside, they aroused comment and indignation.[78]

The revolt against the Victorians never compared in sheer intensity to the revolt of the Thermidorians against the Revolution and the *ancien régime;* as Barton tartly notes:

> A century from the time when the liberated citizeness of Paris threw away her corset and her high-heeled shoes, her descendant (and all the feminine Western world after her) constricted her middle to an orthodox eighteen inches and squeezed her feet into patent leather shoes with toothpick toes and heels higher than Marie Antoinette's.[79]

For men, it was still the detail that counted—the monocle, the stick, and the like—and the man was still swaddled in clothes. The refinement of details of men's dress, as in the starched collar, often made the clothing more restrictive than it had been twenty years before. Women had freed their thighs but not the rest of their bodies: the corset remained as tight as ever.

However, the true measure of the distance between Thermidor and the 1890's was not how far women in this later era could undress themselves. It is rather in what people of the 1890's conceived they expressed with these innovations, however limited.

It is worth looking in some detail at a passing fashion of the early 1890's—the piercing of a woman's nipples so that gold or jeweled pins could be inserted. Here is a letter written to a women's magazine of the time in which the author tries to explain why she went through this excruciating operation:

> For a long time I could not understand why I should consent to such a painful operation without sufficient reason. I soon, however, came to the conclusion that many ladies are prepared to bear passing pain for the sake of love. I found that the breasts of the ladies who wore rings were incomparably rounder and fuller developed than those who did not . . . so I had my nipples pierced and when the wounds were healed I had rings inserted. . . . I can only say they are not in the least uncomfortable or painful. On the contrary, the slight rubbing and slipping of the rings causes in me a titillating feeling.[80]

For the same reason women pierced their nipples, they also began to wear silk petticoats which, supposedly, rustled in a seductive fashion.

They began to marcel their hair in order to make themselves "alluring"; they even began to use makeup. What idea of sexuality did they hope to convey? The laceration of the breasts, the use of rustling undergarments and some forms of makeup, meant that sensual appeal came through preparations which were hidden by clothing or which, as in the case of cosmetics, hid the face. No one sees those rings unless they see the woman undressed, the petticoats can be heard up close but not seen. In place of the shielding clothes of the 1840's, the idea of the attractive clothes of the 1890's was to add a layer over the body but under the visual exterior. A symbol of emotional freedom like the nipple ring is still *invisible*. What image of a woman's body itself, however, would a man call to mind when he heard the rustle of five layers of petticoat? It might seem logical that a revolt against stiffness in clothes in the 1890's would have meant simpler garments; in fact, clothes during this decade became more complex and symbolic. They did not release women from constraints; rather, dressing the body now involved adding a new, sexual layer.[81]

The reason for this difficulty in freeing feminine clothes was that sexuality, created by a clothing layer, continued the very clothing idea which took form in the middle of the century, that the clothes are expressions of individual personality.

In the 1890's, the pierced nipples, petticoats, and cosmetics were codes of character which the observer needed to know how to read. An example: the number of rustling petticoats under the dress was in the mid-1890's supposed to indicate how much importance a woman attached to a given social situation in which she appeared. If she positively crackled, that meant she wanted to be at her very best. But she could easily overdress this way as well, appearing too seductive for a given situation, showing in turn that she had misjudged the "quality" of her companions. How to nuance such minutiae, how to balance one's body, was as problematic an activity in the 1890's as it was in the 1840's.

Attempts to be sexual by means of hidden devices like nipple rings, petticoats, or perfume applied beneath the outer garments indicated a very particular, and forbidden, character. To be sexually free was to be a demimondaine, a high-class prostitute. The use of cosmetics had throughout the 19th Century been associated with courtesans. In the 1890's, such famous *horizontales* as Emilie d'Alençon and La Belle Otero were expert in the use of creams and perfumes. As late as 1908, Helena Rubenstein said,

> Make-up was used exclusively for stage purposes and actresses were the only women who knew anything of the art, or who would dare to be seen in public wearing anything but the lightest film of rice powder.

This is an exaggeration. In the 1890's makeup was being mass-produced and discreetly advertised in women's magazines. What is correct is that using such devices to make the body attractive seemed like the woman was committing some kind of crime. Here is Gwen Raverat's memory of cosmetics in the 1890's:

> However, obviously, less favored ladies did use powder with discretion; but never young girls. And never, never rouge or lipstick. That was definitely only for actresses or "certain kinds of women," or the wickedest sort of "fashionable" lady.

This sense of committing a crime is why, in adding a sexual layer to the body, middle-class women tried to make so much of it invisible. The body spoke, but in secret. Cosmetics were the only bold defiance of Victorian mores.[82]

For women ideologically committed to emancipation in this period, clothing became a symbol of a different sort. These women wanted to be free of the idea that their bodies existed for the purpose of attracting men; they wanted their dress to be independent of sexual images. The clothing they chose to express this freedom, however, was the clothing of men; body gestures became mannish as well. In the eyes of those whom they encountered in their parades, all this display of liberation was a display, supposedly, of lesbian taste. The physical appearance of women emancipating themselves from sexual roles and the physical appearance of women trying to make themselves more sexual led to the same end: they appeared to others to be engaging in illicit activity.[83]

In sum, revolt on these terms becomes in society an act of deviance. Deviance is per se an act of abnormality. Feeling free to express oneself, deviance, abnormality: these three terms become absolutely linked once the public medium becomes a field for the disclosure of personality. In the Thermidor, the natural body was a statement of what people in general should look like on the street; the shock this near-nudity could arouse was not couched in terms of the *incroyable* or *merveilleuse* committing a crime. Whereas in the 1890's it was by transgression that a woman, or a man like Oscar Wilde, was free. In a culture of personalities, freedom becomes a matter of not behaving and appearing as others are; freedom becomes idiosyncratic expression rather than an image of how humanity as such can live.

Self-consciousness must play a heightened role in any revolt of this sort, and directly at the expense of spontaneity. The memoirs of the Thermidorians tell what life was like on the streets. The memoirs of the rebels of the 1890's tell what my clothes made me feel like. When the Thermidorian man was self-conscious about his appearance, it was for purposes of mockery, a social purpose, a matter of laughing with others at himself. Personality self-consciousness is rather more inhibiting; experiments with clothes became dangerous or subject to checks in the play of fantasy, because each experiment is a statement about the experimenter.

Deviations have a curious effect of reinforcement on the dominant culture. When people commented on Oscar Wilde's tastes in scarves and cravats, in the years before his homosexuality trial, they were wont to acknowledge his individuality and at the same time to remark that such tastes were a clear definition of how the ordinary gentleman ought not to appear. Kai Erikson has argued that when a society can identify certain people as deviant, it has acquired the tools also for defining who or what is not deviant; the deviant confirms the norms of the others by making clear in a striking fashion what is to be rejected. The irony of the revolt against homogeneous, monochromatic clothes beginning in the 1890's is that each stage of revolt "interests" those not in revolt, and also gives them a concrete image of what not to look like if they don't want to be outcasts.

The clearest sign of the inhibitions on personal revolt in a culture of personality comes in the relations between codes of belief on the stage and among the audience. The artist is forced ever more into a compensatory role in the eyes of his audience, as a person who really can express himself and be free. Spontaneous expression is idealized in ordinary life but realized in the domain of art. The theater costume of the 1890's seemed truly revolutionary at the time precisely because it created expression for the body which went beyond the terms of deviance and conformity. The audience found an unrestricted liberty in stage costume which they could not find in their own street clothes.

In 1887 Antoine, the great proponent of stage realism, launched his Théâtre-Libre in Paris. He sought the most precise reconstruction of "real life" on the stage: if a character, for example, was supposed to be at the stove cooking, eggs and bacon were actually fried on stage. His was the last gasp of that search for verisimilitude which began forty years before. Antoine's theater was soon attacked by painters calling themselves Symbolistes, a group which touched but did not perfectly coincide with the ideas of the poets associated with Stéphane Mallarmé. Led by Paul Forte, these Symbolistes founded the Théâtre d'Art.[84]

The Théâtre d'Art (soon to change its name to Théâtre de l'Oeuvre) sought to make all the elements of the play as free and harmonious with each other as possible. They abandoned the "real world" and its sights and smells as a standard of reference; they saw instead that the form of a drama had a structure, a symbol or symbols, which defined how the scenery should relate to the costumes, the costumes to the light, and so on. Physical appearances should express that form as sensually and immediately as possible.

Through the Théâtre d'Art, Parisians began to see bodily appearances in which expression became fluid, cut loose from the tyranny of ham-and-eggs realism. They saw the body become plastic, and in this sense free of the world, but more than just a statement of rejecting the world. In the theater, the body could adopt as many forms of expression as the symbolic world of the play suggested.

The Théâtre d'Art was avant-garde, but this new sense of body imagery spread to the popular stage as well. The Harvard Theatre Collection has photographs of Sarah Bernhardt in many different roles she played in the 1890's. As a boy troubadour in Coppée's *Le Passant,* she wears tights which expose all of her legs and thighs, a fantastic cloak, and a loose vest. She is neither an accurate historical model of a boy troubadour, as a costumer of the 1840's might have made her, nor is she a fantastication of ordinary street dress, as she would have been in the 1750's. She is rather a composite of real and fantastic elements combined with so much imagination and freedom that her costume has no meaning in terms of outside referents or sources. As *Phèdre,* she appears in classic, flowing robes. They are, again, neither the robes an archaeologist would describe nor an extension of a currently fashionable mode. A belt of gold scales holds these robes at the waist. Every time Bernhardt moves, the robes assume a new form. The body builds an expression, it builds a symbol of the classic heroine: the costumes are an extension of the actress's body at work.[85]

If the 1840's were a period in which people turned to the theater to solve the problematics of the street, at the end of the century people turned to the theater to find images of spontaneity, an expressive freedom not tied to simple repudiation of the street. In both cases, formal dramatic art accomplished for the audience what the audience could not accomplish in everyday theatrics. In the 1840's this accomplishment meant the audience became a spectator to truth—they watched it, they did not enact it. By 1900 this passivity has grown stronger. The spectator at the theater sees freedom of expression, but like the spectator in the theater of fifty years before, he does not see something about his own perceptions clarified. An alternative form of perception is instead presented to him.

This gap is most striking in a phenomenon which steps beyond 1900 by nine years—the appearance of the Ballets Russes in Paris. It is difficult to evoke in retrospect the electricity generated by the appearance of this troupe. They were extraordinary dancers; their movements had nothing conventional, nothing "balletic," but the body seemed to be totally at the service of primal emotion. It was this animal expressiveness of the bodies, and not the Oriental or exotic "atmosphere" of the Ballets Russes, which seized the imagination of the public.

The costumes of Léon Bakst done for the Ballets Russes were at once a summary of all that the Théâtre d'Art hoped to create and yet more insistent, more elemental. Seen in a gallery or display by themselves, they appear heavy and cumbersome. Seen mounted on the human body, as in both photographs and Bakst's fine drawings, the garments and the body become one; what the body does and how the garment drapes it are perfectly united, so that every motion of the dancer has both a kinesthetic and a "photographic still" meaning.[86]

In a way, the Ballets Russes was the Thermidorian city come to life on the stage—but a city now never to be experienced outside the theater hall. There was a famous moment in the history of the Ballets, when Nijinsky, the principal male dancer, made an extraordinary exit from the stage in a ballet in which he played a faun. He leaped offstage, appearing to ascend to an impossible height just before he disappeared behind the side cloth. His costume accentuated every line of the motion. He was like someone who was free from gravity, whose whole appearance symbolized weightless, effortless floating. The audience went wild; yet what chance had Proust, swaddled in his fur coat, what chance had the ladies laced into their corsets and the gentlemen with their canes, high collars, and crushed hats, ever to catch sight of, much less to enact themselves, that freedom of expression when they walked back out to the street?[87]

SUMMARY

Personality in the last century was composed of three terms: unity between impulse and appearance, self-consciousness about feeling, and spontaneity as abnormality. The root of personality was a new kind of secular belief; transcendent Nature was replaced by immanent sensation and immediate fact as the hard core of reality.

In Balzac's work, these terms of personality were made into codes for understanding society, and were related to the material conditions of his times. In the clothing of the midcentury, these terms of personality intruded into the public realm, and there entered into a dialogue with the forces of industrial production and distribution. In the nuclear family of the time, for all the desire to stabilize personal relations and withdraw from society, these same terms of personality disturbed the family process. And in the rebellions against the public culture of the midcentury, the compulsive interest in personal expression in public remained unchallenged, inhibiting both the scope and the spontaneity of rebellion, and widening the gap between appearances in everyday life and appearances on the stage.

Out of this entrance of personality into society and its intersection with industrial capitalism in public, there were produced all of the signals of psychic distress about the new terms of public culture: fear of involuntary exposure of character, superimposition of public and private imagery, defensive withdrawal from feeling, and increasing passivity. No wonder a sense of foreboding, no wonder a darkness hangs over this period. As the reality people could believe in transformed itself to what they could immediately experience, a kind of terror about the immanent entered their lives.

The very drama of public life takes us back to Balzac. The respectable woman dressing worries that "revealing details" of her appearance might suggest bad things about her character; the bankers scrutinize each other for clues of gentlemanliness. While his subjects were thus deforming the idea of a public appearance which they inherited, so that they were becoming more serious and less expressive everyday actors than their forefathers, Balzac took these terms and wrought from them a truly new *theatrum mundi*, a *comédie humaine*.

It is an irony: the modern reader, encountering Balzac's world, is led consistently and purposefully by the writer to think "this is what Paris is like; here is an example of how the world works." Balzac's contemporaries used the same tools of perceiving, and with them had greater and greater difficulty in understanding how the world works. Only a great artist now could accomplish the tasks of public expression which in the 1750's had been accomplished in everyday life.

Donald Fanger has summarized the task of novelists of the city like Balzac and Dickens very well. In his words,

> each was admonishing his readers, in effect, "The old assumptions, the old categories are no longer valid; we must try to see afresh." The comfortable certainty of Fielding, for instance, that he could take as his subject human nature and simply illustrate it . . . was no longer available to them. Theirs was not the familiar daylight world; Apollo did not reign there, and beauty itself was dethroned.[88]

CHAPTER 9

THE PUBLIC MEN
OF THE 19ᵀᴴ CENTURY

When personality entered the public realm, the identity of the public man split in two. A few people continued to express themselves actively in public, continued the imagery of man-as-actor which oriented the *ancien régime*. These active few had by the mid-19th Century become professionals at it, though; they were skilled performers. Another identity grew up alongside this one; it was that of the spectator. And this spectator did not participate in public life so much as he steeled himself to observe it. Unsure of his feelings and convinced that, whatever they were, they were expressed wholly beyond his will, this man did not desert public society. He clung to the belief that outside the home, in the cosmopolitan crowd, there were important experiences for a person to have; unlike his predecessor in the *ancien régime,* for him this fulfillment in public was to be not of his social being, but of his personality. If he could only prepare himself, above all if he could discipline himself to silence in public, things would happen to his feelings which as an individual he could not make happen for himself.

Passive in public yet still believing in public life, the spectator shows how by the middle of the last century a new secular order intersected with a surviving *ancien régime* belief. From all that has been said of the effects of immanence and immanent personality, it is easily seen that the public man might feel more comfortable as a witness to someone else's expression than as an active conveyor of expression himself; in different ways this attitude appeared in the costuming tastes of the 1840's and the 1890's. And so, the sheer survival of belief in public life might seem to be a necessary survival, a means for the spectator of having a realm in which to observe. But the survival of that public geography, when allied to personality, produced something more.

The spectator, an isolated figure, hoped to accomplish tasks of personality which he felt he could not accomplish when he actively exchanged with others. In his social interactions his feelings became confused and unstable; by making himself passive, he hoped he would be aroused to feel more. This hope was more than a desire for titillation, for sensory stimulation by keeping still. In public, people, especially males, hoped at least to witness what life was like outside the rigidities of the propriety they experienced in the family. In silence, watching life go by, a man was at last free. Thus, the survival of a public realm on the new terms set up a fundamental antithesis of modern life: the modes of free personal development as opposed to, at war with, the modes of social interaction, as embodied in the family. This survival of public life, ironically, permitted personality and sociability to become mutually hostile forces.

In the last century the impact of personality on the public identity of the few who were active caused a remarkable change. Politicians began to be judged as believable by whether or not they aroused the same belief in their personalities which actors did when on stage. The content of political belief recedes as in public, people become more interested in the content of the politician's life. Wilkes foreshadowed this; a century later the political personality is now defined by crowds in specific terms, those of the purity of his impulses, and what the politician believes has become less and less important in deciding whether or not to believe in him.

The public actor is misleadingly simple a figure if we speak of him as dominating a crowd of silent spectators. The public personality does dominate the silent spectators in a brute sense—they no longer "point" or "settle" him. But the term "domination" has two misleading overtones. The silent spectators need to see in the public actor certain traits of personality, whether he possesses them or not; they invest in him in fantasy what he may lack in reality. So to speak of him dominating their feelings is not quite correct, because the frustrations this audience experiences in their own lives arouses in them a need, and that need they project onto the public actor. Again, the image of domination suggests that without the actor there can be no spectator. But the silent observer remains in public even when there is no one personality to focus on. The needs projected onto him are then transmuted; the spectators become voyeurs. They move in silence, in isolated protection from each other, and release themselves through fantasy and daydreaming, watching life go by on the streets. Degas's pictures of the silent, single person at the cafe catch the quality of their lives. And here is in germ the modern scene of visibility in public yet interpersonal isolation.

Finally, the public actor of the 19th Century is a complex personage because, if a performing artist, the appearance of personality factors in his work was more than just a cultural influence upon his own sense of himself. Expression in the performing arts inevitably raises a complex question of personality. Diderot tried to solve the question by denying personality much of a role. In the Romantic era, performers began to try solving it another way.

In this chapter, we shall begin by looking at the Romantic performer's encounter with the new code of immanent personality; he created a new identity in public for himself from this encounter. We shall then look at his audience; this audience of silent spectators survived and grew entrenched, even as the first generation of Romantic enthusiasm ebbed from society. And finally we shall look at the silent spectators in public without one performer in front of them, voyeurs on the streets. In the next chapter, we shall return to the public personality, now as politician rather than artist.

THE ACTOR

In the last chapter we found it better to speak of the culture of personality "encouraging" sexual fear rather than "causing" it. These fears run so deep in Western society that no one age can take responsibility for their existence, only exacerbate or lighten their burden. In the same way, the culture of personality encouraged the performing artist to see himself as a special kind of human being, but did not make him so. For in Western society the performer has a text upon which to base his work, and in the problem of text is contained a source for him to think of himself as having a peculiar character. What happened by the 1830's and 1840's was that the culture of personality had so strengthened this belief, in his own eyes and the eyes of others, and strengthened it in such a way, that the professional performer became the only active public figure, the only person who could arouse others to feel strongly in the public realm.

Every actor and musician has a text upon which to base his art, but he can treat the text in one of two ways. The difference lies in how much the performer believes his own work can be "notated." In music, this means asking how far the system of musical signs printed on the page can actually represent the music the composer heard in his head. If you believe these signs—the notes, loud and soft markings, tempo indications—are an adequate language, then in performing the piece you concentrate on realizing in sound what you, the performer, read. If you believe music cannot be adequately notated, then your task in the performance is to find what is missing from the printed page. The actor has a similar choice. He can treat the text either as a set of suggestions for a character in Shakespeare's or Ibsen's mind, suggestions which cannot be ignored, but leave him much freedom, or he can treat the text as a bible which, once understood, will tell him how to act. In ballet the problem is crucial: can you write down the movements of the body, and if you can, how much should this notation be taken as an absolute guide?[89]

Therefore, the performing arts always have this problem with text: the degree to which a language of notation is adequate as a language of expression. On this hinges the presence of the performer's personality. To the extent that the notation seems to have an intrinsic meaning, to that extent the performer need not feel he must intrude himself; he is an agent, an instrument, a middleman who, if he performs his job with sufficient skill, will make it possible for the spectator to make contact with the meaning contained in the notation. There is a limit to this power of notation. There are very few musicians who would claim that the experience of reading a score is equivalent to hearing it; almost no choreographers who in poring over even the most sophisticated of dance-movement figures would claim they are experiencing dancing. Because of the indirect qualities of performance notation, the fact that the notes, figures, and lines are only guides to another kind of action, the performer can never think of himself simply as a "mirror" or as a faithful executor.

In the history of music, attitudes toward notation and personality polarized into two warring schools in the opening decades of the 19th Century. They did, in part, and ironically, because composers were beginning to notate on the printed page more and more directions than they did in the 18th Century about how the music was to be played. In the Bach Sonatas for Viola da Gamba and Continuo, for example, the composer set down no markings of where the music was to be played loud or soft, and only very rough tempo indications; in the Beethoven Sonata for Cello and Piano, opus 69, by contrast, there are very elaborate markings about volume and tempo at different points in the score. Even more important, literary terms were being brought in by the composer to explain what he felt the classical musical notation could not convey about his music. Such marks as "calmato" or "molto tranquillo" began to make a regular appearance; they became more elaborate in Beethoven's later years, and after his death composers began to use as prefaces whole poems to suggest what is in the music, or like Schumann in his *Kinderszenen,* they used complicated titles for pieces of music. By the end of the century, the composer's attempt to note the character of his music by literary means had become either baroque, as in the case of Debussy, or self-mocking, as in the case of Satie.[90]

How were performers to cope with this increasing complexity of notation? In dealing with the problem, two mutually hostile schools arose. In the first was Schumann and Clara Wieck, and after them, Brahms and Joachim in Central Europe; sometimes Bizet, then Saint-Saëns, Fauré, and Debussy in France. All believed that, no matter how complex or extramusical the markings, the text as such was the only guide to what the music should be; if the language of music expanded, it became a better language, more complete, if also less easy, a guide.[91]

The other school began to take form in the early 1800's, and it is this school which began to connect the work of performing with special qualities of personality in public. It is a school which conceived of music as in essence beyond the power of notation; it viewed the increasingly complicated notation of music as but an admission of this fact. The performer was the central figure in this school. The performer was the creator—the composer almost like his coach. Fidelity to text had no meaning for the more extreme performers of this school, because the text has no absolute affinity to music. Why should they faithfully mirror the scores of Mozart when these printed scores do not mirror the music Mozart made? To bring that music to life, the performer has, as it were, to become a Mozart himself; he is like a magician bringing a figure to life by rubbing a magic lantern. This school began to treat music, therefore, in two ways: first, it was an art with immediate meanings, rather than frozen textual meaning; it thus became an art based on the principle of immanence. Second, the performance depended on the strong disclosure of strong feelings in the performer when he was playing. The new relationship between performer and text was embodied in Franz Liszt's famous remark, "The concert is—myself." The specific actions of the artist, the note or musical line beautifully shaped, were now thought the product of an artistic personality rather than a highly skilled worker.[92]

A similar link between immanent art and personality developed in all the arts under the sway of Romanticism. In *Culture and Society,* Raymond Williams has shown, for instance, how the very words associated with creative activity changed in the 1820's under the Romantic aegis:

> ... The emphasis on skill [as defining an artist] was gradually replaced by an emphasis on sensibility; and this replacement was supported by the parallel changes in such words as *creative... original...* and *genius...* From *artist* in the new sense there were formed *artistic* and *artistical,* and these by the end of the nineteenth century, had certainly more reference to temperament than to skill or practice. *Aesthetics* ... stood parent to aesthete, which again indicated "a special kind of person."[93]

The performing artist had to be, however, a different kind of "special person" from the Romantic poet, painter, or essayist. The performing artist had to elicit a direct response from an audience, a different situation from that of a poet, who may in isolation conceive of his imagery and rhymes as creating a noble self. In addition to the direct presence of his audience, a Romantic conversion of art from skill to self had to be different for the pianist than for the painter because of the performer's different relationship to his medium. No matter how personal he makes it, the Romantic pianist is still tied to a text, often not of his own making, created at a moment other than the moment right here and now in which he is bringing it to life before the audience. The Romantic performer, in making music an immanent experience, has therefore to play a text but also convert it into himself.

Contemporary reviews suggest how we would hear a Romantic musician working to make music seem immanent: pauses, retards, rubato would make the moment a sound was produced important; the deformation of rhythm would usually be at the expense of long lines, disciplined ensemble work with the orchestra, and a concern for the balance and tight weaving of parts. Those, in any event, would be concerns only of a performer presenting a text. The immediate attack, the sensuous tone, the stunning chord—such were the techniques for making music right now absolutely real.

What kind of personality was a musician who could do this perceived to have? On August 23, 1840, Franz Liszt wrote an obituary notice of Paganini's death. He opened his essay with these words:

> As Paganini . . . appeared in public, the world wonderingly looked upon him as a super-being. The excitement he caused was so unusual, the magic he practiced upon the fantasy of hearers, so powerful, that they could not satisfy themselves with a natural explanation.

These words do not exaggerate the public reception of Paganini. This violinist, born in a small town in Hungary, by 1810 was given constant adulation not only by bourgeois audiences but by workers as well. He became the first musician to be a popular hero.[94]

Paganini had an extraordinary technique and was devoid of musical taste. All his work on stage was focused on drawing attention to himself. The audience at a typical Paganini concert might witness the violinist break one, two, or finally three strings on his violin, so that by the end of a difficult concerto, all the notes were being played off a single string. They would certainly hear him improvise cadenzas which were so complicated that any resemblance to the original themes was effaced; the listeners were to be dazzled by a sheer rain of notes. Paganini liked to appear suddenly in front of the audience from a hiding place within the orchestra, rather than waiting in the wings offstage; once visible, he would wait one, two, or three minutes, staring silently at the audience, bringing the orchestra to an abrupt halt, and all at once begin to play. Paganini loved best to start with a hostile audience, ready to boo him, and then reduce them to blind adulation by the force of his playing. With the exception of one English tour, he was universally acclaimed, but the critics could never say what was so extraordinary about him. "One knows he is great, but not why," wrote one critic. He made performing an end in itself; his greatness, in fact, was to make his audiences forget about the musical text.[95]

Paganini captured the imagination of men who at the same time were appalled by his vulgarity. Berlioz, who loved the "idea" of Paganini, was often revolted by his music. This "idea" was that Paganini made the moment of truth in music the moment of performance. Immanent music, however, is tense experience. The performance became a matter of shocking the listener, of making him suddenly hear as he had never heard before, of taking over his musical senses. Just as the composer was trying to make what he set down on the paper live by adding all sorts of descriptive literary terms, the performers of the Paganini school were trying to make their concerts live by making the audience hear dimensions of even the most familiar music that they had not heard before. The immanent and a sense of shock: Paganini's performance of the most familiar piece was like hearing a wholly new work.[96]

The heroic vulgarian thus showed musicians it was possible to reject Schumann's dictum that "the original manuscript remains the authority to which we must refer." It was possible to bring the technical fireworks of *bel canto* singing to an orchestral instrument, the drama and excitement of the opera world within the concert hall.[97]

The essential personality trait of an artist who makes music immanent is his shocking quality: he administers shocks to others, he is himself a shocking person. Doesn't a man who has this power qualify as a "dominant" personality?

When a dominant personality in society is spoken of, the term can have three different meanings. It can mean someone who does for others what they cannot do for themselves; this was Weber's notion of charisma, in analyzing the life of ancient kings. It can mean someone who appears to do for others what neither he can do for himself nor they can do for themselves; this was Erikson's notion of charisma, in analyzing the life of Luther. Or finally, a dominant personality can be someone who shows others that he can do for himself what they ought to do for themselves; he feels in public. True, he shocks his audience into feeling. But they can in no way take this feeling out of the theater and back into their everyday lives. They cannot "routinize" the power of the dominant figure, as Weber's ancient kings were so institutionalized, nor can they form themselves into a community with him, as did Erikson's Luther with his brethren. Under the modern terms, those who fall under the performer's sway can only watch him "be" in public. His extraordinary powers give him the appearance of spontaneous feeling and the ability to arouse momentary feeling in others. He is unlike them, as are all charismatic figures, but he is also permanently isolated from anyone he arouses. This view appears poignantly in Liszt's tribute to Paganini:

> . . . this man, who created so much enthusiasm, could make no friends among his fellowmen. No one guessed what was going on in his heart; his own richly blessed life never made another happy. . . . Paganini's god . . . was never any other than his own gloomy, sad "I."[98]

What are the tasks of personality which this isolated yet dominant figure accomplishes? For the spectator he creates feelings which are both abnormal and safe. He appears to feel spontaneously in public, and that is abnormal; through his shock tactics, he makes others feel. But momentary shock is safe because of his very isolation. Here is no emotional experience the audience must measure against their own powers; after all, he is an extraordinary man. Thus appear both the public identities produced by personality in public: on one side, an extraordinary actor; on the other, spectators who can be comfortable in their passivity. They have lesser gifts than he, but he does not challenge them. He "stimulates" them.

This situation is far different from the control *ancien régime* audiences exercised over their actors and musicians, where what's real for them and known to them limited what the performer could do. When Madame Favart shocked them, they made her change her costume. Paganini's audience becomes enthusiastic at the point when he administers shock. This is one measure of the change from a bridge between stage and street to a new condition of dependence on the stage for images of public feeling. What the taste for accurate costuming suggests in one way—that appearances in this realm tell the truth—or for liberated costuming in another—that only people on stage feel freely—the virtuoso performer synthesizes.

An active public personality depended on a special kind of power. Among Romantics in the arts who qualified as active public personalities this extraordinary power was a matter of unusual technique. Since the union of believable public personality with power itself is going to occupy us more and more as we move closer to politics, it is worth looking in some detail at its first appearance in the formal performing arts.

The necessity of pushing one's personality forward in order to play great music requiring extraordinary technique set Liszt, Berlioz, and the others of the school of serious egoism off from their tutor, Paganihi. Of all who observed the Romantic performer laboring under this necessity, no one captured its musical meaning better than Robert Schumann, who for himself found it alien and impossible. The *Études* of Liszt *"must be heard,"* he wrote, for enormously difficult pieces

> were wrung from the instrument with the hands; and hands alone can make them resound. And one ought also to see the composer play them; for just as the sight of any virtuosity elevates and strengthens, so much more does the immediate sight of the composer himself, *struggling with his instrument, taming it, making it obey. . . .*[99]

What was serious about serious egoism was that the medium itself seemed refractory; immense efforts appeared necessary to wrest music from sound—that is, immense struggle is necessary to make the immediate moment expressive when the raw sound desired was so difficult to produce. From the sense of the refractoriness of the expressive media came quite logically the emphasis on the virtuoso. It is not that the virtuoso is a *better* artist than other artists; only the very exceptionally gifted can be an artist *at all* in this scheme, because only very exceptional gifts will make sound music.

Virtuosity had a social consequence: it was a means of gaining mastery over those who will never understand what one feels or suffers or dreams. Virtuosity was taking charge of that unworthy mob (whose praise one may crave, but this was a shameful secret); just as it is a physical seizing of the medium which is so ungiving, it compels the audience to feel by focusing them on the artist's physical struggle. We are today inclined to smile at this Romantic self-inflation—and yet is it not true that we still believe that only an exceptional performance is an "alive" performance, do we not speak of art as a struggle, do we not think we experience a different Mozart F Major quartet when we hear it played by the Budapest Quartet than when we hear it played by an honest, serious, but uninspired crew? We remain under the spell of the Romantic performers' code that art transcends text, but we lack their passion, and a certain innocence with which they took themselves so seriously.

Being expressive and having extraordinary talent—that was the formula on which personality entered the public realm. This formula was not peculiar to the arts of musical performance; it occurred also in the theater. Most strikingly, special powers, public expressiveness, and a believable personality in public were joined in the melodrama, as the melodramatic texts of the 1830's and 1840's were performed by great Parisian actors like Marie Dorval and, above all, Frédérick Lemaître.

In the last chapter we saw that the essence of writing a melodrama lay in making up a "pure character type," a person on the stage who could immediately be recognized as fitting into the category of villain, virgin, young hero, landlord, young artist, dying girl, rich patron—all examples of kinds of people, rather than singular personalities. The irony of Parisian melodrama was that in the 1830's there appeared actors like Dorval and Lemaître to play these parts who were persons of great individuality; in performing these stock roles, the actors managed to use the texts as vehicles to put across a sense, as the press never tired of repeating, of their own "ineffable personalities."

Dorval and Lemaître began to change the acting of melodramas around the time they appeared together in a play of Goubaux's, *Trente Ans,* in June 1827. In it, they began to speak naturally, rather than in the stentorian full voice which was conventionally expected at moments of passion or crisis. They began to concentrate on details of stage business, to infuse details of action with new meaning. Frédérick Lemaître, in particular, was the first great actor of the 19th Century to realize that audiences could be immensely moved by details of pantomime action. For instance, the classic entrance of a villain was supposed to consist of walking onstage with short, mincing steps, as though afraid to be seen by the audience; from the moment he appeared, you thus knew who he was. When Lemaître appeared in familiar melodramas of the 1830's in the role of villain, he simply strode onto the stage naturally, as though he were just like any of the other characters. This caused a sensation among the audience and was thought to be a *grand geste:* they knew what he was in the play, of course, but by altering such details of stage business, he, Frédérick Lemaître, was thought to show his own creative personality—and not to show something about the hidden depths of the villain's part in the text.[100]

The plays presented on the Boulevard du Crime (the district of popular theater) became occasions to see Lemaître perform. Good melodramas and Romantic plays by 1839 had a chance of popular success only if Frédérick Lemaître played in them, but if he did, then they were thought important plays. This elevation of the text was perhaps most striking in a play Frédérick himself had a large hand in composing, *Robert Macaire,* the most popular drama of the 1830's, in which melodrama, Romantic ideas of revolt against society, and the picaresque hero were first and most successfully united—or were they? Here is Gautier's description of the play:

> *Robert Macaire* was the great triumph of the revolutionary art which followed on the July Revolution. . . . There is something special about this particular play, and that is the sharp, desperate attack it makes on the order of society and on mankind as

a whole. Around the character of Robert Macaire, Frédérick Lemaître created a genuinely Shakespearean comic figure— a terrifying gaiety, sinister laughter, bitter derision . . . and on top of all that, an astonishing elegance, suppleness and grace which belongs to the aristocracy of vice.

And yet the play is today forgotten. Indeed, it is unplayable because there is no Frédérick Lemaître. We cannot say a critic like Gautier was so dazzled by the artist that he failed to see the defects of the text—that is a critical statement which ignores the art Gautier was seeing: it was the creation of a meaningful text by the power of an extraordinary actor.[101]

Frédérick Lemaître received the same passionate acclaim that musicians like Liszt received; he was, unlike Liszt, a popular hero in the sense that the audiences he played to were more mixed audiences in Paris, and the actor was perceived to be a man of the people. The work of an actor like Lemaître also has to be taken into account when we consider the meaning of virtuoso performance in the 19th Century, because it serves as a corrective and a caution to taking only heroic vulgarians like Paganini as models. Paganini's art was founded on exaggeration; Lemaître's, on naturalness. It took as much art, as much exceptional skill, to seem to act naturally in public as it did to twist and deform precisely written musical lines. Virtuosity lay in the power to make the moment of performance seem completely alive, not in the practice of any one particular technical trick.

In becoming the only active public persons, then, the images of these performers consisted of the following elements: they used shock tactics to make the moment of performing all-important; those who could arouse shock the audience perceived as powerful persons and, therefore, as of superior status, rather than in the servant status of the 18th Century performer. In this way, as the performer came to rise above his audience, he came to transcend his text.[102]

THE SPECTATOR

The people who were witnesses to these performers saw their powers at a comfortable elevation. But it would be a great mistake to think therefore of the silent spectator as a comfortable man. His silence was the sign of a profound self-doubt. As the first Romantic generation of public personalities disappeared, the spectator's self-doubt, ironically, grew. Let us take him first when he is focused upon a public personality, and then when he is focused only upon himself.

"Do you want to know something disgusting?" asks M. Pierre

Véron, in his *Paris S'Amuse*, a popular guide to the city in the 1870's. At the Théâtre de la Porte St.-Martin,

> right here in the 19th Century, there still exist primitive creatures who are pushed to the incontinence of tears by the unhappiness of some stage heroine at the hands of a traitor. Don't go to this theatre just to witness the crying candour of these forthright workers, these honest petits-bourgeois. . . . let them amuse themselves in becoming desolate. They are happy in their despair!

To sneer at people who showed their emotions at a play or concert became *de rigueur* by the mid-19th Century. Restraint of emotion in the theater became a way for middle-class audiences to mark the line between themselves and the working class. A "respectable" audience by the 1850's was an audience that could control its feelings through silence; the old spontaneity was called "primitive." The Beau Brummell ideal of restraint in bodily appearance was being matched by a new idea of respectable noiselessness in public.[103]

In the 1750's, when an actor turned to the audience to make a point, a sentence or even a word could bring immediate boos or applause. Similarly, in the 18th Century opera, a particular phrase or high note beautifully performed could rouse the audience to demand that the little phrase be immediately sung again; the text was interrupted and the high note hit once, twice, or more. By 1870, applause had acquired a new form. One did not interrupt actors in the middle of a scene but held back until the end to applaud. One did not applaud a singer until the end of the aria, nor at a concert between movements of a symphony. Thus, even as the Romantic performer transcended his text, the behavior of audiences was moving in an opposite direction.[104]

To cease to express oneself immediately when one was moved by a performer was allied to a new silence in the theater or concert hall itself. In the 1850's, a Parisian or London theatergoer had no compunction about talking to a neighbor in the midst of the play, if he or she had just remembered something to say. By 1870, the audience was policing itself. Talking now seemed bad taste and rude. The house lights were dimmed too, to reinforce the silence and focus attention on the stage: Charles Kean began the practice in the 1850's, Richard Wagner made it an absolute law at Bayreuth, and by the 1890's, in the capital cities, darkness was universal.[105]

Restraint of one's feelings in a dark, quiet hall was a discipline. It is important to know its dimensions. In the latter decades of the 19th Century, audience self-discipline reached into the popular street theaters, but it was stronger and developed earlier in the bourgeois legitimate theaters, the opera houses, and the concert halls. The audiences of the 19th Century could be moved to instant, active expression when they felt themselves subjected to "outrages" on the stage, but as the century wore on, "outrage" became more and more an exception.[106]

The discipline of silence was a distinctly cosmopolitan phenomenon. In provincial houses both in England and in France, spectators tended to be more noisy than in London and Paris, to the disgust of visiting stars from the capitals. These provincial houses, usually one or two to a town, did not clearly separate the working class and middle class, but all were gathered together in the audience. In turn, it was the "gaffe of the provincial," in Edmund Kean's phrase, to respond demonstratively when he or she went to the theater in Paris or London. Véron's image of the boor at the theater, quoted above, was thus both of a lower-class person and of a provincial from nowhere—nowhere being Bath, Bordeaux, or Lille.

The 19th Century was, in Paris, London, and other large European cities, a time for building new theaters. These theaters were much larger in seating capacity than the 18th Century houses; 2,500, 3,000, even 4,000 people were now jammed within the hall. Their size meant that the audiences had to keep quieter than in a small house in order to hear, but their silence is not so easily disposed of, even in a big theater with bad acoustics like Garnier's Opéra. The architectural conception of the theater building itself was oriented to a new idea of spectatorship. Let us compare two very different theaters completed in the 1870's, Garnier's Opéra in Paris and Wagner's Opera House in Bayreuth. By opposing means they arrived at the same end.[107]

Garnier's Paris Opéra is by modern standards a monstrosity. Like an enormous wedding cake sagging under the weight of its decorations, it is an immense, squat edifice ornately decorated in Greek, Roman, Baroque, and Rococo style, depending where one is looking at the moment. It is magnificence raised almost, but not quite, to the level of farce. "The spectator's progress," Richard Tidworth comments, "from the pavement of the Place de l'Opéra to his seat in the auditorium is an exhilarating experience—destined possibly to be his most exhilarating experience of the evening."[108]

This building reversed all the terms of the Comédie Française built in 1781. The Opéra building was not a cover which enclosed people, nor a façade against which the audience consorted with each other, nor a frame in which the actors appeared; the building exists to be admired independently of any of the people or the activities in it. People are to notice it rather than each other. The immense interior spaces especially serve this end. A hawk would be the only creature who would easily recognize individuals in the audience in this vast space, or perceive clearly what was happening on stage. The interior is so ornate that it becomes scenery which overpowers any scenery mounted on the stage.

The magnificence of the Paris Opéra left no room for ordinary social intercourse. Talk and intimate chatter in the lobby were to erode in a building whose sole purpose was to command a "silent awe," in the architect's words. Of his building, Garnier also wrote:

> The eyes begin to be gently charmed, then the imagination follows them into a sort of dream; one drifts into a feeling of well-being.[109]

Such theater-as-narcotic would define Richard Wagner's notion of the evil his Bayreuth Opera House would defeat. But the environment he built arrived, by an opposite route, at the same imposition of silence. Bayreuth was begun in 1872 and completed in 1876. The outside of the building was bare, almost bleak, because Wagner wanted all attention focused on the art being performed within. The interior was striking in two ways. First, all the seats were arranged on the model of an amphitheater. Every member of the audience had an unobstructed view of the stage; a clear view of other members of the audience they did not have, because that was not what Wagner wanted them to go to the theater for. The stage was everything.

In an even more radical departure, Wagner hid the orchestra from the audience's view by covering the orchestra pit with a hood of leather and wood. The music was heard, therefore, but never seen produced. Further, Wagner built a second proscenium arch over the edge of the orchestra pit, in addition to the arch over the stage. Both these arrangements were to produce what he called the *mystische Abgrund*, "the mystic gulf." Of this idea, he wrote:

> It makes the spectator imagine the stage is quite far away, though he sees it in all the clearness of its actual proximity; and this in turn gives rise to the illusion that the persons appearing on it are of larger, superhuman stature.[110]

Discipline in this theater was produced by the attempt to make the stage complete and total life. Theater design was of a piece with the continuous melody in Wagner's operas; both were to be tools for disciplining those who listen. The audience was never to be free to leave the music, for the music never ends. The audiences of Wagner's time did not really understand his music. But they knew what he wanted from them. They could understand they might have to submit themselves to the music, whose unbroken continuity and length would give them, in the words of one critic, a "vision which before the opera existed in their lives they could not have." Both at Bayreuth and in Paris, the audience becomes the witness to a rite, "larger" than life; the role of the audience is to see, not to respond. Its silence and stillness during the long hours of the operas is a sign it has made contact with Art.[111]

Those who were to witness the full, free, and active experience of a public performer prepared themselves by an act of self-suppression. The performer aroused them; but to be aroused they have had first to make themselves passive. The origin of this peculiar situation was a self-doubt which haunted the spectator.

In public, he did not know how to express himself; it happened involuntarily to him. In the domains of theater and music, therefore, by the middle of the 19th Century, people wanted to be told about what they were going to feel or what they ought to feel. This is why the explanatory program note, whose first successful practitioner was Sir George Grove, became so popular at both plays and concerts.

The music criticism of Robert Schumann in the 1830's had the tone of a friend talking to other friends in print about common enthusiasms, or about something new the writer has found he wants his friends to share. The music criticism that took form with Grove, and dominated the rest of the century, had a different character, or, rather, three different forms which led to the same end.

The first explanation to people of what they should feel was the "feuilleton," the program note or newspaper piece in which the writer told his readers how Art made him palpitate. Carl Schorske captured its glorification of subjective feeling this way:

> The feuilleton writer, an artist in vignettes, worked with those discrete details and episodes so appealing to the 19th Century's taste for the concrete.... The subjective response of the reporter or critic to an experience, his feeling-tone, acquired clear primacy over the matter of his discourse. To render a state of feeling became the mode of formulating a judgement.[112]

Or the critic, like Grove, explained how the music worked or the musician played, as though both critic and listener, sensible people, were faced with a strange gadget which wouldn't work without an instruction booklet. Or the critic, like Eduard Hanslick, was professorial; music was viewed as a "problem," to be unraveled only with the aid of a general theory of the "aesthetic." Judgment and "taste" demanded now a process of initiation. Each of these three forms of criticism was a form of initiation.[113]

All were, for their readers, modes of reassurance. These interpretive intermediaries grew up in music because the public was losing faith in its own capacity to judge. Old and familiar music was subject to the same treatment as the new music of Brahms or Wagner or Liszt. The explanatory program note—which from the 1850's flourished in the theater as well—and the critic who unraveled the "problems" of music or drama were the complement of the audience who want to be sure that characters on the stage are exactly as they should be historically. The mid-19th Century audience, at both concert and theater, worried about embarrassment, about being ashamed, about "making fools of themselves" on terms and to a degree that would have been incomprehensible to the audiences of Voltaire's time, who were enjoying themselves thanks to the efforts of a high class of servants. The anxiety about being "cultured" was pervasive a century ago; but in the public performing arts those fears were especially intense.[114]

Alfred Einstein points to a blindness on the Romantic musician's part: he knew he was isolated from the public, but forgot they also felt isolated from him. Audience isolation was in a way comforting, because so easily interpreted as philistinism. The audience, as Rossini remarked, was profoundly worried that all the harsh words directed against it were true.[115]

It was perfectly reasonable for men and women who were having trouble "reading" each other in the street to worry about feeling the right emotions in the theater or concert hall. And the means of dealing with this worry were similar to the shielding people practiced on the street. To not show any reaction, to cover up your feelings, means you are invulnerable, immune to being gauche. In its dark aspect, as a mark of self-doubt, silence was a correlative of 19th Century ethology.

The Romantic performer as a public personality was such that he invited audience fantasy about what he was "really" like. The self-disciplined spectator survived even as the first and most flamboyant generation of Romantic performers passed from the scene. This fantasy investment in a public personality survived along with the passive spectator; indeed, the investment of fantasy in people who have public personalities grew ever stronger and more political in its terms. The terms of this fantasy were double: the self-disciplined spectator places a burden of fantasied authority on the public personality and erases any boundaries around that public self.

We have an intuitive notion of personality "authority" as a trait; it is of a leader, someone whom others want to obey rather than have to obey. But when a silent follower, or a silent spectator, needs to see authority in those who express themselves in public, the fantasy of authority follows a particular path. A man who can both show and control his feelings must have a compelling self; in the eyes of his audience he is in control of himself. This stabilization of himself implies power even greater than, as in the first Romantic era, the power to shock.

Nineteenth Century music shows us this fantasy gradually gathering strength in the changing public images of the personality of orchestra conductors. Many late 18th Century orchestras were without conductors, and most of the musical societies which sponsored public concerts lacked a professional "musical director." In the 19th Century, a special person began to be assigned the task of leading a large group of musicians in public. Berlioz's *Memoirs* shows the composer struggling in the early decades of the century with various conductors, whom he treats with scant respect, as do musicians in his orchestras and the public at performances. A typical insult, appearing in a newspaper of the 1820's, speaks of conductors as "time keepers wound up by nerves and food."[116]

Later in the century, conducting became a recognized musical craft, as the size of orchestras and problems of coordination grew. In Paris, the first great 19th Century conductor on these lines was Charles Lamoureux. He established the principle of the conductor as a musical authority, rather than as a timekeeper; he developed many of the signs that conductors have since used to control the orchestra; in 1881, he established his own orchestra. Other conductors in Paris, notably Edouard Colonne, worked along similar principles. Lamoureux and Colonne were treated far differently from the conductors Berlioz had known in his youth. The question is not whether conducting is a legitimate enterprise but why by the 1890's was so much personal authority invested in this one figure. The respect accorded the late 19th Century conductor by his audience was wholly deferential; in the case of Lamoureux, it approached a kind of hero worship. People spoke of feeling "abashed" in his presence, of feeling "inadequate" to the meeting, sentiments the sons of Johann Sebastian Bach would have never encountered.

These men were not Romantic "stars," that is, prodigies or wizards who won public approval by extraordinary feats. They acted and were treated like kings rather than princes. The conductor created discipline, he controlled a diverse group of musicians; to make them play, he must possess self-control. It seemed logical indeed, as it would not a century before, that a conductor should act like a tyrant. This new category of performer was the appropriate authority for an audience keeping itself silent.[117]

In the same way that authority was invested in the personality of the public person, the boundaries around his public self were erased by those who watched him act. It is instructive, for instance, to contrast the way the French public viewed the actress Rachel, who lived from 1821 to 1858, with the view they had of Sarah Bernhardt, who began acting in Paris four years after Rachel died. Rachel was a marvelous actress, especially of tragedies, and honored as such. The public knew of her private life, found it disreputable (she was kept by Dr. Véron), but separated the actress from the private woman. A generation later, actresses like Bernhardt and Eleonora Duse had no private lives in the eyes of their public. Audiences wanted to know everything they could about the actors and actresses who appeared before them; these creatures were like magnets. "Sarah's real achievement," one critic writes, "was the part of Sarah Bernhardt: personal *mise en scène.*"[118]

Sarah Bernhardt's audience was fascinated with her, yet indiscriminately. Her makeup, her opinions on events of the day, her malicious gossip were all devoured by the popular press. Since the audience had no declared expressive character of its own, how can it be critical, how can the performer be objectified, judged, and put in perspective? The age of gossip about one's servants was over. What would it be like to be able to wear a genuinely expressive mask, to display one's feelings? One devours the details of Bernhardt's life to find the secret of her art; there are no longer boundaries around the public self.

In both the fantasy of authority and the erasure of limits on the public self, we are seeing the spectator invest the public performer with a personality. And that is why in the end it is not quite right to talk about the relation of spectators and actors as the dependence of the many upon the few. The weakness of the many led them to search out and invest qualities of personality in the special class of people who were once their servants.

Let me put this another way: The performer did not make the spectators dependent upon him—that notion of dependence comes from a traditional notion of charismatic power appropriate for describing a religious figure but not a modern artistic personality. The forces which intruded personality into the public realm robbed most of those who lived in public of the conviction that they possessed "real" personality, and so these people went in search of a few who did, a search to be concluded only by acts of fantasy. One fruit of this was a new image for "the artist" in society; another will be a new form of political domination.

The rules for passive emotion which people used in the theater they also used out of it, to try to comprehend the emotional life of a milieu of strangers. The public man as passive spectator was a man released and freed. He was released from the burdens of respectability he carried in the home, and even more, he was released from action itself. Passive silence in public is a means of withdrawal; to the extent that silence can be enforced, to that extent every person is free of the social bond itself.

For this reason, to understand the spectator as a public figure we have finally to understand him outside the theater, on the streets. For here his silence is serving a larger purpose; here he is learning that his codes for interpreting emotional expression are also codes for isolation from others; here he is learning a fundamental truth of modern culture, that the pursuit of personal awareness and feeling is a defense against the experience of social relations. Observation and "turning things over in your mind" take the place of discourse.

Let us see how the focus on a professional performer was first transferred to the focus on a stranger on the street. In "The Painter of Modern Life," an essay on Constantin Guys, Baudelaire probed the figure of the *flâneur*, the man of the boulevard who "dresses to be observed," whose very life depends on his arousing the interest of others in the street: the *flâneur* is a person of leisure who is not an aristocrat at ease. The *flâneur* Baudelaire takes to be the ideal of middle-class Parisians, just as Poe, in "The Man of the Crowd," takes him to be the ideal of middle-class Londoners, just as Walter Benjamin later took him as the emblem for the 19th Century bourgeois who imagined what it would be like to be interesting.[119]

How does this man showing himself off on the boulevards, this creature attempting to catch the attention of others, make an impression, how are others to respond to him? A story by E. T. A. Hoffmann, "The Cousin's Corner Window," gives a clue. The cousin is paralyzed; he looks out his corner window at the great urban crowd passing him by. He has no desire to join the crowd, no desire to meet the people in it who succeed in catching his attention. To a visitor he says he would like to induct the man who can use his legs "to the principles of the art of seeing." The visitor is made to realize that he will never understand the crowd until he too is paralyzed, until he watches but does not move himself.[120]

That is how the *flâneur* is to be appreciated. He is to be watched, not spoken to. To understand him, you must learn "the art of seeing" which is to become like a paralytic.

This same value placed on observation of, rather than interaction with, phenomena ruled much of the positivistic science of the time. When the researcher intruded his own values, "spoke to his data," he distorted it. Within psychology itself, the first practitioners of talking therapies explained their work to the public by a clichéd contrast to the solace offered by priests: the priests don't really listen; they interfere too much by bringing in their own ideas, and so can't really understand the problems brought to the confessional. Whereas the psychologist who passively listens without immediately offering advice understands the patient's problems better because he hasn't interfered with their spoken expression by "coloring" or "distorting" it with his own speech.

It is at the psychological level that this idea of silence and appreciation engages our attention. There was in the last century an intimate relationship between taking appearances to be signs of personality and becoming a silent spectator in ordinary life. At first glance, the relationship seems illogical, because to take someone's appearances seriously as signs of self implies active intrusion, even of prying, into his or her life. Recall, however, the changes in the everyday theatrics of buying and selling which occurred in the department stores: here too was the union of a person's silence with an act of concentration; similarly, in the theater, on the street, at a political gathering, the new codes of personality demanded new codes of speech. Public expression could be understood only through the imposition of restraints upon oneself. This meant subservience to the few who act; it was also more. This discipline of silence was an act of purification. One wanted to be stimulated fully, without the adulteration of one's own tastes, history, or desire to respond. Out of this, passivity came logically to seem a requisite for knowledge.

Just as there was a relationship between silence and social class in a theater audience, so was there a relationship between the two in a street crowd. Public silence among workers was thought by the bourgeoisie to be a sign that, if not content, the urban worker was at least submissive. This belief came out of an interpretation first made by the 19th Century bourgeoisie about the relationship between revolution and freedom of speech among workers. The interpretation was simple. If workers were allowed to congregate together, they would compare injustices, scheme and conspire, foment revolutionary intrigues. Thus, laws like those of 1838 in France came into being which forbade public discussion between work peers, and a system of spies was set up in the city to report on where the little molecules of laborers congregated— in which cafes, at which times.

In order to shield themselves, workers began to pretend that their get-togethers in cafes were only for the purpose of heavy and sustained drinking after the day's labor. The expression *boire un litre* ("drink a liter" of wine) came in the 1840's into usage among workers; it meant, loudly declaimed in the hearing of the employer, that the boys were going to lose themselves in drink at the cafe. There is nothing to fear from their sociability; drink will have rendered them speechless.[121]

Restrictions on the right of workers to congregate were not formalized in England in the 1840's to the degree they were in France; but the fears of the middle classes were the same, and in London the police seemed to have enforced informally the curbs on association which in Paris were matters of decree. The same boasting of alcoholism, the same camouflaging of association, was therefore found in working-class London as in Paris, even though, legally, there was no need for it.

No one can deny the escapist drinking of many workers in Paris, London, and other large cities of the 19th Century. Whatever the balance between real and simulated alcoholism, the camouflage is important because it reveals the connections that middle-class Parisians and

Londoners made between social stability, silence, and the proletariat.

When the cafe became a place of speech among peers at work, it threatened the social order; when the cafe became a place where alcoholism destroyed speech, it maintained social order. Condemnation of low-class pubs by respectable society has to be looked at with a jaundiced eye. While these condemnations were no doubt sincerely meant, most instances of the closing of cafes or pubs occurred not when riotous drinking got out of hand, but when it became evident that people in the cafes were sober, angry, and talking.

The relationship between alcohol and public passivity goes a step farther. Thanks to the work of Brian Harrison, maps can be drawn in 19th Century London of where off-sale liquor stores and on-sale pubs were located in different parts of the city. In working-class residential districts, there were, in late 19th Century London, a great number of pubs and not a great concentration of off-sale stores. In the upper-middle-class districts, there were few pubs but quite a large concentration of off-sale stores. Along the Strand, then largely an office worker's area, large numbers of pubs existed and were used at lunch. The release the pub and its booze provided at lunchtime was respectable; it was a release from work. The pub as a release from home was by contrast degrading. Harrison tells us that by the 1830's

> London tradesmen, however, were by then drinking at home,
> and private, as opposed to public, drinking was becoming a
> mark of respectability.[122]

The ability to exclude pubs, places of noise and conviviality, was a test of the ability of a neighborhood to pass as respectable. Although much less is known about this exclusion process in 19th Century Paris than in London, it is reasonably certain that the *taverne,* or worse, the local *cave* below a retail wineshop, was one of Haussmann's targets in rebuilding the city; he did not want to eliminate them, but rather to get them out of the bourgeois neighborhoods. Silence is order, because silence is the absence of social interaction.

The idea of silence within the bourgeois stratum itself had a related meaning. Take for example the changes in English clubs since Johnson's day. In the mid-19th Century, people went to clubs so that they could sit in silence, without being disturbed by anyone; if they wanted, they could be absolutely alone in a room filled with friends. In the club of the 19th Century, silence had become a right.[123]

This phenomenon was not limited to the great London clubs; in the lesser clubs, silence had become a right as well. But this was distinctively a London phenomenon; visitors from the provinces spoke of feeling intimidated by the silence of the London clubs, and frequent comparisons were drawn between the conviviality which reigned in the provincial clubs of Bath, Manchester, or even Glasgow, and the "deathly stillness at White's."[124]

Why this silence at the big-city clubs? There is a simple explanation; to wit, that London was harassing and fatiguing and people went to their clubs to escape it all. That in large measure is probably true, but poses its own question: why was "relaxation" a matter of ceasing to speak to other people? After all, these gentlemen on the street were not exactly babbling freely with all the strangers they chanced to meet. Indeed, if the metropolis was the impersonal, blind monster popular mythology makes it, then one would assume the way to escape all this impersonality of the street would be to find a place where you could talk unrestrainedly.

To make sense of this puzzle, it will help to compare the London club with the nonproletarian Parisian cafe. Of course, the comparison is maladroit. The cafes were open to anyone who could pay; the clubs were exclusive. But the comparison is also apt because both cafe and club began to operate by similar rules of silence as a public right of protection against sociability.

From the middle of the 19th Century, cafes in various quarters began to sprawl out onto the streets. The Café Procope in the 18th Century did put chairs and tables outside on a few occasions, such as after a big night at the Comédie Française, but the practice was unusual. In the wake of the building of the *grands boulevards* by Baron Haussmann in the 1860's, cafes had much more room to spread out into the street. These *grand boulevard* street cafes had a diverse middle- and upper-class clientele; unskilled and semiskilled workmen did not frequent them. In the decades after the *grands boulevards* were finished, an enormous number of people sat in spring, summer, and fall out of doors, and in winter behind plate-glass facing the street.

Apart from the boulevards there were two centers of cafe life. One was around Garnier's new Opéra; near each other were the Grand Café, the Café de la Paix, the Café Anglais, and the Café de Paris. The other center of cafe life was the Latin Quarter. The most famous were the Café Voltaire, the Soleil d'Or, and the François Premier. In the boulevard, Opéra, and Latin Quarter cafe, the backbone of trade was the habitué, rather than the tourist or the elegant out with a demimondaine. It was this clientele that used the cafe as a place to be in public and alone.[125]

We look at Degas's "Absinthe Drinker" and we see a woman sitting at a Left Bank cafe alone, staring into her drink. She is perhaps respectable but nothing more; she sits insulated totally from those around her. Pointing to the middle class, Leroy-Beaulieu, in his *Question Ouvrière au XIX Siècle*, asked of the bourgeoisie at leisure in Paris, "What are those rows of cafes doing on our boulevards, overflowing with idlers and absinthe drinkers?" We read of the "great silent crowds watching the street live" in Zola's *Nana;* we look at Atget's photographs of the cafe which is now the Sélect Latin on the Boulevard St.-Michel, and see single figures sitting a table or two apart and staring into the street. It seems a simple change. At the cafe for the first time, there were large numbers of people massed together, relaxing, drinking, reading, but divided by invisible walls.[126]

In 1750, Parisians and Londoners conceived of their families as private domains. The manners, speech, and dress of the great world began to feel inappropriate within the intimacy of the home. One hundred and twenty-five years later, this divorce between the home and the great world had, in theory, become absolute. But again the historical cliché is not quite accurate. Because silence created isolation, the public/private distinction would not hold as a pair of opposites. The silent spectator with no one in particular to watch, shielded by his right to be left alone, could now also be absolutely lost in his own thoughts, his daydreams; paralyzed from a sociable point of view, his consciousness could float free. One escaped from the family parlor to the club or cafe for this privacy. Silence therefore superimposed public and private imagery. Silence made it possible to be both visible to others and isolated from them. Here was the birth of an idea which the modern skyscraper, as we have seen, brings to a logical conclusion.

This right to escape to public privacy was unequally enjoyed by the sexes. Even into the 1890's, a woman alone could not go to a cafe in Paris or a respectable restaurant in London without arousing some comment, occasionally being rejected at the door. She was denied, supposedly, as a matter of her greater need for protection. For a worker to accost a gentleman on the street for the time, or street directions, was no cause for anger; if this same worker were to have accosted a middle-class woman for the same information, it would have been an outrage. Put another way, "the lonely crowd" was a realm of privatized freedom, and the male, whether simply out of domination or greater need, was more likely to escape in it.

The 19th Century rules for understanding appearances moved beyond the rules through which Rousseau analyzed the city. He could imagine the cosmopolitan public as alive only by portraying everyone in the city as an actor; in his Paris everyone was engaged in self-inflation and the pursuit of reputation. He imagined a perverse opera in which everyone hammed his or her part for all it was worth. In the 19th Century capitals, the appropriate theatric form was instead the monologue. Rousseau hoped for a social life in which masks would become faces, appearances signs of character. In a way, his hopes were realized; masks did become faces in the 19th Century, but the result was the erosion of social interaction.

In the 1890's, a form of social entertainment grew up in Paris and

London which perfectly embodied the new rules. Massive public banquets became popular in the city; hundreds, and on occasion thousands, of people were brought together, most of whom knew only a few other people in the room. A uniform dinner was served, after which two or three people would make speeches, read from their own or other people's books, or otherwise entertain the crowd. The banquet ended what the coffeehouse two centuries before began. It was the end of speech as an interaction, the end of it as free, easy, and yet elaborately contrived. The massive banquet was the emblem of a society which clung to the public realm as an important realm of personal experience, but had emptied it of meaning in terms of social relations.[127]

For these reasons, by the end of the 19th Century the fundamental terms of audience had changed. Silence was the agent of dependence in art, of isolation-as-independence in the society. The whole rationale of public culture had cracked apart. The relation between stage and street was now an inverted one. The sources of creativity and imagination which existed in the arts were no longer available to nourish everyday life.

CHAPTER 10

COLLECTIVE PERSONALITY

Having come this far in the history of public life, it may be useful to ask, how did the 19th Century lay the groundwork for our present-day problems? Today, impersonal experience seems meaningless and social complexity an unmanageable threat. By contrast, experience which seems to tell about the self, to help define it, develop it, or change it, has become an overwhelming concern. In an intimate society, all social phenomena, no matter how impersonal in structure, are converted into matters of personality in order to have a meaning. Political conflicts are interpreted in terms of the play of political personalities; leadership is interpreted in terms of "credibility" rather than accomplishment. One's "class" seems to be a product of personal drive and ability rather than of a systematic social determination. Faced with complexity, people reach for some inner, essential principle amid the complex, because converting social facts into symbols of personality can only succeed once the complex nuances of contingency and necessity are removed from a scene.

The entrance of personality into the public realm in the 19th Century prepared the ground for this intimate society. It did so by inducing people to believe that interchanges in society were disclosures of personality. It did so by framing the perception of personality in such a way that the contents of personality never crystallized, thus engaging men in an obsessive and endless search for clues as to what others, and themselves, were "really" like. Over the course of the hundred years, social bonds and social engagement have receded in the face of inquiry about "what am I feeling?" Indeed, the tasks of developing personality have come to appear antithetical to the tasks of social action.

The differences between the last century and our own lie in the fact that the last century believed that certain tasks of personality, above all the arousal of spontaneous feeling, occurred only in an impersonal milieu, even if this arousal did not occur through a process of active social participation. Maintenance of a belief in the public realm was linked to a strong desire to escape the family and its rigors. We may today condemn this escape into impersonality, because men were given much more freedom to do it than women, but as the public itself has been erased from our minds and our behavior, the family has become steadily more demanding. It is our only model for defining what emotionally "real" relationships are like. Except for those of us who are very rich, we know no cosmopolitan alternatives. The voyeuristic escape from the family available in the last century should not, therefore, be totally dismissed; at least some people got to escape.

Intimate society is organized around two principles, one which I have defined as narcissism, the other which I shall define in the course of this chapter as destructive gemeinschaft. This social-science barbarism has, unfortunately, a useful but non-translatable meaning. The entrance of personality into the public life of the last century paved the way for each one.

Narcissism, it will be recalled, is the search for gratification of the self which at the same time prevents that gratification from occurring. This psychic state is not created by a cultural condition; it is a possibility of character for any human being. But narcissism may be encouraged by cultural developments and can vary in expression from era to era, so that in some circumstances, it may seem tiresome, in others, pathetic, in others, an affliction shared in common.

Narcissism depends on an elementary part of the psychic apparatus going into suspension. This is "enlightened self-interest," or what is technically called a "secondary ego function." To the extent a person can form in his own mind an idea of what he wants, what serves his own interests, what does neither, he tests reality in a particular way. He judges what's in it for him, rather than if it is him. The word "enlightened" in the economic jargon catches this more clearly than does the psychoanalytic jargon. Any particular reality is "lightened" of the burden of having to sum up a state of being, having to suffice as an expression of the person in it. Once "lightened" this way, it will not be found systematically wanting, as occurs when a person tries to use concrete, limited relations to symbolize himself. Enlightened self-interest also has the connotation of bringing light to bear on a situation, putting it in perspective, finding out what real pleasure a situation offers by defining the limits of the situation itself. I have often thought that the best definition of an ego-function might be derived from this: it is learning how to take rather than to desire. That sounds possessive and domineering; in fact, however, those who have learned to take are more modest than those who are rooted in the narcissism of unfocusable desire.

For a culture to encourage narcissism, it has therefore to discourage people from taking; it has to divert them from a sense of their own self-interest, suspend the faculty of judging new experience, and stimulate the belief that this experience at each moment is absolute. This diversion of judgment is what the entrance of personality into the public realm in the last century began.

We saw in the last chapter how the personality of the artist in public was allied to a problem of "text"; he focused attention away from the text being played. Now we are to see how, when it is a politician who is the public personality, he also focuses attention on himself to the degree that he focuses interest away from a "text." That text is the sum of the interests and needs of his listeners. To the extent that a politician in public arouses credence in himself as a person, to that extent those who are credulous lose a sense of themselves. The suspension of judgment by the modes of passivity and self-doubt we have already seen at work in an artistic public context. Instead of judging him, his listeners want to be moved by him, to experience him. The same thing is true of a political "personality"; his listeners lose a sense of themselves too. They focus on who he is rather than what he can do for them. This process I shall call the suspension of the ego interests of a group—not an elegant phrase, but a useful combination of the economic and the psychoanalytic. This process began to appear in the political life of the 19th Century capitals.

The second characteristic of present-day intimate society is its strong emphasis on community. In its garden-variety definition, a community is a neighborhood, a place on the map; this definition makes good common sense now precisely because of the atomizing of the city which took place in the 19th Century, so that people living in different places in the city lived different kinds of life. This garden-variety definition is much too narrow, however; people can have all sorts of experiences of community which do not depend on living near one another.

The sociologist Ferdinand Tönnies tried to portray the non-geographical sense of community in contrasting gemeinschaft to gesellschaft. The first is community in the sense of full and open emotional relations with others. In opposing this idea of community to gesellschaft (society), Tönnies meant to create an historical contrast, rather than depict two different states of living which can exist at the same time. For him, gemeinschaft existed in the pre-capitalist, pre-urbanized world of the late Middle Ages, or in traditional societies. Gemeinschaft, the full and open emotional communication with others, is possible only in a hierarchical society. Gesellschaft relations by contrast are appropriate to modern society, with its division of labor and unstable classes rather than fixed statuses. Here people will apply the principle of division of labor to their feelings, so that in each of the encounters they have with other people they will engage themselves only partially. Tönnies regretted the loss of gemeinschaft but believed only a "social Romantic" could ever believe it would ever appear again.

We have become the "social Romantics" Tönnies wrote about. We believe that disclosure of oneself to others is a moral good in itself, no matter what the social conditions which surround this disclosure. Recall those interviewers described at the opening of this book; they believed that, unless they revealed themselves every time their clients disclosed something, they would not be engaged in a humane and authentic relationship with the clients. Instead, they would be treating their clients like an "object," and objectification is bad. The community idea involved here is the belief that when people disclose themselves to each other, a tissue grows to bind them together. If there is no psychological openness, there can be no social bond. This principle of community is the very opposite of the "sociable" community of the 18th Century, in which the acts of disguise, the masks, were what people shared.

Any kind of community is more than a set of customs, behaviors, or attitudes about other people. A community is also a collective identity; it is a way of saying who "we" are. But if the matter is left there, any social grouping, from a neighborhood to a nation, could be considered a community, as long as the people in the group could come up with a picture of themselves as one whole. The question is how these pictures of collective identity become formed, what are the tools people use to forge a sense of who "we" are.

The simplest way in which a communal identity is formed is when a group is threatened in its very survival, such as a war or other catastrophe. While taking collective action to meet this threat, people feel close to one another and search for images that bind them together. Collective action nourishing a collective self-image: this alliance stretches from the ideals of Greek political thought to the speech of 18th Century coffeehouses and theaters; the shared speech yielded people the sense of constituting together a "public." In general, we can say that the "sense of community," of a society with a strong public life, is born from this union of shared action and a shared sense of collective self.

But in times when public life is eroding, this relationship between shared action and collective identity breaks down. If people are not speaking to each other on the street, how are they to know who they are as a group? You may say, in that case they will simply stop thinking of themselves as a group; the conditions of public life in the last century show that this is not so, at least in modern times. Those silent, single people at cafes, those *flâneurs* of the boulevards who strutted past but spoke to no one, continued to think they were in a special milieu and that other people in it were sharing something with themselves. The tools they had to work with in constructing a picture of who they were as a collectivity, now that neither clothes nor speech were revealing, were the tools of fantasy, of projection. And since they were thinking of social life in terms of personality states and personal symbols, what they began to do was create a sense of a common personality in public created by, sustainable only in, acts of fantasy. Given the fact that the symbols of personality were in actuality so unstable, that the act of reading personality was so difficult, it makes sense that the enlarging of the terms of personality to encompass the personality of a collective group could work, if at all, only through acts of fantasy and projection.

This, then, is the form of community we are going to study: a community which has a collective personality, a collective personality generated by common fantasy. It is a long way from the garden-variety meaning of community in the city as local life, but then, that garden-variety definition is a long way from encompassing the depth and seriousness of the phenomenon of community itself. Furthermore, we are going to try to see what this sense of community as shared personality has to do with the questions of group ego interests discussed above. Between the phenomenon of projected collective personality and the loss of group interest there stands a direct relationship: the more a fantasied common personality dominates the life of a group, the less can that group act to advance its collective interests. This brutal cause-and-effect took form in the last century, most obviously and seriously in the politics of class warfare.

What has emerged in the last hundred years, as communities of collective personality have begun to form, is that the shared imagery becomes a deterrent to shared action. Just as personality itself has become an antisocial idea, collective personality becomes group identity in society hostile to, difficult to translate into, group activity. Community has become a phenomenon of collective being rather than collective action, save in one way. The only transaction for the group to engage in is that of purification, of rejection and chastisement of those who are not "like" the others. Since the symbolic materials usable in forming collective personality are unstable, communal purification is unending, a continual quest after the loyal American, the authentic Aryan, the "genuine" revolutionary. The logic of collective personality is the purge; its enemy, all acts of alliance, cooperation, or United Front. Broadly stated, when people today seek to have full and open emotional relations with each other, they succeed only in wounding each other. This is the logical consequence of the destructive gemeinschaft which arose when personality made its appearance in society.

Since both the suspension of ego interests and the fantasy of collective personality are politically loaded topics, because they invite rhetoric, I want to deal with each of these seeds of an intimate society in terms of specific events and persons. The suspension by a public personality of the ego interests of a group is studied at one of its first appearances, in the early days of the revolution of 1848 in Paris; that appearance is briefly contrasted with the work of a revolutionary priest in Renaissance Florence. The formation of collective personality is studied principally through an analysis of the language of community in the Dreyfus Affair, in particular Zola's "J'Accuse."

1848: INDIVIDUAL PERSONALITY TRIUMPHS OVER CLASS

A new mode of politics paralleled the rise of the orchestra conductor. At moments of great stress, the bourgeoisie was sometimes able to employ codes of personality in public as a tool to dominate workers in revolt. This transpired through a new agency: the politician who had become a believable, moving public performer, a personality of authority who could impose on his working-class audience that discipline of silence which the bourgeois audience normally imposed on itself in the domain of Art. The result was the temporary, but often fatal, suspension by workers of their own demands.

To speak of the bourgeois politician as a performer dominating the workers is to raise an uncomfortable problem. It is all too easy to look at politicians as conscious manipulators of the public, or as people who understand their own powers. A picture of class struggle in the 19th Century society results, then, filled with bourgeois villains and working-class virgins seduced. But the great, and the true, drama of class domination in the last century lay precisely in the blind imposition of rules of cognition on those below which the bourgeoisie used to dominate and suppress itself. The fact that these rules produced effective passivity during revolutionary stresses, those who employed them understood and appreciated no more than they understood the business cycle that made them rich, or indeed understood that their fears of being found out by their physical appearance formed part of a whole social psychology.

The revolution of February to June 1848 marks the appearance of two new forces in conjunction with each other; 1848 was a moment at which 19th Century terms of culture and of class intersected. It is the first moment at which the codes of ethology, silence, and isolation—the codes of bourgeois public culture—were sufficiently developed to affect the experience people had of a revolution. It was also the first revolution in which questions of class and class conflict were consciously on the minds of those engaged in the upheaval.

In any revolution or any social movement, an observer who desires can discern class interests playing a role. Situations in which the actors themselves speak openly of their own class interests are a different matter. The appearance of a consciousness of class sets off 1848 from the prior revolution in France, that of 1830, in which class was not on the minds of those who may have been motivated by class nonetheless. Capitalist industrial production itself only began to flower in the eighteen years preceding 1848; it was only natural that certain issues present to those who struggled in 1848 were not consciously present to those who struggled in 1830.

It is common to call the revolution of 1830 a "bourgeois revolution." The term is misleading if we then imagine that the bourgeoisie composed the street crowds of Paris, or was at one with those deputies engaged in the constitutional struggle with the Restoration government. This was a revolution led by middle-class journalists and politicians, which gathered behind it in the streets of Paris manual laborers with different grievances all their own; the crowds were a motley group, wherein there were absent only the extremes of the very poor and the very rich. But the term "bourgeois revolution" is accurate if it is taken to represent a certain view of the "people" which permitted this diverse assemblage to draw together for the moment.[128]

Delacroix's *Liberty Guiding the People,* painted in 1831, is the most famous representation of this community called "the people." Up over the barricade, across sprawling dead bodies, come three living figures; in the center is an allegorical "Liberty," a woman in a classical pose but with a flag in one hand and a gun in the other, urging the people on who come behind her. The "people" are, most prominently, on the left, a gentleman in top hat, black broadcloth coat, and on the right, a young worker with shirt open at the throat and two pistols in his hands. The "people" are thus composed of two representative figures led by an abstraction, an allegorical Liberty. It was the solution of the problem of Wilkes's time—the human representation of liberty—in terms of a composite myth of the "people." But it was a myth of the "people" that could not survive. In his brilliant book *The Absolute Bourgeois,* T. J. Clark concludes a study of this painting with the following words:

> That was the trouble with the bourgeois myth of revolution. The very terms of the myth—the story the bourgeois told himself—suggested its own dissolution. . . . If the new revolution really was heroic and universal, if it went to make a new definition of man, if people and bourgeois were true allies, then the people must be represented—and the bourgeois was going to find himself in their midst, one against four, or one against a hundred, a colonial planter surrounded by slaves.[129]

By 1848, this image of the "people" as one body no longer constituted a believable revolutionary community. In the visual arts, there were a few attempts to use Delacroix's 1831 painting as an icon of sorts for 1848; a few anonymous painters tried to revive Delacroix's figures to depict the new revolution, but the attempts were unpopular, and visual disasters. The middle classes gradually disappear from representations of the revolution—even though in 1848, as in 1830, they play a dominant role in leadership. When hostilities first broke out in February of 1848, Daumier moved from the 1831 imagery (as in *The Uprising,* c. 1848) to images of the "people" as the destitute, or the disciplined manual laborer (as in *Family on the Barricades,* c. 1849).[130]

What happened in painting happened in the writings of workers themselves and their intellectual champions. In 1830, *journaux de travail* would speak of their interests as "distinct" from those of the men of property. In 1848 they spoke of their interests as "antagonistic" to those of the bourgeois classes. To be sure, "working class," "proletarian," *"menu peuple,"* and the like had little consistent meaning; the Marxian definitions of these terms were not dominant, or even relatively popular. But it was in 1848 that many workers became suspicious for the first time of middle-class intellectuals who wanted to act as their champions. The worker-writers who founded *L'Atelier,* for instance, expressly excluded white-collar sympathizers from the management of this popular newspaper.[131]

People from all social strata could be found in revolt, then, but only those from the working classes could be imagined to be. The liberal bourgeois in 1848 is truly a man in the middle. He can be opposed to vestiges of the *ancien régime,* he can be for constitutional government, for the expansion of industry, for reform, but at the same time he is on the defensive. He is at once a rebel and the object of rebellion; he is for a new order, but he is for order in and of itself.

Revolutions distort time. In the minds of those who live through them, immense changes appear to be wrought in the social fabric overnight; manners and habits which have been practiced for years or centuries are suddenly abandoned; it is almost impossible to judge the meaning of events, to know whether they are of cataclysmic importance or may mean nothing a day later. The very turmoil of revolutionary events prompts people to disconnect one moment from the next; each exchange of fire, each impromptu speech becomes a world of its own; one wants to plumb it for clues about what is happening, and yet there is no time. Fighting has broken out in the next street, or a speech is to be made across the city, or one simply has to flee.

In revolution, therefore, the questions of how one will make sense of momentary encounters, how one will know whom to believe, become all-important. Codes for making sense of appearances by strangers acquire an inflated importance as history is speeded up and time suspended.

In times of revolutionary disarray, it is common for codes of meaning to remain operative but to jump their normal channels. Aristocrats can suddenly see with the eyes of workers, and feel what in untroubled times they would be too blind even to notice. Conversely, those in revolt can during the moments of upheaval suddenly begin to see with the eyes of those above them, and this vision can obscure a sense of themselves. One may suddenly try to understand what is happening by reference to the world-view of the seemingly more self-assured and educated groups, to make sense of one's own interests—which may be to destroy the groups above. Such a displacement of cognition is what occurred in 1848.

Alphonse de Lamartine played a crucial role in that displacement. Lamartine was, by the 1830's, recognized as a great Romantic poet. He did not fall accidentally into politics; from the late 1830's on, he had interested himself deeply in national affairs. Throughout the 1840's, he was spoken of as a man of finer stuff, more worthy to lead the nation than the bourgeois king, Louis Philippe. When a revolution broke out in Paris, he became the personality most in the eye of the Parisian crowds.

On February 22 and 23, 1848, discontents which had been smoldering for years against Louis Philippe's rule suddenly burst into revolution. Everyone thought of the great days of 1830, the great years after 1789, but this revolution of 1848 was at the outset virtually bloodless. There was something almost gay about it; to Marx, the period after February was "dramatic" rather than real:

> This was the February revolution itself, the common uprising with its illusions, its poetry, its imagined content and its phrases.

In March, April, and May, disorder within Paris grew stronger and stronger. In June, with great turmoil in the streets, the Parisians were put down by violent "forces of order" under General Cavaignac. The nephew of Napoleon I arrived on the scene; by December 1848, he was the overwhelming victor in national presidential elections, and soon after began to prepare the way for becoming dictator of France.[132]

Lamartine, a man of the February days, was supreme in March and April; by June, worn out; in December, he received 17,000 votes for president against the young Napoleon's 5,500,000. Lamartine was no revolutionary plotter in the early days, although his *Histoire des Girondins*, appearing in 1847, revived the memory of the Great Revolution among wide sections of the bourgeois public, making the fall of the *ancien régime* seem a humane event.[133]

To understand why a public personality should give a man power to pacify aroused workers, it is necessary to understand the importance of words in this February revolt, what Marx scorned as "its illusions, its poetry." Theodore Zeldin tells us:

There was suddenly the liberty to speak as one pleased, without fear of the police, to publish any book one liked, to issue newspapers without tax, caution, money or censorship.

An enormous number of newspapers suddenly sprang up, three hundred in Paris itself, with huge circulations. The cloak of silence which we have observed workers to wear in cafes was for a moment thrown off. That Lamartine was valued for his ability to speak in public made sense in this milieu where it was for once possible to speak unrestrainedly.[134]

Let us follow Lamartine through one day, the day of February 24, 1848. All through that day, the provisional government was meeting in the Hôtel de Ville, the building surrounded by an enormous mob of people. The people of this crowd were not the dregs of Paris; they were workers from all strata of skilled and unskilled labor, and most were unacquainted with each other. They were intensely angry; anyone who attempted to hold the reins of power seemed suspect.[135]

Seven times that day Lamartine came out to address the crowd. By evening many of his listeners were drunk; eyewitnesses tell of pistols suddenly being cocked, of a man hurling a hatchet at him. Each time, when he initially appears, the crowd jeers at him; in the evening someone calls for his head. Lamartine's response in the evening, as throughout the day, is extraordinary. He does not plead with the mob or seek to mollify them. He challenges them instead. He recites poetry, he tells them *he* knows what it is to be alive at a revolutionary moment. He calls them fools, he tells them flatly that they do not understand what is happening. He is not condescending; he is outraged by them and lets them know it.[136]

The logic of the situation is that, after the first sentence he speaks showing his contempt, Lamartine ought to be dead. But it is exactly this show of contempt, this refusal to truck with them, which quiets the mob in the evening as it has done all day. Whitehouse, Lamartine's biographer, tells us that Lamartine's defiance abashed the crowd. They became "fascinated" by Lamartine as a person, and began to act penitently. Elias Regnault, an eyewitness, recalled that Lamartine acted "proudly, imperiously"; but it was difficult for him to remember what Lamartine said.[137]

Lamartine's triumphs in February, March, and April were those of a man who disciplined mobs who were calling once again for liberty, equality, and fraternity—by calling them rabble to their faces. He told them he was better than they, because he could express "restraint and power," while they could only emote like animals. When he showed them just how fine and noble were his own sentiments, they became subdued and respectful. Their own demands they put aside in his presence; that is, his personality in public repressed the expression of their interests. He was their conductor.

The events of the next day, February 25, show all the ingredients of this authority in public crystallized: the emphasis on the immediate moment when a politician speaks to a crowd; their sense that his rhetoric is the revelation of a superior personality; the imposition of silence; the temporary abandonment by the crowd of its own interests.

All revolutions have moments in which some trivial issue acquires momentous symbolic value. It can be the pulling down of a statue of an old leader, the destruction of a monument built to glorify a past battle. At the end of February 1848 it was the color of the flag: should the flag be red, symbolizing revolution, or the tricolor, symbolizing the nation? Foreign governments are on the move, plots and counterplots abound, but the color of the flag is passionately debated. On February 29, again a great crowd of angry workers draws around the Hôtel de Ville. Again Lamartine becomes the emissary of the government to quell the mob, so that the representatives of the People can deal with the metaphysical meaning of red cloth.

But Lamartine does not speak to them directly about the flag. He speaks about his own feelings; he compares the red cloth to a banner of blood, and then recites a poem he has made up about banners of blood waving in the sky. Above all, he speaks to them about how he and they are separate and unequal, as long as they resist his poetry. In his memoirs he recalls that he ended his speech by saying:

> As for me, never will my hand sign this decree you seek. Until
> death overtakes me I will refuse to accept this banner of blood.
> And you ought to repudiate it just as emphatically as I do.

Perhaps it was easy for Lamartine to remember these lines; he had written them once before, in his *Histoire des Girondins,* where they were put in the mouth of one of the principal Girondists of 1791. Thanks to the researches of Barthou on Lamartine's oratory, we know that most of his speeches were rehearsed, and that Lamartine often worked in front of a mirror. He gave the appearance of spontaneous inspiration, but this appearance was as minutely calculated as Garrick's study of the tones of his own voice.[138]

What were the signs of crowd passivity? A hostile eyewitness, the woman aristocrat whose pen name was Daniel Stern, gives a detailed account. The crowd had to pay attention to the flow of his words to get what he was up to, she reported, since it was not an ideological question with him, not a matter of what position he took, but how he spoke. What they got when they paid attention was something very static; a glimpse of him feeling. Coming under the power of his performance, Stern tells us, the crowds on these days became "irrationally still." They forgot their own grievances, their own interests. When he told them he could feel without shouting, that he was in control of himself, there was a humiliating contrast to their own noisy, unfocused protests. "He subjugated the . . . passion of the mob by the force of incomparable eloquence alone," we are told. No one really cared what he said, they cared that he could be so poetic and fine. When we say the mask became the face of such a man, we mean that simply being able to generate emotion in public showed that the person acting had a superior, because "authentic," personality.[139]

In this way, the politician used personality as an anti-ideological force; to the extent that he could arouse interest, respect, and belief in the quality of his appearances in public, to that extent he could divert his audience from dealing with either his or their own position in the world. It is this power of personality which horrified Tocqueville, even though he was more conservative than Lamartine and thus the beneficiary of these restorations of public order from February to the middle of May. Tocqueville wrote:

> I do not believe that ever anybody inspired such keen enthusiasm as that to which [Lamartine] was then giving rise; one must have seen love thus stimulated by fear to know with what excess of idolatry men are capable of loving.[140]

Lamartine at work was like De Gaulle at work in the Fifth Republic or, in a bastardized form, Richard Nixon at work defending himself against charges of corruption. If the leader can focus attention on his capacity to feel in public, he can delegitimize the demands of those who press in upon him. But the parallel is inexact in one way. In this 19th Century revolutionary upheaval, the leader succeeded in imposing what were middle-class standards of propriety—that is, silence in the face of art—on a working-class audience, outside the theater and at a moment when the working classes were thoroughly aroused. The modern politicians worked the same suppression on an audience diverse in its class structure. Moreover, no longer is flowery rhetoric itself the fashion; but it is the use, the function, of this rhetoric which connects past and present. What we are seeing in Lamartine during these early fierce days is the power of the culture of personality over class interest. Marx made an appalling error in dismissing the "poetry and fine phrases" of this revolutionary movement as irrelevant to the "real struggle," because it was poetry and fine phrases which defeated the class struggle.

Tocqueville was too unkind to Lamartine, to see him only as the performing puppet of the regime; Lamartine served as its Foreign Minister, and in the judgment of a modern historian, William Langer,

. . . proved himself a hardheaded realist . . . in substance [Lamartine] proclaimed a policy of peace, as Palmerston at once recognized. British opinion, as well as the foreign secretary, paid tribute to Lamartine, who was obviously a man of sense.

But these abilities were not what made him popular with the revolutionary crowd of Paris; in fact, his foreign policy was highly unpopular and considered to be weak. What one has to imagine through the early months of the revolution is that the frequent public appearances of Lamartine served as measures of restitution and rebalancing of the public favor which Lamartine's hardheaded foreign policy destroyed.[141]

One difference between 1830 and 1848, we have seen, was that by 1848 the People seemed no longer a community whose heterogeneous interests could be served by common measures. By 1848, the bourgeoisie were at once the leadership class of the revolution and the enemy in the eyes of the crowd. Lamartine believed in the People in principle, but was unhappy with them in the flesh. He believed the "sentiment of nobility" should govern a nation, but waffled on whether noblemen best embodied the principle. He believed that "poetry" made a nation great, but was uncertain what relationship verse had to twelve hours of labor six days a week, or an apartment infested with rats. Men of Lamartine's class had great trouble, therefore, in understanding the events they led. They were not false Republicans; they were genuinely ambivalent men.

In speaking to the Parisian crowd, Lamartine faced the extreme edge of popular, working-class sentiment during the revolution. In the elections of April 1848, the Parisian working classes often voted for middle-class candidates: only twelve socialist deputies were elected, and prominent radicals like Blanqui and Raspail failed. Yet the sense of antagonism between classes was everywhere. The most antagonistic were the most vocal and active on the streets; they were ready to seize those chance opportunities by which even a popular regime can be destroyed. Lamartine's ability to silence these extreme elements is a testament to the power of personality in public, but also a sign of an ironic limit on public personage itself. In having finally come to terms with the necessity for order day by day, after mid-May the people of the streets quickly tired of Lamartine. They became indifferent, as though they had exchanged their own willingness to be dominated for his person; by May's end, they had squeezed him dry.[142]

If we seek to trace back to its source this power of personality to suspend group interest, we come again upon the doctrine of immanence, the belief in the immediate, which came to rule in the 19th Century. The power of personality is one in which a public appearance at a given moment can suddenly diffuse the weight of the past, the memory of old injuries, the convictions of a lifetime. For a crowd to be pacifiable on these terms, the appearance and behavior of a forceful person must be taken as an absolute situation. Loss of memory occurs when the crowd ceases to measure and test the public figure in terms of his actions, his achievements, his ideology. Such judgment of substance, such attention to "text," would form the ego interest of a group. Codes of immanent meaning are inimical to the exercise of this ego interest. These codes are the terms of modern secularism.

It is common to assume that the crowd is always fickle, a mob easily brought to heel if only a strong man stands up in it. This common-sense assumption is incorrect.

How crowds are controlled, the way in which they submit to a leader, depends on the very principles of belief governing a society. To understand personality dominant over class interests in a modern crowd, I think we have therefore to go back to the differences between secular and religious belief. Let us take as an example the differences between the political personality of Lamartine and a revolutionary priest at work in Renaissance Florence.

In 1484, a young friar sat in the monastery of San Giorgio in Florence, waiting for a friend. He suddenly had a vision of a terrible punishment to be inflicted on the Church by God. Someone would then rise up to lead the afflicted, and, sitting in the monastery garden, Savonarola had a strong intimation that the person would be himself. Within a decade he became, in fact, the leading force of public opinion in Florence. The city was threatened with foreign domination in 1494, and Savonarola, emerging as the representative of the city in dealing with Florence's enemies, became as well the moral voice within the city's walls. He called upon the Florentines to put aside their sumptuous vanities, to burn pictures, books, and clothes which were not chaste. Among the many who responded was Botticelli, consigning many of his paintings to the flames. But Savonarola, like Lamartine, saw his career as popular leader terminate abruptly, saw his power to discipline the urban masses suddenly disappear.[143]

To compare popular leaders separated by four centuries is mixing water with oil. But these two men shared so many similar experiences that certain differences between them stand out in relief. Both Lamartine and Savonarola ruled by power of oratory, neither because he was titular head of a government. The popularity of both was based on the same rhetorical stance: they were the chastisers, the discipliners of those whom they led. Neither appealed to the crowds who gathered to hear them; their message was always rebuke and moral censure. Both arrived at a language of rebuke which was suited to large crowds where few people knew each other; that is, both orators created a rhetorical language that would work with a city crowd—as opposed to a priest speaking to the flock in church or the poet declaiming in a salon. Lastly, their downfalls were similar.

The difference between them we shall focus on is that one was a priest speaking in a culture still pious; the other, a poet speaking in a culture that treated religion as a polite convenience. The divide is not between belief and unbelief; it is between transcendent and immanent belief in the person of a public figure. What difference does this difference in meaning make in the behavior of the crowds themselves?

When Jakob Burckhardt wrote his *Civilization of the Renaissance in Italy,* he put forward a thesis that has been debated for the hundred years since the book appeared. Burckhardt treated the Renaissance city-states as the first secular cities, awakened from the dreamlike faith of the Middle Ages. Burckhardt's analysis was based on the views of such Renaissance leaders as Marsilio Ficino, who wrote:

> This is an age of gold, which has brought back to life the almost
> extinguished liberal disciplines of poetry, eloquence, painting,
> architecture . . . and all this at Florence.

After a century of research, Burckhardt's picture appears historically incomplete, because side by side with this proud worldliness existed feelings much darker and more rooted in the medieval past.[144]

Robert Lopez speaks of a persistent "depression" and "pessimism" about mankind among the thinkers of the Renaissance, a depression not only among the clergy but among politicians like Machiavelli and artists like Leonardo and Michelangelo. The cultured elite is said to have had an "eschatological hunger," rationalists like Pico della Mirandola spending long hours studying the mystic signs of the Cabala. Among the masses of the city, belief in the Church and medieval religious imagery remained strong.[145]

The religious bond was one of the few elements which held the Florentines together. Florence of the late 1400's was a city of great diversity; many non-Tuscans—that is, non-citizens—lived in it, some exiles from their own city-states, others displaced persons come to the city as war refugees. In addition, among the Tuscan population itself, the high death rate of each generation growing up in the city was compensated for not by a high rate of births, but by a high rate of migration into the city from the countryside. The Florentine whose parents were Florentines was a minority figure.[146]

It was to this collection of strangers, whose religion was their common bond, that Savonarola spoke. He was himself an outsider, born into the middle ranks of society in Ferrara in 1452. Twenty-three years later he entered the Dominican monastery at Bologna; the Dominicans called themselves preaching friars, and made the study of rhetoric a religious duty. Savonarola was thus led to work on his oratory as a matter of faith. After some checks in his career in the 1480's, he was ensconced in Florence in 1490, became prior of San Marco in 1491, and for the next four years served as the moral conscience of the city.

Savonarola was no more a clear or original thinker than Lamartine. Felix Gilbert points out that Savonarola's intellectual life was an amalgam of many disparate sources, and his theological dogmas were well-tried clichés. People did not flock to hear him because he gave them a special view of the world.[147]

What he did give them was a simple message about how shameful their lives were, and a simple message about what they needed to do to change. Savonarola's speeches dramatize all the petty details of the corrupt and luxurious life. His favorite device was mimicry: "If I wore furs, look at how silly this robe would be on me." He held up a mirror to those who listened by making them concentrate on him as a person; having shown them how appalling their vices were when they looked at them embodied in him, he would then turn the tables suddenly, chastise them for acting this way themselves, and tell in minute detail how they ought to reform.[148]

Savonarola's listeners were often hostile, violently so, when he began to speak. He talked not only in churches but in public squares, giving impromptu sermons during market hours. Like Lamartine, he put them to shame by focusing all attention on his person and by making every minute exhibition of his own feelings the subject of the sermon. But the priest differed from the poet in two ways.

First, he sought more than the conquest and silence of his listeners. He sought to spur them into action, to change their behavior. Lamartine sought only to pacify. The priest sought a response from the audience; the poet sought only its submission. After all the differences of time and place, of circumstance and purpose, are taken into account, there remains an elemental, structural reason why the priest could speak in terms of reform and the poet in terms of renunciation. This priest, like any priest, is only an instrument of a higher power. All the meaning which is attached to his personality in public comes from another world. As priest, his appearances, no matter how immediately gripping, are never self-contained in meaning. His rhetorical powers always lead beyond his own personality; the audience shows him he is effective by themselves participating in the divine through ritual acts. Recall Bossuet's words: If you are moved by eloquence, you should be more devout.[149]

In Lamartine's world, nothing stands beyond the moment. Appearances are self-contained, real on their own terms; the result is that the audience, once disciplined, becomes passive. All the audience sees is that the speaker is superior to themselves; how then are they justified in anything but submissive approval of him? Because the priest is an instrument of a power beyond the world of appearances, his audience does not become imprisoned in the immediate situation, which is that they are made ashamed, and look to the priest as their superior.

The most famous actions this particular priest spurred were the burning of "vanities" in the city. In 1496 and 1497 Savonarola set aside a day, reviving an old custom which had fallen into disuse, on which the children of Florence would go from house to house gathering up profane or luxurious pictures, furs, clothes, and books. These were brought to a central point in the city and, with much extemporaneous prayer, burned. It was to these children's raids that Botticelli is supposed to have contributed his pictures for fuel.[150]

In Thomist thought, there is a distinction drawn between internal ceremony and external theater. Men and women need external ceremony because they are imperfect beings; the common prayer, the incense, the music are roads to the inside, where the celebration of God takes place. The external theater poses "enamorative virtue." What Savonarola did was move the stage for external theater from the church to the city.[151]

The price for doing away with this magic, with dogmas of the transcendental, with priests and all their mumbo-jumbo, is that the people are highly susceptible to becoming narcotized by a great political speaker. There are no standards of reference, there is no reality, outside the quality of his performance. The priest, however, is always tied to his role as representative of a transcendent power. He may embody divine grace; he can never claim to own it. The priest brings mental idiocy to those who believe in him, but leaves free their expressive powers—indeed, encourages them to share God with him by all the dramatic acts which go under the name of ritual. The secular politician gives his followers faith in the absolute reality of the concrete, the immediate moment, and in so doing destroys their powers to express themselves and their own ego interests. Under religious and secular conditions, the people are taking two different kinds of drugs, the first blocking their heads, the second, their will.

When a discipliner, be he priest or secular orator, says to a crowd, "You are vile," or "You need me," who is the "you" he refers to? The priest refers not to the whole human being, because the human being is not wholly involved in that dramatic relationship, or in any worldly affair. A part of him, the part that God can touch, is always at a remove from the world, and the person's sins of the world. Paradoxically, this is why the priest like Savonarola could say that you are vile and expect you to redeem yourself; part of the "you," your will, is at a distance from your sins.

In modern secular culture, in which the immediate is the real, when a crowd is convincingly told, "You are vile," how are they to cease being so? All of the self feels indicted. The only way to cease being vile is therefore to cease asserting oneself. When the orator says, "You need me," if you believe him then for the moment you surrender to him fully. People are rendered vulnerable to suppressing their ego interests as a group. The issue of emotional inequality stands out more and more in the relations of the orator and his audience. Because this inequality is felt as so absolute in the relationship, the lesser party falls silent. And the anticlericals, natural scientists, philosophers of the phenomenal—all those who have made the immediate and empirical the standard of truth—have unwittingly sharpened this political instrument.

The word "charisma" means that Grace has entered into a person. For a priest, the meaning of "Grace" is that God's power temporarily infuses him, while he administers a ritual, an office, or a rite. For a priest of the streets like Savonarola, we would want to modify this somewhat and say that he demonstrated his charisma by inducing in his audience those feelings which make them want to change their lives. As long as he serves as a catalyst to their own actions of reform, he seems to them a messenger of God.

If it makes any sense to call Lamartine a charismatic performer, we would have to say that he can induce in his listeners a feeling that he has something as a person they absolutely lack. But what this something is, what his Grace consists of, is a mystery to them. "Everyone was moved by M. Lamartine," Ledru-Rollin wrote to a friend, "but I cannot recall his words or his subject." Ledru-Rollin, a leader of the Left-center, did have a strong text to preach to the workers in 1848, a text which spoke to their interests and demands. But he aroused precious little enthusiasm, week after week, compared with Lamartine, whose words and subjects were so hard to remember.

In the years from 1825 to 1848, politicians began to think about their rhetoric and their public appearances in relation to the appearances of stage artists—particularly male actors and male musical soloists. Lamartine, friend and admirer of Liszt, was jealous of Liszt's enormous public reputation, and fascinated by the ways in which, as he remarked, the "popular enthusiasm you draw might be used to rule the world." Ledru-Rollin studied the impact of the actor Frédérick Lemaître on the public, and counseled his followers that they ought to learn why Frédérick was a hero to the Parisian masses if they wanted the Left to triumph in France. Geraldine Pelles has written of a general "transfer" of heroic symbols which occurred in western Europe in the 1830's. The excitement people of diverse views once felt about politics they began to "transfer" to the arts. As the Napoleonic legend faded, the Artist took his place as the image of a really believable public personage. Once that transfer was made, politicians subsequently modeled themselves on the public idea of what artists suffered and how artists behaved, for this suffering and behavior constituted a new standard of heroism.[152]

Lamartine was the first representative figure of the politicians who followed in the wake of this transfer of charismatic imagery. The distance Lamartine's society had traveled from the days of Napoleon was great. After the victory at Austerlitz, Napoleon was praised by a former enemy for a "courage and daring" unknown since Caesar; after the debacle in Russia, the same man criticized him for a vanity bordering on lunacy. Napoleon's character was deduced from what he did, whereas Lamartine needed to do nothing in the public eye. The rules of performance in the formal arts led to a transcendence of text; politicized, these rules divorced the performer from his acts. Personality, no longer read by Lamartine's generation in terms of action, acquired an independent status of its own. That divorce is what makes his age the germ of ours.

The hidden power of a speaker like Lamartine is that he harnesses mystification. He has no text, and so escapes being measured by any outside standard of truth or reality. He can make the quality of his intentions and sentiments a self-sufficient basis of his legitimacy to rule, and thus, if he is a Goebbels, make large numbers of normally intelligent people believe that Jews are both Communists and international bankers. Whether this is more or less mystical than convincing large numbers of people of a virgin birth is an open question.

The age of proletarian revolutions is over; so is the age of the Romantic performer. Without the color, the passion, the bombast, what has survived is the cognitive structure: a believable public event is created by a believable public person rather than a believable action. The genuine aesthetic qualities of the meeting of politics and the arts having disappeared, what remains is only the obscurantist, paralyzing effect of a "politics of personality."

GEMEINSCHAFT

Lamartine's experience can be read as a lesson to the Left: belief in personality can destroy the working class's sense of itself and its own interests. The lesson would be that personality, such as it is conceived in modern culture, is the enemy of a truly political community. But this lesson is too simple. The very materials of personality, the very symbols of self-expression used by a Lamartine, can be used collectively by groups caught up in a political struggle. The warring camps can see themselves as warring persons: you belong to one camp or the other by your resemblance to other persons in one camp or another; you construct this resemblance not by observing how they behave and comparing it to your own behavior, nor by deciding whether their needs resemble your needs. You construct an idea of your resemblance to others, your shared identity, by what was called in Chapter 8 "decoding."

Decoding means you take a detail of behavior as a symbol for an entire character state. Just as, say, the color of a scarf or the number of buttons undone on a blouse may symbolize a woman's sexual looseness, so small details of appearance or manner can symbolize a political stance. These details seem to indicate what kind of person espouses the ideology. If, for instance, a working-class speaker happens to be elegantly dressed, you focus on this incongruity in his personal appearance in such a way that you come to believe whatever he is saying is an illusion. In this case, you have decoded what he means by how he looks.

A sense of political community can be built out of such acts of decoding. You look for details of behavior among the persons espousing one view or the other to decide which best corresponds with your sense of yourself. Those details become for you a revelation of the true character of the conflict; they symbolize what the conflict is about. As ideology becomes measured as to whether it is believable or not through these details of behavior, political struggle itself becomes more personal. Political language becomes miniaturized, little moments or events seeming of immense importance, because through these details you are learning who is fighting, and therefore on which side you belong.

A political community formed in this way is a gemeinschaft. People are seeking for others to disclose themselves in order to know where to belong, and the acts of disclosure consist in these details which symbolize who believes what, rather than what should be believed. Baring of a self becomes the hidden agenda of political life. And when, in fantasy, these details revealing who is fighting are then blown up to stand for a collective person, political community becomes moralistic rather than ideological in tone.

A society with a very low level of interaction between its members, dominated by ideas of individual, unstable personality, is likely to give birth through fantasy to enormously destructive collective personalities. Fantasy of the collective person tends to be grandiose, because there is very little actual knowledge of others like oneself, only a small number of symbolic details. The collective person has abstract characteristics, for the same reason. This collective figure goes easily out of focus, in part because of his abstractness, in part because the very modes of perceiving personality destabilize the personality perceived. And finally, once formed, collective action for the community is difficult because people's constant worry is who belongs and who is to be excluded from this grandiose, unstable identity. Such a community is hostile to outsiders, and competition is rife among those within over who is "really" an embodiment of the collective personality, who is really a loyal American, a pure-blood Aryan, a genuine revolutionary.

The fractures in public culture during the last century encouraged this kind of destructive communal fantasizing to take form. The entrance of personality into the public realm meant that a collective person seemed as though it ought to be in essence like a concrete person. Conversely, a concrete person ought to be able to recognize himself in the collectivity; in this scheme, social relations do not transform the nature of personality. This is one reason why, by the midcentury, Delacroix's allegorical Liberty leading a revolutionary community no longer aroused belief; an allegorical personage transmutes personality; in its place, there has to be a fantasized collective person who could be concretized as a single individual. Those who recognize themselves in this individual need not talk directly to each other; indeed, the 19th Century taught them that they have a right to be left alone, in silence. And thus was the basis of destructive gemeinschaft laid: emotional relations with other people as a state of being, rather than as actions shared. Community in society became akin to an engine which runs only in neutral gear.

The destructive effects of communal feeling we shall probe in two areas. The first is the language of belonging and of conflict with those who do not belong, as it appeared in the Dreyfus Affair, especially in January 1898. The other is in how middle-class radicals struggled with a language of legitimately belonging to a proletarian community.

In conflict and in radical politics, the language of community made institutional or ideological issues into psychological questions. As the masks people wore in conflict or radical leadership came to seem disclosures of their personality, these issues could quickly metamorphose into attempts to justify one's appearance; one's stand on the issues became a matter of justifying oneself. Common stands and common beliefs then could become confused with common selves. These communities in politics are not "urban" in the sense that the political fights or revolutionary struggles go on in the great city and nowhere else. These political communities are urban in the sense that a code of interpreting appearances which arose among strangers in the city came to influence general political language. The politics are "urban" in the second of the two senses of the word, that of a mode of cognition which originates in the capital city and then spreads out through the whole of society, so that regardless of geography, people come to see with the eyes of those who come from a special place.

THE DREYFUS AFFAIR: DESTRUCTIVE
GEMEINSCHAFT

The Dreyfus Affair has been called "a double drama of detection and ideological conflict." The detection was basically a spy story: Was a certain army officer, the Jewish captain Alfred Dreyfus, conspiring with the Italians and Germans against France? If he was not, then who had made him appear to be a spy, and why had they done so? As each stage in this spy-story detection unfolds, a conflict unfolds about what the evidence means. The longer the Affair goes on, however, the less the parties involved are concerned with what the evidence tells about an act of espionage, the more they are concerned with using the evidence to define two communities in conflict. At a certain moment the line is crossed where the spy story loses any interest other than as fuel for community via confrontation. That moment occurs in January 1898.[153]

The stages of detection are enormously complex. If we keep our attention on what made Dreyfus seem a spy and then what raised questions about his guilt, the spy story was as follows:[154]

In September 1894, a letter, supposedly destined for the German military attaché in Paris, was discovered. This letter, called the *bordereau,* revealed certain military information about the French Army and appeared to be written by a French officer. The handwriting appeared to be that of Captain Alfred Dreyfus. He was arrested; after his arrest, other incriminating evidence suddenly appeared in military files, including a letter from the German military attaché to his Italian counterpart referring to the spy by the initial "D." Dreyfus was tried before a secret military tribunal beginning December 1894. He was found guilty. On January 5, 1895, he was subjected to a ceremonial public degradation, in which his medals were stripped off him and his officer's sword broken, and he was then shipped to Devil's Island for a life sentence; all who would come in contact with him in prison were instructed to avoid speaking to him.

In March 1896, the new commandant of French Military Intelligence, Colonel Picquart, received some discarded documents which had been stolen from the German attaché's wastebasket by his cleaning lady—a secret agent of the French. Among these was a *petit bleu* (a handwritten, special-delivery telegram); this *petit bleu* was addressed to another French officer, Colonel Esterhazy, and led Picquart to suspect Esterhazy might be a spy. In the course of his investigation of Esterhazy, he obtained some samples of the man's handwriting. These looked familiar to him; he thought he recognized the writing to be the same as in the *bordereau* attributed to Dreyfus. After some further research, by the end of August he decided that Esterhazy was the spy in both affairs and that Dreyfus had been unjustly imprisoned.

In 1897, by dint of news leaks and the efforts of the Dreyfus family, the vice-president of the Senate, Scheurer-Kestner, had also become interested in helping Dreyfus. 1897 was a year of indecisive maneuvering and little real advance in the actual detection work. Nevertheless, by its close, public pressure had made a trial of Esterhazy necessary. His court-martial began on January 10 of the new year, 1898, and ended the next day, January 11. He was unanimously acquitted. On January 12, Picquart was arrested for disloyalty to the army; he was later convicted. On January 13, in the face of these terrible reverses for the Dreyfusards, Zola published "J'Accuse."

In a sense, the detection ended on August 13 of that year. On that night a government official discovered that one of the pieces of evidence against Dreyfus was a forgery—a middle line of one letter by Dreyfus had been inserted into another by him. Only one man was in a position to have done this: Colonel Henry, a high-ranking officer. Confronted, he confessed that he had forged this and other evidence against Dreyfus. On August 31, the public learned that Henry had cut his throat in prison while awaiting trial, that Esterhazy had fled to England rather than face a new trial for his part in the faking of evidence, and that one of the heads of the French Army, General Boisdeffre, had resigned. After this, a new trial for Dreyfus was a certainty. It took place in Rennes in August 1899; eventually Dreyfus was freed, and in 1906 he was rehabilitated and restored to rank.

It is difficult in retrospect to understand how this spy story alone could so have aroused the French public that François Mauriac could say in 1965 that "I was a child at the time of the Dreyfus Affair, but it has filled my life," or that Léon Blum would think of it as "the basic question" out of which all the political questions of modern France arose. From 1898 on, every new twist in the Affair prompted street riots in Paris and in some of the provincial cities; from 1898 to 1900, cafes would often erupt into pitched battles when a person pro or contra Dreyfus would hear someone on the opposite side discussing the Affair at a neighboring table. A famous cartoon published in *Figaro* on February 14, 1898, shows a family dinner turned into a melee when the talk turns to the Affair; and from numerous memoirs comes testimony that the cartoon little exaggerated the facts.[155]

As long as the only factors in the picture are the details of the detection story, the affair was not the Affair. Equally, as long as the Affair is said to be a matter of conflict between different forces in French society, the passions remain inexplicable. The ideological conflict is usually portrayed as that of an "old France" representing the Army, Church, and high bourgeoisie clashing with a "new France" representing the heirs of three French revolutions. There were many occasions in the years after the Commune and the Franco-Prussian War when these forces clashed, yet on no such occasion did passions rise to the same point or in the same way as in the Dreyfus Affair. It was the formation of a collective personality based on conflict which escalated these passions to a fever pitch.

Why did old France want to destroy Dreyfus? The ideological answer cites old France's own defeats, its own discreditation in the years following the Franco-Prussian War. Many people, of many political persuasions, suspected that the French officer corps lost the war with the Prussians in 1871 through sheer incompetence. The French troops were ferocious fighters in that war, greatly respected even by the Prussians; people could explain the defeat only as bungling by those who commanded the troops. That lingering distrust was reinforced in the late 1880's, when General Boulanger, a wildly popular officer on the verge of staging a *coup d'état* against the Republic, abandoned his supporters and, with his mistress, fled across the Belgian border. The suspicion grew that the army was a betrayer of the national trust. The army leaders themselves felt the sting of these doubts. They very much wanted to vindicate themselves in some way.

At the end of the 1880's, there grew up among these leaders of old France, as among the devout peasantry and much of the urban petite bourgeoisie, a campaign to rid France of the Jews. Jews are, of course, a classic scapegoat, but they are not a constant target. At the end of the 1880's a new campaign against the Jews arose because the lapses of old France began to be seen by its supporters as the work of alien and traitorous elements. One need not think of the leaders of this campaign as Machiavellian; they wanted to explain to themselves as much as to others why, seemingly, sinister forces beyond their control had made them impotent.

A community forged in confrontation requires opposing sides. You can feel truly a sense of fraternity only when you and your brothers have an enemy in common. But the opposing sides in the Dreyfus Affair developed at an uneven rhythm. For many years, the forces of old France were developing a rhetoric that would make it possible for them to participate in a dramatic confrontation, but a concrete, living enemy whom they could confront remained elusive until 1898. In the decade before that, old France had to deal with chimeras of secret plots, betrayals, and the like, all sponsored by the Jews—but the Jew by his very nature, went the anti-Semitic doctrine, never showed himself openly for a fight. He was a weasel, a secret worker who smiled and courted you and then sold national secrets behind your back. So that, in the decade before January 1898, there existed a community *in posse*, one side ready for confrontation but denied, by its own stereotypes of the enemy, from ever having that confrontation.

Let us see how the language of community began to develop on the anti-Semitic right. The leading anti-Semite of the 1880's and early 1890's was Edouard Drumont, who founded the paper *La Libre Parole*. For Drumont, and followers like the Comte de Rochefort, Dreyfus was the perfect summation of the fantasy of the Jewish traitor: he had weaseled into the very ranks of the army; he was not an open enemy, but an impostor. In an article in *La Libre Parole* of December 26, 1894, "The Soul of Captain Dreyfus," Drumont therefore puts Dreyfus beyond the pale of crime:

> [Dreyfus] has committed an abuse of confidence, but he has not committed a crime against his country. In order for a man to betray his country, it is necessary first of all that he have a country.

The essence of a Jew, however, is that he cannot belong to any country and therefore, in Drumont's words, "the Jews cannot help it" when they sell French secrets for cash.[156]

At an ideological level, a language of anti-Semitism like this arises to expiate the sins of the anti-Semites in the past. In hating the Jew, they are cleansed. But this language is tied to another. Already, in Drumont's prose and the prose of other anti-Semites in the years 1894 and 1895, there is a dramatization of the personality of a man willing to confront the elusive Jews. This self-advertisement appears, for instance, in the way Drumont closes his article "The Soul of Captain Dreyfus." It ends with Drumont's thoughts about himself, rather than with a summary of his thoughts about Dreyfus. We are told:

> I have always been the most feeble of men, the most sentimental, the most easy to discourage. The courage I have shown in awakening my country, you [the other anti-Semites] have given me. . . . My books have rendered an immense service to our dear France, in revealing to her the Jewish peril. . . . I could not write them alone. I have merely obeyed the voice of a superior will: "Speak!" I have spoken.

Anti-Semitism is to Drumont a badge of his personal worth, his integrity. How can anyone speak to him of moderating his position, of making compromises? He would be compromising his integrity. The Dreyfus Affair is for Drumont a symbol of the very man he, Drumont, is himself.[157]

In the wild, baboons give unknown baboons signals of friendly intentions and trustfulness by rubbing the stranger's rump or plucking blades of grass for him. In Paris in the mid-1890's, a similar phenomenon developed, symbolically only, presumably. The hatred of the Jew metamorphosed into confessions of hate, like that of Drumont, and these confessions metamorphosed into clichés of one's own deepest feelings about France, one's own decency and courage in the face of schemers; the confessions in turn signaled to others that one was a friend, a person you could trust. Out of these signs was a sense of community born. Memoirs of the time tell of dinner-party conversations in which the people at tables circle around one another, sniffing out by hints and code words whether the other guests might also be sympathetic; if the ground seems favorable, one then has a flood of confession, of horror at the Jews; fists bang down on the table to emphasize the point that France must be saved from its enemies within; there is a great rush of feeling in the room, people are visibly moved, and yet, in the words of a banker:

> It is all so curiously impersonal. One assents to these intimate disclosures, or keeps silent, and then one leaves the table, full of cigar and cognac, with no sense of who was this man who poured out his heart so insistently to one.[158]

But although the language of anti-Semitism provided the materials for a temporary sense of community, the full feeling had yet to be built because there was in fact no real response. Those who had doubts about Dreyfus's guilt were small in number, and in no way inflamed as the persecutors of Dreyfus were. For the defenders of this man to acquire the same passion, we must wait really until January 1898.

The spy story, we recall, by January 1898 had led to the trial of Esterhazy, and immediately upon his acquittal to the arrest of his accuser, Picquart. In the previous year, defenders of Dreyfus had gradually appeared in the press; the trials themselves aroused much more interest in Dreyfus's case, but opinion in his favor was diffuse, fragmentary, and contradictory.

On January 12, the Affair seemed at an end: Esterhazy had been acquitted, Picquart arrested for accusing him. The importance of Émile Zola's "J'Accuse," appearing in *L'Aurore* of January 13, was that it infused life into this aborted movement by defining the terms of discourse in such a way that a community of Dreyfusards could take form. Zola succeeded in finding images of who "we" are, as Dreyfusards, equal and opposite to the imagery of the anti-Dreyfusards. He did so by using the techniques of melodrama to characterize who a Dreyfusard was as a person. Thus was completed a static confrontation, composed of two enemies who could not henceforth exist without each other.

The excitement of the special edition of *L'Aurore* was immense. Three hundred thousand copies were sold out in a few hours, people literally fighting each other for possession of one. Zola's name was everywhere, and his article was posted throughout provincial France by newly energized Dreyfusards. To analyze this text, step by step, is to see Zola cross the line from political argument to a new kind of communal language. (The text is printed in its entirety as an Appendix to the present volume.)[159]

"J'Accuse" is in the form of a letter to Félix Faure, President of the Republic. Why address it to him? The obvious reason is that Faure is head of state, but this obvious reason is wrong. The purpose of "J'Accuse" was to get its author arrested under the libel and defamation law of 1881, so that a new trial of the Dreyfus Affair could be launched under the guise of trying Zola for lying. Faure could neither institute nor stop such a trial. The real rhetorical point of this address to M. Faure is that he is "the first magistrate of the country" (Paragraph 4); he represents all Frenchmen as judges (although, in legal point of fact, the President was not the leading judge—he hadn't the power of ultimate pardon, for instance, which the American President does).

This setting is important because of the way in which Zola speaks to Faure in the first four paragraphs. It is man to man. In these first four paragraphs, Zola warns Faure and forgives him. The warning is a brilliant stroke:

> But what a mud stain on your name—I was going to say on your reign—is this abominable Dreyfus affair! (Paragraph 2)

France has twenty-five years ago done with kings and emperors; don't think of yourself as a ruler, because that would mean you think of yourself as a part of the old France; think of this affair in terms of your personal honor, your integrity as a man. Equality means no distance between selves. Placing the Affair in these two contingent terms is continued in Zola's terms of forgiveness: "Because of your honor I am convinced you are ignorant of [the truth]." Who is Émile Zola, naturalized citizen from Venice, to forgive the French President, if they are not speaking as intimates?

Zola sets up his own interest in the same terms. Émile Zola knew neither Dreyfus nor any of the military, nor was he in any way previously threatened by the Affair. Why has he taken a hand? In Paragraph 3, Zola thrusts himself on the reader as follows: First, he says he will "dare" to speak, "dare to tell the truth." In other words, the first sign of his presence in this Affair shows us a brave man. More: "It is my duty to speak; I will not be an accomplice." Whoever thought he was? The point of this sentence is that anyone who becomes involved shows he has real character; non-involvement is taken as a lack of personal courage. This assertion of courage prepares the way for a peculiar confession of conscience; if Zola did not dare to speak,

My nights would be haunted by the specter of the innocent man, who is atoning, in a far away country, by the most frightful of tortures, for a crime that he did not commit.

What's involved in a journalist speaking of his courage and his "haunted nights" is not whether he is sincere. What's involved is the way in which these convictions, no matter how deeply felt, are conveyed to an audience. In "J'Accuse" the man of conscience begins by calling attention to the fact of his heroism; he dramatizes the fact that he has a conscience—surely an odd way to begin the defense of another man, and identical in form to the anti-Dreyfusard language of Drumont.

Once we understand the peculiar rhetorical atmosphere of this beginning, we can begin to make sense of the subsequent arguments which have struck so many modern commentators, looking at Zola's text from a logical and legal point of view, as absolutely empty. They have a logic in terms of 19th Century views of public personality.

Paragraphs 5 through 11 comprise Zola's assertion as to who had framed Dreyfus. It's simple. One man

has done it all—Colonel Paty du Clam. He is the entire case. (Paragraph 4)

Zola's proof? Of legal, factual proof he has none. In Paragraph 5 he tells us that when a "sincere" investigation is made, it will be proven. "I have not to tell the whole; let them look, they will find." In the middle of Paragraph 6, Zola proclaims "it is sufficient to say" that Paty du Clam entered the scene as soon as it seemed possible that Dreyfus could be framed. But Zola is not after legal, factual proof, because Right and Wrong in this affair is to be read only in terms of personality. If he can make us feel that Paty du Clam is a disgusting person, then, of course, Paty must have framed Dreyfus. Thus, immediately after accusing Paty du Clam, Zola launches into a baroque description of his character, as a schemer, a romantic, a man who delights in intrigues and midnight meetings with mysterious ladies (Paragraph 5). And the reason Paty du Clam succeeded in his frame-up is not that institutional forces demand a victim, or that the officer class must vindicate itself. No, it is because Paty du Clam has the personal power to hypnotize other people,

for he concerns himself also with spiritualism, with occultism holding converse with spirits. (Paragraph 6)

Mystification completes the ring of character; there is a devilish person at work, a heroic person out to expose him, a judge between them who

is honorable but ignorant—and, rather incidentally, there is the institu- ›
tional process which has put a man in jail.

After fingering the villain, Zola proceeds to transform all the evidence into personal terms. For instance, there is the *bordereau;* how
does Zola deal with it? "I deny this document; I deny it with all my
might" (Paragraph 10). Analysis of what the document means is eschewed; the writer, by stressing that "I" deny it, "with all my might,"
destroys its truth value. A little further in that paragraph, Zola works
the escalation again. After saying that whatever the substance of the
document is, it is unrelated to national security, he immediately proclaims:

> No, no; it is a lie and a lie the more odious and cynical because
> they lie with impunity, in such a way that no one can convict
> them.

"It," the *bordereau,* suddenly becomes "they," the enemy. Even
though we have just been told that the *bordereau* concerns trivial
affairs, and therefore presumably is just a piece of paper which "they"
have put to false uses, now it becomes their manufacture, and it is
impossible to discuss it as real or phony because "they lie in such a way
that no one can convict them."

Thus, from making the Affair a drama of personal morality, Hero
contra Devil, Zola makes all discussion of evidence count only so far as
it relates to the personality of the antagonists. The evidence has no
reality apart from its psychological symbolism.

In Paragraphs 12 to 22, the events from the beginning of the Esterhazy phase up to the day before publication of "J'Accuse" are subjected to this treatment. The critical moment when the army officials
had to decide on Esterhazy's prosecution is presented as a "psychological moment, full of anguish." The officials, having taken the decision
belatedly, are attacked by Zola in the most personal terms—"And
these people sleep, and they have wives and children whom they
love!" (Paragraph 14). What is the meaning of this extraordinary statement? There is no world, no web of bureaucracy, cross-conflicts of
power and authority, no checks on desire in Zola's Affair: there are
only absolutes of self. How can you be human if you disagree with
me? Every worldly appearance, every specific action, becomes an indicator of these absolutes. A man's mask is a true guide to his essential
character, and thus, for Zola as for Drumont, there can be no shifting
of these worldly positions, no interaction, for how can one barter with
one's integrity?

Thus we arrive at the inner rationale of the famous statement at the
end of Paragraph 18, which an English jurist at the time called the

"essence of irrationality in the name of rational justice." This is Zola's summation of the respective fates of Esterhazy and Picquart:

> . . . the proclamation of the innocence of men who are ruined with debts and crimes, while honor itself, a man of stainless life, is stricken down. When a society reaches that point it is beginning to rot. (Paragraph 18)

Zola is speaking literally: the popular press made a great deal of the fact that Esterhazy owed many people money, while Picquart was debt-free. This passage is the essence of trial by character, and of character assassination. Trial by character is the only way politics can proceed, once the line between public life and personal life has been erased.

"J'Accuse" shows one consequence of the change in rhetoric made visible between Napoleon's and Lamartine's generation. Once character became independent of action, once Lamartine could present himself to the people as a leader without leading them in any action, the way was prepared for this reversal, in which the public world of action has lost all meaning except in subordination to personal motivation.

Zola now reaches for the dramatic high point of the piece, the list of accusations beginning at Paragraph 26. Each one opens with the form "I accuse," rather than "X is guilty of." Indeed, "I" is the most prominent word in the entire accusation. It is not so much that an injustice is being challenged or that these men are being exposed, for in fact Zola has said that he won't engage in that sort of thing; it is up to the authorities. The important thing is that "I" am accusing them. Of what? Here is Zola's list of the men and their crimes:

> Paty du Clam—"diabolical workman"
> Mercier—"weakness of mind"
> Billot—"lèse humanity" and "lèse justice"
> Boisdeffre—"clerical passion"
> Gonse—"excess of friendship"
> Pellieux—"rascally inquiry"
> handwriting experts—"lying and fraudulent reports"
> war ministry—"abominable campaign" in press
> council of war—"violating the law"

Only Boisdeffre's crime, his clerical passion, and the crime of the council of war, violating courts-martial law, are institutional. All the rest are crimes of personality. And that is why it is so important that "I accuse" them, or, equally, why when "I accuse" is the rhetoric, crimes of personality are what will most likely be found.

Zola's conclusion to "J'Accuse" has a disturbing parallel to Drumont's conclusion to "The Soul of Captain Dreyfus." Zola, in Paragraph 28, assures us that his is a pure passion, unmotivated by gain or party. In Paragraph 29, like Drumont, he informs the reader of how moved he is personally; we get a reading on the state of his feelings: "My fiery protest is simply the cry of my soul." Paragraph 30 shows Zola, like Drumont, presenting to the reader a last image, which is of Zola, rather than of Dreyfus or of France. Zola is defiant and fighting. The hero's motto that he writes for himself, describing his attitude toward his own future trial for defamation, is: "I await it." This declaration of Zola's moral fortitude is how the plea for Dreyfus ends.

If we ask why this essay sold three hundred thousand copies in a day; why it roused a large section of French men and women to Dreyfus's defense; why, even after Zola's trial, when he fled to England with his mistress and a wad of banknotes rather than face a year in jail, and so was personally discredited as a leader of the cause, "J'Accuse" remained the basic text of the movement; if we ask why, even after Henry's suicide and the consequent necessary vindication of Paty du Clam, "J'Accuse" remained a compelling document to large numbers of people, we can only answer that they wanted what Zola offered them, which was a language of belonging to a collective struggle, rather than a set of logical reasons why Dreyfus should be free.

The real content of "J'Accuse" is what kind of person would defend the Jewish captain, what kind of person would attack him. That person never crystallizes into one leader, on either side. Zola's swift trial and even swifter departure disqualified him, and indeed, the characters prominent in the Affair after January 13, 1898, are shuffling on and off the stage so quickly that no one man or group of men ever appears in control of events. But this instability at the top does not mean that the lines between Dreyfusard and anti-Dreyfusard shift below. The two camps harden among the populace; Henry's forgeries, for instance, are quickly taken up by the anti-Dreyfusards as an act of supreme nobility and self-sacrifice, because if Dreyfus isn't guilty, he ought to be. In fact, as the detective work slowly brings Dreyfus to a point of vindication—without ever conclusively establishing who the "D" of the *bordereau* was—each new step becomes only the occasion for renewed mob action in the streets between the warring factions.

After 1902, when the overt violence between the two camps had died down, there was never any process of conciliation. The Ferry Laws secularizing French education were spoken of on both sides as a sort of "revenge" for the conviction of Dreyfus, since the priests were allied with the army. Such writers as Charles Maurras and such groups as the Camelots du Roi owe their inspiration to the anti-Dreyfusards, and it has become accepted among historians outside France that some of the impulse for French collaboration with the Nazis arose out of old wounds to the army and hatred of the Jews stirred up by this affair. The Dreyfus Affair is a classic case of how, when a community based on an abstract, diffuse collective personality takes form, an irremediable schism opens up in a society. No change in material conditions, in history, can alter the position of opponents, for what is at stake in the conflict seems to both sides to be not an issue, but integrity, honor, the collectivity itself.

After the community formed there was nothing the participants could learn from the action. Henry's suicide does not shake the world-view of the enemies of Dreyfus; the event is quickly reinterpreted as yet another act of heroism by a loyal Catholic member of the army. Paty du Clam's vindication by Henry's suicide does not crack the shell of Dreyfusards. Zola's "plot" idea was immediately saved by the Dreyfusards, who claimed that Paty du Clam, master hypnotist that he was, took Henry to a cafe one night and mesmerized him into performing the forgery.

The Dreyfus Affair is a historical example of the logical extreme, the end point of the code that makes appearance into indices of self. The mask reveals a common face; for the community to exist, the faces of all to be recognizable in this common face, it must remain rigid and still. There is community on both sides only so long as their appearances to each other are inflexible.

On the stage, you know every action of Dr. Weltschmerz is determined by his moral character; in the streets, you also believe that every mark of justice shown toward Dreyfus is the effect of a Jewish conspiracy to destroy the decent people of France; but—as does not happen in the theater—because their characters are indecent, you deny the villains, Jews and their defenders, any right to exist. In a culture anxious about the believability of appearances, melodrama off the stage has the inevitable logic of suggesting that you can believe in yourself only if you destroy your enemies. If they can believe in themselves, how do you keep up belief in your own appearance? Your own membership in a community? If every act is an emblem of personality—if that is the point of being pro- or anti-Dreyfus—then those who do not appear wearing one's own emblem must be inauthentic, liars, phony, and therefore should be destroyed. Stage melodrama has no outcome, induces no change in the characters, but political melodrama has a singular outcome, suggesting that the ultimate way to stabilize one's own appearance is to destroy one's enemy. Purge is the logic of a collective personality.

From this identification of community feeling as a sharing of a personality, it becomes quite natural to see the language of negotiation, bureaucracy, and management relations as all in a different realm. Thus, there developed by the opening of the present century the rationale for thinking that the life of a community and the life of the state were different *in kind*.

If the community is itself worth caring about, it is ruled by a perverse domino theory. Negotiation becomes the great threat to community: change positions or alter them, and the communal spirit itself is weakened. It becomes more important to declare who you are than to traffic with others unlike yourself. This is why, in the midst of the great passions a crisis like the Dreyfus Affair engendered, there was at heart as static and wooden a set of human relationships as the dead submission Lamartine induced among the Parisian masses.

WHO IS A REAL RADICAL?

This language of community began to appear in the last century in a domain where it should have been forbidden, the domain of radical politics. It served bourgeois radicals as a way to think of themselves as having a legitimate place in proletarian movements. Let us see why collective personality ought not to have appeared in Marxian movements in particular, and then how in fact it did.

Perhaps the greatest inheritance of the 19th Century still untaxed today is a view of history in which events follow logically, even if not inevitably, from social conditions. This idea included as believers those who imagined nations had "destinies," many 19th Century anarchists, some followers of Saint-Simon, most of the social Darwinists, as well as those who followed Marx. To speak of a Marxian dialectic of history is to speak of stages of experience, each produced out of contradictions in the stages which have come before. We have become so familiar with this idea that it can be recited as a catechism: a thesis exploding into its antithesis, where the same situations and persons are viewed in a new light, and this antithesis exploding again, yielding either a synthesis after a period of revolution, or yet another antithesis, an anti-antithesis, in a ceaseless wheel of material and intellectual re-formation.

Ironically, having learned this catechism by heart, we have also witnessed events that discredit it. Over half the world is ruled by governments subscribing to the doctrines of Marx, modified one way or another, yet the societies these governments rule are the precise opposite of the societies he, along with Fourier and Saint-Simon, believed ripe logically for revolution. They have been colonized, or as yet undeveloped industrially, or in some other way peripheral to the European situations where Marx could deduce a logic of historical development from immediate social structure.

No single generation, and certainly no single book, can explain the paradox of this displaced destiny. Yet the cycle of urban culture traced so far in these pages can throw light on at least one dimension of the paradox: the psychological deformation culture works on those who are committed to radical, dialectical change, so that they become defensive when history flies in the face of theory.

Marx throughout his writings conceived of the dialectical forces in history leading people to reformulate their beliefs under the impact of new events. The slogan that material conditions determine consciousness is, and has been, easily vulgarized. At his best, Marx meant by it that every new material situation in society forces a reformulation of belief only because the world informing those beliefs has altered.

What does it take, psychologically, for a person to be able to reformulate his beliefs? To think dialectically? If a belief has become to its espouser so deeply and intensely personal, if what a person believes has come to define his or her identity, then any change in belief involves a great upheaval in the self. The more personal and self-involving belief becomes, that is, the less likely it is to be changed.

Thus, a dialectical consciousness seems to require an almost impossible human strength. Here is an ideology of passionate concern about the world, a passionate commitment against its injustices, and yet an ideology which demands that as historical situations change, the nature of those commitments must be suspended, rethought, and re-formed. Belief is to be at once intensely held and yet at a distance from the self, so that the belief can be changed without carrying the burdens of personal loss or a sense of intimate jeopardy.

When the matter is put this way, we realize that what Marx imagined as a dialectical imagination is close to a concept we have explored in terms of city life: the concept of public behavior. To be dialectical in one's perceptions, one must be out in public, away from the symbolization of personality through belief or social action. If Rousseau was an enemy of man in public, Marx is his champion.

Yet, there is the all too familiar creature who calls himself Marxist and detests this flexibility. Sometimes he is termed an "ideologue," sometimes a "dogmatist"—convenient labels to subsume a radical movement by the character structure of its worst exponent. He is more accurately and narrowly a person from the middle classes who out of humane motives or anger at his past, or anger at himself, becomes a radical, identifying the interests of justice and right in the society with the working class. If his motives for championing the oppressed vary from case to case, his problem in relationship to the working classes does not: how is he legitimately a part of their movement, how does this man with his education, his sense of decorum, his sense of propriety, legitimate his presence in the community of the oppressed?

Marx and Engels knew him because his problem was theirs. He solved the problem of legitimating himself as a radical through the codes of appearances of the bourgeois culture from which he sprang. Every position he took, each topic he discussed, was burdened with the weight of his own identity as a revolutionary. Debate about "correct" strategy quickly became for him a characterological conflict: who is "really" revolutionary? In the midst of seeming to argue about what are good revolutionary tactics, the real argument was, who is a legitimate radical? One's opponents, in having the wrong strategy, belonging to the wrong faction, taking the wrong line, are really not radicals at all. They do not therefore belong to the radical community because of ideological "error."

Questions about his legitimacy were asked by the members of working-class radical communities themselves from 1848 on. We have seen how in that revolution, working-class groups like *L'Atelier* began to deny this dispossessed middle-class revolutionary a place in their own struggle. In England in the 1850's there could be observed the same hostility toward the bourgeois intellectual who comes to help in the revolution on the part of those in whose name and in whose interests the revolution was to be made. Indeed, class antagonism within the ranks of the revolutionary cadres remains the great unwritten history of 19th Century radical politics.

This sectarian passion is directly a product of the secular codes of immanent personality. A believable appearance is one in which a personality is disclosed—but here it is of necessity a displaced personality. His very displacement, his very past, can only make those whom he hopes to join as comrades perceive him as alien. The terms for belonging to which he then resorts are those which define him as a new person by virtue of the strength of his beliefs. His mask must be immobile, must be fixed, for him to believe in himself. If he converts radical intellection into puritanical passion, he does so not because he has an "authoritarian" personality, although in particular cases this may be true, but because he wants to legitimate himself in an alien community. To belong he must make his positions the sum and substance of himself; they become disclosures of him; they are burdened with the weight of his desire to be "a revolutionary," rather than to be "revolutionary." The modern ideologue takes every stand as non-negotiable because on each hinges the troubled question to him of whether he really *is* as he appears, whether he legitimately has a place in the legions of the oppressed.

As early as the First International, this figure was visible; by the Second, he was a major force. In late 19th Century France, his problem was most fully displayed in the life of Jules Guesde. Guesde is supposed to have forcefully introduced Marxian ideas into the socialist movement in France in the late 1880's. He was the perfect petit bourgeois (his father was a schoolteacher) provincial intellectual. As a youth, periods of self-doubt, voluntary poverty, and arrest all were marked by an "envy of the integrity of workers." Guesde took a version of Marxian theory and applied it rigidly to French life (it was a version Marx himself became unhappy with, although the two originally collaborated). And with this simple, fixed version of Marxism, Guesde legitimated his position as a radical leader. He came to power in rivalry with a real worker, Jean Dormoy, a steelworker equally radical but more supple in mind. Guesde was firm when Dormoy showed himself openly confused by changes in the French economy in the 1880's, a contrast Guesde used to proclaim himself "more of a genuine revolutionary because more stalwart." By 1898, the movement Guesde forged around himself

> . . . was somewhat irrelevant to French conditions and they made little effort to adapt it to the changing times. They preached that wages were bound to fall even though in France they were quite clearly rising . . . their stress on theory degenerated into a facile repetition of inert dogmas.

Guesde was the very essence of a leader who legitimates himself as a Marxian revolutionary by subverting the idea of dialectical changes in belief.[160]

In France, by the beginning of the present century, there can be seen two different kinds of betrayal of the left. One is incarnate in the rule of Clemenceau from 1906 to 1909; the radical, opposed to the opportunism of those in power, when he comes to power himself abandons his radical beliefs and his old supporters. The betrayal of Guesde is something else. It is betrayal of the revolution by one's sheer passion to be a revolutionary. To be a believable revolutionary, to legitimate this personal position, has by the century's end become a matter of deserting the dialectical ideal.

For a group which has committed itself to orienting its political views to a continuous rereading of social conditions, to commit oneself to an absolute position on, say, the ripeness of a certain country for trade-union organizing, is more self-destructive than the dogmatism of those, say, who believe in a New Jerusalem, because the truth of it is more easily discredited. The loss of distance between public behavior and personal need means more to the secular revolutionary than it does to the Puritan. It means a loss of his very reason for acting.

Someone alive to the dangers of Stalinism might here strongly object, saying that ceasing to consider personal needs in relation to public questions can wind up in a barren world where the "needs of the revolution" dehumanize society. But I am here after something else. The tragedy of 19th Century politics, and it is a tragedy, lay in the fact that forces of culture so often imprisoned those who revolted, just as they imprisoned those who defended the existing economic order, in a ferocious self-declaration through political means. This culture could make radicals inhumane. Further, there was increasing paralysis of consciousness among the political intelligentsia; this paralysis arose from destructive tendencies in cosmopolitan culture, not in the supposedly absolutist features of revolutionary dogma.

The culture of the 19th Century capital cities set in motion a powerful weapon against change. When the mask became the face, when appearances became indices of personality, self-distance was lost. What freedom have people when they are as they appear? How can they engage in those acts of self-criticism and change which depend on self-distance? Belief is too loaded. The culture of bourgeois urban life undermined the freedom of too many bourgeois radicals. This culture robbed dialectical ideology of its dialectic, by accustoming people to think of their rhetorical positions, their ideas stated in public, as disclosures of themselves psychologically. The people on the left increasingly found themselves in the position of defending personal "integrity," "commitment," "authenticity," in defiance of changing material conditions. They exchanged dialectic for the sense of belonging to a radical community, a Movement. Again, we arrive at the same inward-turning language which typified the Dreyfus Affair; rigidity for the sake of feeling bound up in a group, a defiance of the dissonances of history for the sake of community.

Far from destroying fraternal community, 19th Century cosmopolitan culture made community seem too valuable. Cities appear in present-day clichés as the ultimate in empty impersonality. In fact, the lack of a strong, impersonal culture in the modern city instead has aroused a passion for fantasized intimate disclosure between people. Myths of an absence of community, like those of the soulless or vicious crowd, serve the function of goading men to seek out community in terms of a created common self. The more the myth of empty impersonality, in popular forms, becomes the common sense of a society, the more will that populace feel morally justified in destroying the essence of urbanity, which is that men can act together, without the compulsion to be the same.

PART FOUR

THE INTIMATE SOCIETY

CHAPTER 11

THE END
OF PUBLIC CULTURE

One way to picture the past is through images of the rise and fall of a prized way of life. These images naturally produce a sense of regret, and regret is a dangerous sentiment. While it produces empathy for the past, and so a certain insight, regret induces resignation about the present, and so a certain acceptance of its evils. I have not assembled this picture of the rise and fall of secular public culture in order to produce regret; I have assembled it to create a perspective on beliefs, aspirations, and myths of modern life which seem to be humane but are in fact dangerous.

The reigning belief today is that closeness between persons is a moral good. The reigning aspiration today is to develop individual personality through experiences of closeness and warmth with others. The reigning myth today is that the evils of society can all be understood as evils of impersonality, alienation, and coldness. The sum of these three is an ideology of intimacy: social relationships of all kinds are real, believable, and authentic the closer they approach the inner psychological concerns of each person. This ideology transmutes political categories into psychological categories. This ideology of intimacy defines the humanitarian spirit of a society without gods: warmth is our god. The history of the rise and fall of public culture at the very least calls this humanitarian spirit into question.

The belief in closeness between persons as a moral good is in fact the product of a profound dislocation which capitalism and secular belief produced in the last century. Because of this dislocation, people sought to find personal meanings in impersonal situations, in objects, and in the objective conditions of society itself. They could not find these meanings; as the world became psychomorphic, it became mystifying. They therefore sought to flee, and find in the private realms of life, especially in the family, some principle of order in the perception of personality. Thus the past built a hidden desire for stability in the overt desire for closeness between human beings. Even as we have revolted against the stern sexual rigidities of the Victorian family, we continue to burden close relations with others with these hidden desires for security, rest, and permanence. When the relations cannot bear these burdens, we conclude there is something wrong with the relationship, rather than with the unspoken expectations. Arriving at a feeling of closeness to others is thus often after a process of testing them; the relationship is both close and closed. If it changes, if it must change, there is a feeling of trust betrayed. Closeness burdened with the expectation of stability makes emotional communication—hard enough as it is—one step more difficult. Can intimacy on these terms really be a virtue?

The aspiration to develop one's personality through experiences of closeness with others has a similar hidden agenda. The crisis of public culture in the last century taught us to think about the harshness, constraints, and difficulties which are the essence of the human condition in society as overwhelming. We may approach them through a kind of passive, silent spectatorship, but to challenge them, to become enmeshed in them, is thought to be at the expense of developing ourselves. The development of personality today is the development of the personality of a refugee. Our fundamental ambivalence toward aggressive behavior comes out of this refugee mentality: aggression may be a necessity in human affairs, but we have come to think it an abhorrent personal trait. But what kind of personality develops through experiences of intimacy? Such a personality will be molded in the expectation, if not the experience, of trust, of warmth, of comfort. How can it be strong enough to move in a world founded on injustice? Is it truly humane to propose to human beings the dictum that their personalities "develop," that they become "richer" emotionally to the extent that they learn to trust, to be open, to share, to eschew manipulation of others, to eschew aggressive challenges to social conditions or mining these conditions for personal gain? Is it humane to form soft selves in a hard world? As a result of the immense fear of public life which gripped the last century, there results today a weakened sense of human will.

And finally, the history of public life calls into question the mythology built up around impersonality as a social evil. Beginning with the crack in the balance of public and private produced by the Wilkesite movement, fully displayed in the control Lamartine exercised over the Parisian proletariat, the mythology that men are more important than measures (to use Junius's phrase) is revealed really as a recipe for political pacification. Impersonality seems to define a landscape of human loss, a total absence of human relationships. But this very equation of impersonality with emptiness itself creates the loss. In response to the fear of emptiness, people conceive of the political as a realm in which personality will be strongly declared. Then they become the passive spectators to a political personage who offers them his intentions, his sentiments, rather than his acts, for their consumption. Or, the more people conceive of the political realm as the opportunity for revealing themselves to each other through the sharing of a common, collective personality, the more are they diverted from using their fraternity to change social conditions. Maintaining community becomes an end in itself; the purge of those who don't really belong becomes the community's business. A rationale of refusing to negotiate, of continual purge of outsiders, results from the supposedly humanitarian desire to erase impersonality in social relations. And in the same measure this myth of impersonality is self-destructive. The pursuit of common interests is destroyed in the search for a common identity.

In the absence of a public life, these supposedly humane ideals hold sway. To be sure, these diseased beliefs did not begin when the public ended; the very crisis in public life engendered them in the last century. Just as the 19th Century public culture was linked to that of the Enlightenment, the present absence of belief in publicness is linked to its confusion in the 19th Century. The connection is twofold.

To speak of an end of public life is first to speak of a consequence, issuing from a contradiction in culture of the last century. Personality in public was a contradiction in terms; it ultimately destroyed the public term. For instance, it became logical for people to think of those who could actively display their emotions in public, whether as artists or politicians, as being men of special and superior personality. These men were to control, rather than interact with, the audience in front of whom they appeared. Gradually the audience lost faith in itself to judge them; it became a spectator rather than a witness. The audience thus lost a sense of itself as an active force, as a "public." Again, personality in public destroyed the public by making people fearful of betraying their emotions to others involuntarily. The result was more and more an attempt to withdraw from contact with others, to be shielded by silence, even to attempt to stop feeling in order for the feelings not to show. The public thus was emptied of people who wanted to be expressive in it, as the terms of expression moved from the presentation of a mask to the revelation of one's personality, of one's face, in the mask one wore in the world.

To speak of an end of public life is secondly to speak of a denial. We deny there was any value, indeed any dignity, in the repressiveness the Victorian world imposed upon itself as the confusion of public behavior and personality grew more acute. Yet we attempt to "liberate" ourselves from this repression by intensifying the terms of personality, by being more straight, open, and authentic in our relations with one another; we are confused when this seeming liberation produces distress akin to that the Victorians felt in their repressive efforts to create emotional order. We deny, again, that there ought to be any barriers in communication between people. The whole logic of 20th Century communications technology has been bent to this openness of expression. And yet, though we have enshrined the idea of ease of communication, we are surprised that the "media" result in ever greater passivity on the part of those who are the spectators; we are surprised that under conditions of audience passivity, personality becomes more and more an issue on the air, especially in terms of political life. We do not connect our belief in absolute communicativeness to the horrors of the mass media, because we deny the basic truth which once formed a public culture. Active expression requires human effort, and this effort can succeed only to the extent that people limit what they express to one another. Or again, in sheer physical terms, we deny any limits on physical motion in the city, invent a transport technology to facilitate this absolute personal motion, and then are surprised that the result is a disastrous deadening of the city as an organism. The Victorians struggled with the idea of a boundaryless self; it was the very essence of the discontent produced by the confusion of public and private. We simply deny, in these various ways, limits upon the self. But to deny is not to erase; in fact, the problems become more intractable because they are no longer being confronted. Through contradictions inherited from the past and through the denial of the past, we remain imprisoned in the cultural terms of the 19th Century. Thus the end of a belief in public life is not a break with 19th Century bourgeois culture, but rather an escalation of its terms.

The structure of an intimate society is twofold. Narcissism is mobilized in social relations, and the experience of disclosure of one's feelings to others becomes destructive. These structural characteristics also have links to the 19th Century. For narcissism to be mobilized in a society, for people to focus on intangible tones of feeling and motive, a sense of group ego interest must be suspended. This group ego consists in a sense of what people need, want, or demand, no matter what their immediate emotional impressions. The seeds of erasing a sense of group ego were planted in the last century. The revolution of 1848 was the first appearance of the dominance of a culture of personality over these group ego interests, expressed then as the interests of a class. For destructive gemeinschaft to arise, people must believe that when they reveal their feelings to each other, they do so in order to form an emotional bond. This bond consists of a collective personality which they build up through mutual revelation. And the seeds of this fantasy of being a community by sharing a collective personality were also planted by the terms of 19th Century culture. The question then becomes, what is the effect on our lives of being in bondage to the past, to a culture whose effects we deny, even as we do not challenge its premises?

The clearest way to answer this question would be to see how each of the structures of an intimate society has grown upon its 19th Century roots. The suspension of ego interests has grown into a systematic encouragement of narcissistic absorption by centering social transactions on an obsession with motivation. The self no longer concerns man as actor or man as maker; it is a self composed of intentions and possibilities. Intimate society has entirely reversed Fielding's dictum that praise or censure should apply to actions rather than actors; now what matters is not what you have done but how you feel about it. The sharing of collective personality traits has grown into a systematically destructive process as the size of the community which can share this personality has shrunk. The Dreyfus Affair involved the formation of community feeling at a national level; in contemporary society, this same formation of community is now tied to localism. The very fear of impersonality which governs modern society prompts people to envision community on an ever more restricted scale. If the self is narrowed to intentions, the sharing of this self is now narrowed to exclude those who are much different in terms of class, politics, or style. Absorption in motivation and localism: these are the structures of a culture built upon the crises of the past. They organize the family, the school, the neighborhood; they disorganize the city and the state.

Although tracing these two structures would make an intellectually clear picture, it falls short, I think, of conveying the trauma which the reign of intimacy produces in modern life. Often against our own knowledge, we are caught up in a war between the demands of social existence and the belief that we develop as human beings only through contrary modes of intimate psychic experience. Sociologists have unwittingly invented a language for this warfare. They speak of life in society as a matter of instrumental tasks—we go to school, to work, on strike, to meetings because we must. We try not to invest too much in these tasks because they are "inappropriate" vehicles for warm feeling; we make of our life in them an "instrument," a means rather than a reality in which we make commitments of our sentiments. Against this instrumental world, sociologists then contrast affective or holistic or integrative experience; the jargonistic terms are important because they reveal a certain mentality, a belief that when people are really feeling (affective), really alive to the present moment (holistic), fully disclosing themselves (integrative)—in sum, when they are engaged—they are having experiences that are antagonistic to experiences of survival, struggle, and obligation in the world at large. Not unnaturally, the scenes in which sociologists speak of this affective life transpiring are intimate scenes: the family, the neighborhood, the life passed among friends.

It is necessary to see narcissism and destructive gemeinschaft organizing this warfare, giving the struggle between instrumental and affective social relations a form. But the quality of the warfare itself can be brought to life by posing two questions, and organizing our inquiry around the answers to them. How is society injured by the blanket measurement of social reality in psychological terms? It is robbed of its *civility*. How is the self injured by estrangement from a meaningful impersonal life? It is robbed of the expression of certain creative powers which all human beings possess potentially—the powers of play—but which require a milieu at a distance from the self for their realization. Thus the intimate society makes of the individual an *actor deprived of an art*. The narcissistic focus on motivation and the localization of communal feeling give a form to each of these issues.

It is difficult to speak of civility in modern life without appearing to be a snob or a reactionary. The oldest meaning of the term connects "civility" with the duties of citizenship; today "civility" means either knowing which years of Cos-d'Estournel to decant or refraining from noisy and unseemly political demonstrations. To recover that obsolete meaning of civility and relate it to the frame of public life, I would define civility as follows: it is the activity which protects people from each other and yet allows them to enjoy each other's company. Wearing a mask is the essence of civility. Masks permit pure sociability, detached from the circumstances of power, malaise, and private feeling of those who wear them. Civility has as its aim the shielding of others from being burdened with oneself. If one were religious and believed that the impulse life of man was evil, or if one took Freud seriously and believed the impulse life of man an internal war, then the masking of the self, the freeing of others from being caught up in one's inner burden, would be an obvious good. But even if one makes no assumptions about, or has no belief in, an innate human nature, the culture of personality which has arisen in the last century and a half would give civility this same seriousness and weight.

"City" and "civility" have a common root etymologically. Civility is treating others as though they were strangers and forging a social bond upon that social distance. The city is that human settlement in which strangers are most likely to meet. The public geography of a city is civility institutionalized. I do not think people now need await a massive transformation of social conditions or a magic return to the past in order to behave in a civilized way. In a world without religious rituals or transcendental beliefs, masks are not ready-made. The masks must be created by those who will wear them, through trial and error, through a desire to live with others rather than a compulsion to get close to them. The more such behavior takes form, however, the more would the mentality of, and love for, the city revive.

To speak of incivility is to speak of reversed terms. It is burdening others with oneself; it is the decrease in sociability with others this burden of personality creates. We can all easily call to mind individuals who are uncivilized on these terms: they are those "friends" who need others to enter into the daily traumas of their own lives, who evince little interest in others save as ears into which confessions are poured. Or we can easily imagine instances of this same incivility in intellectual and literary life, such as those autobiographies or biographies which compulsively bare every detail of the sexual tastes, money habits, and character weaknesses of their subjects, as though we are supposed to understand the person's life, writings, or actions in the world better by the exposure of his or her secrets. But incivility is also built into the very fabric of modern society itself. Two of these structures of incivility will concern us.

One is the appearance of incivility in modern political leadership, particularly in the work of charismatic leaders. The modern charismatic leader destroys any distance between his own sentiments and impulses and those of his audience, and so, focusing his followers on his motivations, deflects them from measuring him in terms of his acts. This relationship between politician and followers began in the mid-19th Century in terms of the control of one class by the leader of another; it now suits the needs of a new class situation, one in which the leader must shield himself against being judged by those whom he represents. The electronic media play a crucial role in this deflection, by simultaneously overexposing the leader's personal life and obscuring his work in office. The incivility which this modern charismatic figure embodies is that his followers are burdened with making sense of him as a person in order to understand what he is doing once in power—and the very terms of personality are such that they can never succeed in that act. It is uncivilized for a society to make its citizens feel a leader is believable because he can dramatize his own motivations. Leadership on these terms is a form of seduction. The structures of domination especially remain unchallenged when people are led into electing politicians who sound angry, as if ready to change things; these politicians are, by the alchemy of personality, freed from translating angry impulses into action.

The second incivility which will concern us is the perversion of fraternity in modern communal experience. The narrower the scope of a community formed by collective personality, the more destructive does the experience of fraternal feeling become. Outsiders, unknowns, unlikes become creatures to be shunned; the personality traits the community shares become ever more exclusive; the very act of sharing becomes ever more centered upon decisions about who can belong and who cannot. The abandonment of belief in class solidarity in modern times for new kinds of collective images, based on ethnicity, or *quartier*, or region, is a sign of this narrowing of the fraternal bond. Fraternity has become empathy for a select group of people allied with rejection of those not within the local circle. This rejection creates demands for autonomy from the outside world, for being left alone by it rather than demanding that the outside world itself change. The more intimate, however, the less sociable. For this process of fraternity by exclusion of "outsiders" never ends, since a collective image of "us" never solidifies. Fragmentation and internal division is the very logic of this fraternity, as the units of people who really belong get smaller and smaller. It is a version of fraternity which leads to fratricide.

The war between psyche and society is fought on a second front, within the individual person himself. He loses the capacity to play and playact, in a society which allows him no impersonal space in which to play.

The classic tradition of *theatrum mundi* equated society with theater, everyday action with acting. This tradition thus couched social life in aesthetic terms, and treated all men as artists because all men can act. The difficulty with this imagery is that it is ahistorical. The whole history of public culture of the 19th Century was of people who were gradually losing a belief in their own expressive powers, who on the contrary elevated the artist as someone who was special because he could do what ordinary people could not do in everyday life; he expressed believable feelings clearly and freely in public.

And yet the vision of social life as aesthetic life which governed the classical imagery of *theatrum mundi* contains a truth. Social relations can be aesthetic relations, because they share a common root. That common origin lies in the childhood experience of play. Play is not art, but it is a certain kind of preparation for a certain kind of aesthetic activity, one which is realized in society if certain conditions are present. This may seem an involuted way to make a simple statement, but it is necessary because so much of the current psychological investigation of "creativity" proceeds in such generalized terms that it is difficult to connect specific creative work to specific experiences in a life history. Play prepares children for the experience of playacting by teaching them to treat conventions of behavior as believable. Conventions are rules for behavior at a distance from the immediate desires of the self. When children have learned to believe in conventions, then they are ready to do qualitative work on expression by exploring, changing, and refining the quality of these conventions.

In most societies, adults realize and elaborate these strengths of play through religious ritual. Ritual is not self-expression; it is participation in expressive action whose meaning ultimately steps beyond immediate social life and connects with the timeless truths of the gods. The public behavior of the 18th Century cosmopolitans shows that religious ritual is not the only way people can playact; the pouf, the point, the rodomontade speech are signs that people can playact with each other for purposes of immediate sociability. But the terms on which they do so are still of contriving expression at a distance from the self; not expressing themselves, but, rather, being expressive. It was the intrusion of questions of personality into social relations which set in motion a force making it more and more difficult for people to utilize the strengths of play. This intrusion in the last century burdened an expressive gesture to others with a self-conscious doubt; is what I'm showing really me? The self seemed present in impersonal situations, beyond the power of the self to control. Self-distance was on the way to being lost.

As belief in the public domain has come to an end, the erosion of a sense of self-distance, and thus the difficulty of playing in adult life, has taken one more step. But it is an important step. A person cannot imagine playing with his environment, playing with the facts of his position in society, playing with his appearances to others, because these conditions are now part and parcel of himself. The problems of middle-class ideologues in working-class movements at the end of the 19th Century derived from one difficulty with having no self-distance; such middle-class radicals were prone to be rigid in their positions lest, through changes in their ideas, they might change or delegitimate themselves. They could not play.

To lose the ability to play is to lose the sense that worldly conditions are plastic. This ability to play with social life depends on the existence of a dimension of society which stands apart from, at a distance from, intimate desire, need, and identity. For modern man to have become an actor deprived of an art is thus a more serious matter than the fact that people prefer listening to records rather than playing chamber music at home. The ability to be expressive is at a fundamental level cut, because one tries to make one's appearances represent who one is, to join the question of effective expression to the issue of authenticity of expression. Under these conditions, everything returns to motive: Is this what I really feel? Do I really mean it? Am I being genuine? The self of motivations intervenes in an intimate society to block people from feeling free to play with the presentation of feelings as objective, formed signs. Expression is made contingent upon authentic feeling, but one is always plunged into the narcissistic problem of never being able to crystallize what is authentic in one's feelings.

The terms on which modern man is an actor without an art oppose play to narcissism. At the conclusion of this study, we shall try to bring out this opposition in terms of class. To the extent that people feel their social class is a product of their personal qualities and abilities, it is hard for them to conceive of playing with the conditions of class—they would be changing themselves. Instead, especially in classes which are neither proletarian nor bourgeois but messily in the middle, people are more prone to ask, what is it in themselves which has led them to occupy this nondescript, faceless position in society? Class as a social condition, with rules of its own, rules which can be changed, is lost as a perception. One's "capabilities" determine one's standing; play with the facts of class becomes hard, because one would seem to be playing with facts very close to the inner nature of the self.

Having explored how an intimate society encourages uncivilized behavior between people and discourages a sense of play in the individual, I want to end this book by asking, in what sense is intimacy a tyranny? A fascist state is one form of intimate tyranny, the drudgery of making a living, feeding the children, and watering the lawn is another, but neither of these is appropriate to describe the peculiar trials of a culture without a public life.

CHAPTER 12

CHARISMA BECOMES UNCIVILIZED

Civility exists when a person does not make himself a burden to others. One of the oldest usages of "charisma" in Catholic doctrine was to define such civility in religious terms. Priests might be corrupt or weak men; they might be ignorant of true dogma; some days they might want to perform their religious duties, other days they might be listless or skeptical. If their powers as priests depended on what kind of persons they were, or how they felt at a given moment, they would become a burden to their parishioners, who had entered the church in search of communion with God but found, because the priest was nasty or not feeling well, that they could not make contact with God. The doctrine of "charisma" was a way around this problem. When he uttered the holy words, the "gift of grace" entered into the priest, so that the rituals he performed had meaning no matter what the state of his person. The doctrine of charisma was eminently civilized; it was tolerant of human frailty at the same time that it proclaimed the supremacy of religious truth.

As charisma has lost its religious meaning, it has ceased to be a civilized force. In a secular society, when "charisma" is applied to a forceful leader, the origin of his power is more mystifying than in a sacred society. What makes a forceful personality forceful? The culture of personality of the last century answered this question by focusing on what the person felt, rather than on what he did. Motives can be good or bad, of course, but in the last century, people stopped judging them in this way. The sheer revelation of someone's inner impulses became exciting; if a person could reveal himself in public and yet control the process of self-disclosure, he was exciting. You felt he was powerful but couldn't explain why. This is secular charisma: a psychic striptease. The fact of revelation arouses; nothing clear or concrete is revealed. Those who fall under the spell of a forceful personality become themselves passive, forgetting their own needs as they are moved. The charismatic leader thus came to control his audience more fully and more mystifyingly than in the older, civilized magic of the Church.

Anyone who lived through the 1930's, and observed left-wing as well as fascist politicians, has an intuitive sense of the incivility of such a secular charismatic personality. But this intuitive sense can be misleading. It suggests that the charismatic figure is identical with the demagogue, the power of his personality such that he leads his audience to violence, if not practiced by themselves at least tolerated when practiced by him and his henchmen. What is misleading about this intuitive idea is that it may prompt us to believe that when violent demagoguery is absent, the power of charisma is dormant in politics. In fact, the leader himself need have no titanic, heroic, or satanic qualities in order to be charismatic. He can be warm, homey, and sweet; he can be sophisticated and debonair. But he will bind and blind people as surely as a demonic figure if he can focus them upon his tastes, what his wife is wearing in public, his love of dogs. He will dine with an ordinary family, and arouse enormous interest among the public, the day after he enacts a law that devastates the workers of his country—and this action will pass unnoticed in the excitement about his dinner. He will play golf with a popular comedian, and it will pass unnoticed that he has just cut the old-age allowance for millions of citizens. What has grown out of the politics of personality begun in the last century is charisma as a force for stabilizing ordinary political life. The charismatic leader is the agent through whom politics can enter on a smooth course, avoiding troublesome issues or divisive questions of ideology.

This is the form of secular charisma we have to understand. It is not dramatic, it is not extreme, but it is in its own way almost obscene.

If a successful politician, like Willy Brandt, has the misfortune of real ideological commitment, his positions will be managed and shaped by his subordinates so that on television and in the press they lose their force, and therefore their threatening quality; the managers concentrate on showing what a fine, upstanding man he is. If he is good, then what he espouses must be good. Suicide in modern politics lies in insisting that "you need know nothing about my private life; all you need to know is what I believe and the programs I'll enact." To avoid suicide, one must surmount the disability of appearing to have a purely political will. How is this deflection from political belief to motivation accomplished? The politician who, in focusing our attention on his impulses —his Giscardian or Kennedy sophistication, his Enoch Powell rage, his Brandtian kindness—becomes a plausible leader by giving the appearance of spontaneously behaving according to these impulses, and yet being in control of himself. When this controlled spontaneity is achieved, the impulses seem real; therefore the politician is someone you can believe in. In ordinary life, impulse and control seem in conflict, a conflict derived from the belief reigning in the last century in the involuntary, uncontrolled expression of emotion. Thus the politician can seem an active man even if he doesn't do anything in office.

The best way to explore narcotic charisma is to begin by looking at the two reigning theories of charisma in this century, those of Weber and Freud. These theories in turn provide a perspective on the experience of charismatic politics of a particular modern class, the petite bourgeoisie. We need to look at the relation of electronic technology to this charisma. And finally, to understand secular charisma, it will be helpful to pursue the comparison between stage and street which has oriented the historical studies in this book. Is a modern charismatic politician like a rock star or opera diva?

THE THEORIES OF CHARISMA

A sense of something dangerous in the excitement politicians could arouse over the most trivial aspects of their private lives gave birth to the formal study of charisma. The fear of this power of personality dominated the thinking of Max Weber, who was the first sociologist to isolate the term "charisma" and to analyze its social origins. This effort occupied Weber from 1899 to 1919, during which time he was writing his major work, *Economy and Society.* As the book progressed, the idea of charisma was formulated and reformulated until, at the opening of the third part of the work, Weber finally formed a complete theory.

The term "charisma" does not appear in Freud's *The Future of an Illusion,* written in the 1930's, nor does Freud make reference to Weber's work. Literal-minded caution in saying Freud was not concerned with charisma would be, however, obtuse pedantry. Freud's theme is the same as Weber's: how can a person, by force of personality rather than inherited right or promotion within a bureaucracy, gain power and seem a legitimate ruler?

In analyzing the force of personality as political power, Weber and Freud assumed the electrifying personality who took form in the middle of the 19th Century to be the model of a charismatic figure throughout history. An electrifying personality succeeded in becoming so by throwing a cloak of mystery over himself. This "illusion" that Freud and Weber saw the charismatic figure weaving comes out of a profound disbelief both shared. Neither believed that God in fact does send down His grace into the world. When someone appears as a transcendental agent, therefore, his personal force must be an illusion, prompted by worldly forces and worldly needs. That is to say that neither man could leave transcendental beliefs in a society unchallenged; both sought to translate these beliefs into secular needs which would cause men to believe.

One need not believe in God to analyze a religious society, to be sure, but Freud's and Weber's unwillingness to take religion on its own terms created for both an illusion all its own. This was that a charismatic figure was someone who took charge of his subject's feelings in a strong way, that he was a figure of domination who dealt in intense passions. Because religious Grace was in truth an illusion, the charismatic person was in touch with the "irrational" in society. Therefore, both made a fatal exclusion: to bar from the rational and routine matrix of society desires for a charismatic figure. Both could imagine the intense power of charisma making order or losing its force and becoming routinized; neither imagined that charisma could be a force for the trivialization rather than the intensification of feeling, and as such the lubricant of a rational, orderly world.

Freud's and Weber's failure to see charisma as a trivializing force is perhaps inevitable, given where they begin; each writes that charisma arises under conditions of disorder and stress. But on the specific meaning of "disorder" they disagree.

The disorder Weber has in mind is group conflict which can't be resolved. In these moments, Weber thought, people are apt to invest someone with the aura of godlike power so that he can appear to have the authority to deal with the situations others cannot handle. Weber's emphasis is on why people need to believe in a charismatic figure, rather than on the elements in the leader's own personality which make him a likely candidate to be chosen. Weber's wariness of charismatic figures follows logically from this, because their presence indicated upheavals in social life which people had given up hope of solving rationally.[1]

Whereas Weber saw moments of disorder as sporadic, Freud's *The Future of an Illusion* sees disorder as the state of nature toward which the masses of mankind are continually veering. Freud puts this in strong language:

> . . . the masses are lazy and unintelligent, they have no love for instinctual renunciation, they are not to be convinced of its inevitability by argument, and the individuals support each other in giving full play to their unruliness.

A reasonable person would know that self-denial and renunciation are the only means by which he or she could survive in the company of other men or women who have conflicting needs. This the masses cannot bring themselves to see.[2]

The masses need, therefore, to be ruled by a minority or by a single leader:

> It is only by the influence of individuals who can set an example, whom the masses recognize as their leaders, that they can

be induced to submit to the labours and renunciations on which the existence of culture depends.

Now the problem is, how does the leader "induce" them to renounce their passions? Here is where Freud introduces the charismatic illusion.[3]

Renunciation is the task of religion. Religion generates the belief that the laws of survival and justice in society come from a superhuman source, and therefore are beyond human reason and human questioning. The terrors of the state of nature are replaced by terror of the gods' wrath. But the presence of the gods must be directly felt in the world; they are believable only if they show themselves through extraordinary persons, through leaders. The "Grace" of the leader gives him emotional power over the masses; only leaders who appear to have Grace can demand that men renounce their worst passions, can ask them to be good rather than just to obey.

For Freud, then, charismatic leaders must be always present in society, for without them the masses are ever ready to plunge society into chaos. For Weber, such leaders occur sporadically, because only at certain times is society plunged into disorder it feels it cannot resolve by itself, requiring help from Above. Out of this difference between the two theories comes a profound split: Freud believes the charismatic figure is an emotional dictator creating order. Weber believes that once he appears on the scene, the charismatic leader himself makes the chaos worse. Weber's Jesus is anarchic; for instance, he escalates all the group conflicts to a higher symbolic level, a struggle between groups that are enlightened and those that are not. And in this heated state the followers of a charismatic leader are likely to turn on him at any time:

> Charismatic authority is naturally unstable. The holder may lose his charisma, he may feel "forsaken by his God" . . . it may appear to his followers that "his powers have left him." Then his mission comes to an end, and hope expects and searches for a new bearer.[4]

Why does charisma inevitably falter? In answering that question Weber resorts again to the image of illusion. The followers of a charismatic leader expect him to "bring well-being" to them, but the charismatic leader is unable to translate his intentions to do so into acts of well-being, because his aura is only a shared illusion; thus he must fail and end by being discarded as a phony. Weber relates the story of the Chinese emperor who in response to floods prays to the gods; when the floods do not cease, his followers regard him as a mere person just like themselves, and they punish him as a fraud who has usurped power.

This is the internal contradiction of charismatic illusion; but, Weber says, the laws of economic rationality also make charisma falter:

> Every charisma is on the road from a turbulently emotional life that knows no economic rationality to a slow death by suffocation under the weight of material interests; every hour of its existence brings it nearer to this end.

As society "flows back into the channels of workaday routines" people lose their desire to see divine intervention in human affairs. Weber's argument is that boredom and the spirit of routine kill off the desire for a charismatic leader. Charisma does not arise as a fantasy release people need from their mundane tasks.[5]

When a charismatic leader is destroyed, Weber argues, the phenomenon of charisma itself does not disappear. It becomes "routinized," by which he means that the office or position the charismatic leader held acquires an echo of the excitement which once attached to his person. It is only at this point of transfer from the fallen man to the office that charisma could be thought of as a stabilizing force; the office arouses some feeling because people have the memory of the great man who once filled it, and so the office acquires a certain legitimacy. But this "afterlife" of charisma is only a faint echo of the passion which surrounded the leader, and at the time when the leader is alive, the force of charisma is disruptive and anarchic.

Freud looked at the relation of illusion to order in society in a way Weber did not. "We call a belief an illusion," Freud wrote,

> when wish fulfillment is a prominent factor in its motivation, while disregarding its relations to reality, just as the illusion itself does.

Since the masses do not wish to have their instinctual passions curbed, what wish is it that the charismatic leader fulfills for them by illusion, prompting a desire for order on their part?[6]

Freud answered this question with an explanation that today reads like all the clichés of psychoanalysis rolled into one. Every child at some point in his or her development replaces mother as the prime parent to love with father. The child is ambivalent about this replacement; he fears the father as much as he longs for and admires him; he still thinks of the father as a dangerous outsider, intruding on child and mother. When the child grows up and enters the hostile world outside the family, he reinvents these traits of the father, he

> creates for himself the gods, of whom he is afraid, whom he seeks to propitiate, and to whom he nevertheless entrusts the task of protecting him.

That illusion is charismatic: the father love-fear is the wish the leader fulfills. Religion is the social organization of fatherhood.[7]

Such ideas of repetition and reinvention have become so familiar that the strength of Freud's work is often obscured. Freud asks us to believe that belief in the gods is at work in any society, whether its overt religious symbols are deeply espoused, or merely allowed to exist as polite fictions to which no one pays much attention, or actively condemned. Philip II's Spain, Kennedy's America, Mao's China are all religious societies, and all in the same way. An infantile displacement governs all three. All three have charismatic leaders. Where Weber asks us to treat charisma as a historical event, Freud asks us to view it as a structural and functional constant. The success of a charismatic state for Freud is that the leader promises not a state of well-being, but a chance to become psychologically dependent again, as one was once as a child.

The contrast between the discipline Savonarola imposed on the Florentines and the discipline Lamartine imposed on the Parisians, drawn in Chapter 10, suggests what is obscured in each of these global visions. Belief in transcendent or in immanent values makes a great difference in the kind of order the leader produces in society. Savonarola's followers were "dependent" on him, it is true, but the result of their dependence was action, a theatrical form of action; in becoming obedient to him, they did not become passive. "Renunciation" in a culture governed by transcendent terms of meaning is more than ceasing to act badly or destructively; it is to act in new ways more in accord with the values which transcend the squalor of the secular world. Further, Savonarola's role as spiritual father was not that of master; he was only an instrument of a Power outside the world, and so his rule over his subjects was not complete.

Weber's theory cannot explain either why Savonarola gave energy to his subjects or why Lamartine could pacify his. The priest and the poet both created crowd discipline through their charisma, but discipline of an opposite sort. Although he is ostensibly talking about religion, Freud's model of a charismatic leader is exactly in the mold of the secular charisma embodied by Lamartine. Dependency without reference to outside standards of truth, dependency through shame, dependency which produces passivity—all these supposed marks of the religious father figure were marks of the secular charismatic personality. Yet the impact of believing in such a personality was not to harness and channel vicious, anarchic passions. It was to take challenges to injustice, representations of class interest, and trivialize them, by diverting attention onto the impulse life of the father-leader.

Charisma is imagined to be Dionysian by both writers; in a secular society, it is something more tame—and more perverse. Modern charisma is a defensive weapon against impersonal judgment of the state which might lead to demands for change. The defense works by disguising power through projecting the motivations of the leaders; ordinary routine workings of the state are thus maintained. Its archetypal moment is not a catastrophe which prompts people to invent a fiery god, or a renunciation ritual in which people invent a father-god. When the gods are dead, the archetypal moment of charismatic experience is the moment of voting for an "attractive" politician even though one doesn't like his politics.

Secular charisma is so far from being a Dionysian experience that it can create a condition of crisis all its own. In its most recent, televised form, charisma deflects the masses of people from investing much feeling in social issues at all; one is so taken up with the President golfing or dining with an ordinary family that one doesn't pay attention to issues until they arrive at a crisis point, beyond rational solution. It is difficult to imagine the institutions of modern society which act as agents of stability as the very institutions which put social issues eventually beyond the pale of rational control. But charisma, like bureaucracy, is exactly such an institution. By diverting attention from politics to politicians, secular charisma keeps people from worrying about unpleasant facts—that a war has broken out around the globe, that the oil is running out, that the city is running a deficit—just as the absorption of each of these problems into agencies or ministries with "experts" to handle them keeps them out of mind. They come to mind when the war is catastrophic, the oil impossibly expensive, the city broke, all too far gone to be dealt with rationally.

This suggests, I think, the real confusion in theories of charisma based, as Freud's and Weber's are, on an idea of charisma as a *response* to disorder. Modern charisma is order, peaceful order—and as such it creates crises. Like any genuine social theory, the ideas of these two writers on charisma invite criticism and reformulation. What they show us, by equating charismatic personality with passion and illusion and opposing these to rationality, is a certain illusion about rationality itself. The illusion is that rationality is antithetical to the production of disorder. Secular charisma is rational; it is a rational way to think about politics in a culture ruled by belief in the immediate, the immanent, the empirical, and rejecting as hypothetical, mystical, or "premodern" belief in that which cannot be directly experienced. You can directly feel a politician's sentiments; you cannot directly feel the future consequences of his policies. For that, you would have to remove yourself from direct "engagement" in reality, you would have to imagine a reality at some distance from the here and now, from the moment, a reality at some distance from the self. You would have to try, when a politician full of righteous indignation tells you he is going to remove "welfare chiselers" from the public dole, to imagine what in the next depression it would be like if you were on welfare. When a man who has been in jail ten years under a fascist regime announces, after he is out and ready to seize power, that under a proletarian dictatorship there will be no tyranny because everything will be in the interests of the People, you will have to think, not about how courageous a man he was to stand up to the fascists for his beliefs, but rather about what these beliefs would mean if realized. When an uptight and self-righteous crook is succeeded in office by a warm and friendly man, but equally conservative, you would have to disengage yourself from the immediate moment and ask whether things really have changed in any significant way. All these acts involve a certain amount of suspension from immediate reality, they involve a certain play of the mind, a certain kind of political fantasy. They are, in ordinary experience, a form of irrationality, when rationality itself is measured by the empirical truth of what you can see and feel.

CHARISMA AND *RESSENTIMENT*

Secular charisma on these terms serves especially well the needs of a certain kind of politician in his dealings with a certain class of persons. He, a politician of humble origins, founds a career on whipping up the public in attacks against the Establishment, the Entrenched Powers, the Old Order. He does not do so as an ideologue, although in some of his American appearances he shows signs of populist sympathy. His is not a commitment to some new order, but rather a pure resentment, *ressentiment,* against the order which exists. At heart his is the politics of status, of slights to dignity, of exclusion from the right schools; the class to which he appeals detests those who are privileged, but has no idea of destroying privilege itself. In battering against the Establishment, they hope to open a crack in its walls through which each one alone might climb. *Ressentiment* is based on a half-truth, half-illusion which explains why the petite bourgeoisie occupy the place in society they hold. Because a small, disdainful group of insiders controls the strings of power and privilege, they, the petite bourgeoisie, can get nowhere; yet somehow those who have the good things of life unfairly hoarded can put the little bookkeeper, the shoe salesman, to shame if and when they meet face to face. There is nothing egalitarian in this *ressentiment;* shame and envy combine to lead people suffering status injuries to hope that by some lucky break, some accident of mobility, they personally can escape. On this combination of envy and shame, the politician plays.

An odd theory of conspiracy results from *ressentiment:* the very top and very bottom of society are in collusion to destroy those in the middle. Thus Senator McCarthy attacked the bastions of the American Establishment for harboring Communist-anarchists; Spiro Agnew attacked the "bleeding hearts" of the rich American suburbs for being the secret sponsors of black protest. Post-World War II French anti-Semitism is almost a pure case of this sense of a conspiracy from above and below to destroy the beleaguered petite bourgeoisie. Somehow the Jew as usurious banker, Middle Eastern imperialist, fuses with the image of Jew as Communist plotter, outsider, a criminal bent on weakening good Catholic homes, even, as in a recent wave of anti-Semitism in Orléans, bent on murdering the children of Christian families.

It has become a fashion in historical research to see the politics of *ressentiment* at work as a constant force in history. If the middle classes are portrayed to be rising ceaselessly, then they must be always resenting the old order, really worried about status insults when they are clamoring for economic or political rights. The trouble with exporting the politics of *ressentiment* back wholesale into history is more than a lumbering lack of focus; resentment of status inferiority may be a universal human trait, but *ressentiment* has two peculiarly modern features which apply only to advanced industrial society.

The first is that the petite bourgeoisie is forced to invent this Establishment of persons in an impersonal economy. When power becomes bureaucratized, as in a multinational corporation, it becomes difficult to pin down responsibility for any one act to one individual. Power becomes in advanced capitalism invisible; organizations protect themselves from accountability by their very administrative complexity. Now a sophisticated analysis could show that in fact a small network of people move at the top of this administrative order, and in fact personally do wield enormous power. But this view of power is not what arouses the ire of *ressentiment*.

The Establishment of persons is rather a belief that an abstract, invisible class of people have agreed to keep out the world below through unfair means, and the term "unfair" is the key to the myth. Social place in a bureaucracy ought to be determined by merit; the notion of careers open to talent voiced in the late 18th Century is here brought to its greatest point. But there are people at the top who don't have talent; they survive by banding together, by keeping the people of talent out. Thus if you are down below, your lack of status is not your own fault; they took what is your right away from you. This self-serving aspect of the myth does not define the whole of the feeling of *ressentiment*. For what the Establishment of persons had developed is a style of self-assurance; they don't need to keep worrying about themselves, worrying about face, whereas the little man is always burdened with the feeling that he is pushing his way in. Status anxiety, composed of this sense of the proper (i.e., meritocratic) hierarchy betrayed and the fears about becoming pushy, is reported as similarly and strongly felt in the lower white-collar sectors of the French, English, and American occupational structure.

It could be said that the increasing invisibility of actual power in the advanced capitalist countries forces people to invent this myth in order to explain what's happening. It could also be said that as these countries move from a manufacturing to a personal skills–service economy, the issue of personal merit in relation to social position becomes stronger. On either count, the *ressentiment* is peculiar to our own times, something which can't be exported to all human history.

A second modern characteristic of this *ressentiment* is its antiurban bias. Some research on the *ressentiment* felt among petit bourgeois Germans in the 1920's shows a correlation between the sense of a conspiracy against the ordinary man from above and below and a sense that the great city is the source of this evil. The anti-urban character of American *ressentiment* is especially pronounced, a recent VicePresident, for instance, drawing loud applause from a group of veterans by saying that America would be a "healthier" place for decent people if New York City were floated out to sea. Anti-urbanism follows logically from the theory of conspiracy; in order to get together and conspire, the Establishment needs a place where no one knows much about anyone else; it needs a place of secrets and strangers. The city is a perfect mythological locale.

The politician who rides the tide of this *ressentiment* must, however, inevitably face a threat to himself. The more successful he is as an organizer of *ressentiment*, the more powerful, the richer, the more influential he becomes. How then is he to keep his constituency? Doesn't he by the very act of gaining power cross the line, betray those who put him in office as a challenger to the Establishment? For he becomes a part of the very system his supporters resent.

He can deal with this threat to his "credibility" by becoming a charismatic figure on secular terms. The successful practitioner of this status anger must in fact continually turn people's attention away from his political actions and position and instead absorb them in his moral intentions. The existing order will continue then to sleep peacefully because his apparent anger at the Establishment is perceived wholly in terms of his impulses and motives, rather than what he does with his power. The political leader of *ressentiment* must play on all the attitudes about personality which took form in the middle of the last century, if he is to survive as he moves higher and higher in government.

Nixon is an apt figure for study as a political actor seeking to harness the power of *ressentiment*. From his earliest political battles, he consistently pictured himself as a fighter against the Establishment, an establishment of the very secure in cahoots with Communists and traitors. The fight he waged against Alger Hiss was a fight against the Old Guard on the East Coast who were, supposedly, sheltering Hiss. His campaign for Congress against Helen Gahagan Douglas was waged as a campaign against a socialite snob who was "soft" on Communists.

Very soon in Nixon's career, however, the problem of the successful petit bourgeois leader began to make itself apparent. Nixon's first encounter with the problem of his own power surfaced in the campaign scandal of 1952. Wealthy businessmen had covertly given him money for a "slush fund" to be used for political purposes. Such secret funds are something every American is familiar with in terms of the workings of big-city machines; indeed, such scandals when they came to light in the late 1940's concerning city politicians were taken lightly or easily covered up. But Nixon's secret money—relatively small in actual dollars —became a major issue. The stance of this get-the-Establishment, law-and-order politician was personal and vindictively moralistic: he will purify things, and discipline those who have been getting away with murder. Suddenly he stands accused of being just another politician.

Nixon's successful solution to this threat in 1952 is the solution all political figures who become powerful as a result of inflaming *ressentiment* must resort to. In the famous "Checkers speech," Nixon diverted public attention from the facts of the situation to his intimate motives, to the quality of his perceptions and his good intentions. Before millions of TV viewers he cried, but not too long to seem out of control, just enough to show he was really feeling, and so a real, believable person. He spoke of his wife's "Republican cloth coat," he told the public that he was a man who loved dogs, like his own dog Checkers. He was a good man; therefore, they should forget about the money.

The induction of amnesia is a task secular charisma can easily fulfill. Nixon administered his anesthetic by focusing public attention on his impulse life, and more particularly on the fact that he could show his impulses openly. This meant he must be for real. No matter that the feelings are banal. Indeed, banality is precisely part of the prescription; diverting the public from the politician's actions to his psychological motives works only by a focus on spontaneous trivia. The Checkers speech was as great an act of political pacification as Lamartine's February speeches to the Parisian workers. The difference is that where the Romantic artist made an emblem out of his capacity to feel—called it "public poetry"—the same rhetorical stance in Nixon was disguised as simple psychological revelation. The response which the Checkers speech aroused taught Nixon a lesson which served him well for nearly twenty-five years: *ressentiment* can be harnessed, and the public deflected from scrutiny of a politician's personal power and wealth, if he will only learn to wear his heart on his sleeve before strangers.

Focus on motives is a technique open to any politician, and certainly not the only rhetorical stance available. But for the entrepreneur of *ressentiment* it is a necessity for success; otherwise the public which put him in office will end by turning on him as one of the Enemy. The seriousness of secular charisma lies in the fact that the politician, no less than his audience, *believes* in these moments of deflection.

One difference between Talleyrand, say, and Nixon is that the former, successively Bishop of Autun, Revolutionary power broker, Napoleonic minister, anti-Napoleonic minister, flatterer of Charles X, servant of Louis the Bourgeois, had a clear and cynical sense of his own distance from each of these roles, whereas Nixon in each of his incarnations believed in each one of his appearances as really him. That belief comes out of the fundamental idea of secularity. The modern politician of *ressentiment* is no mere contriver of façades to divert the public. His masks of virtue are for him at each moment true; these avowals of good intentions or strong feelings are for him justifying, even as he acts without reference to them or without reference to the needs of the angry shopkeepers and plumbers who put him in office. What makes the Watergate scandals in the United States so interesting is not that the President lied to the public, but that each one of those lies about the facts was surrounded by strong statements about his sense of honor and his own good intentions, and these statements the President himself truly believed. These professions blinded him to the fact of lying, just as for nearly a year they succeeded as an emotional "cover-up." Or there is the famous scene in which Perón told a Buenos Aires audience he had been accused of taking five million dollars out of Argentina. He immediately began to talk of his great love for the workers of the city, his joy at being from time to time out on the Pampas, his attachment to the "idea of Argentina," and he began to weep. It was not necessary to bring up the little matter of the five million dollars again, but on the other hand, those tears were genuine.

In general, a politics of personality consists of the revelation of intentions unrelated to the world of action. The charisma of a *ressentiment* politician is one step more complicated; it is of necessity an illusion, in that the facts of the politician's increasing power are being obscured by his professed motives, but he practices the illusion on himself as well as on his listeners.

Nixon is representative of Poujade, of Perón, of other Americans like Wallace, in the imagery of power that is used to disguise the facts of personal power. Power struggles become wars of contempt. On the one side there is someone against the Establishment who dramatizes his motivations rather than his acts; he is contemptuous of the Establishment, whose feelings are hollow because always shielded by decorum and pretension. On the other hand, this mythical Establishment of persons act contemptuously toward the little man, but they don't deserve their self-assurance; further, they are in conspiracy, somehow, with the scum which wants to tear apart the whole society.

The 19th Century conservative politician who could "talk sense to the workers" was a man who made his audience feel for a while under the sway of middle-class codes of propriety; show that working-class audience how fine your sentiments are and they will become deferential. The modern entrepreneur of status envy has no need to catechize his audience in propriety; the technique of showing them how fine his feelings are is rather bent to the end of making them forget. What is common to both 19th Century conservative crowd control and modern *ressentiment* is the split between action and personal impulse, with the leader's legitimacy in the eyes of his listeners arising from the latter.

To explain that cultural continuity, we need to understand how the electronic media have taken the 19th Century terms on which a speaker in the street would deal with a crowd of strangers and made those terms no longer limited to urban gatherings but regnant in national and international affairs.

ELECTRONICS ENTRENCHES THE SILENCE OF THE PAST

The media encourage secular charisma, but within a larger context. They have a special relation to the basic theme of our study, the rise and fall of public life. Electronic communication is one means by which the very idea of public life has been put to an end. The media have vastly increased the store of knowledge social groups have about each other, but have rendered actual contact unnecessary. The radio, and more especially the TV, are also intimate devices; mostly you watch them at home. TVs in bars, to be sure, are backgrounds, and people watching them together in bars are likely to talk over what they see, but the more normal experience of watching TV, and especially of paying attention to it, is that you do it by yourself or with your family. Experience of diversity and experience in a region of society at a distance from the intimate circle; the "media" contravene both these principles of publicness. Having said this, I am uncomfortable with it as a self-contained formula. For the impulses to withdraw from public life began long before the advent of these machines; they are not infernal devices, according to the usual scenario of technology as monster; they are tools invented by men to fulfill human needs. The needs which the electronic media are fulfilling are those cultural impulses that formed over the whole of the last century and a half to withdraw from social interaction in order to know and feel more as a person. These machines are part of the arsenal of combat between social interaction and personal experience.

Let us first see in what way the electronic media embody the paradox of an empty public domain with which we began, the paradox of isolation and visibility.

The mass media infinitely heighten the knowledge people have of what transpires in the society, and they infinitely inhibit the capacity of people to convert that knowledge into political action. You cannot talk back to your TV set, you can only turn it off. Unless you are something of a crank and immediately telephone your friends to inform them that you have tuned out an obnoxious politician and urge them also to turn off their TV sets, any gesture of response you make is an invisible act.

In the parliamentary speeches of the mid-18th Century, as in the theater, a phrase well done, a pregnant sentence, could be "pointed" by the audience, that is, repeated by demand. For this reason, English parliamentary speeches often lasted much longer when spoken than the modern reader would guess from reading them. To achieve the same effect under modern conditions of political performance, you would have to phone your local station, requesting that such a sentence be repeated; at the end of his speech, your hapless politician would by some miracle have all the phone calls for repetition tabulated and would announce, as a sort of instant referendum, that he has had 30,000 calls for repeat of the fourth paragraph, 18,000 for repeat of the section on national honor at the middle of the speech, and 13,000 for repeat of the section on national honor just before the end. He will be able to repeat just the first two paragraphs because of time limitations, but could he just say a word to the 13,000 whom unfortunately he must disappoint by not repeating? He knows how much they care about this issue. . . .

For the spectator, the radio and the tube do not permit audience interruption; if you start reacting while the politician is on the air you miss part of what he or she says next. You've got to be silent to be spoken to. The only possible means of response is to have a TV commentator select what shall be repeated and discussed. The commentator then assumes exactly the function of the critic who interpreted for those silent audiences of the last century the performances they watched live, but the commentator has more complete control because his is instantaneous. Passivity is the "logic" of this technology. The mass media intensify the patterns of crowd silence which began to take form in the theaters and concert halls of the last century, intensify the idea of a disembodied spectator, a passive witness, whom E. T. A. Hoffmann observed on the city's streets.

No member of the audience perceives the political process on the tube as a triad, composed of viewer/politician as intermediary/another viewer. The relationship is a dyad, and the politician's appearance, the impression he or she makes, the quality of the mask, is the center of viewer interest. How can a person in New York know more about a person in Alabama when both are watching a politician on the tube being sincere? Political campaign workers thus have found that TV is a very poor instrument for organizing political committees, voter registration drives, and the like; personal organizing, though less sweeping, produces more results.

Out of this dyad and the logic of passivity built into the electronic media, the paradox of visibility and isolation appears. Its terms are comparable to the technology of modern construction: one sees more and interacts less.

The first consequence of this paradox in communications is that the politician on the air must treat his audience on peculiar terms of equality. When twenty million people watch a politician give a speech on TV, he has usually to treat them all as belonging to one category, that of citizen. In any industrial nation, the mosaic of class and ethnic groups is rich enough so that the politician performing on TV at best could appeal to diverse groups only in the simplest terms. "To those of you under thirty, I would like to say . . ." and so on. Whereas he must appear open and be concrete if he wants to make a good impression, the very size of the audience means that he must treat it in abstract terms. Experts in media speak of the danger of overspecialized appeals as a result. But in fact it is no danger. Equality on these terms encourages the politician not to be concrete and specific about his programs, encouragement he is all too ready to receive. Treating one's audience as equals becomes the means of avoiding ideological questions, and leads to a focus on the politician's person, the perception of his motives being something which everyone can appreciate and share. The mass media are continually attacked for concentrating so much on the personality of the politicians whom they cover, as though this absorption in political personality were a caprice of a few directors, a choice of emphasis erasable if only the media were more "serious" and "responsible." Such comments miss the structural constraints, the very necessity for concentration on motivation, inherent in these forms of communication.

When it is said that TV journalism is "compulsively" personalistic, always making the private life of the politician the center of interest, the statement is true only to the degree that the true nature of a compulsion is admitted. Compulsion is a denial which in turn produces a magnified interest in persons or personalities who are not similarly denied. The complete repression of audience response by the electronic media creates the logic of the interest in personality. In a darkened room, in silence, you watch actual people; this is no novel or entertainment which requires an effort of imagination on your part. But the reality of politics is boring—committees, hassles with bureaucrats, and the like. To understand these hassles would make active interpretive demands on the audience. This real life you tune out; you want to know "what kind of person" makes things happen. That picture TV can give you while making no demands on your own responsive powers if it concentrates on what the politician feels.

Compulsive interest in the personality of performers grew up in the 19th Century among those large urban audiences, attending the theater or concerts in massive numbers, where silence was becoming the rule of respectable behavior. The modern media remove this interest from the arena of a class—the bourgeois class—and make it a technological consequence for all people watching, regardless of their social station. The perception of personality is the logic of equality, in a medium which can make no demands on the perceiver.

Clearly, then, the electronic media are well suited to the defensive shielding the *ressentiment* politician must engage in once he has power. Consider a famous televised appearance of George Wallace, standing in the school door blocking black children from going to an integrated school. With Wallace, the symbol of resistance to blacks was always tinged with a penumbra of even stronger hatred for "nigger lovers"—that is, outsiders, the Government, rich Northerners—the range of enemies suggested was so enormous it was unfocused. When the news focused on the man, therefore, it became enmeshed in a vicious circle: it tried to understand the personal history, motivation, and feelings of Wallace himself in order to uncover these hidden layers of resentment. The media lost sight increasingly of the fact that the protest was meaningless in terms of actual resistance; the politician succeeded in a transfer of attention so that his personality became a code to be broken, without reference to the power of that personality to act. Indeed, interpreting his intentions as incarnations of hidden forces in the society, the media succeeded in legitimating him as a person worth listening to, no matter what he did. In this way, the "symbolic" protest of an entrepreneur of *ressentiment* was metamorphosed so that the intentions never had to be tested by their consequences, efficacy, or, indeed, their morality.

The compulsive interest in personality aroused by the electronic media and the need for deflection of the successful politician of *ressentiment* meet neatly. In the words of one media consultant to politicians, "Your Wallace type usually makes the media work well, much better than the liberals who look so impersonal and bland," a statement we will read more into than the media consultant meant. But this happy marriage between the technological promotion of secular charisma and the politician of *ressentiment* can also end in abrupt disaster for the politician.

Because all the referents are motivational, an act of weakness, or a crime, or a moral failure in any one realm makes every other aspect of the politician's life suspect. Nixon is perhaps the best example of a leader who crucified himself in this way. For the sake of argument, say this was a leader who defused the possibility of nuclear war with Russia; shouldn't he be allowed a few million dollars in graft, an illegal burglary, and ten or twelve different lies to the public? But that would be a realistic scale which Nixon himself had never before used. Having all his life sought legitimacy through his rage against the Establishment, when he became supreme as ruler, he suddenly expected the public to judge him in terms completely different from and more realistic than the terms in which he hoped them to judge his political enemies on the way up.

The absorption in motivation, necessary for the politician of *ressentiment,* reinforced by the media, creates the only real threat to the tenure of these figures, in that they are continually risking delegitimation because failings in one sphere of their lives are taken as signs that the whole person is no good. Just as personality politics is a deflection of public interest away from measuring personal character in terms of effective public action, so, as all the elements of character become symbolic without any real referents, any flaw can suddenly become the instrument of self-destruction.

Again, the force of this phenomenon is lost if we conceive of the politician only as a poseur who gets caught. Because the politician believes that each moment of appearance is a reality, that every mask he wears is a sign of his true character, he can quickly be tied up in trivial issues, blowing them up to immense crises, in fact making them so in the eyes of the public who until the politician began fretting hadn't noticed. The so-called "land scandals" in Britain in 1973 were a classic instance of this feeling of total threat by events that only distantly, and in a minor way, bore on the work of the prime minister himself.

As a general rule, it can be said that fewer and fewer issues arouse the public because of their intrinsic merit or danger, as people care more and more about the personality of the leaders who are supposed to cope. A certain constriction of *ressentiment* since World War II follows logically from this more general narrowing of political concerns.

Unlike the wholesale transformation of political discourse in the 1930's into the language of injured dignity, the postwar politicians of *ressentiment* are finding fewer and fewer issues which can be converted to this use. If the floating of public bonds, energy problems, matters of trade imbalance, public health or safety are not easily perceived to be real until they become crises, it is also true that they are not easily packaged as a conspiracy of the unfair in cahoots with the scum of society to make decent people suffer. The field of maneuver now available to politicians of *ressentiment* concerns almost entirely the definition of insiders versus outsiders: Asians in Britain, *pieds noirs* or Jews in France, black children in white suburban schools.

To speak of secular charisma as a trivializing force in modern society, in sum, is not to say that the hunger for a charismatic leader is itself a minor or negligible desire. In a perverse way, it is the search for a believable hero, given modern terms of personality. In *A Century of Hero Worship* Eric Bentley analyzed the hunger for believable heroes which arose in the middle of the 19th Century, and concluded that one of the marks of modern society was that, in it, the discovery of heroes had become a constant and constantly frustrating preoccupation. The fall of impersonal public life in modern society is one reason why that search can have no reward: as the hero's motives became the source of his appeal, the content of heroism has become trivial.

The narrowing of content in political discourse matters in itself, and also because it defines an important difference between a politician surviving on the basis of his personality and an artist who is perceived to be a public personality.

THE STAR SYSTEM

In the *ancien régime,* a bridge existed between what was believable onstage and what was believable in everyday life. It may appear that the perception of a public figure in terms of personality is a new kind of bridge between stage and street; indeed, the impact of television on politics is usually discussed in terms of the politician having to behave as though he were an actor. This cliché is true in one way but profoundly misleading in another.

What is believable about the politician as a personality are his motives, his sentiments, his "integrity." All these are at the expense of concern about what he does with his power. The content of politics is thus narrowed by the perception of personality in it. That narrowing of content does not occur in the performing artists when the performer is perceived to be a strong personality. Mick Jagger and Bruce Springsteen project hypnotic personalities on stage, but this in no way detracts from the fact that they are great rock musicians. Similarly, the perception of Casals as a great man did not violate his art as a cellist. In looking at the problem of performer and artist in relation to text which emerged in the last century, we saw the issue not to be of personality at the expense of the "content" of music, drama, or dance. Rather, a different kind of dance, drama, or music is produced when the immediate work of the performer, and of the performer as a personality, takes precedence over the written text. In politics, however, the presence of personality "subtracts" political content.

The growth of personality politics thus may be condemned on ethical grounds. It is an uncivilized seduction of people away from thinking about what they might gain or change in society. A similar ethical judgment of artistic personality would be misplaced. The content of a performing art is not trivialized by the perception of a personality at work in it. The break between the modern stage and street lies in this discontinuity; it is a break in the very substance of expression in the two realms.

In terms of social structure, however, there is a connection between politics and the arts today, one directly created by the culture of personality. The connection lies in the consequences of the star system in both realms.

In all ages there have been famous performers and obscure ones, and people have wanted to see the former more than the latter. The "star system" refers to the profits which accrue by maximizing the distance between fame and obscurity, such that people lose the desire to see a live performance at all if they cannot see someone who is famous. Throughout the 20th Century serious musicians and actors have railed at the state of affairs which has made the public less and less willing to watch or listen live to those whom it does not know; the protests, and the alternative media the protests spawned, have largely failed. Indeed, in the 1960's, with the growth of rock music supposedly signifying a challenge to the mores of bourgeois culture, the star system became an iron law of wages. To understand how this star system works, we shall concentrate on people who want it least, young concert pianists who are more "liberated" from its seductions than rock musicians, and yet get caught up in the economics of the star system despite their best efforts.

It is estimated that there are eight hundred classical pianists in New York trying to have full concert careers; there are five concert halls in the city which "count"; in a given year, from thirty to thirty-five of the eight hundred will appear solo in these halls. Of the thirty, at least half are so well known that they appear year after year. Around fifteen new pianists get a hearing in New York each year, the hall often paid for by themselves; it is very difficult for them to fill up even a small auditorium like the Recital Hall of Carnegie Hall, and the wise pianist will have distributed many free tickets to friends of friends and to every conceivable relative. These new pianists get a paragraph in the *Times* which describes them as "promising" or "accomplished," and then they sink back into obscurity.[8]

The young pianist *must* go through such a concert appearance; he must hope that, in the first place, he will be noticed by a newspaper reviewer at all, and second that the review's variations on "promising" and "accomplished" will arouse the interest of an important agent. For it is only through an agent that he can hope to make the contacts in other cities, and organize them, so that he can go on tour. A tour will give him a minimum income, but more important, it means he can practice his art steadily in public. However, the chances are slim. The number of concert halls in New York has been decreasing steadily since 1920; the number of newspapers has been decreasing steadily since 1950, and the space allotted to music reviews of new artists has grown less and less. There are also fewer agents, and they make their money on big names. Further, although audience attendance has grown *in toto* for serious music in the city, it has done so through the increasing sale of tickets at the major halls and houses—and their size has been increased—while attendance at minor halls like MacMillan Theatre of Columbia University has in general dropped off.

The basic principle of the star system is that there is a direct correlation between the audience's desire, in the musical "center," to hear the live performance of any music and the fame of the music's player. Players who get to go on tour are those few who benefit from this correlation. New York should be placed between Paris and London in the operating strength of this principle. Of all the European capitals, the aspiring pianist or violinist will have the hardest time in Paris finding a good hall to play in, even at his own expense, getting reviewed, and, most importantly, attracting an audience. In London he will have the least trouble, although it will still be much harder for him to give two concerts a year in a London hall which counts than in the main halls of Hull or Leeds. An audience of 1,500 people in Long Beach, Leeds, or Lyons will be more socioeconomically diverse; the New York, London, Paris audience more class-homogeneous and composed of "repeaters." The system works in such a way that the provincial booking agents and managers orient themselves to the musical centers. In western Europe (with the exception of southern Germany), as in America, more aspiring musicians forsake residence in smaller towns, where there are numerous opportunities for playing steadily before a receptive public, for the capital cities, in which they have less opportunity to play, to a more jaded public, on the long-shot chance they may make it big.

The extreme difficulty of gaining access to a metropolitan audience arose for concert pianists as a direct consequence of the belief in the artist as an extraordinary, electrifying personality, a belief formed in the last century. Again, the pianist's experience is an instructive guide to the experience of other performers working as individuals. When the pianist at the end of the 18th Century lost a patron or small group of patrons, he was forced to become something of an entrepreneur in the musical capitals to make his way. Very few bureaucratic positions, as members of orchestras, were available, and the economics of splitting fees for chamber music performances made this an impossible specialty for many people to survive in.

In this situation, the mass of pianists, cut off from a permanent patron at court or château, found it harder and harder to work at all. The situation in Austria is clearest statistically. Between 1830 and 1870 the size of the average Viennese piano recital audience increased by 35 percent, often overcrowding the available halls, while the number of piano concerts fell sharply. One estimate is that the proportion of musicians able to earn a living full-time by performing fell by half during these years. Several factors contributed to this unemployment, but, above all, public interest in music shifted to hearing those pianists who had more than Viennese reputations, who were international celebrities—and that usually meant they had been heralded in Paris, London, and Berlin. The result was massive concert audiences, and fewer and fewer pianists at work. It is the contemporary situation of the New York pianists in germ.

The very essence of the new code of performance was to intensify inequality: if 500 people are famous, no one is, and so to find someone you can call a recognizable personality, a man who stands out, at least 490 must be pushed into the background. This is not benign neglect. Those 490 must be positively unrewarded in the same measure the 10 are rewarded; by denial as much as approval, a few people will then be brought forward as recognizable individuals.

The public of the great capitals thought they saw a great man revealed by the greatness of his ability to perform, and it was the man whom they responded to, paid, and courted, the man whom they made famous. The state of affairs beginning to develop a century ago lessened people's desire to hear music performed for the sheer pleasure of hearing music; the extraordinary quality of the performer became a precondition for going to hear music at all. The behavior of Viennese, Parisian, and to a lesser extent London audiences signaled a basic change in their very approach to musical art.

In looking at Paganini's influence on musicians of better taste than himself, we remarked that his ideas of playing had an appeal transcending the rewards of egoism. This appeal was that music in the hands of a great performer became immediate, direct, and present; music became an experience, almost a shock, rather than the reading out of a score. This is the idea of music as an immanent phenomenon.

In the present century that idea has ripened as follows: There is no musical phenomenon unless the performance is phenomenal. This is the principle of performance which stands behind the gradual disinterest of big-city audiences in just going to hear music. This principle puts enormous pressure on every soloist at work; his performances won't mean anything unless they are accorded the status of "extraordinary." Any sympathetic observer of younger pianists watching them agonize about being singled out as *Wunderkinder* has finally to conclude that the issue is more than a matter of personal advancement. The economics of trying to make it in an all-or-nothing game become coupled to a sense that you aren't any good at all unless you are very special.

The advent of electronic recording of performances has in a certain way extended the logic of the star system beyond the musical capitals. I do not mean that only a small number of soloists ever get the chance to record their repertoire, although that is the case; electronic recording has intensified the problem at a more elemental level.

The essence of live performance is that no matter what mistakes one makes one keeps going. Unless one has great presence, and great public esteem, to stop in the middle of a piece and begin again is an unforgivable sin. Recordings, however, are very seldom made by reading straight through a piece. Small sections are recorded, rerecorded, edited by technicians, as well as the artist, so that every recording is a collage of perfect details. Many musicians believe that some of the power and focus a player gains by having to keep going straight through a piece is thereby lost, but the loss, if it does occur, is idiosyncratic; a performer like Glenn Gould, who now only makes recordings, could hardly be charged on these counts. The problem with recordings is rather their very perfection.

By these electronic means, it becomes possible to establish standards for the listener which in live performance can be met by only a very few musicians. Since the economics of making money in the recording industry are even more stringent than they are in live music, only a very few of the artists who have been good or lucky enough to establish concert reputations will wind up recording. The best of the best, in the recording studio, get an opportunity to produce musical performances of a finish that even they in live performances can seldom equal. Thus, under the most casual circumstances at home, brushing one's hair or doing a crossword puzzle, one's ear becomes accustomed to listening to music of absolute polish. It is an odd situation: the performance standards of a Paganini are reinforced without any effort or awareness on the listener's part that he is hearing something abnormal. By virtue of modern electronics' power of collage, phenomenal performances are absorbed into intimate routine, as a part of the background. Thus the system of phenomenal performance is reinforced; recordings put additional demands on the performer to shock the listener who has bestirred himself to go to the concert hall into paying attention, through an extraordinary performance, because the listener is so familiar with an impossibly finished standard.

In sum, the star system in the arts operates on two principles. The maximum amount of profit is produced from investment in the smallest number of performers; these are the "stars." Stars exist only by checks to the majority of artists practicing their art. To the extent that a parallel exists in politics, the political system will work on three principles. First, behind-the-scenes political power will be strongest when the power brokers concentrate on a very few politicians to promote, rather than on building a political organization or machine. The political sponsor (corporation, individual, interest group) reaps the same benefits the successful modern impresario does; all the sponsors' efforts go into building a "product" which is distributable, a salable candidate, rather than building and controlling the system of distribution itself, the party, just as lesser profits in the performing arts accrue to those who control provincial halls and subsidiary bookings. When the political system works as a star system, its second attribute is that maximum power is gained by limiting the public exposure of candidates themselves; that is, the fewer times they appear to more people, the more they appeal. If Van Cliburn plays four nights in succession in Paris, his total profits can be less than if he plays only once; being less rare and exceptional an event, many fewer people would think of paying very high prices for seats. Similarly, the fewer contacts the candidate has with the public, the more his appearance is a special occasion, the more "appeal" he has. Such an issue is raised by political strategists when they consider the problem of "overexposure" to which a politician can succumb. Finally, a parallel between the star system in the arts and in politics means that inequality is maximized by combining the first two principles. The system becomes a zero-sum game with a vengeance. Whatever power one political figure gains through arousing interest in his personality will lessen the interest of the public in other politicians, and so reduce their access to power.

To the extent that these two systems are parallel, to that extent the seriousness with which people took appearances, beginning in the 1840's, has reached a perverse fulfillment. Mill's science of ethology, the essence of 19th Century culture, extends a dead hand over the conduct of political life in the 20th, more powerful for the very fact that most of the rules by which a politician is thought to be credible or exciting are hidden from the consciousness of those who fall under his influence.

Charisma is an act of enervation—this is what the "gift of grace" becomes in a secular culture. In political life, these charismatic figures are neither titans nor devils, neither Weber's ancient kings nor Freud's father subduing the unruly passions of his children. It is the little man who is now the hero to other little men. He is a star; neatly packaged, underexposed, and so very straightforward about what he feels, he rules over a domain in which nothing much changes until it becomes an insoluble crisis.

CHAPTER 13

COMMUNITY BECOMES
UNCIVILIZED

Ever since the work of Camillo Sitte a century ago, city planners have committed themselves to the building or preservation of community territory in the city as a social goal. Sitte was the leader of the first generation of urbanists to revolt against the monumental scale of Baron Haussmann's planning for Paris. Sitte was a Pre-Raphaelite of cities, arguing that only when the scale and functions of urban life returned to the simplicities of the late medieval era would people find the kind of mutual support and direct contact with each other which makes the city a valuable environment. Today we would dismiss this idealization of the medieval town as an escapist romance, but it is curious how the essentials of the first urban Pre-Raphaelite's vision has come to dominate the modern urbanist's imagination. Or rather, the belief in small-scale community has become ever more powerful an ideal. Whereas Sitte, or in an allied way the visionaries of the "garden city" in England, imagined community relations to transpire within a properly designed city, today planners have largely given up hope on properly designing the city as a whole—because they have come to recognize both their own limits of knowledge and their lack of political clout. They instead have enshrined working at a community level, against whatever interests of money and politics dominate the shaping of the whole city. Sitte's generation conceived of community within the city; today's urbanist conceives of community against the city.

In Chapter 10, we explored how non-territorial ideas of community arise, and what influence on these senses of community the culture of personality had in the 19th Century. Now we are going to consider the relation between a communal, collective personality and the concrete territories of community in the modern city—the neighborhood, the *quartier.*

The thread between Sitte's generation and our own is an assumption about impersonality, as it is experienced in the city, which makes face-to-face contacts in a territorial community seem so important. This assumption is that impersonality is a summation, a result, a tangible effect of all the worst evils of industrial capitalism. The belief that impersonality manifests the ills of capitalism is so prevalent among the public at large as well as among urban planners that it is worth looking at the idea in some detail, for it leads to a bizarre end.

Industrial capitalism, we all know, divorces the man at work from the work he does, for he does not control his own labor, but rather must sell it. Therefore, we all know, the fundamental problem of capitalism is dissociation, called variously alienation, non-cathectic activity, and the like; division, separation, isolation are the governing images which express this evil. Any situation which puts a distance between people must therefore reinforce, if it does not directly result from, capitalistic forces of dissociation. The very idea of the unknown can modulate into seeming one form of the problem of capitalism; just as man is distant from his work, he is distant from his fellows. A crowd would be a prime example; crowds are bad because people are unknown to one another. Once this modulation occurs—and it has a consistency in emotional terms if not in pure logic—then to overcome the unknown, to erase differences between people, seems to be a matter of overcoming part of the basic illness of capitalism. To erase this strangerhood, you try to make intimate and local the scale of human experience—that is, you make local territory morally sacred. It is celebration of the ghetto.

Now precisely what gets lost in this celebration is the idea that people grow only by processes of encountering the unknown. Things and persons which are strange may upset familiar ideas and received truths; unfamiliar terrain serves a positive function in the life of a human being. The function it serves is to accustom the human being to take risks. Love of the ghetto, especially the middle-class ghetto, denies the person a chance to enrich his perceptions, his experience, and learn that most valuable of all human lessons, the ability to call the established conditions of his life into question.

Of course, the capitalist system does dissociate man from his work. But it is important to see the ways in which this system, like any other, controls not only the ideas of those who are its defenders, but shapes the imagination of those who are in revolt against its evils. All too often, what is "self-evidently wrong" about a social system is self-evident precisely because the critique fits nicely into, and does little damage to, the system as a whole. In this case, the celebration of territorial community against the evils of impersonal, capitalist urbanism quite comfortably fits into the larger system, because it leads to a logic of local defense against the outside world, rather than a challenge to the workings of that world. When a community "fights" city hall on these terms, it fights to be left alone, to be exempted or shielded from the political process, rather than to change the political process itself. And this is why the emotional logic of community, beginning as a resistance to the evils of modern capitalism, winds up at a bizarre kind of depoliticized withdrawal; the system remains intact, but maybe we can get it to leave our piece of turf untouched.

But, it might be argued, you are too idealistic: sheer survival in a harsh world is a virtue. If people can reasonably do no more than defend their local communities, then why criticize this—especially as the public world of that larger city is so empty and uninhabitable? What I want to do in the following pages is show that we have no choice but to try to make that larger world habitable; the reason is that, given the terms of personality which have developed in the modern period, the experience of other people's personalities in an intimate communal territory is itself a destructive process. Modern community seems to be about fraternity in a dead, hostile world; it is in fact all too often an experience of fratricide. Furthermore, these terms of personality which govern face-to-face relationships in a community are likely to cut down the desire of people to experience those jolts which might occur in a more unfamiliar terrain. These jolts are necessary to a human being to give him that sense of tentativeness about his own beliefs which every civilized person must have. The destruction of a city of ghettoes is both a political and a psychological necessity.

Perhaps I put the matter so strongly because I and many other writers in the New Left during the last decade so erroneously believed that the rebuilding of local community was the starting point for politically rebuilding the larger society. Ours could be called "experiential fallacy": if in direct experience there were radical changes in belief and behavior, then the people so altered would gradually collectivize this experience, bringing light and change to others.

Today, the patronizing and upper-class character of this belief in intra- as interpersonal change is excruciatingly clear. Even if the idea of building a community sharing intimately new forms of experience had been initiated by the oppressed, or sustained by them, I think the results would have come to the same dead end. For what is wrong about the notion of building a community against the world is that it assumes that the very terms of intimate experience would indeed permit people to create a new kind of sociability, based on the sharing of their feelings.

BARRICADES BUILT AROUND A COMMUNITY

The larger society, of which radical community organizers form an unwitting part, has focused attention on small-scale community life in two ways. It has first done so practically, and second, ideologically.

The real estate ideas of Baron Haussmann in the last century were based on homogenization. New districts in the city were to be of a single class, and in the old central city rich and poor were to be isolated from each other. This was the beginning of "single function" urban development. Each space in the city does a particular job, and the city itself is atomized. In the American middle-class suburbs of the 1950's, single-function planning reached an extreme instance; houses were built en bloc in vast numbers, with the services for families in those houses located somewhere else: a "community center," an "educational park," a shopping center, a hospital "campus." Large-scale planners in the rest of the world were quick to deride the emptiness, tastelessness, and the like of these suburban tracts, and at the same time have blithely proceeded to build in the same manner. Take settlements as diverse as the new city of Brasília in Brazil, Levittown, Pennsylvania, and the Euston Center in London, and you will find the results of planning in which one-space, one-function is the operant principle. In Brasília, it is building by building, in Levittown it is zone by zone, in Euston Center it is horizontal level by horizontal level.

Although these planning ideas may be profitable to put into practice—for there is a single and coherent investment in a known quantity—they are not practical to use. For one thing, if the functional needs of the localized area change historically, the space cannot respond; it can only be used for its original purpose, or be abandoned, or be prematurely destroyed and remade. The difficulties of Brasília are well known in this respect, but the process has a larger dimension than single plans which fail. Think, for instance, of what a city of atoms, with a space for each class to live, for each race to live, for each class and race to work, means for attempts at racial or class integration, either in education or in leisure: displacement and invasion must become the actual experiences involved in the supposed experience of intergroup rapprochement. Whether such forced mixings would ever work in racialist or highly class-segregated societies is an open question; the point is that a city map of single-functions, single-spaces makes all such problems worse.

The atomizing of the city has put a practical end to an essential component of public space: the overlay of function in a single territory, which creates complexities of experience on that turf. The American urbanist Howard Saalmon once wrote that the planning effort Haussmann initiated put an end to the modal urban scene: the interweaving of the necessities of work, of child nurturance, of adult sociability, and of impersonal encounter in and around a single house. Saalmon had in mind the preindustrial urban households in which shops, offices, and living quarters were located in the same building, but the rebuke is just in terms of the larger city as well. To destroy the multiplicity of function in it and so design that usages of space cannot change as the users of it change, is rational only in terms of initial investment.

Part of the ultimate cost which has to be reckoned in this destruction of public space is the paradoxical emphasis on community it creates. For even as the atomizing of the city makes it difficult, say, for mothers or fathers watching their children at play also to work, this same erasure sets up a hunger for human contact. In American suburbs, this hunger is met by resort to voluntary associations; under cover of engaging in a common task, or pursuing a single experience, people get a chance to overcome the wounds of geography imposed by the planners of their communities. Thus, among people who tell researchers they are areligious, there are found an enormous number who belong to suburban churches; thus, as the post-World War II baby boom ends, many of the parents who now have adult children continue to belong to parent-teacher associations. A long and essentially fruitless debate among American urbanists has gone on in the last two decades about whether the suburbs are "real" communities or not; the important thing is that the issue is raised at all, that community has become a problem on people's minds. For the terms of modern urban development make community contact itself seem an answer to the social death of the city. These patterns of urban development have not aroused a desire to remake the city itself in a new image: "alternatives"—that is, flight—is the response.

We know from the history of public life in the 19th Century that the decline in this realm was matched by a contradictory and painful growth in the terms of its opposite number—the psychological sphere. The forces that caused the decline of the one encouraged the rise of the other. The attempts to create community in cities are attempts to make psychological values into social relations. The real measure of what the imbalance of impersonal and psychological life has done to community relations thus lies beyond the fact that the search for community life has become compulsive; it lies also in the expectations people harbor in the desire they have for close, open relations face to face with other people in the same territory.

The larger society has shaped these expectations in an ideological as well as a practical way. It has done so through the images of crowds. For these images have come to be distinct in people's minds from images of community; in fact, community and crowd seem now to be antithetical. The bourgeois man in the crowd developed in the last century a shield of silence around himself. He did so out of fear. This fear was to some extent a matter of class, but it was not only that. A more undifferentiated anxiety about not knowing what to expect, about being violated in public, led him to try to isolate himself through silence when in this public milieu. Unlike his *ancien régime* counterpart, who also knew the anxiety of crowd life, he did not try to control and order his sociability in public; rather he tried to erase it, so that the bourgeois on the street was in a crowd but not of it.

The imagery of crowds regnant today is in one way an extension of this 19th Century idea of isolation. The works of Lyn Lofland and Erving Goffman have explored in great detail, for instance, the rituals by which strangers on crowded streets give each other little clues of reassurance which leave each person in isolation at the same time: you drop your eyes rather than stare at a stranger as a way of reassuring him you are safe; you engage in the pedestrian ballets of moving out of each other's way, so that each of you has a straight channel in which to walk; if you must talk to a stranger, you begin by excusing yourself; and so forth. This behavior can be observed even in the relaxed crowds at sporting events or political rallies.

But, in another way, modern images of the crowd have so extended the 19th Century fear that a wholly new principle of dealing with, and thinking about, crowds has appeared. It is that the crowd is the mode in which the most venal passions of man are most spontaneously expressed; the crowd is man the animal let off his leash. This image of the crowd has come to have an explicit class character: the people actively expressing their feelings in crowds are seen usually as the *Lumpen-proletariat*, the under-classes, or dangerous social misfits. In the urban riots in Paris in the late 1960's, as in the urban riots in American cities in the same decade, the conservative press and its audience would describe the "bad" students and the "bad" blacks as stirring up crowd sentiments, and these were, in the first case and in the words of *Figaro,* "students from destitute or broken homes," and in the second case and in the words of the then Vice-President, "nothing but drunken bums." Thus danger from below and danger from the vocal crowd become united; but this conjunction itself will not quite explain the fear of spontaneous feelings unleashed which seem to make the crowd into a monster. Respectable people who voice these fears are not talking in a racialist way only about poor bad blacks who have more spontaneity; investigators in the wake of the American riots often found people who criticized the rabble ending up with the rueful comment that anyone might go out of control in a crowd. In this case, the crowd appears as a cause of vicious spontaneity, as well as the medium in which a vicious class expresses itself.

The literature of the social sciences offers instances of this fear of spontaneous crowd violence, exemplified in greater depth than popular feeling, but still within the same orbit. The discipline of social psychology itself dates back to the work of Gustave Le Bon, who at the beginning of this century used the transformations crowds were supposed to cause in individual feelings, making an ordinary upright citizen into a monster, as his prime example of how the "psychology" of a human being depended on whether he was considered as a single creature or considered as part of a social group. The crowd unleashed spontaneous violence in its members, which none of them would exhibit in their ordinary dealings with other people. Le Bon made no scientific claims for his view, but a group of animal experimenters with a similar outlook have. These experimenters, working with rats, proclaim that a "behavior sink" is induced in rats when they are crowded together in the laboratory. The rats, supposedly, become terribly vicious, each defending its territory against all comers; crowding is supposed to induce a kind of psychotic frenzy. These scientific claims turn out to be rather paltry, whether or not one believes one can infer human behavior from the behavior of other animals. Although psychotic during the day, crowded rats, like all other rats, sleep huddled as close together at night as possible; stray rats who can't snuggle are insomniacs. Few other animals respond to crowding in the same way; caged rats do not respond to crowding—which for all they know is permanent—the way rats in their own habitats do; and so on. What is important about this "scientific" theory of crowding is not its defects, but the cultural suppositions which led the researchers involved to expand a very peculiar situation into a general metaphor of the psychological evils of crowds. What is implicitly affirmed is that only a simple, clearly demarcated space, with contact between very few individuals, keeps order.

Modern images of crowds have consequences for modern ideas of community. In the more simplified environment there will be order, because individuals know other individuals, and each knows his territorial place. Your neighbors will know if you go out on a spontaneous rampage, whereas in a crowd no one knows you. In other words, community has a surveillance function. But how could it also be a place where people are open and free with each other? It is exactly this contradiction which creates the peculiar roles played out in modern community life, roles in which people are attempting at once to be emotionally open with each other and to control each other. The result of this contradiction is that the experience of local community life, seemingly an exercise in fraternity in a hostile milieu, often becomes an exercise in fratricide.

Fratricide has two meanings. It first and directly means that brothers turn on each other. They reveal themselves to each other, they have mutual expectations based on those self-disclosures, and they find each other wanting. Fratricide secondly means that this mentality is turned toward the world. We are a community; we are being real; the outside world is not responding to us in terms of who we are; therefore something is wrong with it; it has failed us; therefore we will have nothing to do with it. These processes are in fact the same rhythm of disclosure, disappointment, and isolation.

When this rhythm of community began to be heard in the last century, it was still as in a large hall. The conflicts in the Dreyfus Affair, the fights over who really belongs to the radical left, were still governed by a sense of large issues at stake. The logic of a gemeinschaft community will push it over time into becoming more and more local in its terms. That is what has happened in the last half century. Community has become both emotional withdrawal from society and a territorial barricade within the city. The warfare between psyche and society has acquired a real geographical focus, one replacing the older, behavioral balance between public and private. This new geography is communal versus urban; the territory of warm feeling versus the territory of impersonal blankness.

BARRICADES BUILT FROM WITHIN

It is instructive to look at a case of this withdrawal from the outside world, in a neighborhood where initially no one wanted the process to occur. I have in mind the Forest Hills dispute in New York, little known outside the city but immensely disruptive within it. For in Forest Hills a community group took form to pursue exclusively political goals, and gradually evolved into a self-enclosed refuge. The psychological transactions between people in the community became more important than challenge to the operating procedures of the city. In one way, the Forest Hills affair has a direct relationship to the Dreyfus Affair; for in both, community gradually took form around a collective personality whose care and feeding became the main business of the people in the community. But this modern communal struggle shows also the cumulative effects of the atomizing of the city.

Forest Hills is a middle-class, mostly Jewish section of the borough of Queens, threatened a few years ago with the influx of black families through a housing project New York City planned to build in the area. Thanks to a journal kept by a city mediator, Mario Cuomo, during the course of the dispute over this housing, it is possible to follow step by step the response of the citizens to this event. The history of the Forest Hills dispute began in a nearby community, Corona. This working-class Italian neighborhood in the middle 1960's waged a bitter struggle with the city, first to prevent a low-income housing project from being built, and then to scale down the size of a school the city proposed. At long last the Corona residents, with Cuomo as their lawyer, forced the city to abandon its original plans.

From this struggle the people of Forest Hills largely held aloof. "It," the poor black and his culture, didn't seem likely to happen to them. They were as well a community of well-educated, liberal voters, the kind of citizens that had looked with favor on the civil rights movement.

Then "it" struck Forest Hills too—a plan of the city that would locate 840 units of low-income housing in three twenty-four-story towers in the midst of this area of private homes and small apartment buildings.

Now the middle-class Jews encountered what the working-class Italians had faced. The city hearings were farces; in one, for example, a board member who was absent sent a subordinate to cast his vote and read a statement summarizing his "reactions" to the issues the community had raised. As an exercise in omniscience, such behavior convinced Forest Hills, as it had Corona, that politicians and their commissions didn't care what the people of the affected neighborhoods thought.

For the people of Forest Hills, recognition by the city that they had legitimate objections was especially important. We are not racist bigots, they insisted; slum families have a high incidence of crime; we are afraid for our own children; physically our neighborhood will be destroyed.

The more concerned the people of Forest Hills became, the closer the city machinery of community consultation, Board of Estimate hearing, and the like moved the project toward completion—indifferent to the complaints of the residents. Finally, all the legal formalities were completed, and building began. The residents resorted to the one resource they had left: the media. They staged publicity demonstrations; the residents hounded Mayor Lindsay even down to Florida, where he was campaigning for the Democratic presidential nomination, waving hostile signs at his rallies and following him around in view of television cameras.

This publicity campaign scared City Hall. As the conflict between the city and the neighborhood became increasingly complex, Mayor Lindsay assigned Mario Cuomo the role of fact finder and independent judge. Cuomo resolved to set down as precisely as possible what people said, and how they behaved; this record is all the more valuable, perhaps, because it is straightforward, innocent of any theory of what was happening.[9]

What happened to Cuomo was in a way quite simple. He observed, talked, and debated; he drew up a compromise favorable to Forest Hills. The compromise was reluctantly adopted by the Mayor and then by the responsible governmental group, the Board of Estimate. But these practical gains had by that time ceased to matter to the community. In the same way that the Dreyfus combatants passed from a political drama to conflict for the sake of the community, the people in this racial-class dispute passed across that line; in the wake of that passage, results obtained through normal political channels felt meaningless. The community became the implacable defender of each member's integrity. It asserted its legitimacy in defiance of the politicians and the bureaucracy, not by maintaining that the community had legally inviolate rights, but by acting as if only the people of the community, the Jews of Forest Hills, knew what it is to suffer; only the people in the community could judge the moral worth of public housing; resistance to the people of the community was immoral and probably anti-Semitic.

The stigma placed on those enrolled in welfare has strong class origins in addition to racial ones. Thus in New York City the Forest Hills housing project aroused few people in the black community in its favor, because many middle-class blacks had themselves little desire to have welfare families as neighbors. The Forest Hills group was aware of this, and occasionally made use of working-class black antipathy to those on welfare to bolster their own case. But those who actively supported the project—mostly upper-class blacks and whites—did so in a way that reinforced the rage the community felt at first against the bungling of the city government.

On June 14, 1972, Cuomo, listening to a coalition spokesman for the city groups favoring the project, noted: "For the most part they're not residents of the community and aren't immediately affected . . . it's easier for these groups to operate from high 'moral principle precepts.'" The supporters appear to be people who can judge morally without having to experience the lower-class intruders; whatever they say must be fraudulent because this relation of appearance to reality is obviously a fraud. Therefore, the suffering community came to think of itself as an island of morality. What Cuomo noticed among the Jews of Forest Hills, the observer of Paris in the 1890's saw among anti-Semites like Drumont: the world being corrupt and blind, only we count.[10]

At the early stages of the conflict, however, such feelings as "nobody understands us" were often manipulated appearances, consciously exaggerated. For in the beginning people in the community were thinking about a specific goal—how to end the project. They played a role of moral outrage to win specific concessions from the city.

On July 12, 1972, Cuomo had, for instance, a meeting with Jerry Birbach, one of the Forest Hills leaders; Birbach announced that unless the project was changed to meet his demands, Birbach would sell his own house to a black man, and then organize a massive emigration of the whites, "tearing down in his wake the whole community." Is Cuomo horrified? Not really, for he knows Birbach, who speaks with ferocious conviction, doesn't mean it. "The approach had been plotted out carefully," Cuomo notes. "Birbach was going to start by coming on strong."[11]

On September 14 Cuomo records the way the ruse of "sandbagging" works. A community group had gotten word to the Mayor that it could accept a compromise in the dispute if the Mayor would first commit himself to it; the community group then would work covertly on the other members of a board on which the Mayor sits to get them to vote against the compromise. In this way, the Mayor would be tricked into supporting something that no one else supported; he would appear isolated and extreme; he would be humiliated. "It was," Cuomo concludes, "a classic case of fraud in the inducement, but then almost everybody actively engaged in the political game-playing appears to regard that kind of tactic as permissible if not *de rigueur.*" Then Cuomo reflects on what he has just said: "That kind of sophistication is disheartening but increasingly it appears naïve to believe it could be any other way."[12]

If the game-playing were only a matter of frauds and deceits, an observer might well conclude that it was high time the fact finder lost his naïveté. Fraud and deception are classic weapons in the political arsenal. Indeed, a contemporary theory of urban structure advanced by the political scientist Norton Long argues that without such games the fabric of the city would break apart. In "The City as an Ecology of Games," Norton Long writes, "The games and their players mesh in their particular pursuits to bring about overall results; the territorial system is fed and ordered." By this, Long does not mean to say that players like Birbach are conscious that their frauds do good; self-interest, as Hobbes once wrote, makes men blind to what lies beyond personal desires. Long's concept of the ecology of games asserts that a balancing of power in the city is what these informal ploys bring. Long views the city as a state of equilibrium produced by conflict; his concept of the city resembles Locke's view of the society at large. The city's inhabitants, says Long, "are rational within limited areas and, pursuing the ends of these areas, accomplish socially functional ends."[13]

Theories of this sort attempt to define role-playing within a community in relation to the powers-that-be outside it. Moral postures, masks of intransigence, and the like are adjusted to fit how much the community has accomplished its ends in the world. What is peculiar about modern community roles, however, is that the masks, supposedly only the means to power, become ends in themselves. The reason is that people are disposed by the very terms of personality which have come to rule modern society to believe that an appearance is an absolute reality. When a group of people are brought together for political purposes, forge some common stances for themselves, and then begin to behave on the basis of that common appearance, they gradually begin to believe in, to cling to, to defend the posture itself. It is on the way to becoming a real definition of who they are, rather than a position taken in a game for power. For powerless groups challenging an institution of power like New York City, the only wearable masks at first are moral ones. It would be unreal, of course, to treat these cries of moral outrage as insincere; that is not the point. Most community groups that begin to fight on this basis use their own genuine moral outrage as a way of legitimating themselves. What happens is that the codes of belief which reign in modern society gradually induce them to believe that this outrage is so precious it can never be compromised or even slaked by real action, because it has become a definition of who they are as a collective person. At this point, politics is replaced by psychology.

There are many other names for this phenomenon—rule by rhetoric, ideological senility—and often these names are invoked as criticisms by people who really want to decry the legitimate demands of the groups themselves. What is malign in the process is not the political demands, but the way in which the cultural terms of personality can take hold of an assertive group and gradually lead the group into thinking of itself as an emotional collectivity. At that point the face turned to the outer world becomes rigid, and the community embarks on an internal course which becomes ever more destructive.

In the Forest Hills affair, the change took about three months. By the middle of September, in the words of the diarist, people were beginning to "believe what they had earlier pretended to believe." Unlike the Dreyfus Affair, there was no single event, or small groups of events, which served as catalyst. The experience of sharing their anger together had rather imperceptibly accustomed more and more people to think of this exhibition as a sort of communion with each other. Sharing anger became a way of talking within the community, and anybody who would not share this feeling was suspect.

A preview of this came to Cuomo through the Gordons and the Sterns, two couples who came to see him on June 13. Gordon was a retired schoolteacher and came prepared with a full set of lecture notes. "He tried to be coolly professional in his delivery but before long he was caught up in his own fear and would end up literally screaming at me." Cuomo tells us, "There was no devil's advocate role possible with him; any probing question that appeared contradictory to his position was pure 'devil' and no advocate. . . . He finished up in a crescendo—'My wife will be mugged and raped and you ask me to be reasonable.' "[14]

In June, he also caught a glimpse of the ethnic terms which will frame these common sentiments. On June 19, a delegation of community women visited Cuomo. They began with a monotonously familiar theme: people who have not "worked for it should not be given 'expensive apartments.' " But their subsequent arguments were rather more striking. They told Cuomo they had been "conspired against by an anti-Jewish mayor"; they told him they were angry at the Italians of Corona for fending off the blacks. They felt as though, once again, the Jew was society's victim.[15]

Jewish paranoia? Ethnic isolation? It is a question of asking what these words mean.

The ethnic dimensions of people's lives are peculiarly susceptible to community processes through which a collective personality is projected. A mask of anger, turned toward a world which has in the past denied the needs of ethnics, becomes a rigid mask, and questions of solidarity and betrayal become painfully confused. It is true that among western European and American urbanites, ethnicity is being discovered as a new, more "meaningful" principle of group life than class principles. Ethnic revolts by bourgeois people against the outer world can be rather comfortably integrated into that world; the people involved get to be angry, implacable, and cohesive; the system gets to go on much as before. The reason ethnicity is so perfect a vehicle for modern community roles is that ethnicity concerns the recovery in emotional terms of a life which cannot be recovered in political, demographic, and above all religious terms. Bourgeois ethnicity is the recovery of personality traits of a lost culture, not of the culture itself.

Forest Hills, like so many other sections of New York, is Jewish in the sense that the people in it are Jews and used to be Jewish. Yiddish is no longer heard and the Yiddish newspapers are gone. A few kosher butchers exist because kosher poultry is the only fresh-killed poultry to be had in the city, but few people keep kosher. Few Jews below the age of fifty can write or speak a sentence of their own in Hebrew, although the words of the services may be known by rote. Among older New York Jews there were, up to a few years ago, great efforts to act contrary to all stereotypes of Jews—not to talk loudly, not to seem "clannish," not to behave aggressively at work or in school—all of which, of course, is to take the stereotypes immensely seriously. The Yiddish word *yenta* originally meant a person who was both aggressively gross and stupid; among Jews now in their twenties, it is used to refer to anyone who acts "Jewish." This sanitizing of ethnicity is an experience most ethnic groups in America experienced, whether upwardly mobile or not. Language, food habits, customs of family deference—all were ambivalent matters, if not outright shameful.

The central experience lost, however, was religious, most of the European and Asian immigrants being, at the point of immigration, peasants or villagers who were strongly devout. When an ethnic group now becomes conscious of itself anew, the customs may be revived, but this heart is missing. The shell of custom around this faith is renewed in order to define a sense of particular and warm association with others. People feel close to each other because as Jews, as Italians, as Japanese in America they share "the same outlook" without sharing, if it can be put this way, "the same inlook"—religious faith—from which mores and customs of the past originated.

How does this sense of community, of sharing the shell of "outlook" and perception, become activated? The simplest way is through resisting attacks from the outside; indeed, when an attack on a group becomes modulated in the group's mind to an attack on its culture, people believe they can rely on each other only. What does an ethnic community share when it comes under attack? Don't be ashamed of being Jewish, people in Forest Hills said, stand up and defend yourself; be angry. But if sharing an ethnic identity is sharing an impulse, who is this collective person, this angry Jew? He is angry. If he ceases to be angry, does he cease to be Jewish? It is a perverse tautology. Reviving the ethnic shell without its center of belief, what people have to share is their desire to feel something with other people. Community on these terms is a state of being rather than believing. It maintains itself only by internal passion and external withdrawal.

So it should not be surprising when Cuomo reports about the women of Forest Hills who began early to perceive an ethnic threat that, like the men, like the leaders, they "simply refused to listen—let alone believe" when he would correct errors of fact in their presentations. Were they to operate as a group open to give-and-take with him, they would lose that momentary strength of feeling committed to one another, fraternal, united, and pure, by virtue of being under attack as Jews.

Cuomo gives us an eloquent description of this rigidification in describing a meeting he attended on September 21:

> The Forest Hills community is convinced that their principal weapon now, as it has been for the past few months, is to persuade the City fathers and the public-at-large that it is impossible to expect tolerance and acceptance on the part of the community. To do this they exaggerate their force and resistance. *And what is initially in part a pose then communicates itself and feeds on itself and eventually the illusion becomes reality.* Yesterday the hundred or so Forest Hills residents who screamed and stomped, cried and shouted, *believed what they had earlier pretended to believe.*[16]

By the end of September, as they became more solidly and emotionally together, people in Forest Hills began to regard the world outside Forest Hills with resignation. "Wait for a miracle," they said—the miracle that the slate of past actions would be wiped clean, and "no project, no way" would come to pass. In the meantime, expose the actual mechanisms of power as frauds. Since real power in a city is always a matter of give-and-take, actual offers from the government began to seem tainted and unclean to the community because these were only partial concessions. The only true power the community could imagine was total gratification—everything is a non-negotiable demand—and such gratification can never be. The community naturally turned against the instruments of power, the commissions, the formal hearings, etc., to destroy these mechanisms, hoping to show the world that they were phony and morally inauthentic. Believing they are false, the community would have nothing to do with them; otherwise it would compromise its own reason for being. The ironic conclusion of the Forest Hills affair was that bureaucratic inefficiency tied up the project for a long time, and the city's mediator Mario Cuomo, whom people in Forest Hills distrusted as an outsider, turned out to be the most effective spokesman for their interests.[17]

A withdrawal from political wheeling-and-dealing because you want to preserve communal solidarity must inevitably confuse the line between solidarity and betrayal. In this particular community, being against any compromise was taken to mean that someone was unashamed of being Jewish. In my own walks around the community at the time, I frequently heard people talking about being for Israel and being against any compromise over the local housing project as the same thing. At meetings people were continually tested for the steadfastness and implacability of their feelings, and those who leaned toward a settlement were taken to be fatally flawed in their morality. Indeed, the Jewish Defense League (a group of militants) scrawled on the business windows of one of these "compromisers" the motto "Never Again!"— a code phrase intimating that a desire to accept a settlement was the same spirit as that of passively walking into the Nazi death camps.

This pleasant, quiet community made itself into a ghetto, built its own walls. Its members acted as though they had a corner on the market of moral outrage. In no sense is the substance of conflict in this community like the substance of ideological conflicts, such as the conflicts we explored among Guesde and his partisans. But the process of conflict is the same, as the taking of a position becomes gradually the taking on of a rigid, symbolic collective self. Closer in time and place, the black community movements of the 1960's, challengers to the middle class, ended by building similar walls, as each of the different factions involved in disputes on tactics or long-range plans gradually came to see itself as a single legitimate voice of "the people." Outsiders, other blacks no less than whites, were to keep away.

THE HUMANE COSTS OF COMMUNITY

Anthropologists have a term for one aspect of territorial, communitarian rigidity. They call it pseudo-speciation, by which they mean that a tribe will act as though it is the only assemblage of human beings who are really human. The other tribes are lesser, are not as human. But if modern community processes were cast simply into this anthropologi-

cal framework, something essential about the process would be lost.
The growth of this intolerance is not a product of overweening pride,
arrogance, or group self-assurance. It is a much more fragile and self-
doubting process, in which the community exists only by a continual
hyping-up of emotions. The reason for this hysteria is, in turn, not a
matter of the innate destructiveness of man unleashed in the act of
solidarity, but precisely that the terms of culture have come to be so
arranged that, without some forcing and prodding, real social bonds
seem so unnatural.

In a society of atomized social spaces, people are always afraid that
they will be cut off from each other. The materials which this culture
offers people to use to "connect" with other people are unstable symbols of impulse and intention. Because the symbols are so problematic
in character, it is inevitable that the people who use them are at the
same time always going to have to test their strength. How far can you
go, how much of a sense of community can you feel? People are going
to have to equate real feeling with extreme feeling. In the Age of
Reason, people gave themselves over to emotional displays which
would be considered embarrassing in a modern playhouse or bar. To
weep in the theater, however, had a meaning in and of itself, no matter
who you were. Whereas the emotion experienced in a modern fraternal
group is part and parcel of declaring what kind of person you are, and
who is your brother. Now the dramatic displays of feeling become
signals to others that you are "for real," and also, by whipping you up
to a fever pitch, convince you yourself that you are "for real."

Let us sum up the fire urban planners play with so carelessly when
they talk about building a sense of community at a local level in the city,
as opposed to reawakening meaningful public space and public life in
the city as a whole.

One need not be a believer in omnipresent conspiracy to perceive
that this struggle for community solidarity serves a stabilizing function
in terms of the larger political structures of the society. Just as charismatic experience becomes a deflection from dealing with those political
structures, the attempt to form community deflects attention from
those structures. The storms and stresses of fratricide are system-main-
taining. Again, as with charismatic experience, it is all too easy now to
confuse personal passion in society with the disordering of society. In
fact the reverse is the case; the more people are plunged into these
passions of community, the more the basic institutions of social order
are untouched. To speak of questions of personal motivation in politics
as seductive—either in charismatic leadership or in forming the basis
of communal feeling—is not to speak of a metaphor but of a systematic
structural fact. People in struggling to be a community become ever
more absorbed in each other's feelings, and ever more withdrawn from

an understanding of, let alone a challenge to, the institutions of power so very willing to have "local participation" and "local involvement."

Most so-called progressive town planning has aimed at a very peculiar kind of decentralization. Local units, garden suburbs, town or neighborhood councils are formed; the aim is formal local powers of control, but there is no real power that these localities in fact have. In a highly interdependent economy, local decision about local matters is an illusion. The result of these well-intentioned efforts at decentralization produces community rhythms, if not as extreme as the crisis in Forest Hills, depressingly similar in structure. Every urban planner will have experienced these local fights in which people, thinking they have in fact power to change something in the community, become engaged in intense struggle about who "really" speaks for the community. These struggles so engage people in matters of internal identity, solidarity, or dominance that when the real moments of power negotiation come, and the community must turn toward the larger structures of city and state which have actual power, the community is so absorbed in itself that it is deaf to the outside, or exhausted, or fragmented.

A society which fears impersonality encourages fantasies of collective life parochial in nature. Who "we" are becomes a highly selective act of imagination: one's immediate neighbors, co-workers in the office, one's family. Identifying with people one doesn't know, people who are strangers but who may share one's ethnic interests, family problems, or religion, becomes hard. Impersonal ethnic ties, no less than impersonal ties of class, don't really make a bond; one feels one has to know others as persons to use "we" in describing one's relations to them. The more local the imagination, the greater becomes the number of social interests and issues for which the psychological logic is: we won't get involved, we won't let this violate us. It is not indifference; it is refusal, a willed constriction of experience the common self can permit in. To think of this localization in narrowly political terms is to lose some of the force of the phenomenon; basically what is at issue is the degree of risk-taking a person is willing to engage in. The more local his sense of a self he can share with others, the fewer risks he is willing to take.

The refusal to deal with, absorb, and exploit reality outside the parochial scale is in one sense a universal human desire, being a simple fear of the unknown. Community feeling formed by the sharing of impulses has the special role of reinforcing the fear of the unknown, converting claustrophobia into an ethical principle.

The term "gemeinschaft" meant, originally, the full disclosure of feeling to others; historically it has come at the same time to mean a community of people. These two taken together make gemeinschaft a special social group in which open emotional relations are possible as opposed to groups in which partial, mechanical, or emotionally indifferent ones prevail. Any community, we have noted, is in some degree built on fantasy. What is distinctive about the modern gemeinschaft community is that the fantasy people share is that they have the same impulse life, the same motivational structure. In Forest Hills, for example, anger showed you were proud to be a Jew.

Impulse and collective life now joined, the fratricidal rhythm is ready to begin. If people have new impulses, the community will then shatter; they will not be sharing the same feelings; the person who changes "betrays" the community; individual deviation threatens the strength of the whole; people have therefore to be watched and tested. Distrust and solidarity, seemingly so opposed, are united. The absence, misunderstanding, or indifference of the world outside the community is interpreted in the same way. Since fraternal feelings are immediate and strongly felt, how can others not understand, why don't they respond in kind, why won't the world bend to emotional desires? The answer to these questions can only be that the world outside the community is less real, less authentic than the life within. The consequence of that answer is not a challenge to the outside, but a dismissal of it, a turning away, into the watchful sharing with others who "understand." This is the peculiar sectarianism of a secular society. It is the result of converting the immediate experience of sharing with others into a social principle. Unfortunately, large-scale forces in society may psychologically be kept at a distance, but do not therefore go away.

Finally, modern gemeinschaft is a state of feeling "bigger" than action. The only actions the community undertakes are those of emotional housekeeping, purifying the community of those who really don't belong because they don't feel as the others do. The community cannot take in, absorb, and enlarge itself from the outside because then it will become impure. Thus a collective personality comes to be set against the very essence of sociability—exchange—and a psychological community becomes at war with societal complexity.

Urban planners have yet to learn a profound truth which conservative writers have perceived but have put to the wrong uses. It is that people can be sociable only when they have some protection from each other; without barriers, boundaries, without the mutual distance which is the essence of impersonality, people are destructive. It is so not because "the nature of man" is malevolent—the conservative error—but because the sum effect of the culture spawned by modern capitalism and secularism makes fratricide logical when people use intimate relations as a basis for social relations.

The real problem with town planning now is not what to do, but what to avoid. Despite the alarms sounding from social psychology laboratories, human beings have potentially a real genius for group life under crowded conditions. The art of planning town squares is not arcane; it has been practiced with great success for centuries, usually without formally trained architects. Historically, the dead public life and perverted community life which afflicts Western bourgeois society is something of an anomaly. The question is how to recognize symptoms of our peculiar disease, symptoms which lie as much in current notions of what humane scale and good community are as in the false notions we have of impersonality per se as a moral evil. In short, when town planning seeks to improve the quality of life by making it more intimate, the planner's very sense of humanity creates the very sterility he should seek to avoid.

CHAPTER 14

THE ACTOR
DEPRIVED OF HIS ART

In this chapter, I want to bring the analysis of public life to bear in a systematic way on the problem of expression. When "art" and "society" are joined, the discussion is usually of the effect of social conditions upon the artist's work or the expression in his work of those conditions. An art *in* society, aesthetic work intrinsic to social processes themselves, is hard to imagine.

The classic ideal of the *theatrum mundi* attempted to convey one union of aesthetics and social reality. Society is a theater, and all men are actors. As an ideal, this vision is by no means dead. In Nicolas Evreinoff's *The Theatre in Life* of 1927, the *theatrum mundi* is asserted in these terms:

> examine any . . . branch of human activity and you . . . will see
> that kings, statesmen, politicians, warriors, bankers, business
> men, priests, doctors, all pay daily tributes to theatricality, all
> comply with the principles ruling on the stage.

In *The Drama of Social Reality* of 1975, Stanford Lyman and Marvin Scott begin an examination of modern politics in these words:

> All life is theatre; hence political life is also theatrical. And rule
> by theatre may be termed "theatrocracy."[18]

The difficulty with this ideal is that it stands outside time. In the middle of the 18th Century a social life did exist in which the aesthetics of the theater were intertwined with behavior in ordinary life. However, this aesthetic dimension in everyday life gradually withered. It was replaced by a society in which formal art accomplished tasks of expression which were difficult or impossible to accomplish in ordinary life. The imagery of *theatrum mundi* shows what is a potential of expression in society; the erosion of public life shows what in fact has become of this potential: in modern society, people have become actors without an art. Society and social relations may continue to be abstractly imagined in dramatic terms, but men have ceased themselves to perform.

Changes in the meaning of expression have followed in the wake of these changes in public identity. Expression in the public world was presentation of feeling states and tones with a meaning of their own no matter who was making the presentation; representation of feeling states in the intimate society makes the substance of an emotion depend on who is projecting it. The presentation of feeling is impersonal, in the sense that death has a meaning no matter who is dying. The representation to another of what is happening to oneself is idiosyncratic; in telling another person about a death in the family, the more he sees of what the death made you feel, the more powerful does the event itself become to him. There has been a movement from belief in human nature to belief in human natures, a movement from the idea of natural character to that of personality.

The differences between presentation and representation of feeling are not between the expressive and the inexpressive, per se. They are rather between the kind of emotional transaction in which people can call upon the powers of a particular art and emotional transactions in which they cannot. The work of presenting emotion is akin to the work an actor does; it is making manifest to another a feeling tone or state which will have a meaning, once it is given a shape. Because this feeling has a conventionalized form, it can be repeatedly expressed; the professional actor who learns to give a good performance night after night is the model. But in holding an inquest on one's personality, the power of the actor is not so easily available. For this inquest is about what is specific and unique in a life; from moment to moment the meaning changes, and one's energies are directed toward finding out what it is one feels, rather than making the feeling clear and manifest to others.

The actor deprived of the art of acting appears when the conditions of public expression have so eroded in society that it is no longer possible to think of theater and society, in Fielding's words, as "indiscriminately" intertwined. He appears when the experiencing of human nature during the course of a lifetime is replaced by the search for a selfhood.

But placing this figure in such broad historical terms is in its own way misleading. It suggests that this loss of an art in everyday life is very far away in time, that today we live out the consequences but know nothing of the process of loss itself. In fact, within the life cycle of people today, this loss occurs in miniature as well. Strengths of playacting developed in childhood are effaced by the conditions of adult culture.

As he is inducted into the anxieties and beliefs that comprise the adult culture, the growing human being is also losing this childhood strength.

The question of play and what happens to play in adult life is important because the cultural evolution of modern times is peculiar. It is unusual for a society to distrust ritual or ritualized gesture, unusual for a society to see formal behavior as inauthentic. The childhood energies of play are in most societies continued and enriched as ritual, usually in the service of religion. Secular, advanced capitalist society does not call upon, but rather works against, these energies.

"Playing," "playacting," and the "play" have a common linguistic root, and it is not a chance coincidence. But it is important to keep the two apart as well; childhood play is preparation for a certain kind of adult aesthetic work, yet certainly not the same as that work. It is equally important to divorce inquiry into the cultural meaning of play from the current celebration of play as a revolutionary principle. This celebration identifies play with spontaneity, and that is wrong. The element of aesthetic training that goes on in play lies in accustoming the child to believe in the expressivity of impersonal behavior, when it is structured by made-up rules. Play for the child is the antithesis to expressing himself spontaneously.

The relationship between childhood play and the adult culture which today enervates it can be cast in the form of a conflict between two psychic principles. One of these is the principle which leads children to invest a great deal of passion in an impersonal situation governed by rules, and to think of expression in the situation as a matter of the remaking and the perfecting of those rules to give greater pleasure and promote greater sociability with others. This is play. It conflicts with the principle which has come to govern the state of adult culture which leads adults to invest a great deal of passion in uncovering their own motives for action and the motives of others with whom they come into contact. These discoveries of inner reasons and authentic impulses are seen to be the freer, the less people are impeded by abstract rules, or forced to express themselves in terms of "clichés," "stereotyped feelings," or other conventional signs. The mark of the seriousness of this inquest is the very difficulty in undertaking it; pain rather than pleasure is its legitimation, and a withdrawal from surface sociability into a "deeper" life, usually at the expense of companionship and casual friendship, is its product. The psychic principle governing this adult culture is narcissism.

And thus, in probing how the actor without an art came to be, we arrive at an image of a conflict between play and narcissism, the forces of narcissism, now mobilized by the culture, defeating the strength to play which the human being had before he grew up and entered "reality."

PLAY IS THE ENERGY FOR PUBLIC EXPRESSION

The immense literature on play tends to fall in two schools. One treats play as a form of cognitive activity; it examines how children form symbols through their play and how these symbols become more complex as children at play grow older. The other school treats play as behavior, is less concerned with symbol formation, and concentrates on how children learn cooperation, express aggression, and tolerate frustration through playing together.

Those in the cognitive camp have occasionally shown an interest in the relationship of play to creative work, but these forays have suffered on two accounts. One is that many writers have identified play and "the creative act" as virtually synonymous; the strict adherents of Freud have done so in imitation of such sentiments as the following from their master:

> The creative writer does the same as the child at play. He creates a world of phantasy which he takes very seriously, that is, which he invests with large amounts of emotion, while separating it sharply from reality. . . .

—a dictum which led Freud to the conclusion that

> The opposite of play is not what is serious but what is real.[19]

Those whose studies of play have led them to question this Freudian opposition of play-creativity to reality often phrase their arguments in equal if opposite terms. Play and creativity are spoken of as "at work in reality, not on it," as a process of drawing logical connections which cannot be drawn by the particular processes of deductive logic, and so forth. But the play and creativity are spoken of interchangeably still. Thus it becomes difficult to distinguish the specific qualitative differences between a child who, banging on the black keys of the piano, suddenly discovers they form a pentatonic scale, and Debussy, who, one summer doing finger exercises, discovers possibilities in the pentatonic scale none of his contemporaries had before imagined. To say the two activities are similar in kind easily meshes into saying they are "fundamentally" the same, and then an essential quality in each realm becomes obscured: judgment. If Debussy is "fundamentally" playing around the same way as a child, the quality of his judgment about his experiments with the pentatonic scale is obliterated; "any child could do it," then. But the point is, no child could.

An allied problem in the cognitive school of play-studies is the term "creativity" itself. It is appealing to proceed on the theory, as Arthur Koestler does, that there is a general biological propensity which can be called creativity, that one can speak as he does of a unitary process knitting together "scientific discovery, artistic originality, and comic inspiration." The problem is that artists, at least, are not "being creative." They are doing specific work in a specific medium. All too often the theories which link creativity and play result in a picture of what was original about what an artist did, and how this result resembles the results of play for children, but does not explain the steps by which this result was arrived at in the artist's work, and the relationship of that process to the internal activities of a child at play.[20]

Theorizing about play and creative work is worthwhile, but it has to have a focus. One has to see play activities preparing for creative activities, in order to maintain a sense of the differences about the quality of the results. One has to link specific action within play to specific kinds of creative work. Such an approach should overcome the distance between play viewed as a cognitive activity and play viewed as behavior. In Ernst Kris's happy phrase, the relationship between specific acts of play and specific artistic actions is a matter of "ancestry" rather than of "identity."[21]

The ancestry of performing we shall seek out in child's play is the learning children do about self-distance—specifically, how self-distance helps children work on the quality of the rules by which they play. In his study of play, *Homo Ludens,* Johan Huizinga defines three aspects of play. Play is, first of all, a purely voluntary activity. It is then what Huizinga calls "disinterested" activity. It is finally secluded, by which he means play has special spaces and time periods which set it apart from other activities.[22]

The second of these three conditions, play as disinterested activity, is related to the question of self-distance. Disinterested does not mean uninterested. Children at sport could hardly be called bored. Huizinga means disinterested in the sense of stepping away from immediate desire or instant gratification. That stepping away permits people to play together. Disinterested play appears in the life cycle long before children play formal games with each other, however; it begins in the later months of the first year of life.

To Jean Piaget, disinterested or self-distanced play begins at the third sensorimotor stage of life; that is, at the end of the first year. He gives a wonderful example of it when, in sitting next to his daughter's crib, he watches her toy with objects suspended over her crib. She sees a pattern of light formed by the sunlight pouring over these objects, she reaches up to them, moves them, a new pattern of light appears, and she is delighted. She flops the objects over once again. Yet another pattern appears.[23]

If babies were all voracious desire, then the moment a pleasurable pattern had been obtained, the baby would cease to act, would become retentive of the pleasure. Or if it did keep moving the discs around, and produced a pattern unlike what it knew first, the infant would cry out in pain at the loss of the pleasing pattern. When such a loss is not experienced, retentive pleasure is suspended and something more complex than sure gratification governs the baby's acts. Possession by the self, in the sense of a pattern made and then stably kept, is loosened, so that the infant can take the risk of finding a new pattern—a pattern which may or may not give pleasure. Piaget has observed that when infants do not like the new patterns they make in such situations, they do not attempt to re-establish the first, but instead try again for a third alternative. Such attempts are play. In play the infant has put a distance between his or her desire for retention. In this sense, the baby engages in self-distanced activity.

Self-distance evolves again at the point when children begin to play games with each other. A game is best defined as an activity children engage in together, with principles of action consciously acknowledged or agreed upon by the children. The game as a social contract appears in different year-stages, depending on the different cultures children live in; but by the fourth year almost all known child cultures engage in such compacts.

Here is how self-distance works in the game of marbles, played by children of four and one half, five, and six (the following observations come from work done by the author some years ago at the Laboratory of Social Psychology at the University of Chicago). A game of marbles is a competitive situation in which the aim is for one of the players to get all the marbles of the other players, or, under a different set of rules, to wipe the other players' marbles off the playing field. If the adult observer tries to simplify the rules of the game, he encounters resistance from the children. What they like are attempts to make the rules more and more complex. If the game were just a means to an end, their behavior would make no sense. Acquisition is the reason children play, but not the play itself; the complication of rules children favor instead delays the acquisitive end as long as possible.

It is also true that no game is "free" for children in the sense that they feel comfortable about play simply for the sake of play. There *must* be an end, be it a rule of winning, as in most Western games, or simply a rule about when the game is finished, as in current Chinese games. Huizinga's definition of play as "secluded" comes to mind; a special sense of time, of termination, sets this activity off from non-game behavior. For children in a modern American setting, winning a game of marbles legitimates the act of play. The specific acts in play, however, are all aimed at the delay of winning, delay of termination. The tools which permit children to delay, to remain in a state of play, are the rules.

A game of marbles is thus a complicated affair. It is only by erecting rules that the children keep themselves free of the outside, non-play world. The more complicated the rules are, the longer the children are free. But freedom as an endless state is not what the children aim at; the marbles rules often have messy beginnings, baroque middles, but always have clear termination points.

These rules are acts of self-distance for two reasons. The first is that mastery over others is put off. It is striking how angry children become when one person in a game of marbles is detected cheating. When one child tries to gain a more immediate dominance over the other children than he or she could have in sticking to the rules, the play seems spoiled for everybody. Thus the conventions of a child's game put the child's pleasure in dominating others at a distance, even though domination is the reason the game is played, even though domination is strongly desired throughout.

The second way rules become acts of self-distance concerns the control of inequalities of skill among the players. Long-distance marbles, for example, is a game requiring good muscular coordination in order to shoot the marble straight. A child of four and a half is physically at a disadvantage here with a child of six. When small children are put with older children and asked to play long-distance marbles, the older children immediately decide to change the rules so that the little ones will not be instantly eliminated. The older children invent a "handicap" for themselves, to establish equality among the players, and thus prolong the game. Again the rules take the children away from direct assertion of themselves, from immediate mastery. Self-distance here too gives structure to play.

In game play, the malleability of rules creates a social bond. When a six-year-old wanted to stop a four-year-old from having a toy in the nursery, she hit him over the head or took the toy away from him by brute force. When she wanted to play long-distance marbles with him, she "made up" a situation in which that difference in strength did not exist between them, even though she kept her aggressive desire to triumph over him in the end. To play requires a freedom from the self; but this freedom can be created only by rules which will establish the fiction of initial equality in power between the players.

Infant and child play arrive at the same end by opposite means. The infant arrives at self-distance by a suspension of retentive pleasure, by breaking the patterns on the crib. A child of six in play with other children arrives at self-distance by making up patterns, patterns which at once delay his mastery over others and creates a fictive community of common powers.

What is the relation of child play to the frustration children experience because of their physically and emotionally incomplete development? For infants, every encounter with the environment is fraught with enormous risks; the infant has no way of knowing what the possibilities are for injuring or pleasing himself by doing what he has not done before. Play behavior is the point where the fear of frustration is surmounted by the desire to take risks. But the risk-taking is easily defeated. If Piaget's child in turning over her colored discs had accidentally focused the sun in her eyes, pain would ensue, and in all probability the infant would abandon the string of discs for the time being. The acquisition of a verbal language is a critical stage in reducing the risk of unknown experiences, for the infant can then learn from others about risk, rather than having to rely on trial and error or on inexplicable parental prohibitions. However, group play among children of four to six retains the risk-taking quality. A child aged four is in ordinary social situations going to be excluded from much that a child aged six can and wants to do. In play, however, he gets the opportunity to interact with her as an equal, and so explore a kind of social situation he otherwise could not know.

This question of risk-taking is important, because it is the means of understanding another complexity of the self-distance children learn in play. Much of the Freudian-based literature on play treats the pleasures of game-play especially as contrary to the frustrations and constraints children experience in "reality." In fact, the risks in play produce anxiety, and in games where children consistently lose, a great deal of frustration. But they do not, as a result, stop playing, as if "called back to reality" (Freud's phrase). The frustrations get them ever more involved in the play. Precisely because in this special region there is distance from the self, the familiar syndromes of frustration-causing-withdrawal, frustration-causing-apathy do not appear.

We tend to assume that only very sophisticated adults can experience all at the same time frustration in a situation, sustained attention to what is happening in the situation, and some pleasure from the situation. Children do experience this complexity through play, but then it gets lost in many adult lives because there are so few adult settings in which to continue playing on these sophisticated, balanced terms. The very social compact children engage in when they agree to play contains a nuanced mixture of risk, frustration, and gratification. Children attempt to reduce frustration by focusing their attention on the situation itself, treating the rules of the game as a reality of its own. When a kid consistently loses a particular game of marbles, for example, the frustration is not reduced by his demanding that another type of game be played, which would be the logical thing to do if the object of play were to get away from the frustrations of "reality." Instead, he will often caucus with the other players about ways to change the rules so that the chances of winning equalize. In the caucus itself, everyone will go into a kind of suspension in which the rules are discussed at a highly abstract level. The frustration reinforces self-distance, and, in the words of Lionel Festinger, "attachment to the situation."[24]

The work on the quality of the rules of play is pre-aesthetic work. It is focus on the expressive quality of a convention. It teaches a child to believe in these conventions. It prepares the child for a specific kind of aesthetic work, performing, because the child learns to orient himself to the expressive content of a "text." Play teaches a child that, when he suspends his desire for immediate gratification, and replaces this by interest in the content of rules, he achieves a sense of control over and manipulability over what he expresses. The farther away he gets in play from an immediate calculus of pleasure and pain, the more baroque these acts of control of a situation can become. Musicians talk of developing the "third ear." This is an ability to hear oneself so that in practicing one does not woodenly repeat the same patterns again and again; in getting the self-distance from one's own actions so that one seems almost to be hearing a performance by someone else, one can gradually shape and reshape a line until it conveys whatever one wants it to. Childhood play is a preparation for adult aesthetic work by developing the belief in, and the first experience of, the "third ear." Play rules are the first chance to objectify action, to put it at a distance and change it qualitatively.

Play prepares for performing in another way besides preparing for belief in the "third ear." It accustoms children to the idea that expression can be repeated. When one asks children in a laboratory situation to talk about their play, and define its differences from "just hanging around," the commonest response one gets is that "you don't have to start all over again" in a game, by which I have found them to mean that activities which have a repeatable meaning exist when they play games, whereas in just hanging around they have to go through all sorts of testing operations with each other (for six-year-olds it is mostly testing who gets to control which toys or other similar possessions). Play in a game has an instantaneous meaning because the rules exist. However, one finds in games which have gone through several changes of rules in a week or two that children *au courant* with the latest rules initiate new children by going through the whole history of the changes in rules, so that the new kids know exactly what the expressive state of the current rules is; since rules are productions, not absolute givens, children socialize each other by explaining how the production occurred. Once that has happened, the rule can be repeated.

In Diderot's theory of expression, two claims are made: first, that aesthetic expressions are repeatable, and second, that the individual has enough distance from his expressions to work on them, correcting and improving them. The origins of this aesthetic work lie in the learning about self-distance which occurs in childhood play. Through self-distanced play the child learns that he can work and rework rules, that rules are not immutable truths but conventions, under his control. The ancestry of emotional presentation is in games rather than in what is usually learned from parents. Parents teach obedience to rules; play teaches that rules themselves are malleable, and that expression occurs when rules are made up, or changed. Immediate gratification, immediate retention, immediate mastery are suspended.

Self-distance creates a certain attitude about expression; in equal measure it creates a certain attitude about other people. Children at play learn that the relationship of being together depends on making rules together. In a maze game, for example, children normally highly aggressive toward each other suddenly felt uncompetitively close at the point they had to change the pattern of the maze. The relationship between sociability and rule-making also appears in the six-year-old's arrangements with the four-year-old about the proper "handicap" she should impose on herself so that they could play.

It is true, as the behaviorists argue, that play is a response to the child's frustrations in the world, due to his general lack of power to cope with the environment: the child in play makes a controlled environment. But this environment survives only by the self-denial of observing rules. If one child spontaneously changes the rules to make them immediately gratifying to himself—an easy aim, for instance—he spoils the game. In play the child thus replaces generalized frustration with a more localized and specific form of frustration, that of delay, and this structures the play and gives it internal tension, its "drama." The tension itself sustains the child's interest in his playing.

Ironically, the content of childhood play is often much more radically abstract than the adult games. The child shuts out the world beyond the play realm when he is playing; in Huizinga's words, he "secludes" it. This is why children at play so often pretend the objects and toys at hand are something else. The adult at play need not engage in play as an alternative world; the same symbols and meanings of symbols in the non-play world can remain, but they are subject to a process of redefinition so that their effects are different. In the coffee-house, for example, the elaborate speech patterns were not alternatives to the patterns of speech employed in other social settings, but they were used for a purpose to which they were specially suited, that of permitting discourse to flow freely among people of unequal rank. The result was a social fiction; people acted "as if" the differences between themselves did not exist—for the moment.

As we saw in Chapter 5, within the *ancien régime* itself the child's world of play began to seem unlike the play world of the adult. The child with his toys had drawn apart from the man, who now had special games of his own. As the *ancien régime* principles of playacting and the presentation of emotion gradually eroded in adult society, within the life cycle a new rhythm was born. The passage from childhood to adulthood became the loss of play experience as the child was inducted into the serious business of adult culture. As Huizinga once remarked, when we are adults we can think of watching others play as "relaxing," we can become passionate about sport, but we inhabit a world in which such relaxations are rests from serious "reality." The loss of a sense of play in reality, as embodied by that remark of Freud's at the opening of this section, is the loss, or more exactly the repression, of a childhood power to be sociable and to be concerned with the quality of expression at the same time.

In what way does the culture into which the child enters repress this artfulness? What psychic forces has the historical loss of an impersonal realm mobilized, to engage in warfare with the strengths of play?

NARCISSISM ENERVATES THIS ENERGY

The most common problems alienists in the 19th Century saw were problems of hysteria. The common and mild forms of hysteria were the various "complaints," the physical betrayal of tension which people, especially bourgeois women, could not succeed in suppressing. Something more than Victorian sexual prudery explains the existence of these nervous disorders; we have seen their cultural setting to be one of great pressure to maintain stable appearances within the family, so that the family itself could be a principle of order in a chaotic society. Set against this regulation of appearances were the belief in and fear of involuntary disclosure of emotion. Hysterical disorders were, in sum, the symptoms of a crisis—and the word is not too strong—in the distinctions between, and stability of, public and private life.

The foundations of psychoanalytic theory were laid in the study of these hysterical symptoms, and logically so. A theory that reaches for the hidden, the involuntary, the uncontrolled, can with reason begin with clinical data which concern eruptions from below a surface of control and order. The theory of the unconscious was not an original perception of Freud's—the idea goes as far back as Heraclitus. What was original was his connecting the theory of unconscious psychic processes to repression on the one hand and sexuality on the other. Freud was the first to see that an absence of consciousness was a two-dimensional psychic phenomenon, a way of repressing what could not be handled in ordinary life and a form of life (libidinal energy) which had no need of conscious articulation in order to exist.

In the present century, the clinical data on which psychoanalysis was founded have gradually eroded. Hysterias and hysterical formations still exist, of course, but they no longer form a dominant class of symptoms of psychic distress. An easy interpretation of why "complaints" no longer so routinely appear would be that the sexual fears and ignorance of the last century no longer hold sway. This would be an inspiring interpretation, except that sexual difficulties have not disappeared; they have taken on new forms, as part of what are called "character disorders." What is meant by this is psychic distress which does not show itself through behavior which clearly labels the person involved as suffering, as having made his distress into a tangible symbol. Rather, the distress lies exactly in formlessness: a sense of disconnection, or dissociation, of feeling from activity—the extreme of which may produce schizophrenic language, but the routine form of which creates a sense of meaninglessness in the midst of activity. The experience of emptiness, of an inability to feel, is not easily encompassed by mechanical notions of repression. This shift in ordinary symptomology has challenged psychoanalytic thinking to find a new diagnostic language, and to expand terms which in the early years of psychoanalysis were poorly thought out, because the then dominant clinical experiences of distress did not demand their articulation.

As a way of coming to grips with the character disorders of disconnection and a sense of emptiness, one group of psychoanalytic writers has begun to expand the notions of narcissism which played a subordinate role in earlier theory. Freud's first full-dress treatment of this subject in 1914 was a peculiar part of his early work, oriented to his debate with Jung, and so limited by a hidden agenda in which the theory of narcissism is used as a weapon to discredit the Jungian theory of archetypal images in primary process; Freud wanted to show these images couldn't exist.[25]

Some sense of what the new concern with narcissism is about can be gained by going back to the ancient myth upon which it is based. Narcissus kneels over a pool of water, enraptured by his own beauty reflected on the surface. People call to him to be careful, but he pays no heed to anything or anyone else. One day he bends over to caress this image, falls, and drowns. The sense of the myth is something other than the evils of self-love. It is the danger of projection, of a reaction to the world as though reality could be comprehended through images of self. The myth of Narcissus has a double meaning: his self-absorption prevents knowledge about what he is and what he is not; this absorption also destroys the person who is so engaged. Narcissus, in seeing himself mirrored on the water's surface, forgets that the water is other and outside himself and thus becomes blind to its dangers.

As a character disorder, narcissism is the very opposite of strong self-love. Self-absorption does not produce gratification, it produces injury to the self; erasing the line between self and other means that nothing new, nothing "other," ever enters the self; it is devoured and transformed until one thinks one can see oneself in the other—and then it becomes meaningless. This is why the clinical profile of narcissism is not of a state of activity, but of a state of being. There are erased the demarcations, limits, and forms of time as well as relationship. The narcissist is not hungry for experiences, he is hungry for Experience. Looking always for an expression or reflection of himself in Experience, he devalues each particular interaction or scene, because it is never enough to encompass who he is. The myth of Narcissus neatly captures this: one drowns in the self—it is an entropic state.

The attempt to give new meanings to the idea of narcissism has appeared most fully in the writings of Heinz Kohut. And what is so suggestive about his struggle to find a new language to describe this phenomenon, like the increasing prominence of narcissistic character disorder itself, is how much larger social processes are implicated, how much it resonates as a language for describing the results of a long-term evolution of culture. Much of the writing on narcissism is sociological description—but those who do it are unaware of the fact, and write as though they are only uncovering and explaining a dimension of psychic life which previously has been inadequately treated.

In Kohut's discussion of how the "grandiose self" relates to "objects" in the world (and by this is meant both physical things and persons) he argues that such a personality configuration leads the self to treat the world in terms "of the control which he expects over his own body and mind [rather] than the grownup's experience of others and of his control over them." The consequence is that this interpretation of the world in terms of the self "generally leads to the result that the object of such narcissistic 'love' feels oppressed and enslaved by the subject's expectations and demands." Another dimension of this same relation of grandiose self to objects becomes "mirror" transference in therapy, and more generally a view of reality in which the Other is a mirror of the self.[26]

The self formed on these terms begins to resonate with the history of personality and culture which has concerned us; this is a self for whom the boundaries of meaning extend only as far as that mirror can reflect; as reflection falters and impersonal relations begin, meaning ceases. These resonances grow stronger in a second way. Much of the analysis of clinical data on narcissism has focused on a split between activity and impulse. "What am I really feeling?" becomes a question which, in this personality profile, gradually detaches itself from and overrides the question "What am I doing?" The diagnostic profile assembled by Otto Kernberg depicts a personality type in which action is negatively valued and in which feeling tone becomes all-important. The questioning of the motives of others similarly works to devalue their actions, because what matters is, not what they do, but fantasies one has of what they are feeling when they do it. Reality is thus rendered "illegitimate," and as a result, in perceiving others in terms of fantasied motives, one's actual relations with them become apathetic or colorless.[27]

This too is familiar to us. It is the self-as-motivation; a self measured by its impulse life rather than its acts began to appear in political form in the middle of the last century at a moment of class struggle, and now serves as a more general canon of political legitimacy. The sharing of impulses rather than the pursuit of common activity began to define a peculiar sense of community at the end of the last century, and is now tied to the localization of community—so that one shares only as far as the mirror of self reflects.

What is unasked, however, in the psychoanalytic formulations is what happens when "reality" itself is governed by narcissistic norms. The canons of belief in this society are such that it becomes a logical view of "reality" to interpret social realities as meaningful when they mirror imagery of the self. Given the sheer increase of narcissistic character disorders appearing in the clinics, it is surprising that analysts do not ask whether, in addition to their being now able to perceive narcissism, the society in which the self moves is not encouraging these symptoms to come to the fore. (As a word of balance, it should be said that psychologists like D. W. Winnicott, in being less wedded to the peculiar definitions of psychoanalysis, are more willing to ask such questions.[28])

Just as hysteria was mobilized in social relations by a culture caught in the last century in a crisis of public and private life, narcissism is now mobilized in social relations by a culture deprived of belief in the public and ruled by intimate feeling as a measure of the meaning of reality. When issues like class, ethnicity, and the exercise of power fail to conform to this measure, when they fail to be a mirror, they cease to arouse passion or concern. The result of a narcissistic version of reality is that the expressive powers of adults are reduced. They cannot play with reality, because reality matters to them only when it in some way promises to mirror intimate needs. The learning about self-distance in childhood through the experience of play, learning which is about what is expressive and sociable at the same time, is overpowered in adult life by the cultural activation of a contrary principle of psychic energy.

To the classical analyst this will seem to be a complete hash of his terms, adulthood and self-distanced knowledge appearing to him the transcending of the archaic, narcissistic energies of childhood. I want to make a hash of his terms because the analyst's sense of social and historical reality is deficient. In modern social life adults must act narcissistically to act in accordance with society's norms. For that reality is so structured that order and stability and reward appear only to the extent that people who work and act within its structures treat social situations as mirrors of self, and are deflected from examining them as forms which have a non-personality meaning.

As a general process, the creation of narcissistic concern and unease by social institutions occurs along two lines. First, boundaries are erased between the person's actions in the institution and the judgments the institution makes of his innate abilities, character strengths, and the like. Because what he does appears to reflect what kind of person he is, action at a distance from the self is rendered difficult for the person to believe in. The second way narcissism is mobilized occurs when the focus upon the innate qualities of the self is on potentials for action rather than specific actions accomplished. That is, judgments are made about a person's "promise," about what he could do, rather than is doing now or has done. To the degree the person so judged takes this seriously, he will deal with himself and interpret the world in terms of non-differentiation of objects and absorption in unrealized action; these traits an analyst would be prone to see as signs of an individual character disorder.

Let us, as an example of these social norms, look more closely at how narcissistic concern is induced in the realm of class, particularly in the realm of the emergence of a new middle class in the technological bureaucracies of the 20th Century.

THE MOBILIZATION OF NARCISSISM AND THE APPEARANCE OF A NEW CLASS

The 20th Century is commonly spoken of as an age of non-manual, bureaucratic labor. It is true that the number of persons who perform manual, industrial labor has declined as a percentage of the work force in most industrialized countries. It is also true that the expansion of white-collar work has been in the lower echelons of the bureaucratic structure; what is perceived to be the disappearance of manual labor is really its transposition into routine work of a secretarial, filing, or service nature.

Some writers attempt to portray this change by speaking of a transformation of the bourgeois classes into the middle classes, the *classes moyennes.* They point to the fact that it is no longer possible to speak of the shadings from accountant to banker as differences of tone within one class, the gap between routine and managerial work in offices has so widened. One must conceive of a class structure within the white-collar world, they say, with its own internal proletariat, artisanat, petite bourgeoisie, and managerial class.[29]

A special kind of class has appeared with this division of labor within the white-collar world. It is composed of people who do quasi-technical, quasi-routine work: computer programmers, accounts-receivable flow analysts, the lower levels of control and stock processing in brokerage houses, and the like. Neither in control of the use of their own skills, nor performing tasks which are so routine anyone off the street could immediately do them, the members of this special category of the *classes moyennes* have as yet no group identity, no class culture in which to picture themselves. They are a class of arrivals. They are also, in North America and western Europe, the most rapidly expanding sector of the work force.[30]

The members of this class are subject to institutional definitions of their work which are to a large extent also an institutional definition of their personalities. Against this institutional process, they have few countervailing traditions or artisanal standards; instead, these arrivals to a new class accept the institutional definitions of themselves as valid, and seek to work out patterns of defense and meaning within a situation in which class circumstances and personality are so closely allied. Corporations treat their white-collar technical workers so that both of the norms of narcissistic absorption are produced; boundaries between self and world are erased because that position at work seems a mirror of personal power; the nature of that power resides, however, not in action, but in potential. The result of this mobilization of narcissism in their lives is that the technical workers' ability to challenge the rules of dominance and discipline which govern their class is destroyed. Class becomes too much a part of themselves to be played with. The mobilization of narcissism by an institution has succeeded in rendering impotent the element of expressive play, that is, play with and remaking of impersonal rules which govern their actions.

Boundaries between the self and work are first of all erased by the patterns of mobility in the corporation. The expansion and proliferation of these white-collar jobs has very little to do with functional necessity, and quite a lot to do with providing new avenues of promotion, demotion, or make-work for the white-collar bureaucracy as an ongoing organism. The essence of the internal logic of bureaucratic expansion is that the new work be unlike or unrelated to the old; thus, a promotion consists not in getting more financial rewards for something you do well, but in ceasing to perform that work and instead supervising others who do the work. Demotion consists not in being forced to stay with a task until it is completed better than you have done it in the past, but in being put to work at a new task in which you start all over again. Technological innovation has a curious relationship to bureaucratic expansion. For instance, a study of computerization of hospital record-keeping in an American city reveals that the advent of the computer steadily decreased the efficiency of the bills rendered and paid in the hospital. The computer cost so much to install and activate, however, that it forced the hospital to create a whole new staff for its care and feeding, which in turn stimulated the hospital to engage in a major fund-raising campaign, which in turn produced a large amount of new contributions, which were then diverted to the building of a new hospital wing. The deficits for the bureaucracy as a whole piled up, but the expansion and subdivision of white-collar labor convinced those in charge that, thanks to the computer, the hospital was "modernizing." As Keynes predicted a half-century ago, the essence of modern bureaucracy is that a stable, balanced system, producing steady profits without resort to expansion of capital, personnel, or output, is likely to inspire horror in those who manage it and likely to be seen more generally by the society as a "dead" operation.[31]

Bureaucratic enlargement for the sake of growth rather than functional necessity has had a peculiar effect upon this class. They have technical skills learned on the job, but not professional skills, skills so specialized or rare that they can be resistant to being moved around within the organization as its internal structure subdivides and proliferates. Instead they have what could be called a "protean" work experience. They move from task to task within the corporation, learning new skills at every move, or they maintain one position formally, but the contents of work in this position shift as the corporate structure becomes elaborated. The programmer may suddenly find himself doing work which is in fact a form of bookkeeping, even though he does it upon a familiar machine; or a new computer may be introduced into the office and as a result, because he does not know how to program in a new language, his superiors may put him in charge of printout processing, which has to do with the packaging of results rather than initiating the process of making the machine work. Or if a salesman deals with technical goods, when a new line is introduced it may be decided that he is no longer valuable as a salesman of these wares he has not sold before, and so is shifted elsewhere in the organization.[32]

As a result of such processes, his ability to maintain his position in the bureaucracy has little to do with how well he performs a particular skill, but rather how likely he is judged to be able to perform many skills, most of which he has yet to learn. The emphasis in protean work is on the "innate" ability of the worker, as well as his interpersonal "skills" of cooperation, empathy, and give-and-take as a human being. Ironically, the less a person's place is identified with a sense of his craft —using the word in its broadest sense—the more he is valued for basic traits of ability and companionability.

The refusal to change positions often is a form of suicide in large bureaucracies, whether in the state system or in private enterprise. It shows that a person does not have initiative, but even worse, that he is not "cooperative." Just as being a "valuable" worker means that one has the ability to perform a variety of tasks, being a part of the team, being cooperative and pliant means that one has the right interpersonal skills to be of value to the bureaucratic structure. "Flexibility" is the positive name for this value. It covers the fact that the man at work has lost any distance, functionally, from his material conditions. He is being judged upon his nature as a human being—his "potential."

How does a person so treated make sense of the erasure of the distance between personality and class position? In 1946, in a famous article, C. Wright Mills was the first to begin to answer the question. In "The Middle Classes in Middle-Sized Cities" he argued that the more people connected the facts of class to their own personalities, the less did injustices of class arouse them to political action, or even anger. He focused particularly on bureaucratic workers and other middle men in his analysis, and observed that when education, work, even income, became felt as ingredients of personality, it became difficult for these people to rebel against injustices they perceived in their education or work. When, Mills said, class passed through the filter of personality, what emerged were problems people perceived "in getting along with each other." Class problems became human puzzles; Mills particularly noticed a kind of absorption in matters of how others felt, what their impulses were in the midst of action, which deflected people from pursuing organizational or impersonal aims.[33]

In the postwar period, labor organizers often have described the lower middle ranks in bureaucracies as the hardest to organize, the most easily diverted from questions of cash, benefit, and mutual assistance to questions of personal "status" in the organization. The willingness to endure far poorer work conditions than manual-labor groups—secretaries are usually cited as the prime example—exists because these low-level white-collar jobs are "respectable" and therefore "personal." In the words of an English labor organizer, the perception of "respectable work in terms of being a respectable person makes office workers unwilling to think of their lives in institutional terms." Instead there is an unwillingness to pursue group interests, a sense of personal isolation, broken down only by hard effort on the organizer's part.

It has become a cliché among writers on the new classes to talk about such responses as a "false consciousness," when people believe social position to mirror the self. Perhaps it would better be said that the belief that one's work, unstable and protean as it is, is an expression of one's personality is the consciousness of a certain bureaucratic process, the reflection of that process in the consciousness of the worker himself. This image of work position as a mirror of the self, yet a mirror in which nothing fixed can ever be reflected, is the first stage in the induction of narcissistic feeling out of the class system.

But alone the erasure of distance between self and position would not create that sense of never being present in one's action, that passivity in the midst of interaction, which is the special mark of dissociated feeling which appears in this character disorder. Oddly enough, such passivity arises among the technological *classes moyennes* as they attempt to create a psychological shield for themselves against the rather naked light in which they appear at work. They resist by manipulation of language, a pattern of describing the self at work which appears in studies of manual laborers who do service work for large companies as well as in studies of white-collar bureaucrats themselves. The self at work is split into an "I" and a "me." The "I," the active self, is not the self the institution judges; the "I" is the self of the worker's motivations, his feelings, his impulses. Paradoxically, the self which accomplishes and is rewarded is described by passive language, by reference to events which happen to the "me." The "I" does not accomplish them.[34]

Thus, in an American study of such workers, one hears them describe a promotion as something an abstract "they" gave to "me" and seldom hears workers speak as follows: "I did X or Y" and so "earned" a promotion. When workers in these middle-rank jobs use the "I" forms in their speech about work, it is directed toward fraternal relations or feelings about other workers. Outside of the substance of work, an active "I" is present; within the substance of it a passive "me" frames the self.

Acting passive serves a functional purpose. In a material situation which equates person and worker, to act as though it really is something that comes to one, that one hasn't caused, is protective. Yet the difficulty with this divorce of the active "I" from the actor involved in being judged, rewarded, or criticized is that when the job itself seems a result of the exercise of one's abilities, one is caught in a contradiction: on the one hand, position is a product of personality; on the other, one protects oneself at work by treating one's experience there as though one's personality were a passive recipient of the bureaucratic functioning.

The splitting of the self into an "I" and a "me" comes from terms which originate in the larger culture of belief. The real self is the self of motivations and impulses; it is the active self. But it is not active in society; instead a passive "me" exists there. This very defense disposes people to act in ways which Mills and the labor organizers quoted above perceived as apathetic. There is nothing maladjusted or non-normal about this split, as certain industrial psychologists who have seized upon the literature of character disorder to analyze the "listless worker" are now proclaiming. It is a logical way to feel in a society whose logic is to absorb people into questions of self-adequacy; work and other social relationships of inequality are structured around that imagery.

In societies where class position appears to be impersonal or imposed, to occupy a nondescript position in society is no source of personal shame; to better one's position as a worker can easily be seen as linked to bettering the position of others as well, as a class. When class becomes a projection of personal ability, however, the logic of self-respect is upward mobility; to fail to be mobile, for all that one knows the institutional odds are against it, seems somehow due to a failure to develop one's personality and personal capabilities. Thus worry over class position, and especially about the question of mobility out of a class, and worry over the adequacy of having a real and developed personality are joined. In such a condition of belief, it is hard to identify with others in a similar position—in the abstract one may recognize common interests, but between a mutual recognition of interests and a group acting upon them intervenes a comparison of personal adequacy. If one were really using one's abilities, one wouldn't have to be "demeaned" by impersonal actions with others. Yet one's abilities are never concretized and made manifest.

Technical workers inhabit a culture in which the conflation of self and social class is believable, because life in an institution has a meaning only when it reflects the self. A French study of computer programmers came up with a neat formula for this; people experience not "alienation" from the institution but "compulsive bonding" to it, so that even the most trivial doings of the corporation engage their wholehearted interest. The result is to disturb at a profound level the sense of self-esteem people have in society. They are not obviously denied, they are not obviously accepted; they are instead continually testing themselves by attempts to find validation in a reality which in truth admits of no coherent limits to the self. It is because this protean selfhood is believable that institutional processes such as the creation of a new class of protean technological workers become feasible. But equally, this belief that self and position are reflector images of each other is no mechanical derivative of the power system's needs. As with the relationship between machine production and the willingness to believe in commodities as "fetishes" which we analyzed in Part Three, so with this relationship between the institutional need for protean workers and the workers' belief in a protean self. These are two dimensions of a single cultural process. Together they produce the signs of passivity at work; it is this class structure in combination with a culture of belief which mobilizes the psychic energies of narcissism.

We have spoken of the energies of narcissism and the energies of play as contradictory. The concept of play has direct relevance to a phenomenon like "compulsive bonding." People in this passive state do not think of challenging or playing with the corporate rules; the corporation is an absolute and fixed reality in which they must make their way by using their abilities. The issue is whether they accept the corporate structure as a given, not whether they like it. To the extent they accept it, they cannot "problematize" its rules. This is when play has failed.

Play involves some pleasure working on the quality of rules. Narcissism, on the contrary, is ascetic activity. To understand why it is, and how this asceticism corrodes the expressive powers of those under its sway, we need again to take the concept out of the hands of the psychiatrists and place it in a social and historical setting.

NARCISSISM IS THE PROTESTANT ETHIC OF MODERN TIMES

We earlier remarked that an egoist who aggressively seeks pleasure in the world, who enjoys what he has and what he is, a person who knows how to take, would not appear in the clinical profile of narcissism. This paradox, however, is no unique discovery of analytic theory. For it is exactly the formulation Weber used in his classic *The Protestant Ethic and the Spirit of Capitalism;* he opposed egoism to "worldly asceticism." The parallels between Weber's analysis of worldly asceticism and what appears now as a "new" psychiatric phenomenon are so strong that we are forced to inquire whether the resemblance is more than accidental, more than a happy coincidence of imagery, and instead if the cultural forces which have produced this narcissistic self-absorption have not in some way revived the Protestant Ethic on new terms.

The Protestant Ethic is probably the best known and most misunderstood of all Weber's ideas, and the responsibility for the misunderstanding is as much his fault as his readers'. As many critics have pointed out, his language is confused, so that sometimes he speaks of Protestantism as the origin of capitalism, sometimes not; he wavers between considering his work as an actual history or as an intellectual abstraction of certain general ideas from the historical record. But if we read, as I think we ought, this work as a kind of moral tale, then the work acquires the strength of its best and most passionate moments. What is Weber's myth? The loss of a ritual religion (Catholicism) and the rise of capitalism lead to a common end: it is denial of gratification for purposes of validating the self. This is "worldly asceticism." By denying oneself pleasure in concrete experiences, one shows one is a real person. The ability to delay gratification is the sign, supposedly, of a strong personality. In Protestant terms, it is denying oneself the pleasure of ritual, especially absolution for sins; in capitalist terms, it is denying the gratification of oneself sensually by use of one's money in the company of others. Worldly asceticism thus erases sociability through ritual or through expenditure. The impulse is more inward-turned. Denying oneself pleasure in the world makes a statement to oneself, and to others, about what kind of person one is. Weber is getting at not the nature of asceticism but the nature of a secular ethos. A monk chastising himself before God in the privacy of his cell thinks not of his appearance to others; his is the asceticism of erasure of self. In Weber's Calvin or Ben Franklin we have ascetics who want to make perfectly clear in this world that they are worth something as persons.

Worldly asceticism and narcissism have much in common: In both, "What am I feeling?" becomes an obsession. In both, showing to others the checks and impulses of oneself feeling is a way of showing that one does have a worthy self. In both, there is a projection of the self onto the world, rather than an engagement in worldly experience beyond one's control.

If we ask why Weber constructed this idea of a Protestant Ethic, one answer is that it was his way of showing the combined results of secularism and capitalism on the psyche; it is no accident he should have chosen these two forces. They lead to an erosion of belief in experience external to the self. Together they have eroded the self as an aggressive, confident force, and instead made its very worthiness the object of obsessive anxiety. Together, they have eroded public life.

The ascetic impulses Weber discerned, ascetic behavior for the purposes of self-justification, are important clues to understanding how narcissistic energies may be converted into interpersonal experience. Narcissistic impulses become social by being formulated in terms of ascetic self-justification. The result of these self-justifying impulses—as in the desire to demonstrate one's abilities at work—is to withdraw from others, and more particularly, to withdraw from activity in concert with them that does not draw attention to the self. The result of this withdrawal, in turn, is that the very idea of acting, the very perception that life is a set of conventions, is dethroned.

Since common sense, that most fallible of guides, tells us that self-absorption and asceticism are contrary, it may help to give a concrete example of how they mesh. The erotic fears of the last century would seem to be the ultimate in ascetic behavior. But it would be entirely wrong to think a woman took some secret pride in her chastity, that she wore her virginity as an "advertisement for myself." All the fear of sex as dangerous, all the self-loathing involved in it would be lost if 19th Century eroticism were pictured in those terms. And those terms are the sense of Weber's worldly asceticism; they are a self-denial which calls attention to the self. By contrast, the terms of sexuality which rule the present, seemingly more liberated age draw closer to this constant denial of pleasure which is really an assertion of the primacy of the self. Women's fears of not having an orgasm or men's fears of not having enough ejaculations often appear, as in a study conducted in New York in the late 1960's, to have little to do with the fear of not satisfying one's partner. If sexual behavior is altered so that more orgasms or ejaculations are experienced, the level of expectation about how much is enough is correspondingly escalated; the person still is not then experiencing "enough" for the sexual behavior to be truly "fulfilling," "meaningful," etc. It was this kind of self-denial that Weber had in mind as asceticism, and which Kohut describes as the oppressive demands of narcissism. Because one is unfulfilled, one's energies are focused upon oneself.

The ascetic character of the narcissism mobilized in modern society results in two of the qualities of feeling which appear in the clinical literature. One is the fear of closure, the other is blankness.

Continual escalation of expectations so that present behavior is never fulfilling is a lack of "closure." The sense of having reached a goal is avoided because the experiences would be then objectified; they would have a shape, a form, and so exist independently of oneself. For it to be unbounded, the person must practice a form of asceticism—or, as Weber wrote of Calvin's fears of rituals of piety, concretized reality must appear suspicious. The self is real only if it is continuous; it is continuous only if one practices continual self-denial. When closure does occur, experience seems detached from the self, and so the person seems threatened with a loss. Thus the quality of a narcissistic impulse is that it must be a continual subjective state.

The second trait of narcissism in which asceticism plays a role is blankness. "If only I could feel"—in this formula the self-denial and self-absorption reach a perverse fulfillment. Nothing is real if I cannot feel it, but I can feel nothing. The defense against there being something real outside the self is perfected, because, since I am blank, nothing outside me is alive. In therapy the patient reproaches himself for an inability to care, and yet this reproach, seemingly so laden with self-disgust, is really an accusation against the outside. For the real formula is, nothing suffices to make me feel. Under cover of blankness, there is the more childish plaint that nothing can make me feel if I don't want to, and hidden in the characters of those who truly suffer because they go blank faced with a person or activity they always thought they had desired, there is the secret, unrecognized conviction that other people, or other things as they are, will never be good enough.

The ascetic qualities of narcissism are important elements in making this psychic state inimical to certain kinds of expressiveness. Expression to others of what one is feeling comes to seem at the same time very important and very formless; shaping, objectifying expression seems to rob the feelings expressed of their authenticity. That is, narcissism is the psychological rationale for the form of communication we have called representation of emotion to others, rather than shaped presentation of emotion. Narcissism sets up the illusion that once one has a feeling, it must be manifest—because, after all, "inside" is an absolute reality. The form of feeling is only derivative from the impulse to feel.

Out of fear of objectifying impulses, of producing signs, the person sets up his expressive life so that he is bound to fail to re-present to others what is present to himself, and bound to blame them for the failure. After all, they can see that he is feeling, but his very fear of objectifying his emotions means they cannot see what it is he feels. Emotional ambiguity arises in narcissistic situations because emotional clarity is a threat. But for the person who refuses to objectify, the very impulse to tell, if only one could, is genuine. If the act of trying to tell others about oneself is real and strongly felt, then the failure of others to respond must mean there is something wrong with them: one is being genuine, they are not understanding, they are failing one, they are not adequate to one's needs. Thus there is reinforced the belief that one's own impulses are the only reality upon which one can rely. To find out what one feels becomes a search for oneself; it is with almost an attitude of negligence that one deals with the problem of making this search meaningful to others. If one tells them one is searching, surely they ought to understand.

We saw in Part Three how the belief in representation of emotion came in the last century to be linked to the idea of involuntary disclosure of emotion. Recall Darwin's dictum: what one feels shows beyond the power of one's will to control. Narcissism takes the idea of the involuntary disclosure of character to its logical extreme.

To the extent, in sum, that a society mobilizes narcissism, it gives rein to a principle of expression entirely contrary to the expressive principle of play. In such a society it is only natural that artifice and convention will seem suspect. The logic of such a society will be the destruction of these tools of culture. It will do so in the name of removing the barriers between people, of bringing them closer together, but it will succeed only in transposing the structures of domination in the society into psychological terms.

THE TYRANNIES
OF INTIMACY

There are two images which easily come to mind as intimate tyrannies. One is a life limited by children, mortgages on the house, quarrels with one's spouse, trips to the vet, the dentist, the same hours for waking, catching the train to work, returning home, the careful drinking of two martinis and smoking of eight cigarettes which is each day's ration, the worry over bills—a catalogue of domestic routine soon produces one image of intimate tyranny; it is claustrophobia. Intimate tyranny can also stand for a kind of political catastrophe, the police state in which all one's activities, friends, and beliefs pass through the net of governmental surveillance. This intimate oppression involves the constant fear that one may betray opinions which lead instantly to jail, that one's children may be indiscreet at school, that one may unwittingly commit crimes against the state which the state makes up as it goes along. *Madame Bovary* is an emblem of the first sort of intimate tyranny; the Stalinist legend of the good little Communist who turned his errant parents in to the secret police, the emblem of the second.

Both of these images are inadequate. Domestic obligation falls short of defining the sense of claustrophobia which oppresses so many people today. Fascist surveillance is an image which easily misleads; when fascism is absent it is easy to imagine intimate political controls to be weakened, whereas in fact they become different in form. The reason both these images fall short is that both are tyrannies of brute coercion. But tyranny itself can be something more subtle.

One of the oldest usages of the word "tyranny" in political thought is as a synonym for sovereignty. When all matters are referred to a common, sovereign principle or person, that principle or person tyrannizes the life of a society. This governing of a multitude of habits and actions by the sovereign authority of a single source need not arise by brute coercion; it can equally arise by a seduction, so that the people want to be governed by a single authority who stands above them all.

Nor need this seduction involve one person as tyrant. An institution can rule as a single font of authority; a belief can serve as a single standard for measuring reality.

Intimacy is a tyranny in ordinary life of this last sort. It is not the forcing, but the arousing of a belief in one standard of truth to measure the complexities of social reality. It is the measurement of society in psychological terms. And to the extent that this seductive tyranny succeeds, society itself is deformed. I have not tried to say in this book that we intellectually understand institutions and events exclusively in terms of the display of personality, for that obviously is not so, but rather that we have come to care about institutions and events only when we can discern personalities at work in them or embodying them.

Intimacy is a field of vision and an expectation of human relations. It is the localizing of human experience, so that what is close to the immediate circumstances of life is paramount. The more this localizing rules, the more people seek out or put pressure on each other to strip away the barriers of custom, manners, and gesture which stand in the way of frankness and mutual openness. The expectation is that when relations are close, they are warm; it is an intense kind of sociability which people seek out in attempting to remove the barriers to intimate contact, but this expectation is defeated by the act. The closer people come, the less sociable, the more painful, the more fratricidal their relations.

Conservatives maintain that the experience of intimacy defeats the expectations people have of intimate encounter because "the nature of man" is in its interior so diseased or destructive that when people reveal themselves to each other, what they show are all the private little horrors which in less intense forms of experience are safely hidden. I think the defeat that intimate contact deals to sociability is rather the result of a long historical process, one in which the very terms of human nature have been transformed, into that individual, unstable, and self-absorbed phenomenon we call "personality."

That history is of the erosion of a delicate balance which maintained society in the first flush of its secular and capitalist existence. It was a balance between public and private life, a balance between an impersonal realm in which men could invest one kind of passion and a personal realm in which they could invest another. This geography of society was governed by an image of human nature based on the idea of a natural human character; this character was not created by the experiences of a lifetime, but was revealed in them. It belonged to Nature and was reflected in man. As both secularity and capitalism arrived at new forms in the last century, this idea of a transcendent nature gradually lost its meaning. Men came to believe that they were the authors of their own characters, that every event in their lives must have a meaning in terms of defining themselves, but what this meaning was, the instabilities and contradictions of their lives made it difficult to say. Yet the sheer attention and involvement in matters of personality grew ever greater. Gradually this mysterious, dangerous force which was the self came to define social relations. It became a social principle. At that point, the public realm of impersonal meaning and impersonal action began to wither.

The society we inhabit today is burdened with the consequences of that history, the effacement of the *res publica* by the belief that social meanings are generated by the feelings of individual human beings. This change has obscured for us two areas of social life. One is the realm of power, the other is the realm of the settlements in which we live.

We understand that power is a matter of national and international interests, the play of classes and ethnic groups, the conflict of regions or religions. But we do not act upon that understanding. To the extent that this culture of personality controls belief, we elect candidates who are credible, have integrity, and show self-control. These personalities appeal, we say, to a wide variety of interests. Class politics are weakened as class itself, especially among the new classes forming in the present century, is made to seem so much the expression of innate personal abilities. Localism and local autonomy are becoming widespread political creeds, as though the experience of power relations will have more human meaning the more intimate the scale—even though the actual structures of power grow ever more into an international system. Community becomes a weapon against society, whose great vice is now seen to be its impersonality. But a community of power can only be an illusion in a society like that of the industrial West, one in which stability has been achieved by a progressive extension to the international scale of structures of economic control. In sum, the belief in direct human relations on an intimate scale has seduced us from converting our understanding of the realities of power into guides for our own political behavior. The result is that the forces of domination or inequity remain unchallenged.

This belief that real human relations are disclosures of personality to personality has, secondly, distorted our understanding of the purposes of the city. The city is the instrument of impersonal life, the mold in which diversity and complexity of persons, interests, and tastes become available as social experience. The fear of impersonality is breaking that mold. In their nice, neat gardens, people speak of the horrors of London or New York; here in Highgate or Scarsdale one knows one's neighbors; true, not much happens, but life is safe. It is retribalization. The terms "urbane" and "civilized" now connote the rarefied experiences of a small class, and are tinged with the rebuke of snobbism. It is the very fear of impersonal life, the very value put upon intimate contact, which makes the notion of a civilized existence, in which people are comfortable with a diversity of experience, and indeed find nourishment in it, a possibility only for the rich and well-bred. In this sense, the absorption in intimate affairs is the mark of an uncivilized society.

These two tyrannies of intimacy, these two denials of the reality and worth of impersonal life, have a common and opposite side. The renovation of the city, the casting off of the chains of localism which were first forged in the 19th Century and have today become a creed, is also the renovation of a principle of political behavior. The extent to which people can learn to pursue aggressively their interests in society is the extent to which they learn to act impersonally. The city ought to be the teacher of that action, the forum in which it becomes meaningful to join with other persons without the compulsion to know them as persons. I don't think this is an idle dream; the city has served as a focus for active social life, for the conflict and play of interests, for the experience of human possibility, during most of the history of civilized man. But just that civilized possibility is today dormant.

NOTES

The source notes that follow are for the benefit of students who may wish to pursue specific topics, especially those of a historical nature, in more detail. No notes are given for Part One, as the works mentioned there are readily available in bookstores; few notes are provided for Part Four, save where the subjects discussed are based on specialized sources. When analyzing the stages of argument in another writer's theory, I have cited specific passages for each idea, as references to "the Darwinian theory," or a "Freudian approach," are in themselves meaningless.

PART TWO

1. Fernand Braudel, *Capitalism and Material Life* (New York: Harper & Row, 1973), pp. 430 ff., for a good discussion of these two *ancien régime* cities.

2. *Ibid.*, p. 431.

3. Louis Chevalier, *Laboring Classes and Dangerous Classes*, trans. Frank Jellinek (New York: Howard Fertig, 1973), p. 176; Alfred Cobban, *A History of Modern France* (3rd ed.; London: Penguin, 1963), I, 48; Pierre Goubert, "Recent Theories and Research in French Population Between 1500 and 1700," in D. V. Glass and D. E. C. Eversley, eds., *Population in History* (Chicago: Aldine, 1965), p. 473.

4. See H. J. Habakkuk, "English Population in the 18th Century," *Economic History Review*, 2nd series, VI (1953), 117 ff.; Robert Mandrou, *La France aux XVII et XVIII Siècles* (Paris: Presses Universitaires de France, 1967), p. 130; Comte de Buffon, quoted in Chevalier, *op. cit.*, p. 178.

5. See E. A. Wrigley, "A Simple Model of London's Importance in Changing English Society and Economy, 1650–1750," *Past and Present*, No. 37, pp. 44 ff.; C. T. Smith, map in *The Geographical Journal*, June 1951, p. 206.

6. Louis Henry, "The Population of France in the 18th Century," in Glass and Eversley, *op. cit.*, pp. 434 ff.

7. Daniel Defoe, *A Tour Through the Whole Island of Great Britain* (London: Penguin, 1971; first published 1724), p. 308.

8. S. Giedion, *Space, Time and Architecture* (Cambridge: Harvard University Press, 4th ed. 1963), pp. 141–42.

9. Haussmann in the next century realized, however, that these vast spaces could quickly fill up with unruly crowds, so that the anti-crowd planning of the 18th Century appeared in the 19th to have set the stage in the city for riotous formations.

10. Paul Zucker, *Town and Square: From the Agora to Village Green* (New York: Columbia University Press, 1959).

11. E. A. Gutkind, *Urban Development in France* (New York: Free Press, 1970), p. 252.

12. Giedion, *op. cit.*, p. 619.

13. *Ibid.*, p. 620.

14. E. A. Gutkind, *Urban Development in Western Europe: The Netherlands and Great Britain* (New York: Free Press, 1971), p. 259.

15. Defoe, *op. cit.*, p. 287.

16. *Ibid.*, p. 295; also Raymond Williams, *The Country and the City* (New York: Oxford University Press, 1973), ch. 2, especially the sections on counter-pastoral.

17. Christopher Hill, *Reformation to Industrial Britain* (Baltimore: Penguin, 1969), p. 226.

18. Jeffry Kaplow, *The Names of Kings* (New York: Basic Books, 1972), p. 7.

19. Karl Polanyi, *The Great Transformation* (Boston: Beacon Press, 1964), conclusion.

20. See Jane Jacobs, *The Economy of Cities* (New York: Random House, 1969).

21. Kaplow, *op. cit.*, p. 36.

22. Williams, *op. cit.*, p. 147; see H. J. Habakkuk, *American and British Technology in the 19th Century* (Cambridge: Cambridge University Press, 1962), for a more general theory of what became of this surplus in the 19th Century.

23. J. H. Plumb, *The Origins of Political Stability: England 1675–1725* (Boston: Houghton Mifflin, 1967), *passim*. For specific changes see Alfred Franklin, *La Vie Privée d'Autrefois* (Paris: Plon, 1887), I, 259–82.

24. See Saint-Simon, *Memoirs* (Paris: Boston, 1899), and also the very interesting asides in H. Baudrillart, *Histoire du Luxe Privé et Public* (Paris: Hachette, 1880), Vol. I, pp. 194–95; see also those moments recorded in

Pepys's diaries when he describes toasts while his companions are drinking.

25. W. H. Lewis, *The Splendid Century* (New York: Morrow, 1971 ed.), pp. 41–48.

26. Lord Chesterfield, *Letters* (London: Dent-Dutton, 1969 ed.; first published 1774), p. 80; there are interesting parallels to the compliments with which Voltaire opens his letters; the same words are addressed to a widely divergent range of people, some of whom answer in exactly the same terms; that the compliments are impersonal in no way detracts from their "courtesy."

27. Marivaux, *La Vie de Marianne*, in *Romans, Récits, Contes et Nouvelles*, texte présenté et préfacé par Marcel Arland (Tours: Bibliothèque de la Pléïade, 1949), pp. 247–48.

28. Chesterfield, *op. cit.*, p. 80.

29. *Ibid.*, p. 32.

30. *Ibid.*, p. 34.

31. When the Estates General met in 1789, the Master of Estates, following the old laws, declared that the members of the Third Estate were not allowed to wear jewelry or rings or to wear ribbons or other bright-colored cloth emblems. This enraged Mirabeau and prompted one of his greatest speeches. See R. Broby-Johansen, *Body and Clothes: An Illustrated History of Costume* (New York: Reinhold, 1968), "18th Century."

32. See James Laver, *A Concise History of Costume and Fashion* (New York: Abrams, Inc., n.d.), "The 18th Century," for an excellent factual summary.

33. Geoffrey Squire, *Dress and Society, 1560–1970* (New York: Viking, 1974), p. 110.

34. Braudel, *op. cit.*, p. 236.

35. François Boucher, *20,000 Years of Fashion* (New York: Abrams, n.d.), pp. 318–19.

36. Max von Boehn, *Dolls,* trans. Josephine Nicoll (New York: Dover, 1972), pp. 134–53.

37. Norah Waugh, *The Cut of Women's Clothes, 1600–1930* (New York: Theatre Arts Books, 1968), p. 123.

38. Quotation from Johan Huizinga, *Homo Ludens* (Boston: Beacon Press, 1955), p. 211; Elizabeth Burris-Meyer, *This Is Fashion* (New York: Harper, 1943), p. 328; R. Turner Wilcox, *The Mode in Hats and Headdress* (New York: Scribner's, 1959), pp. 145–46.

39. Lester and Kerr, *Historic Costume* (Peoria, Ill.: Chas. A. Bennett, 1967), pp. 147–48; quotation from *ibid.*, pp. 148–49.

40. Burris-Meyer, *op. cit.*, p. 328.

41. Maggie Angeloglou, *A History of Makeup* (London: Studio Vista, 1970), pp. 73–74.

42. *Ibid.*, pp. 79, 84; Lucy Barton, *Historic Costume for the Stage* (Boston: W. A. Baker, 1935), pp. 333 ff.; Burris-Meyer, *op. cit.*, p. 328.

43. Wilcox, *The Mode in Footwear* (New York: Scribner's, 1948), illustration page for Ch. 15.

44. Wilcox, *The Mode in Hats and Headdress*, p. 145; quotation in Iris Brooke, *Western European Costumes, 17th to Mid-19th Centuries, and Its Relation to the Theatre* (London: George Harrap & Co. Ltd., 1940), p. 76.

45. Quotation from James Laver, *Drama, Its Costume and Decor* (London: The Studio Ltd., 1951), p. 154; Brooke, *op. cit.*, p. 74.

46. Library for the Performing Arts, Lincoln Center, New York, Research Division, Lecompte Folder in 18th Century Costume section, plates 77 and 104; plate 78.

47. Laver, *Drama*, p. 155.

48. John Lough, *Paris Theatre Audiences in the 17th and 18th Centuries* (London: Oxford University Press, 1957), p. 172; Charles Beecher Hogan, *The London Stage, 1776–1800* (Carbondale, Ill.: University of Southern Illinois Press, 1968), p. ccx; Alfred Harbage, *Shakespeare's Audience*, (New York: Columbia University Press, 1941), Ch. 2.

49. Frederick C. Green, *Eighteenth-century France* (New York: Ungar, 1964), p. 169; Lough, *op. cit.*, pp. 180–84, 226; George W. Stone, Jr., *The London Stage, 1747–1776* (Carbondale, Ill.: University of Southern Illinois Press, 1968), p. cxci; Lough, *op. cit.*, p. 177.

50. Stone, *op. cit.*, p. cxci; Lough, *op. cit.*, pp. 229–30. See also Marmontel, *Oeuvres* (Paris, 1819–20), IV, 833.

51. Phyllis Hartnoll, *The Concise History of Theatre* (New York: Abrams, n.d.), p. 154; quotation from Hogan, *op. cit.*, p. cxci.

52. Hogan, *op. cit.*, p. cxiii.

53. John Bernard, *Retrospections of the Stage* (London: Colburn and Bentley, 1830), II, pp. 74–75.

54. Greene, *op. cit.*, p. 173; Stone, *op. cit.*, p. clxxxiv.

55. See W. H. Lewis, *The Splendid Century* (New York: Anchor, 1957); Hartnoll, *op. cit.*, p. 156.

56. Jean Duvignaud, *L'Acteur* (Paris: Gallimard, 1965), pp. 68–69.

57. *Ibid.*, pp. 69–70.

58. Henry Raynor, *A Social History of Music* (New York: Schocken, 1972), pp. 246, 252, 259.

59. Duvignaud, *op. cit.*, p. 74.

60. *Ibid.*, p. 75; see also Richard Southern, *The Seven Ages of the Theatre* (New York: Hill & Wang, 1963), on the professionalization of the theater. Southern makes the dating for England earlier than that for France, but is less specific than Duvignaud.

61. This sense of symbol joins such different philosophers of language as Cassirer and Chomsky.

62. See R. Fargher, *Life and Letters in France: The 18th Century* (New York: Scribner's, 1970), p. 19, for a discussion of Massillon in this context.

63. Green, *op. cit.*, p. 166; Hartnoll, *op. cit.*, pp. 154–55; quotation from Collé, *Diary*, in Green, *op. cit.*, pp. 166–67.

64. Aytoun Ellis, *The Penny Universities* (London: Secker and Warburg, 1956), p. 223; see Ch. 9 for a marvelous description of coffeehouses in the city.

65. Lewis A. Coser, *Men of Ideas* (New York: Free Press, 1965), p. 19; R. J. Mitchell and M. D. R. Leys, *A History of London Life* (London: Longmans, Green & Co., n.d.), pp. 176–79.

66. Ellis, *op. cit.*, p. 238.

67. Jean Moura and Paul Louvet, "Le Café Procope," *Revue Hebdomadaire*, Année 38, Tome 11, pp. 316–48, is the best serious study of this cafe.

68. Henry B. Wheatley, *Hogarth's London* (New York: Button and Co., 1909), p. 301; A. S. Turberville, *Johnson's England* (Oxford: Clarendon Press, 1933), I, 180–81.

69. James Boswell, *Life of Samuel Johnson*, quoted in Ellis, *op. cit.*, p. 229.

70. Coser, *op. cit.*, p. 24; Wheatley, *op. cit.*, p. 272.

71. Quoted in Ellis, *op. cit.*, p. 230.

72. Turberville, *op. cit.*, p. 182.

73. Emily Anderson (ed. & trans.), *Letters of W. A. Mozart and His Family*, Vol. I (London: MacMillan and Co., 1938).

74. A plate in the collection of the Institut de Chalcographie, Louvre (planche anon. tiré pour le premier fois en 1744, vue des Tuileries), depicts the mixture of business on the Seine and in the Tuileries very well. The gardens are passage and storage points for traffic being taken off the river.

75. Philippe Ariès, *Centuries of Childhood*, trans. Robert Baldick (New York: Vintage Books, 1965), pp. 87–88.

76. *Ibid.*, pp. 97–98.

77. See Bogna Lorence, "Parents and Children in 18th Century Europe," *History of Childhood Quarterly*, II, No. 1 (1974), 1–30.

78. Cited in *ibid.*, p. 23.

79. The best treatment of Enlightenment psychological theory is therefore by historians of philosophy. For these double characteristics, see, for instance, Carl Becker, *The Heavenly City of the 18th Century Philosophers* (New Haven: Yale University Press, 1932), pp. 63–70; see Arthur Wilson, *Diderot* (New York: Oxford University Press, 1972), pp. 250–51 (letter to Landois), as an example of Becker's point; see also Ernst Cassirer, *The Philosophy of the Enlightenment* (Boston: Beacon, 1955), pp. 105–8, 123 ff.

80. Richard Sennett and Jonathan Cobb, *The Hidden Injuries of Class* (New York: Knopf, 1972), pp. 251–56.

81. The major biographies are George Rude, *Wilkes and Liberty* (Oxford: Oxford University Press, 1962); Raymond Postgate, *"That Devil Wilkes"* (London: Constable, 1930); William Treloar, *Wilkes and the City* (London: Murray, 1917); see also an admirable sketch of Wilkes by Peter Quennell in *The Profane Virtues* (New York: Viking, 1945), pp. 173–220.

82. See Joseph Grego, *A History of Parliamentary Elections and Electioneering from the Stuarts to Queen Victoria* (London: Chatto and Windus, 1892), Ch. VI, "John Wilkes as Popular Representative."

83. Quennell, *op. cit.*, pp. 181–82.

84. Wilkes gives an account of the duel in a letter reprinted in Postgate, *op. cit.*, pp. 45–50.

85. Rude, *op. cit.*, pp. 17–73, is the most comprehensive account; Treloar, *op. cit.*, pp. 51–79, is somewhat naïve but contains much primary material.

86. Quennell, *op. cit.*, p. 177; see also the discussion of Sterne's view of sexual relationships, *ibid.*, pp. 169–70; for France, see especially J. J. Servais and J. P. Laurend, *Histoire et Dossier de la Prostitution* (Paris: Éditions Planète, 1965).

87. Quoted in Rude, *op. cit.*, pp. xiii–xiv.

88. Postgate, *op. cit.*, pp. 150–68.

89. Rude, *op. cit.*, pp. 86–89; Postgate, *op. cit.*, pp. 141–42; compare to Bernard Bailyn, *Ideological Origins of the American Revolution* (Cambridge: Harvard University Press, 1967).

90. Postgate, *op. cit.*, pp. 251–58, is a good account.

91. James Boulton, *The Language of Politics* (London: Routledge & Kegan Paul, 1963), p. 24.

92. Boulton, *ibid.*, p. 36.

93. Henry Fielding, *Tom Jones* (London: Penguin, 1966; first published 1749), p. 299.

94. *Ibid.*, p. 302.

95. Lee Strasberg, "An Introduction to Diderot," in Denis Diderot, *The Paradox of Acting*, trans. W. H. Pollack (New York: Hill & Wang, 1957), p. x; Arthur M. Wilson, *Diderot* (New York: Oxford University Press, 1972), pp. 414–16; Felix Vexler, *Studies in Diderot's Esthetic Naturalism* (New York: Ph.D. thesis, Columbia University, 1922).

96. Diderot, *Paradox*, p. 14.

97. *Ibid.*, pp. 15, 24.

98. Quotation from *ibid.*, p. 20; *ibid.*, p. 23.

99. *Ibid.*, p. 25.

100. *Ibid.*, pp. 15 ff.

101. Quotation from *ibid.*, p. 25.

102. *Ibid.*, pp. 32–33, italics added.

103. T. Cole and H. Chinoy, *Actors on Acting* (rev. ed.; New York: Crown, 1970), pp. 160–61.

104. Diderot, *op. cit.*, pp. 52 ff.; K. Mantzius, *A History of Theatrical Art in Ancient and Modern Times* (London: Duckworth & Co., 1903–21), V, 277–78.

105. The dating is established as follows: D'Alembert prepared the article after a visit to Voltaire at his estate outside Geneva; Voltaire had moved to the estate in 1755; the article was slated to appear in 1757; and Rousseau's response to it appeared in 1758. Rousseau, *Politics and the Arts: The Letter to M. d'Alembert*, trans. A. Bloom (Ithaca: Cornell University Press, 1968), p. xv. The title *Politics and the Arts* is an English title for the English translation of the *Letter;* hereafter it will be referred to by the correct title: *Letter to M. d'Alembert;* quotation from d'Alembert, quoted in *ibid.*, p. 4.

106. There are grounds for believing that in so closely rebutting d'Alembert's description of moral and religious life in Geneva, Rousseau was also arguing with himself about the value of a militant ascetic religion for a city. See Ernst Cassirer, *The Question of Jean Jacques Rousseau*, trans. and edited by Peter Gay (New York: Columbia University Press, 1954), pp. 73–76, for Rousseau's religious thought.

107. See "Translator's Notes," in Rousseau, *op. cit.*, p. 149, note 3.

108. *Ibid.*, pp. xxx, 16.

109. *Ibid.*, p. 16.

110. Johan Huizinga, *Homo Ludens* (Boston: Beacon, 1955), pp. 1, 6, 8–9.

111. Lionel Trilling, *Sincerity and Authenticity* (Cambridge, Mass.: Harvard University Press, 1972), p. 64.

112. Rousseau, *op. cit.*, p. 18.

113. This is precisely the point of view of d'Alembert's article. The treatment of religion in the last five paragraphs is a good example, reprinted as an appendix to Rousseau, *op. cit.*, pp. 147–48.

114. *Ibid.*, p. 58.

115. *Ibid.*, pp. 58–59.

116. Not all the instruction in *Émile* is purposive, nor are the incidents of the *Confessions* recorded in terms of a central formal plan based on "utility."

117. Quoted in English translation in M. Berman, *The Politics of Authenticity* (New York: Atheneum, 1970), p. 116.

118. Cassirer, *Question*, p. 43; Rousseau, quoted in *ibid.*

119. Berman, *op. cit.*, pp. 114–15; the idea of reputation as an achieved meaning begins, as Berman points out, with Montesquieu; Rousseau gives the image a new, more negative meaning.

120. Rousseau, *op. cit.*, pp. 59–61.

121. *Ibid.*, p. 60.

122. *Ibid.*

123. *Ibid.*

124. *Ibid.*, pp. 65–75.

PART THREE

1. Joanna Richardson, *La Vie Parisienne, 1852–1870* (New York: Viking, 1971), pp. 76–77.

2. Maxime du Camp, quoted in *ibid.*, p. 77.

3. See Charles Tilly, *An Urban World* (Boston: Little, Brown & Co., 1974).

4. The raw data for the two tables are from Adna Ferrin Weber, *The Growth of Cities in the 19th Century* (Ithaca, N.Y.: Cornell University Press, 1963; first published 1899), p. 73. Alternative data: Louis Chevalier, *La Formation de la Population Parisienne au XIX Siècle* (Paris: Institut National d'Études Démographiques, Cahier No. 10, 1950), pp. 284 ff.

5. Quotation from Asa Briggs, *Victorian Cities* (New York: Harper & Row, 1963), p. 324.

6. Computed from A. F. Weber, *op. cit.*, p. 46.

7. Richard Sennett, data tape for *Families Against the City*, Joint Center for Urban Studies of Harvard and M.I.T., cross-tabs "class and length of residence."

8. David H. Pinkney, *Napoleon III and the Rebuilding of Paris* (Princeton: Princeton University Press, 1958), pp. 6–9.

9. Quotation from *ibid.*, p. 17; for Wirth, see Louis Wirth, "Urbanism as a Way of Life," in Richard Sennett, ed., *Classic Essays on the Culture of Cities* (New York: Appleton-Century-Crofts, 1969), pp. 143–64; for Park, see Robert Park, "The City . . ." in *ibid.*, pp. 91–130.

10. J. H. Clapham, *Economic Development of France and Germany, 1815–1914* (4th ed.; London: Cambridge University Press, 1968), pp. 70–71.

11. See Richard Sennett, *Families Against the City* (Cambridge, Mass.: Harvard University Press, 1970), Chs. 5 and 11, for a fuller discussion of problems of defining "middle class." Roy Lewis and Angus Maude, *The English Middle Classes* (London: Phoenix House, 1949), Part I, Ch. 3, has an excellent, if nonquantitative, discussion of the strength of the middle classes in different settings in England. The data for 1867 are from J. Burnett, *Plenty and Want* (London: Pelican, 1968), p. 77.

12. S. G. Checkland, *The Rise of Industrial Society in England, 1815–1885* (New York: St. Martin's Press, 1966), pp. 425–26.

13. H. Pasdermadjian (also spelled Pasjermadjian), *The Department Store: Its Origins, Evolution, and Economics* (London: Newman, 1954), pp. 3–4.

14. Bertrand Gille, "Recherches sur l'Origines des Grands Magasins Parisiens," in *Paris et Île de France* (Paris, 1955), VII, 260–61; Martin Saint-Léon, *Le Petit Commerce Français* (Paris, 1911), pp. 520–21.

15. See Clifford Geertz, *Peddlers and Princes* (Chicago: University of Chicago Press, 1963), *passim.*

16. Pasdermadjian, *op. cit.*, pp. 4, 12.

17. C. Wright Mills, *White Collar* (New York: Oxford University Press, 1957), p. 178.

18. Pasdermadjian, *op. cit.*, p. 2, note 4; Sennett, *Families Against the City*, Ch. 2.

19. G. D'Avenel, "Les Grands Magasins," *Revue des Deux Mondes*, July 15, 1894.

20. Quotation from Émile Zola in Pasdermadjian, *op. cit.*, p. 12.

21. Gille, *op. cit.*, pp. 252–53.

22. Pasdermadjian, *op. cit.,* p. 32.

23. Karl Marx, *Capital,* trans. Samuel Moore and Edward Aveling (New York: Modern Library; first published 1906), pp. 82–85.

24. Charles Fegdal, *Choses et Gens des Halles* (Paris: Athéna, 1922), pp. 211–20; M. Baurit, *Les Halles de Paris dès Romans à Nos Jours* (Paris: M. Baurit, 1956), pp. 46–48.

25. Jean Martineau, *Les Halles de Paris dès Origines à 1789* (Paris: Mondarestier, n.d.), pp. 214–15.

26. Paul Maynard, *Les Modes de Vente des Fruits et Légumes aux Halles Centrales de Paris* (Paris: Sirez, 1942), p. 35.

27. Fegdal, *op. cit.,* p. 123; Martineau, *op. cit.,* pp. 242–43.

28. Thomas Carlyle, *Sartor Resartus,* edition reproduced in *English Prose of the Victorian Era,* Harrold and Templeman, eds. (Oxford: Oxford University Press, 1938), p. 94.

29. Quotation from Henry James in Donald Fanger, *Dostoevsky and Romantic Realism* (Chicago: University of Chicago Press, 1967), p. 30; quotation from Honoré (de) Balzac, *Splendeurs et Misères des Courtisanes* (Paris: Edition de Béguin, 1947–53), p. 137. English rendition uses both Fanger, *op. cit.,* p. 42, and V. S. Pritchett, *Balzac* (New York: Knopf, 1973), p. 165, for the first quotation, and Pritchett only for the second.

30. Quotation from Honoré (de) Balzac, *Père Goriot* (Paris: Éditions du Pléïade, n.d.), II, 884. English rendition by Peter Brooks, "Melodrama" (manuscript), p. 44.

31. Quotation from Charles Lalo, *L'Art et la Vie* (Paris, 1947), III, 86.

32. Honoré (de) Balzac, *Scènes de la Vie Parisienne* (Paris: Édition de Béguin), XV, 110. English rendition by Fanger in Fanger, *op. cit.,* pp. 37–38.

33. The interpretation is found on pp. 28–64 of Fanger, *op. cit.;* the quotation from Lukacs occurs on p. 17.

34. The interpretation is found in Brooks, *Melodrama,* pp. 1–64.

35. Erich Auerbach, *Mimesis: The Representation of Reality in Western Literature,* trans. Willard R. Trask (Princeton: Princeton University Press, 1968), pp. 469 ff.

36. Quotation from Balzac in *ibid.,* p. 470; quotation from Auerbach, p. 471.

37. Rebecca Folkman Mazières, "Le Vêtement et la Mode chez Balzac" (manuscript), p. 3.

38. Quotation from Squire, *op. cit.,* p. 159.

39. Boucher, *op. cit.,* p. 408; Burris-Meyer, *op. cit.,* p. 273; Wilcox, *The Mode in Hats and Headdress,* p. 213; Wilcox, *The Mode in Footwear,* p. 131.

40. See Boehn, *op. cit.*, Chs. 10 and 11.

41. Boucher, *op. cit.*, pp. 385–86.

42. Burris-Meyer, *op. cit.*, p. 139; Fairfax Proudfit Walkup, *Dressing the Part: A History of Costume for the Theatre* (New York: Appleton-Century-Crofts, 1938), p. 244.

43. Barton, *op. cit.*, pp. 424, 445.

44. Angeloglou, *op. cit.*, p. 89.

45. Barton, *op. cit.*, pp. 425, 444, 395; Burris-Meyer, *op. cit.*, p. 273.

46. Quoted in Steven Marcus, *The Other Victorians* (New York: Random House, 1964), pp. 5–6.

47. Angeloglou, *op. cit.*, p. 96.

48. Quotations from A. Conan Doyle, *The Complete Sherlock Holmes* (Garden City, N.Y.: Doubleday, 1930), p. 96.

49. Quotation from Balzac in Pritchett, *op. cit.*, p. 166.

50. Quotation from Carlyle, *op. cit.*, p. 89; the latter theme is developed further in Chapter 10 of Book One.

51. Quotation from Philip Rosenberg, *The Seventh Hero* (Cambridge, Mass.: Harvard University Press, 1974), p. 46; see this author's superb discussion, pp. 45–55.

52. The edition used in this analysis is Charles Darwin, *The Expression of Emotion in Man and Animals*, Vol. X of *The Works of Charles Darwin* (New York: Appleton, 1896; reprinted by AMS).

53. Quotation from *ibid.*, p. 178.

54. *Ibid.*, pp. 179–83.

55. *Ibid.*, pp. 188–89.

56. Quotation from *ibid.*, p. 353; the latter point is discussed on pp. 183–84.

57. Laver, *Drama*, p. 155; quotation from Smith in Southern, *op. cit.*, p. 257.

58. Laver, *Drama*, p. 209.

59. *Galerie Dramatique*, plates taken from costumes of the Théâtre de la Porte St.-Martin in the collection of the New York Public Library, the Main Branch, plates 131 and 132.

60. Established by comparisons with illustrations in Alan Davidson's *Mediterranean Seafood* (London: Penguin, 1972), Catalogue of Fish.

61. *Galerie Dramatique*, plates 37, 38, 41; Dabney, op. cit., plate 39; see illustrations of melodramatic gesture in "Costumes: English Clippings,"

Envelope C, at the Library for the Performing Arts, Lincoln Center; quotation from Carlos Fischer in Laver, *Drama*, p. 155.

62. P. I. Sorokin, *Cultural and Social Mobility* (Glencoe, Ill.: Free Press, 1959), pp. 270 ff.; Talcott Parsons and E. F. Bales, *Family* (Glencoe, Ill.: Free Press, 1954), and bibliography of Parsons's writings on the family in Sennett, *Families Against the City*, bibliography.

63. Sennett, *Families Against the City*; Juliette Mitchell, *Woman's Estate* (New York: Pantheon, 1971); Ariès, *op. cit.*, conclusion.

64. Allan Janik and Stephen Toulmin, *Wittgenstein's Vienna* (New York: Simon and Schuster, 1973), pp. 42–43.

65. T. G. Hatchard, *Hints for the Improvement of Early Education and Nursery Discipline* (London, 1853), *passim*.

66. Daniel Patrick Moynihan, *Report on the American Negro Family* (Washington, D.C.: U.S. Dept. of Labor, 1965), *passim*.

67. Joseph Hawes, *Children in Urban Society* (New York: Oxford University Press, 1971), *passim*.

68. Anthony Trollope, *The Way We Live Now* (London: Oxford University Press, 1957; first published serially 1874–1875), p. 391.

69. Burris-Meyer, *op. cit.*, p. 91; quotation in Squire, *op. cit.*, p. 135.

70. This interpretation differs somewhat from Squire, p. 135.

71. Behavior all the more unusual as this was one of the coldest winters in France in the 1790's.

72. Boucher, *op. cit.*, pp. 343; Wilcox, *The Mode in Hats and Headdress*, pp. 188–89.

73. *Ibid.*, p. 189.

74. Jean Duvignaud, *Sociologie du Théâtre* (Paris: Presses Universitaires de France, 1965), p. 238.

75. Burris-Meyer, *op. cit.*, p. 90.

76. Boucher, *op. cit.*, pp. 343–44.

77. Barton, *op. cit.*, p. 461; *Eternal Masquerade* (New York Public Library Collection, n.d.), p. 230; Barton, *op. cit.*, pp. 343–44.

78. Nevil Truman Pitman, *Historic Costuming* (London: A. I. Pitman & Sons, 1967), p. 109; Broby-Johansen, *op. cit.*, p. 195.

79. Quotation from Barton, *op. cit.*, p. 498.

80. Anonymous quote in Angeloglou, *op. cit.*, p. 103.

81. *Eternal Masquerade*, p. 209; Wilcox, *The Mode in Hats and Headdress*, p. 266.

82. Helena Rubenstein quoted in Angeloglou, *op. cit.*, p. 107; Gwen Raverat, *Period Piece* (London: Faber and Faber, 1952), 105. This memoir is a marvelous picture of the era.

83. Broby-Johansen, *op. cit.*, p. 200.

84. Laver, *Concise History of Fashion*, p. 216.

85. These are miserably reproduced in Cornelia Otis Skinner's book on the actress, *Madame Sarah* (Cambridge, Mass.: Riverside Press, 1967); the original plates are at the Harvard Theatre Collection, Harvard College Library.

86. A recent sale, in the spring of 1972, of Bakst costumes was held in London, where the garments were beautifully displayed; most are now, unfortunately, dispersed into private collections; Boris Kotchno, *Diaghilev and the Ballets Russes*, trans. Adrienne Foulke (New York: Harper & Row, 1970); *The Drawings of Léon Bakst* (New York: Dover Publications, 1972).

87. For a longer account, see Richard Buckle, *Nijinsky* (New York: Simon and Schuster, 1971).

88. Quotation from Fanger, *op. cit.*, pp. 261–62.

89. These issues are fully discussed in David Barnett, *The Performance of Music* (New York: Universe, 1972).

90. The reader is referred to the Peters editions of the Bach and Beethoven, which in both cases came close to an *Urtext;* in editions like International or Schirmer, modern editors have supplied numerous markings of their own.

91. See, for example, Alfred Einstein's discussion of Mendelssohn in Einstein, *Music in the Romantic Era* (New York: Norton, 1947), pp. 124 ff.

92. Quotation from Liszt in Eleanor Perenyi, *Liszt: The Artist as Romantic Hero* (Boston: Atlantic Monthly Press, Little, Brown & Co., 1974), p. 49.

93. Quotation from Raymond Williams, *Culture and Society*, 1780–1950 (New York: Harper & Row, 1966), p. 44.

94. Quotation from Franz Liszt, "Paganini," in *Gazette Musicale*, Paris, August 23, 1830.

95. The most complete, if uncritical, account of these antics is found in the biography by Renée de Saussine, *Paganini* (New York: McGraw-Hill, 1954), p. 20, for example.

96. See Walter Beckett, *Liszt* (New York: Farrar, Straus, and Cudahy, 1956), pp. 10 ff.

97. Robert Schumann, quoted in Carl Dorian, *The History of Music in Performance* (New York: Norton, 1971), p. 224.

98. Quotation from Liszt in Beckett, *op. cit.*, pp. 10 ff.

99. Robert Schumann, *On Music and Musicians,* trans. Paul Rosenfeld (New York, 1946), p. 150.

100. Robert Baldick, *The Life and Times of Frédérick Lemaître* (Fair Lawn, N.J.: Essential Books, Oxford University Press, 1959), especially pp. 52–54.

101. Quotation from Gautier translated in *ibid.,* p. 141.

102. See Ernest Newman, *The Man Liszt* (New York: Cassell, 1934), p. 284; Sacheverell Sitwell, *Liszt* (New York: Dover, 1967), p. 136.

103. Pierre Véron, *Paris S'Amuse* (Paris: Levey Frères, 1874), p. 36.

104. Hogan, *op. cit.,* p. xcii. The dating of restrained applause is uneven. In some cities different kinds of music elicited different patterns of applause. Thus, in Vienna in the 1870's it was bad taste to clap between the movements of a symphony, but permissible to clap between movements in a concerto.

105. Green, *op. cit.,* p. 168; Simon Tidworth, *Theatres: An Architectural and Cultural History* (New York: Praeger, 1973), p. 173.

106. See, for example, Duvignaud, *L'Acteur.* The uproar over *Le Sacré du Printemps* in 1913 is a good case of the latter point; a special event then, in Garrick's time it would have been business as usual.

107. S. Joseph, *The Story of the Playhouse in England* (London: Barrie & Rockcliff, 1963), Ch. 7.

108. Tidworth, *op. cit.,* p. 158.

109. Garnier, quoted in *ibid.,* p. 161.

110. Richard Wagner, quoted in *ibid.,* p. 172.

111. See Jacques Barzun, *Darwin, Marx, Wagner* (Garden City, N.Y.: Doubleday, 1958), which remains the best study of Wagner's intentions, even if it is spotty musically in a few places.

112. Carl Schorske, "Politics and Psyche in Fin-de-Siècle Vienna," *American Historical Review,* July 1961, p. 935.

113. Arthur Young, *The Concert Tradition* (New York: Ray, 1965), pp. 211, 203.

114. For the contrast to the program announcement of the 18th Century, see Hogan, *op. cit.,* p. lxxv.

115. Einstein, *op. cit.,* pp. 37–40.

116. See Hector Berlioz, *Memoirs,* trans. David Cairns (New York: Knopf, 1969), pp. 230–31, for an amusing instance.

117. Young, *op. cit.,* pp. 236–38.

118. Richardson, *op. cit.*, p. 142.

119. See Walter Benjamin, *Illuminations,* ed. Hannah Arendt (New York: Schocken Books, 1969), "Baudelaire."

120. *Ibid.*, p. 173.

121. Cacérès, *op. cit.*, p. 173.

122. The best current picture of pub life is Brian Harrison, "Pubs," in H. J. Dyos and Michael Wolff, eds., *The Victorian City,* Vol. I (Boston: Routledge & Kegan Paul, 1973); quotation from Brian Harrison, *Drink and the Victorians* (London: Faber and Faber, 1971), p. 45.

123. John Woode, *Clubs* (London: 1900), *passim.*

124. Ibid.

125. Richardson, *op. cit.*, p. 128; see map in David H. Pinkney, *Napoleon III and the Rebuilding of Paris* (Princeton: Princeton University Press, 1958), p. 73; Raymond Rudorff, *The Belle Epoque: Paris in the Nineties* (New York: Saturday Review Press, 1973), pp. 32, 149–50.

126. Leroy-Beaulieu, *La Question Ouvrière au XIX Siècle,* quoted in Richardson, *op. cit.*, p. 88; see Henri d'Almeras, "La Littérature au Café sous le Second Empire," in *Les Oeuvres Libres,* No. 135 (Sept. 1932), for a beautiful description of those who sat and watched the litterateurs who let themselves be watched.

127. Roger Shattuck, *The Banquet Years,* Ch. 1.

128. On crowd diversity: Ernest Labrousse, *Le Mouvement Ouvrier et les Idées Sociales en France de 1815 à la Fin du XIX Siècle* (Paris, 1948), pp. 90 ff.; David Pinckney, *The French Revolution of 1830* (Princeton: Princeton University Press, 1972), pp. 252–58.

129. T. J. Clark, *The Absolute Bourgeois* (Greenwich, Conn.: New York Graphic Society, 1973), quotation on p. 19.

130. *Ibid.*, pp. 9–30.

131. Priscilla Robertson, *The Revolutions of 1848: A Social History* (Princeton: Princeton University Press, 1967), pp. 19–23.

132. Quoted in Georges Duveau, 1848: The Making of a Revolution, trans. Anne Carter (New York: Pantheon, 1967), p. xix; see also Karl Marx, *The 18th Brumaire of Louis Bonaparte,* no translator indicated (New York: International Publishers, 1963), p. 21.

133. Figures from Duveau, *op. cit.*, p. xxi.

134. Theodore Zeldin, *France 1848–1945* (Oxford: Clarendon Press, 1973), quotation on p. 484.

135. Duveau, *op. cit.*, pp. 33–52.

136. H. R. Whitehouse, *The Life of Lamartine* (Boston: Houghton Mifflin, 1918), II, 240.

137. Elias Regnault, *Histoire du Gouvernement Provisoire* (Paris, n.d.), p. 130. (The book was privately printed; extant copies in the Bibliothèque Nationale, Paris, and in the New York Public Library.)

138. Quotation from Lamartine, *Mémoires Politiques* (Paris, n.d.), II, 373; L. Barthou, *Lamartine Orateur* (Paris: Hachette, 1926), pp. 305–09.

139. See Whitehouse, *op. cit.,* pp. 242–45; quotation from Regnault, *op. cit.,* p. 130; see also Whitehouse, *op. cit.,* p. 241; Alexis de Tocqueville, *Recollections,* trans. Stuart de Mattos (London: Harvill Press, 1948), p. 126.

140. *Ibid.,* p. 124.

141. William Langer, *Political and Social Upheaval, 1832–1852* (New York, Harper & Row, 1969), quotation on pp. 337–38.

142. *Ibid.,* pp. 343–44.

143. Donald Weinstein, *Savanarola and Florence* (Princeton: Princeton University Press, 1970), pp. 74–75.

144. Marsilio Ficino, quoted in Ferdinand Schevill, *Medieval and Renaissance Florence,* first published as *A History of Florence* (New York: Harper Torchbook, 1936 and 1963), II, 416; Rucelli, quoted in *ibid.*

145. Robert S. Lopez, "Hard Times and the Investment in Culture," in *The Renaissance, Six Essays,* ed. Wallace Ferguson (New York: Harper Torchbook, 1954), p. 45; Eugenio Garin, *La Cultura Filosofica del Rinascimento Italiano* (Florence, 1961), *passim;* Richard Trexler, "Florentine Religious Experience: The Sacred Image," in *Studies in the Renaissance,* XIX (1972), 440–41.

146. Richard Sennett, "The Demographic History of Renaissance Florence" (paper in preparation).

147. Felix Gilbert, "The Venetian Constitution in Florentine Political Thought," in Nicolai Rubinstein, ed., *Florentine Studies* (London: Faber and Faber, 1968), p. 478.

148. Pasquale Villari, *The Life and Times of Girolamo Savanarola,* trans. L. Villari (London: T. Fisher Unwin, 1888), I, 106 ff.

149. See G. Savanarola, *Prediche sopra Ezechiele,* ed. R. Ridolfi, Vol. I (Rome, 1955).

150. See the excellent account of these burnings of vanities in Ralph Roeder's *The Man of the Renaissance.*

151. Savanarola, *op. cit.,* p. 168.

152. See Geraldine Pelles, *Art, Artist and Society* (Englewood Cliffs, N.J.: Prentice-Hall, 1963).

153. Roderick Kedward, *The Dreyfus Affair* (London: Longmans, Green, 1969), p. 8.

154. The clearest presentation of this part of the Affair is Douglas Johnson's *France and the Dreyfus Affair* (New York: Walker, 1967); see also Guy Chapman's *The Dreyfus Affair*. The literature is, of course, enormous; Joseph Reinach's massive study is still a basic source, even though he was a participant in the Affair himself. The account here is drawn from Johnson, Chapman, and Kedward.

155. Mauriac quoted in Johnson, *op. cit.*, preface; probably the most interesting, if "biased," pictures of upper-middle-class occasions when the Affair was touchy are in Marcel Proust's *Jean Santeuil*.

156. Edouard Drumont, "L'Âme de Capt. Dreyfus," in *La Libre Parole*, December 26, 1894; a condensed translation appears in Louis Snyder, *The Dreyfus Case* (New Brunswick, N.J.: Rutgers University Press, 1973), p. 96.

157. *Ibid.*

158. Arsènne de Marloque, *Mémoires* (Paris: privately printed, n.d.), Bibliothèque Nationale, trans. R.S.

159. Johnson, *op. cit.*, p. 119; since the full text is included in the present book, and since all quotes refer to numbered paragraphs, individual citations will not be given.

160. Quotation from Zeldin, *op. cit.*, pp. 750–51.

PART FOUR

1. Max Weber, *Economy and Society,* ed. Guenther Roth and Claus Wittich (New York: Bedminster Press, 1968), III, 1112.

2. Sigmund Freud, *The Future of an Illusion* (New York: Anchor, 1957), p. 7.

3. *Ibid.*

4. Weber, *op. cit.*, p. 1114.

5. *Ibid.*, pp. 1120–21.

6. Freud, *op. cit.*, p. 54.

7. *Ibid.*, p. 40.

8. A fuller treatment of this system will be found in Richard Sennett, "The Artist and the University," *Daedalus* (Fall 1974).

9. Now in published form: Mario Cuomo, *Forest Hills Diary*, with a preface by Jimmy Breslin and an afterword by Richard Sennett (New York:

Random House, 1974). The analysis that follows is a reworking of the afterword appearing in that book.

10. *Ibid.*, p. 61.

11. *Ibid.*, pp. 103 ff.

12. *Ibid.*, pp. 128–29.

13. Norton Long, "The Local Community as an Ecology of Games," in Edward Banfield, ed., *Urban Government* (Rev. ed.; New York: Free Press, 1969), p. 469.

14. Cuomo, *op. cit.*, pp. 56 ff.

15. *Ibid.*, pp. 67 ff.

16. *Ibid.*, p. 134.

17. *Ibid.*, pp. 147–49.

18. Evreinoff in Stanford Lyman and Marvin Scott, *The Drama of Social Reality* (New York: Oxford University Press, 1975), quoted on p. 112; direct quotation from these two authors on p. 111.

19. Sigmund Freud, "Creative Writers and Day-Dreaming," *The Standard Edition of the Psychological Works of Sigmund Freud*, IX (London: Hogarth, 1959), 144.

20. See Arthur Koestler, *The Act of Creation* (New York: Macmillan, 1964), *passim*.

21. See Ernst Kris, *Psychoanalytic Explorations in Art* (New York: Schocken, 1964), especially pages 173–203 for a discussion of the psychic ancestry of caricature in child's play.

22. Huizinga, *op. cit.*, pp. 7–9.

23. Jean Piaget, *Play, Dreams, and Imitation in Childhood* (London: Heinemann, 1951), *passim*, especially Ch. 1.

24. The psychologist will recognize that this analysis of play frustration is close to Festinger's idea of situation reinforcement in cognitive dissonance. See Leon Festinger, *A Theory of Cognitive Dissonance* (Stanford, Calif.: Stanford University Press, 1957); also "The Psychological Effects of Insufficient Rewards," *American Psychologist*, 1961, Vol. 16, No. 1, pp. 1–11.

25. Sigmund Freud, *On Narcissism* (London: Hogarth, 1957; first published 1914).

26. Heinz Kohut, *The Analysis of the Self* (New York: International Universities Press, 1971), pp. 33–34.

27. Otto Kernberg, "Structural Derivatives of Object Relationships," *International Journal of Psychoanalysis*, Vol. 47, 1966, pp. 236–53; Kernberg, "Factors in the Psychoanalytic Treatment of Narcissistic Personalities,"

Journal of the American Psychoanalytic Association, 1970, Vol. 18, No. 1, pp. 51–85; Kohut, *op. cit.,* pp. 22–23.

28. D. W. Winnicott, "Transitional Objects and Transitional Phenomena," *International Journal of Psychoanalysis,* 1953, Vol. 34, pp. 89–97.

29. This view appears in writers as divergent as Daniel Bell *(The Coming of Post-Industrial Society)* and Alain Touraine *(La Production de la Société),* or in strategists as divergent as André Gorz and Serge Mallet.

30. In the United States, these are often, indeed, the elite of the blue-collar working groups, who think of themselves as having risen out of the working class but are not treated so in bureaucratic personnel charts. See especially the work of Blauner on technological workers. Robert Blauner, *Alienation and Freedom: The Factory and Its Industry* (Chicago: University of Chicago Press, 1967).

31. Jane Veline, "Bureaucratic Imperatives for Institutional Growth: A Case Study" (manuscript).

32. The term "protean work" is derived from R. J. Lifton's "Protean Man," *Partisan Review,* Vol. 35, No. 1 (Winter 1968), pp. 13–27. The best description of protean work appears in Mills, *op. cit.,* and the educational/technological skill question involved in such work is best analyzed in Christopher Jencks and David Riesman, *The Academic Revolution* (Garden City, N.Y.: Doubleday, 1968).

33. C. Wright Mills, "The Middle Classes in Middle-Sized Cities," *American Sociological Review,* Vol. II, No. 5 (Oct. 1946), pp. 520–29.

34. See Sennett and Cobb, *op. cit.,* pp. 193–97.

APPENDIX

"J'Accuse!"

L'Aurore, *January 13, 1898. Translated in* The Trial of Émile Zola
(New York: Benjamin R. Tucker, 1898), pp. 3–14.

LETTER TO M. FELIX FAURE, PRESIDENT OF THE REPUBLIC

Monsieur le Président:

Will you permit me, in my gratitude for the kindly welcome that you once extended to me, to have a care for the glory that belongs to you, and to say to you that your star, so lucky hitherto, is threatened with the most shameful, the most ineffaceable, of stains?

You have emerged from base calumnies safe and sound; you have conquered hearts. You seem radiant in the apotheosis of that patriotic *fête* which the Russian alliance has been for France, and you are preparing to preside at the solemn triumph of our Universal Exposition, which will crown our great century of labor, truth, and liberty. But what a mud stain on your name—I was going to say on your reign—is this abominable Dreyfus affair! A council of war has just dared to acquit an Esterhazy in obedience to orders, a final blow at all truth, at all justice. And now it is done! France has this stain upon her cheek; it will be written in history that under your presidency it was possible for this social crime to be committed.

Since they have dared, I too will dare. I will tell the truth, for I have promised to tell it, if the courts, once regularly appealed to, did not bring it out fully and entirely. It is my duty to speak; I will not be an accomplice. My nights would be haunted by the specter of the innocent man, who is atoning, in a far-away country, by the most frightful of tortures, for a crime that he did not commit.

And to you, Monsieur le Président, will I cry this truth, with all the force of an honest man's revolt. Because of your honor I am convinced that you are ignorant of it. And to whom, then, shall I denounce the malevolent gang of the really guilty, if not to you, the first magistrate of the country?

First, the truth as to the trial and conviction of Dreyfus.

A calamitous man has managed it all, has done it all—Colonel du Paty de Clam, then a simple major. He is the entire Dreyfus case; it will be fully known only when a sincere investigation shall have clearly established his acts and his responsibilities. He appears as the most heady, the most intricate, of minds, haunted with romantic intrigues, delighting in the methods of the newspaper novel, stolen papers, anonymous letters, meetings in deserted spots, mysterious women who peddle overwhelming proofs by night. It is he who conceived the idea of dictating the *bordereau* to Dreyfus; it is he who dreamed of studying it in a room completely lined with mirrors; it is he whom Major Forzinetti represents to us armed with a dark lantern, trying to gain access to the accused when asleep, in order to throw upon his face a sudden flood of light, and thus surprise a confession of his crime in the confusion of his awakening. And I have not to tell the whole; let them look, they will find. I declare simply that Major du Paty de Clam, entrusted as a judicial officer with the duty of preparing the Dreyfus case, is, in the order of dates and responsibilities, the first person guilty of the fearful judicial error that has been committed.

The *bordereau* already had been for some time in the hands of Colonel Sandherr, director of the bureau of information, who since then has died of general paralysis. "Flights" have taken place; papers have disappeared, as they continue to disappear even today; and the authorship of the *bordereau* was an object of inquiry, when little by little an *a priori* conclusion was arrived at that the author must be a staff officer and an officer of artillery,—clearly a double error, which shows how superficially this *bordereau* had been studied, for a systematic examination proves that it could have been written only by an officer of troops. So they searched their own house; they examined writings; it was a sort of family affair,—a traitor to be surprised in the war offices themselves, that he might be expelled therefrom. I need not again go over a story already known in part. It is sufficient to say that Major du Paty de Clam enters upon the scene as soon as the first breath of suspicion falls upon Dreyfus. Starting from that moment, it is he who invented Dreyfus; the case becomes his case; he undertakes to confound the traitor, and induce him to make a complete confession. There is also, to be sure, the minister of war, General Mercier, whose intelligence seems rather inferior; there is also the Chief of Staff, General de Boisdeffre, who seems to have yielded to his clerical passion, and the sub-Chief of Staff, General Gonse, whose conscience has succeeded in accommodating itself to many things. But at bottom there was at first only Major du Paty de Clam, who leads them all, who hypnotizes them,—for he concerns himself also with spiritualism, with occultism, holding converse with spirits. Incredible are the experiences to which he submitted the unfortunate Dreyfus, the traps into which he tried to lead him, the mad inquiries, the monstrous fancies, a complete and torturing madness.

Ah! this first affair is a nightmare to one who knows it in its real details. Major du Paty de Clam arrests Dreyfus, puts him in close confinement; he runs to Mme. Dreyfus, terrorizes her, tells her that, if she speaks, her husband is lost. Meantime the unfortunate was tearing his flesh, screaming his innocence. And thus the examination went on, as in a fifteenth-century chronicle, amid mystery, with a complication of savage expedients, all based on a single childish charge, this imbecile *bordereau,* which was not simply a vulgar treason, but also the most shameless of swindles, for the famous secrets delivered proved, almost all of them, valueless. If I insist, it is because here lies the egg from which later was to be hatched the real crime, the frightful denial of justice, of which France lies ill. I should like to show in detail how the judicial error was possible; how it was born of the machinations of Major du Paty de Clam; how General Mercier and Generals de Boisdeffre and Gonse were led into it, gradually assuming responsibility for this error, which afterward they believed it their duty to impose as sacred truth, truth beyond discussion. At the start there was, on their part, only carelessness and lack of understanding. At worst we see them yielding to the religious passions of their surroundings, and to the prejudices of the *esprit de corps.* They have suffered folly to do its work.

But here is Dreyfus before the council of war. The most absolute secrecy is demanded. Had a traitor opened the frontier to the enemy in order to lead the German emperor to Notre Dame, they would not have taken stricter measures of silence and mystery. The nation is awe-struck; there are whisperings of terrible doings, of those monstrous treasons that excite the indignation of History, and naturally the nation bows. There is no punishment severe enough; it will applaud even public degradation; it will wish the guilty man to remain upon his rock of infamy, eaten by remorse. Are they real then,—these unspeakable things, these dangerous things, capable of setting Europe aflame, which they have had to bury carefully behind closed doors? No, there was nothing behind them save the romantic and mad fancies of Major du Paty de Clam. All this was done only to conceal the most ridiculous of newspaper novels. And, to assure one's self of it, one need only study attentively the indictment read before the council of war.

Ah! the emptiness of this indictment! That a man could have been condemned on this document is a prodigy of iniquity. I defy honest people to read it without feeling their hearts leap with indignation and crying out their revolt at the thought of the unlimited atonement yonder, on Devil's Island. Dreyfus knows several languages—a crime; no compromising document was found on his premises—a crime; he sometimes visits the neighborhood of his birth—a crime; he is industrious, he is desirous of knowing everything—a crime; he does not get confused—a crime; he gets confused—a crime. And the simplicities of this document, the formal assertions in the void! We were told of fourteen counts, but we find, after all, only one,—that of the *bordereau.* And even as to this we learn that the experts were not in agreement; that one of them, M. Gobert, was hustled out in military fashion, because he permitted himself to arrive at another than the desired opinion. We were told also of twenty-three officers who came to overwhelm Dreyfus with their testimony. We are still in ignorance of their examination, but it is certain that all of them did not attack him, and it is to be remarked, furthermore, that all of them belonged to the war offices. It is a family trial; there they are all at home; and it must be remembered that the staff wanted the trial, sat in judgment at it, and has just passed judgment a second time.

So there remained only the *bordereau,* concerning which the experts were not in agreement. It is said that in the council chamber the judges naturally were going to acquit. And, after that, how easy to understand the desperate obstinacy with which, in order to justify the conviction, they affirm today the existence of a secret overwhelming document, a document that cannot be shown, that legitimates everything, before which we must bow, an invisible and unknowable god. I deny this document; I deny it with all my might. A ridiculous document, yes, perhaps a document concerning little women, in which there is mention of a certain D—— who becomes too exacting; some husband doubtless, who thinks that they pay him too low a price for his wife. But a document of interest to the national defense, the production of which would lead to a declaration of war tomorrow! No, no; it is a lie; and a lie the more odious and cynical because they lie with impunity, in such a way that no one can convict them of it. They stir up France; they hide themselves behind her legitimate emotion; they close mouths by disturbing hearts, by perverting minds. I know no greater civic crime.

These, then, Monsieur le Président, are the facts which explain how it was possible to commit a judicial error; and the moral proofs, the position of Dreyfus as a man of wealth, the absence of motive, this continual cry of innocence, complete the demonstration that he is a victim of the extraordinary fancies of Major du Paty de Clam, of his clerical surroundings, of that hunting down of the "dirty Jews" which disgraces our epoch.

And we come to the Esterhazy case. Three years have passed; many consciences remain profoundly disturbed, are anxiously seeking, and finally become convinced of the innocence of Dreyfus.

I shall not give the history of M. Scheurer-Kestner's doubts, which later became convictions. But, while he was investigating for himself, serious things were happening to the staff. Colonel Sandherr was dead, and Lieutenant-Colonel Picquart had succeeded him as Chief of the Bureau of Information. And it is in this capacity that the latter, in the exercise of his functions, came one day into possession of a letter-telegram addressed to Major Esterhazy by an agent of a foreign power. His plain duty was to open an investigation. It is certain that he never acted except at the command of his superiors. So he submitted his suspicions to his hierarchical superiors, first to General Gonse, then to General de Boisdeffre, then to General Billot, who had succeeded General Mercier as Minister of War. The famous Picquart documents, of which we have heard so much, were never anything but the Billot documents,—I mean, the documents collected by a subordinate for his minister, the documents which must be still in existence in the war department. The inquiries lasted from May to September 1896, and here it must be squarely affirmed that General Gonse was convinced of Esterhazy's guilt, and that General de Boisdeffre and General Billot had no doubt that the famous *bordereau* was in Esterhazy's handwriting. Lieutenant-Colonel Picquart's investigation had ended in the certain establishment of this fact. But the emotion thereat was great, for Esterhazy's conviction inevitably involved a revision of the Dreyfus trial; and this the staff was determined to avoid at any cost.

Then there must have been a psychological moment, full of anguish. Note that General Billot was in no way compromised; he came freshly to the matter; he could bring out the truth. He did not dare, in terror, undoubtedly, of public opinion, and certainly fearful also of betraying the entire staff, General de Boisdeffre, General Gonse, to say nothing of their subordinates. Then there was but a minute of struggle between his conscience and what he believed to be the military interest. When this minute had passed, it was already too late. He was involved himself; he was compromised. And since then his responsibility has only grown; he has taken upon his shoulders the crime of others, he is as guilty as the others, he is more guilty than they, for it was in his power to do justice, and he did nothing. Understand this; for a year General Billot, Generals de Boisdeffre and Gonse have known that Dreyfus is innocent, and they have kept this dreadful thing to themselves. And these people sleep, and they have wives and children whom they love!

Colonel Picquart had done his duty as an honest man. He insisted in the presence of his superiors, in the name of justice; he even begged of them; he told them how impolitic were their delays, in view of the terrible storm which was gathering, and which would surely burst as soon as the truth should be known. Later there was the language that M. Scheurer-Kestner held likewise to General Billot, adjuring him in the name of patriotism to take the matter in hand and not to allow it to be aggravated till it should become a public disaster. No, the crime had been committed; now the staff could not confess it. And Lieutenant Colonel Picquart was sent on a mission; he was farther and farther removed, even to Tunis, where one day they even wanted to honor his bravery by charging him with a mission which would surely have led to his massacre in the district where the Marquis de Mores met his death. He was not in disgrace; Gen. Gonse was in friendly correspondence with him; but there are secrets which it does one no good to find out.

At Paris the truth went on, irresistibly, and we know in what way the expected storm broke out. M. Mathieu Dreyfus denounced Major Esterhazy as the real author of the *bordereau*, at the moment when M. Scheurer-Kestner was about to lodge a demand for a revision of the trial with the keeper of the seals. And it is here that Major Esterhazy appears. The evidence shows that at first he was dazed, ready for suicide or flight. Then suddenly he determines to brazen it out; he astonishes Paris by the violence of his attitude. The fact was that aid had come to him; he had received an anonymous letter warning him of the intrigues of his enemies; a mysterious woman had even disturbed herself at night to hand to him a document stolen from the staff, which would save him. And I cannot help seeing here again the hand of Lieutenant-Colonel du Paty de Clam, recognizing the devices of his fertile imagination. His work, the guilt of Dreyfus, was in danger, and he was determined to defend it. A revision of the trial,—why, that meant the downfall of the newspaper novel, so extravagant, so tragic, with its abominable *denouement* on Devil's Island. That would never do. Thenceforth there was to be a duel between Lieutenant-Colonel Picquart and Lieutenant-Colonel du Paty de Clam, the one with face uncovered, the other masked. Presently we shall meet them both in the presence of civil justice. At bottom it is always the staff defending itself, unwilling to confess its crime, the abomination of which is growing from hour to hour.

It has been wonderingly asked who were the protectors of Major Esterhazy. First, in the shadow, Lieutenant-Colonel du Paty de Clam, who devised everything, managed everything; his hand betrays itself in the ridiculous methods. Then there is General de Boisdeffre, General Gonse, General Billot himself, who are obliged to acquit the major, since they cannot permit the innocence of Dreyfus to be recognized, for, if they should, the war offices would fall under the weight of public contempt. And the beautiful result of this prodigious situation is that the one honest man in the case, Lieutenant-Colonel Picquart, who alone has done his duty, is to be the victim, the man to be derided and punished. O justice, what frightful despair grips the heart! They go so far as to say that he is a forger; that he manufactured the telegram, to ruin Esterhazy. But, in heaven's name, why? For what purpose? Show a motive. Is he, too, paid by the Jews? The pretty part of the story is that he himself was an anti-Semite. Yes, we are witnesses of this infamous spectacle,—the proclamation of the innocence of men ruined with debts and crimes, while honor itself, a man of stainless life, is stricken down. When a society reaches that point, it is beginning to rot.

There you have, then, Monsieur le Président, the Esterhazy case,—a guilty man to be declared innocent. We can follow the beautiful business, hour by hour, for the last two months. I abridge, for this is but the resume of a story whose burning pages will some day be written at length. So we have seen General de Pellieux, and then Major Ravary, carrying on a rascally investigation whence knaves come transfigured and honest people sullied. Then they convened the council of war.

How could it have been expected that a council of war would undo what a council of war had done?

I say nothing of the choice, always possible, of the judges. Is not the superior idea of discipline, which is in the very blood of these soldiers, enough to destroy their power to do justice? Who says discipline says obedience. When the Minister of War, the great chief, has publicly established, amid the applause of the nation's representatives, the absolute authority of the thing judged, do you expect a council of war formally to contradict him? Hierarchically that is impossible. General Billot conveyed a suggestion to the judges by his declaration, and they passed judgment as they must face the cannon's mouth, without reasoning. The preconceived opinion that they took with them to their bench is evidently this: "Dreyfus has been condemned for the crime of treason by a council of war; then he is guilty, and we, a council of war, cannot declare him innocent. Now, we know that to recognize Esterhazy's guilt would be to proclaim the innocence of Dreyfus." Nothing could turn them from that course of reasoning.

They have rendered an iniquitous verdict which will weigh forever upon our councils of war, which will henceforth tinge with suspicion all their decrees. The first council of war may have been lacking in comprehension; the second is necessarily criminal. Its excuse, I repeat, is that the supreme chief had spoken, declaring the thing judged unassailable, sacred and superior to men, so that their inferiors could say naught to the contrary. They talk to us of the honor of the Army; they want us to love it, to respect it. Ah! certainly, yes, the Army which would rise at the first threat, which would defend French soil; that Army is the whole people, and we have for it nothing but tenderness and respect. But it is not a question of that Army, whose dignity is our special desire, in our need of justice. It is the sword that is in question; the master that they may give us tomorrow. And piously kiss the sword hilt, the god? No!

I have proved it, moreover; the Dreyfus case was the case of the war offices, a staff officer, accused by his staff comrades, convicted under the pressure of the Chiefs of Staff. Again I say, he cannot come back innocent unless all the staff is guilty. Consequently the war offices, by all imaginable means, by press campaigns, by communications, by influences, have covered Esterhazy only to ruin Dreyfus a second time. Ah! with what a sweep the Republican Government should clear away this band of Jesuits, as General Billot himself calls them! Where is the truly strong and wisely patriotic minister who will dare to reshape and renew all? How many of the people I know are trembling with anguish in view of a possible war, knowing in what hands lies the national defense! And what a nest of base intrigues, gossip, and dilapidation has this sacred asylum, entrusted with the fate of the country become! We are frightened by the terrible light thrown upon it by the Dreyfus case, this human sacrifice of an unfortunate, of a "dirty Jew." Ah! what a mixture of madness and folly, of crazy fancies, of low police practices, of inquisitorial and tyrannical customs, the good pleasure of a few persons in gold lace, with their boots on the neck of the nation, cramming back into its throat its cry of truth and justice, under the lying and sacrilegious pretext of *raison d'État!*

And another of their crimes is that they have accepted the support of the unclean press, have suffered themselves to be championed by all the knavery of Paris, so that now we witness knavery's insolent triumph in the downfall of right and of simple probity. It is a crime to have accused of troubling France those who wish to see her generous, at the head of the free and just nations, when they themselves are hatching the impudent conspiracy to impose error, in the face of the entire world. It is a crime to mislead opinion, to utilize for a task of death this opinion that they have perverted to the point of delirium. It is a crime to poison the minds of the little and the humble, to exasperate the passions of reaction and intolerance, while seeking shelter behind odious anti-Semitism, of which the great liberal France of the rights of man will die, if she is not cured. It is a crime to exploit patriotism for works of hatred, and, finally, it is a crime to make the sword the modern god, when all human science is at work on the coming temple of truth and justice.

This truth, this justice, for which we have so ardently longed,—how distressing it is to see them thus buffeted, more neglected and more obscured. I have a suspicion of the fall that must have occurred in the soul of M. Scheurer-Kestner, and I really believe that he will finally feel remorse that he did not act in a revolutionary fashion, on the day of interpellation in the Senate, by thoroughly ventilating the whole matter, to topple everything over. He has been the highly honest man, the man of loyal life, and he thought that the truth was sufficient unto itself, especially when it should appear as dazzling as the open day. Of what use to overturn everything, since soon the sun would shine? And it is for this confident serenity that he is now so cruelly punished. And the same is the case of Lieutenant-Colonel Picquart, who, moved by a feeling of lofty dignity, has been unwilling to publish General Gonse's letters. These scruples honor him the more because, while he remained respectful of discipline, his superiors heaped mud upon him, working up the case against him themselves, in the most unexpected and most outrageous fashion. Here are two victims, two worthy people, two simple hearts, who have trusted God, while the devil was at work. And in the case of Lieutenant-Colonel Picquart we have seen even this ignoble thing,—a French tribunal, after suffering the reporter in the case to arraign publicly a witness and accuse him of every crime, closing its doors as soon as this witness has been introduced to explain and defend himself. I say that is one crime more, and that this crime will awaken the universal conscience. Decidedly, military tribunals have a singular idea of justice.

Such, then, is the simple truth, Monsieur le Président, and it is frightful. It will remain a stain upon your presidency. I suspect that you are powerless in this matter,—that you are the prisoner of the constitution and of your environment. You have nonetheless a man's duty, upon which you will reflect, and which you will fulfill. Not indeed that I despair, the least in the world, of triumph. I repeat with more vehement certainty; truth is on the march, and nothing can stop it. Today sees the real beginning of the Affair, since not until today have the positions been clear: on one hand, the guilty, who do not want the light; on the other, the doers of justice, who will give their lives to get it. When truth is buried in the earth, it accumulates there, and assumes so mighty an explosive power that, on the day when it bursts forth, it hurls everything into the air. We shall see if they have not just made preparations for the most resounding of disasters, yet to come.

But this letter is long, Monsieur le Président, and it is time to finish.

I accuse Lieutenant-Colonel du Paty de Clam of having been the diabolical workman of judicial error,—unconsciously, I am willing to believe,—and of having then defended his calamitous work, for three years, by the most guilty machinations.

I accuse General Mercier of having made himself an accomplice, at least through weakness of mind, in one of the greatest iniquities of the century.

I accuse General Billot of having had in his hands certain proofs of the innocence of Dreyfus, and of having stifled them; of having rendered himself guilty of this crime of *lèse-humanité* and *lèse-justice* for a political purpose, and to save the compromised staff.

I accuse General de Boisdeffre and General Gonse of having made themselves accomplices in the same crime, one undoubtedly through clerical passion, the other perhaps through that *esprit de corps* which makes the war offices the Holy Ark, unassailable.

I accuse General de Pellieux and Major Ravary of having conducted a rascally inquiry,—I mean by that a monstrously partial inquiry, of which we have, in the report of the latter, an imperishable monument of naive audacity.

I accuse the three experts in handwriting, Belhomme, Varinard, and Couard, of having made lying and fraudulent reports, unless a medical examination should declare them afflicted with diseases of the eye and of the mind.

I accuse the war offices of having carried on in the press, particularly in *L'Eclair* and in *L'Echo de Paris,* an abominable campaign to mislead opinion and cover up their faults.

I accuse, finally, the first council of war of having violated the law by condemning an accused person on the strength of a secret document, and I accuse the second council of war of having covered this illegality, in obedience to orders, in committing in its turn the judicial crime of knowingly acquitting a guilty man.

In preferring these charges, I am not unaware that I lay myself liable under Articles 30 and 31 of the press law of July 29, 1881 which punishes defamation. And it is wilfully that I expose myself thereto.

As for the people whom I accuse, I do not know them, I have never seen them, I entertain against them no feeling of revenge or hatred. They are to me simple entities, spirits of social ill-doing. And the act that I perform here is nothing but a revolutionary measure to hasten the explosion of truth and justice.

I have but one passion, the passion for the light, in the name of humanity which has suffered so much, and which is entitled to happiness. My fiery protest is simply the cry of my soul. Let them dare, then, to bring me into the Assize Court, and let the investigation take place in the open day.

I await it.

Accept, Monsieur le Président, the assurance of my profound respect.

ÉMILE ZOLA

INDEX

INDEX

Malory, Sir Thomas, 16

man, 8, 97; as an actor, 35, 42, 107–22, 127, 142, 195, 217, 313; basic rights of, 73, 89–91, 95, 97; and belief, 33–4, 35, 38–41, 49, 56, 87, 151–2, 157, 195, 252, 253–5, 296, 331, 334, 338–9; corruption of, 116–20; and emotional risk-taking, 31, 295, 310; fantasies of authority in, 196, 210–12; ideology of intimacy of, 259–62, 298, 309–12, 336, 338–9; and motivation, 263–5, 267, 279–81, 284, 287, 315, 326; as passive spectator, 195–7, 202, 205, 209–14, 221, 222, 224, 260–2, 269–70, 275, 283–5; and play, 92–3, 116–17, 118, 120, 264, 267; psychological openness of, 11, 29–30, 222, 223, 255, 259, 261–2; public, 195–218, 261, 287; pursuit of happiness of, 89–90; pursuit of reputation of, 119–20, 121, 217; and the self, 4–6, 7–12, 27, 28–32, 89, 117, 151, 153, 184, 219, 252, 262, 263, 268, 314, 324–35, 339; self-distance in, 264, 281; self-doubt in, 205, 209–10, 221, 267, 309; and war between intimacy and society, 263–8, 283; see also audience; crowds

Manchester, England, 136, 140, 216

Mann, Thomas, 11, 35

Manuel, Frank, 91

Mao Tse-tung, 275

Marcus, Steven, 166

Marivaux, Pierre de, 40, 149; *Paysan Parvenu, Le,* 51–2; *Vie de Marianne, La,* 51–2, 62

Marmontel, Jean, 114

Martin, Jean Baptiste, 71, 72

Marx, Karl, 11, 20, 32, 139, 146, 157, 164, 227, 230, 251–2, 253–4; *Capital,* 145

Mauriac, François, 241

Maurras, Charles, 249

McCarthy, Joseph, 278

media, electronic, 38, 282–5, 302; and compulsive interest in personality, 284–6; passive spectators of, 262, 283–5; and politics, 262, 265, 271, 276, 283–6, 287; and secular charisma, 282–7; and war between intimacy and society, 283

men: appearance of, 68, 69–71, 163–6, 185–6, 187, 188; in family, 165, 178, 180, 196; in public, 23–4, 164–5, 168

Michelangelo Buonarroti, 233

middle class, 48, 49, 74, 100, 133, 216, 268, 282; appearance of, 68, 161, 162–3, 190; children of, 94, 95; ghetto, 295, 297, 301–8; radicals, 239; see also bourgeoisie; *classes moyennes*

Middlemarch (Eliot), 141

Mill, John Stuart, 146, 169, 292

Mills, C. Wright: "Middle Classes in Middle-Sized Cities, The," 330, 331; *White Collar,* 142

Mills, John, 139

Mitchell, Juliette, 178

moeurs, 116–18, 184

Molière, 71

Montesquieu, 110

Moynihan Report, 180

Mozart, Leopold, 85

Mozart, Wolfgang, 85, 199, 203

Murphy, Arthur, 100

music: agents, 289; composers, 197, 198–9; conductors, 211, 224; immanent, 199–205, 290; performers, 197–203, 321; personality in, 199–203; program notes, 209–10; recorded, 288, 291; star system in, 287–92; text in, 197–9, 200, 203, 287–8, 290; virtuosos, 202–3, 205; see also performing arts

Mystères de Paris, Les (play), 175

Nadar (balloonist), 125

Napoleon I, Emperor, 237

Napoleon III, Emperor, 227

narcissism, 4–12, 220, 333; as ascetic activity, 333–6; blankness in, 9, 335; boundaries erased between personality and class, 327, 328–32; as character disorder, 8–10, 324–33; closure in, 335; and enlightened self-interest, 220, 335; and expression, 28, 29, 30, 32, 326, 335–6; and focus on potentials, 327, 328, 329–30, 332; as opposed to play, 267–8, 315, 333, 336; and